Witnessing Witnessing

Witnessing Witnessing

On the Reception of Holocaust Survivor Testimony

Thomas Trezise

FORDHAM UNIVERSITY PRESS

NEW YORK 2013

Copyright © 2013 Fordham University Press

All rights reserved. No part of this publication may be reproduced, stored in a retrieval system, or transmitted in any form or
by any means—electronic, mechanical, photocopy, recording, or
any other—except for brief quotations in printed reviews,
without the prior permission of the publisher.

Fordham University Press has no responsibility for the persistence or accuracy of URLs for external or third-party Internet
websites referred to in this publication and does not guarantee
that any content on such websites is, or will remain, accurate or
appropriate.

Fordham University Press also publishes its books in a variety of
electronic formats. Some content that appears in print may not
be available in electronic books.

Library of Congress Cataloging-in-Publication Data is available
from the publisher.

Printed in the United States of America

15 14 13   5 4 3 2 1

First edition

For Susan
and for Gabriel

CONTENTS

I am inclined to think that no one undertakes the study of trauma unless compelled to do so for personal reasons. At least, I find this a much more plausible motive than mere career advancement, despite the memory of a well-meaning scholar who once remarked to me that I had selected "a good topic." But really, why would you choose to spend years of your life listening and reading and thinking and talking and writing about something so emotionally and psychologically difficult, so fraught with social, political, and moral conflict, so draining and dispiriting to live with—unless you could not do otherwise?

My own apprenticeship in listening to survivors of trauma began more than twenty years ago, when I was suddenly summoned to an ambulance and found, so badly beaten she was unrecognizable, my wife, Susan Brison. Only later did I learn that she had been sexually assaulted and left for dead at the bottom of a ravine. In the ambulance, there was not much Susan could say, since her trachea had been fractured when the assailant had tried to strangle her and she was now breathing through an oxygen mask. Still, she managed to whisper "I'll be okay," offering a reprieve to my pounding heart and the glimmer of a hope that she might not die. Besides, you can also listen to a gaze or the squeeze of a hand.

During the many hours and days, the weeks and months and years that followed, my education inevitably expanded to include listening to Susan's other listeners: medical personnel, police officers, lawyers, crisis counselors, couples therapists, family members, friends and acquaintances, colleagues, a judge and jury; people of different races and nationalities, of both sexes and all ages. At the same time, I learned that I could not study or write about trauma, even of my own, vicarious variety, while still in the thick of its aftermath, which may feel worse than a nightmare because you cannot dispel it by waking up and there's no telling in advance how long you'll remain in its grip. What's more, since trauma is intrinsically silencing and Susan's assault was so clearly gender based, even as time passed I was not about to preempt her by telling the story in public before she herself had the chance to do so.

Only in recent years, well after the publication of her book, *Aftermath: Violence and the Remaking of a Self,* have I begun to find a voice of my own in which to narrate what happened to her and to me and to us. But in the meantime, I still had a profession, which I could not afford to abandon but which I knew could only be salvaged in my own eyes if I managed somehow to wed it to the experience that otherwise made it seem, like so much else, insufferably trivial. Well, you cannot study and teach twentieth-century French or European literature and philosophy without being at least marginally aware of the Holocaust, and if you start reading about trauma, sooner or later the Holocaust will move from the margins to the middle. For me, there was no turning back after reading the testimony of Charlotte Delbo, even if this suggested a certain lack of professional wisdom on my part, confirmed since then by the fact that the book you hold in your hands required what was surely one of the lengthiest gestations in the annals of academic publishing.

Comparisons of the Holocaust with other traumas tend to raise objections, especially where important differences between them are elided, along with the very difference between comparing and equating. So I feel bound to assure you, while expressing my distaste for anything like competition in suffering, that I am well aware of the differences between the Holocaust and the horror inflicted on Susan.

Nevertheless, it is in all the listening mentioned just a moment ago that I now find the seeds of this volume, which I dedicate to Susan and to our son, Gabriel, who brought us new life.

ACKNOWLEDGMENTS

There is no one from whom I have learned more about trauma, survival, and testimony than Susan Brison. It is not only her ground-breaking work and the sharing of her experience with me that have made this book possible, however, but her abiding support of the project, her boundless patience and energetic encouragement along what turned out to be a very long road.

Our son, Gabriel, has afforded me the great joy and consuming interest of being a father, always putting my troubles in perspective and reminding me that life can be lived with passion, curiosity, and hope.

For as long as I can remember, Ross Chambers has taken an enthusiastic interest in this project, supporting it as much by his generous intellectual and personal friendship as by the inspiring example he has set as a critic. Like him, Marie-Hélène Huet and Dominick LaCapra have been steadfast in their encouragement and unfailingly helpful in commenting on the manuscript. Marianne Hirsch, Mark Johnson, and Judith Sanders have also devoted many hours to reading and discussing drafts with me and contributing to improvements for which I am deeply grateful.

Among my colleagues at Princeton, I am indebted not only to Marie-Hélène Huet but to Lionel Gossman, Suzanne Nash, and François Rigolot for their affirmative responses to my work and for having had faith in me when my own was failing, and to David Bellos, André Benhaïm, Sandra Bermann, Eduardo Cadava, Pietro Frassica, Michael Jennings, Sarah Kay, Gaetana Marrone-Puglia, Ronnie Pardo, Volker Schröder, and Froma Zeitlin for their generous professional support and sustained interest in the book.

I have also benefited in the most tangible ways from exchanges with colleagues at other institutions, including Mieke Bal, Karyn Ball, Omer Bartov,

David Caron, Philippe Carrard, T. J. Clark, James Creech, Sidra Ezrahi, Nancy Fraser, Geoffrey Hartman, Lynn Higgins, Thomas Kavanagh, Mary Kelley, Anna Klosowska, Margot Livesey, Annelise Orleck, Sven-Erik Rose, Michael Rothberg, Eric Santner, Debarati Sanyal, Charles Shepherdson, Ann Smock, Leo Spitzer, Jonathan Strauss, Susan Suleiman, Soraya Tlatli, Alain Toumayan, Ernst van Alphen, and Eli Zaretsky.

For computer help at various stages of the project, I am very grateful to Susan Bibeau and Michael Rivera. During my visits to the Fortunoff Video Archive for Holocaust Testimonies at Yale, Joanne Rudof offered invaluable assistance. In Poland, Tomasz Cebulski generously shared his historical research with me during the twelve-hour days we spent visiting Auschwitz I and II, Majdanek, Bełżec, and several other sites. For editorial assistance with an earlier version of Chapter 1, I wish to thank Gadi Algazi and Philippa Shimrat. For research assistance, I am grateful to Matthew Escobar.

My debt is no smaller in the way of personal sustenance and friendship throughout the years when I was working on this book, and even before. In addition to the members of my family, whose loving support has never failed me, I am especially grateful to Melissa Bailey, Gerry Bergstein, John Blake, Gail Boyajian, Sabrina Brown, Ann Bumpus, Hal Cash, Peter Collier, Tim Collins, John Gager, Eric Garnick, Eva Gossman, Ronald Green, Fred Haas, Pascale Hubert-Leibler, Susan Jennings, Alexis Jetter, Gary Karpf, Jeffrey and Eva Kittay, Carol Koffel, John Kulvicki, Kathryn Lachman, Ted Levin, Shifra Levine, Daniel Lieberfeld, Marie-Victoire Louis, André Maman, Esther Marion, Karen McPherson, Monique Middleton, Linda Mulley, Terry Osborne, Nora Paley, Soo Sunny Park, Harold Shapiro, Matthew Shapiro, Nicole Simek, Pi Smith, Catherine Tudish, Annie Weeden, Bob Wetzel, Gretchen Wetzel, Zahi Zalloua, and Yetta Ziolkowski.

Princeton has repeatedly granted me generous leave time to pursue this project, and colleagues at Berkeley, Cornell, Dartmouth, Johns Hopkins, Miami, Michigan, and Notre Dame, among others, have kindly invited me to present the results of my research. When away from Princeton, I have benefited from the collegiality of Katharine Conley, Mary Jean Green, Lynn Higgins, and John Rassias, who, as chairs of the Department of French and Italian at Dartmouth, have supported my status as a visiting scholar with unfettered access to library resources. And I owe a special debt to the National Endowment for the Humanities, not only for granting me a Senior Fellowship but for responding to the evolution of the book with patience and understanding.

Lastly, I wish to thank Helen Tartar for the lively interest she expressed in this project at a much earlier stage, for the enthusiasm with which she greeted news of its completion, and for her scrupulous editing. To Thomas Lay and to Kathleen Sweeney I am also very grateful for the savoir faire that has smoothed the road between completion and publication.

An earlier version of Chapter 1 was published in *History & Memory* 20, no. 1 (Spring/Summer 2008), and portions of Chapter 3, now revised, appeared in *The Yale Journal of Criticism* 14, no. 1 (Spring 2001), and *Modern Language Notes* 117, no. 4 (September 2002).

AA   Charlotte Delbo. *Auschwitz and After.* Translated by Rosette C. Lamont. New Haven: Yale University Press, 1995. *Auschwitz et après.* Vol. 1, *Aucun de nous ne reviendra.* Geneva: Gonthier, 1965. Rpt. Paris: Minuit, 1970. Vol. 2, *Une connaissance inutile.* Paris: Minuit, 1970. Vol. 3, *Mesure de nos jours.* Paris: Minuit, 1971.

AI   Berel Lang. *Act and Idea in the Nazi Genocide.* Chicago: University of Chicago Press, 1990. Rpt. Syracuse: Syracuse University Press, 2003.

BW   Dori Laub. "Bearing Witness, or the Vicissitudes of Listening." Chapter 2 of Shoshana Felman and Dori Laub, *Testimony: Crises of Witnessing in Literature, Psychoanalysis, and History,* 57–74. New York: Routledge, 1992.

DS   Primo Levi. *The Drowned and the Saved.* Translated by Raymond Rosenthal. New York: Simon & Schuster, 1988. Rpt. Vintage International, 1989. *I sommersi e i salvati.* In *Opere,* edited by Marco Belpoliti, 2:995–1153. Turin: Einaudi, 1997.

EE   Emmanuel Levinas. *Existence and Existents.* Translated by Alphonso Lingis. The Hague: Martinus Nijhoff, 1978. *De l'existence à l'existant,* 2nd ed. Paris: Vrin, 1963.

GS   Theodor W. Adorno. *Gesammelte Schriften.* Edited by Rolf Tiedemann. Frankfurt am Main: Suhrkamp, 1997.

GW   Sigmund Freud. *Gesammelte Werke.* Edited by Anna Freud et al. London: Imago, 1940–68.

LL   Jorge Semprun. *Literature or Life.* Translated by Linda Coverdale. New York: Viking, 1997. *L'écriture ou la vie.* Paris: Gallimard, 1994. Rpt. Collection Folio, 1996.

NL   Theodor W. Adorno. *Notes to Literature*. Edited by Rolf Tiedemann. Translated by Shierry Weber Nicholsen. 2 vols. New York: Columbia University Press, 1992.

OB   Emmanuel Levinas. *Otherwise than Being or Beyond Essence*. Translated by Alphonso Lingis. The Hague: Martinus Nijhoff, 1981. Rpt. Pittsburgh: Duquesne University Press, 1998. *Autrement qu'être ou au-delà de l'essence*. The Hague: Martinus Nijhoff, 1974.

RA   Giorgio Agamben. *Remnants of Auschwitz: The Witness and the Archive*. Translated by Daniel Heller-Roazen. New York: Zone Books, 1999. *Quel che resta di Auschwitz: L'archivio e il testimone*. Turin: Bollati Boringhieri, 1998.

RS   Emmanuel Levinas. "Reality and Its Shadow." In *Collected Philosophical Papers*, translated by Alphonso Lingis, 1–13. Dordrecht: Martinus Nijhoff, 1987. "La réalité et son ombre." *Les Temps Modernes* 38 (1948): 771–89.

SE   Sigmund Freud. *The Standard Edition of the Complete Psychological Works of Sigmund Freud*. Ed. and trans. James Strachey. London: Hogarth, 1953–74. Rpt. New York: Vintage, 2001.

TD   Emmanuel Levinas. "Truth of Disclosure and Truth of Testimony." In *Basic Philosophical Writings*, edited by Adriaan T. Peperzak, Simon Critchley, and Robert Bernasconi, 98–107. Bloomington: Indiana University Press, 1996. "Vérité du dévoilement et vérité du témoignage." In *Le témoignage*, edited by E. Castelli, 101–10. Paris: Aubier-Montaigne, 1972.

TEM   Cathy Caruth, ed. *Trauma: Explorations in Memory*. Baltimore: Johns Hopkins University Press, 1995.

TI   Emmanuel Levinas. *Totality and Infinity: An Essay on Exteriority*. Translated by Alphonso Lingis. Pittsburgh: Duquesne University Press, 1969. *Totalité et infini: Essai sur l'extériorité*. The Hague: Martinus Nijhoff, 1961.

UE   Cathy Caruth. *Unclaimed Experience: Trauma, Narrative, and History*. Baltimore: Johns Hopkins University Press, 1996.

I have at times modified published translations when a different wording would better reflect features of the original text that are relevant for my discussion.

Witnessing Witnessing

Introduction

As the last Holocaust survivors age and pass away, the awareness that all living memory of the events themselves will soon be extinguished has fostered in regard to survivor testimony what one could call an anxiety of historical transmission. This anxiety accounts in large part for the accelerated production of testimony in the past two or three decades, most notably through the establishment of extensive video archives but also through the publication of written memoirs. It doubtless helps to explain as well the republication or translation of many important texts. Yet transmission has as much to do with reception as with production, and anxiety is a feeling that pertains to the uncertainty of the future—in this instance, a future in which the fate of Holocaust survivor testimony will depend entirely on its reception by those who "were not there." It is thus no accident that, during these same decades, the wealth of testimony made available to the reading or viewing public has been matched if not exceeded by a proliferation of articles and books, as well as educational initiatives extending from elementary schools to universities, concerned with how such testimony can or should be received.

Of course, this concern should not be traced to the anxiety of transmission alone. But enough time has passed to warrant a critical if necessarily limited assessment of recent scholarship that reflects the concern itself no less than that of texts from a somewhat earlier era whose interest it has renewed or even enhanced. *Witnessing Witnessing* approaches the testimony of Holocaust survivors, therefore, by focusing attention on those who receive it. It challenges widely accepted theoretical views about the representation of trauma in general and the Holocaust in particular, as these are set forth in the work of Dori Laub, Cathy Caruth, Berel Lang, and Giorgio Agamben, and it reconsiders, in the work of Theodor W. Adorno and Emmanuel Levinas, reflections on ethics and aesthetics "after Auschwitz" in their pertinence to the reception of testimony. The term *reception*, chosen in part for its accommodation of listening, reading, and viewing, not only designates the focus of the study but also refers to the model of witnessing on which its interpretive framework is based, a model that includes both the situation of address wherein a survivor bears witness to a listener, reader, or viewer and the position one may take as a witness to their interaction. Thus, whether the theoretical work under discussion has primarily to do with trauma, testimony, or artistic representation relevant to both, and whether the place of the survivor is merely implied or represented instead by specific testimony, I approach the work itself as an *act* or a *practice* of reception and pursue its critique accordingly. It goes without saying that *Witnessing Witnessing* is itself open to critique in the same way.

What brings the first of the above-mentioned figures within the purview of this book (as also, but to a lesser extent or in a qualified manner, Adorno and Levinas) is not just a theorizing impulse in regard to traumatic historical experience and its representation but a set of shared attitudes no less remarkable for the different paths leading to them than for their invariably silencing effect on Holocaust survivor testimony or alternative responses to it. These attitudes constitute major thematic preoccupations of the book, just as their contestation represents one of its major objectives. They include, first of all, the view that the Holocaust is intrinsically unspeakable, whether due to the profound psychosocial incapacitation of its victims (Laub and Caruth), the historically unprecedented "desubjectification" of its witnesses (Agamben), or the collective nature of the event itself insofar as it renders "personal" accounts incongruous at best (Lang). Aside from arguing that this view is epistemically unfounded, I emphasize its potentially inhibitive effect on the giving and especially the receiving of testimony.

In the second place, and closely related to this position, is what can be called the "sacralization" of the Holocaust, which here does not denote the integration of this catastrophe into a new theodicy but a tendency nonetheless to make of it a new, if negative, absolute, as well as the basis of a theorizing whose will to render the extreme, transgressive nature of the event can result in so thorough a preoccupation with its own structures and operations, its conceptual paradoxes and hyperbolic generalizations, as to obscure altogether the very history to which it supposedly refers, not to mention the actual experience of that history's victims. This rhetorical self-involvement, together with a compulsive interest in traumatic reenactment, leads me to consider, third, in Laub and Caruth as in Lang and Agamben, the extent to which and the ways in which theoretical approaches to trauma are prone unwittingly to replicate the very object of their study. Whatever the mechanism of this "acting-out" may be, my aim is to show how, in the reception of testimony, it results either in a pronounced listening impairment or in an unjustifiable appropriation of survivors' experience—or both.

This demonstration is not an end in itself but a means of pursuing another major objective of the study, namely, to clarify impediments that anyone receiving testimony may encounter and to emphasize the degree to which reception depends on how well listeners hear themselves. I stress such self-awareness above all because at stake when we witness a witness to the destruction of community are the assumptions we ourselves make about the nature of community and, by extension, the ways in which we "practice" it. In this vein, I draw attention to the need for survivors to resort to conventional modes of communication in order to convey their traumatic experience to the world at large *and* to the no less forceful need for them to challenge convention so as to avoid either aestheticizing that experience or making too much sense of its senselessness. At issue here are also openly contestable interpretations of particular testimonies or discrepancies between theoretical perspectives and the testimonial evidence to whose authority they appeal, as well as theories certain of whose implications, while arguably unintended, are ethically or politically troubling. Moreover,

I venture my own interpretations of relatively well-known testimonies, beginning with one from the Fortunoff Video Archive for Holocaust Testimonies at Yale University and including texts by Charlotte Delbo, Primo Levi, and Jorge Semprun. And it is in part *as* testimony that I read the work of Adorno and, to a much greater extent, Levinas.

Chapter One, "Frames of Reception," focuses on the work of Dori Laub, a psychiatrist, cofounder of the Fortunoff Video Archive at Yale, and co-author, with Shoshana Felman, of the influential book *Testimony: Crises of Witnessing in Literature, Psychoanalysis, and History*. I examine in particular, in a chapter written by Laub and entitled "Bearing Witness, or the Vicissitudes of Listening," the author's well-known and frequently cited account of both the videotaped testimony of an Auschwitz survivor and the debate it provoked between Laub and certain unnamed historians at an interdisciplinary conference on education and the Holocaust. As a viewer of that testimony and a reader of Laub's text, I discuss at some length the conflict between history and psychoanalysis as frameworks for the reception of survivor testimony, emphasizing the relation between fact and interpretation, the role of performative and constative language, the function of narrative in reference to knowledge, and the interactive nature of testimony. At the same time, I am concerned to show that, while the debate represents an instructive clash of disciplines, its traumatic subject also triggers reactive mechanisms that can result in an impairment of listening. The analysis of this impairment leads to a reassessment of reception in terms of the relational self, the generic hybridity of testimony, and the cognitive uncertainty it arouses.

Chapter Two, "Trauma and Theory," starts out from the premise that the reception of testimony is bound to depend on what we understand about trauma and goes on to offer a sustained critique of the theory advanced by Cathy Caruth in *Unclaimed Experience* and related texts. The first part of the critique pertains to the epistemic status of Caruth's theory and is conducted by way of a contrasting comparison with Freud's view of trauma, on which Caruth claims to base her own. Central to this analysis is Caruth's claim that traumatic experience is inherently unrepresentable and its aftermath but an endless repetition of the event or the experience itself, a claim at odds with Freud's understanding of trauma as a profound disturbance of representation that the very self it alters can nonetheless subsequently integrate, at least to some extent, by narrating it to others. Such symbolic interaction points the way to the second part of my critique, which focuses on the ethically problematic nature of a theory that equates the truth of trauma with its ineffability and the historical reality of traumatic experience with what eludes all conscious awareness.

In the third chapter, "Art after Auschwitz, Again," I begin with a historically contextualized reading of Theodor W. Adorno's famous phrase "to write poetry after Auschwitz is barbaric," as it first appears in "Cultural Criticism and Society" and is subsequently modified in "Commitment" and *Negative Dialectics*. My purpose here is to transpose the tension Adorno articulates between ethics and aesthetics—especially in the statement that "suffering demands the continued existence of the very art it forbids"—to a discussion of testimonial discourse. Following his critical comparison of Sartre and Beckett, I stress what Adorno calls "dismantling" as the means by which the artwork resists the very illusion it creates as well as the pleasure or spurious understanding it may afford at the expense of victims. By way of reflections on community and subjectivity, I turn, in a second section of the chapter, to testimonial memoir, examining the first person singular voice from both a linguistic and a narratological point of view and discussing the fundamental historical questions faced by survivors within the situation of address that frames testimony—questions that ultimately train a spotlight on those who receive it.

A third section of this chapter takes up, in Berel Lang's "The Representation of Evil: Ethical Content as Literary Form," a recent and quite literal interpretation of Adorno's phrase, according to which artistic representations of the Holocaust are morally indefensible. I consider the assumptions underlying Lang's position as well as its consequences, but also attempt to account psychologically for its widespread appeal. The last section of the chapter focuses on the practice of survivor testimony in Charlotte Delbo's trilogy of memoirs, *Auschwitz and After*. Here I concentrate mostly on the framework established in the opening pages of the first volume, *None of Us Will Return*, and attempt in so doing to show how this work calls a position such as Lang's into question and even offers a new perspective on Adorno's statements about art after Auschwitz.

Chapter Four, "Theory and Testimony," is framed by the question of theoretical inquiry after Auschwitz and examines at length the theory of testimony presented in Giorgio Agamben's *Remnants of Auschwitz*, together with the testimonial texts of Primo Levi on which it is largely based, "The Gray Zone" and "Shame" (from *The Drowned and the Saved*). I challenge Agamben's view that the concentration camp was a "gray zone" in which victim and perpetrator were indistinguishable, as well as the birthplace of a "new ethics" devoid of responsibility and judgment, and more centrally pursue a critical reflection on what he calls "Levi's paradox," derived from a statement in "Shame" to the effect that the true witnesses were the camp inmates called "Muslims," the very extremity of whose suffering precluded their bearing witness at all. I show how Agamben's universalizing impulse leads him to convert the historical "Muslim" into the concept of a "desub-jectification" constitutive of *all* subjectivity, whereby his theory risks losing sight of the Holocaust, its victims, and its witnesses in their historical speci-ficity. I then propose a different interpretation of Levi's remark, which views it as an expression of affect rather than a statement of fact, and in which the survivor assumes testimonial responsibility for the silenced while delegat-ing the task of listening to us. The chapter concludes with a reading of Levi's description, in *Survival in Auschwitz*, of the dream of "the unlistened-to story."

In the fifth and final chapter, "The Survivor as Other," I return to the relation between ethics and aesthetics discussed in Chapter Three but this time from the perspective offered by the thought of Emmanuel Levinas. Referring to "Truth of Disclosure and Truth of Testimony," "Reality and Its Shadow," and several of his better-known works, I question Levinas's view of the aesthetic as essentially inimical to the ethical relation with the other that is his central concern and that thoroughly informs his own phi-losophy of testimony. I argue that the ethical and the aesthetic only appear to diverge when Levinas associates "art" with the pleasure yielded by static and potentially idolatrous forms of representation and transposes the whole aesthetic dimension of unpleasure to the ethical relation. This relation, which even for Levinas proves inseparable from the aesthetic insofar as it demands the undoing, in representation, of representation itself, leads me to discuss the aesthetics of his own discourse in *Totality and Infinity* and especially *Otherwise than Being*, where, through an "unsaying" reminiscent of Adorno's "dismantling," he insists on the interlocutory relation that pre-cedes and exceeds any given statement and that frames the interaction we call "witnessing."

That the universalizing language of philosophy is still challenged in its effort to convey the singularity of this situation of address invites a juxta-position of Levinas's discourse with a literary "other" in the testimonial memoir of Jorge Semprun, *Literature or Life*. I focus on the opening pas-sage, where Semprun, just liberated from Buchenwald, encounters Allied officers near the gate to the camp and show how in this scene of reception he attempts to mitigate their fear while also forestalling overidentification with the survivor by alluding to rather than directly naming the atrocity of the world he represents, and how such indexical art conveys to readers, not the horrified gaze initially perceived by the officers, but one that he terms "fraternal." This emphasis on the addressee then brings me to consider Levinas's philosophy as a response in its own right to the millions of vic-tims to whom *Otherwise than Being* is dedicated. I argue that the genesis of memory as he sees it is analogous to the dynamics of self-blame, emphasize his increasingly sacrificial view of responsibility, and, referring to his mem-oirlike "Nameless," propose that Levinas's work be envisioned as a philo-sophical allegory of post-traumatic memory.

In the conclusion, I recall what informs the perspective of the book in its entirety, that is, the tension inherent in a relational conception of the self, and briefly refer to extensions of witnessing witnessing beyond the recep-tion of Holocaust survivor testimony. Above all, I stress that our response to survivors is of a piece with our own practice of community.

Frames of Reception

One of the more noteworthy contributions to our understanding of the reception of Holocaust survivor testimony has been made by Dori Laub, a psychiatrist and cofounder of the Fortunoff Video Archive for Holocaust Testimonies at Yale University. In two influential essays, "Bearing Witness, or the Vicissitudes of Listening" and "An Event Without a Witness: Truth, Testimony and Survival,"[1] Laub, who is also a survivor and has served as an interviewer for the Archive, draws attention to the relational nature of testimony by insisting that the listener, as witness to the witness, plays a crucial role in the elaboration of testimonial narrative. Specifically, he makes it clear that listeners enable witnesses to listen to themselves and hence to become survivors in more than the biological sense of the term by speaking of themselves as formerly silenced victims, to create for themselves a present and a future through the distancing act of narrating their past. At the same time, Laub points out that the ability of listeners to play this role depends to some extent on whether they, too, can listen to themselves. That is, even as they focus on what witnesses say (or do not say) and on how it is said (or not), listeners should be alert to the character as well as to the possible causes and effects of their own responses. They must bear witness at once to witnesses and to themselves. Finally, Laub's work suggests that the reception of Holocaust survivor testimony requires not only attending to the voices of witnesses while remaining aware of one's own but also attending, with equal self-awareness, to the voices of other listeners. Witnessing witnessing assumes a community of respondents no less than of testifying survivors.[2]

Of course, not everyone has the opportunity to listen in person to Holocaust survivors, much less to record interviews with them and thus to collaborate in both the production and the reception of testimony. But none of what I have just conveyed from Laub's work loses any of its pertinence when transposed to the reception of testimony already recorded in one form or another: whether survivors' voices continue to be heard will still depend on whether we enable their testimony to speak, and this in turn will still depend in some measure on how well we listen to ourselves and to other listeners. To be convinced of this, one need look no further than Laub's own account, in "Bearing Witness," of the videotaped testimony of an Auschwitz survivor and of the debate provoked by its viewing at an interdisciplinary conference on education and the Holocaust. This portion of his essay has become familiar to many for its anecdotal illustration of an interpretive conflict between history and psychoanalysis. Yet the very succinctness and simplicity that lend it the aura of a fable may also have discouraged any sustained consideration of Laub's account as a case study in the impairment of listening, not only to other listeners but to oneself and to survivors.[3] If I propose such a consideration here, it is certainly in part because, just as psychoanalysis has always learned more from pathology than from health, so perhaps shortcomings in the reception of Holocaust survivor testimony will prove more instructive than successes. But it is also because only close examination of Laub's text and of the videotaped testimony to which it refers can afford an idea of the extent to which and the ways in which the reception of testimony is a question of framing. The analysis that follows will therefore focus primarily on frames of reception, in the expectation that studying a single but noteworthy instance of witnessing witnessing will warrant, in the last section of the chapter, certain general inferences in the name of a reception at once more attentive and more inclusive.

I turn, then, to "Bearing Witness," where the author recounts how "a woman in her late sixties was narrating her Auschwitz experience to interviewers from the Video Archive for Holocaust Testimonies at Yale." Laub notes that the woman was "slight, self-effacing, almost talking in whispers, mostly to herself. Her presence was indeed barely noteworthy in spite of the overwhelming magnitude of the catastrophe she was addressing. She tread lightly, leaving hardly a trace" (BW, 59). This only heightens, by contrast, the subsequent drama of Laub's account:

> She was relating her memories as an eyewitness of the Auschwitz uprising; a sudden intensity, passion and color were infused into the narrative. She was fully there. "All of a sudden," she said, "we saw four chimneys going up in flames, exploding. The flames shot into the sky, people were running. It was unbelievable." There was a silence in the room, a fixed silence against which the woman's words reverberated loudly, as though carrying along an echo of the jubilant sounds exploding from behind barbed wires, a stampede of people breaking loose, screams, shots, battle cries, explosions. It was no longer the deadly timelessness of Auschwitz. A dazzling, brilliant moment from the past swept through the frozen stillness of the muted, grave-like landscape with dashing meteoric speed, exploding it into a shower of sights and sounds. Yet the meteor from the past kept moving on. The woman fell silent and the tumults of the moment faded. She became subdued again and her voice resumed the uneventful, almost monotonous and lamenting tone. The gates of Auschwitz closed and the veil of obliteration and of silence, at once oppressive and repressive, descended once again. The comet of intensity and of aliveness, the explosion of vitality and of resistance faded and receded into the distance. (BW, 59)[4]

As we shall see, it is the first of the three short sentences in quotation marks that allegedly triggered the debate on which this portion of Laub's essay is focused. But the effort he devotes to staging and imaginatively expanding upon what little the woman is quoted as saying should not escape our attention. For although setting the scene of the interview as the context in which her witnessing took place provides information essential to understanding Laub's text, his use of the past progressive tense (as in "a woman in her late sixties was narrating" or "she was relating") creates a suspense that can only pertain to the narrative re-presentation of this witnessing, while his evocation of her voice before, during, and after her brief account of the

Auschwitz uprising is clearly calculated to accentuate ex post facto the contrast he senses between a moment of vitality and the numbness that surrounds it, between a fleeting presence of passionate intensity and the deathly self-effacement by which it is framed. More remarkable yet, the woman is no sooner said to have fallen silent than Laub begins to speak, in a manner that could hardly be confused with the straightforwardness of her own statement, of "a fixed silence against which the woman's words reverberated loudly, as though carrying along an echo of the jubilant sounds exploding from behind barbed wires, a stampede of people breaking loose, screams, shots, battle cries, explosions," emphasizing that "a dazzling, brilliant moment from the past swept through the frozen stillness of the muted, grave-like landscape with dashing meteoric speed, exploding it into a shower of sights and sounds." At first glance, of course, the transition from quoting to commenting may appear so smooth as to suggest that this passage merely prolongs the "reverberation" of the woman's words. But if the phrase "as though" does not already send a sufficient signal, then the rather inflated and overly insistent prose it introduces should certainly alert us to the fact that the witness's silence has here been superseded by Laub's own highly imaginative and appropriative response to her testimony. To put it simply, what we witness in this case is the witnessing of Dori Laub and not of the woman in question. Taking note of Laub's response is also important, finally, because Laub himself does not explicitly acknowledge it as his own. That is, the generalizing third-person grammar in which he formulates it leaves no room to ask how the other interviewer reacted,[5] even as it imparts to the response itself the function of a prompt to Laub's readers—as though anyone in his position would have responded in precisely the same way.

I will eventually return to Laub's description of the Auschwitz uprising in order to evaluate it in historical terms. My point for now is that the perspective from which he will present the controversy concerning this woman's testimony has already been heavily inflected by his own reception of it. And it is especially important that his readers remain aware of this inflection since, as will gradually become clear, the witness to whom he refers as a single individual is arguably a composite figure based on the videotaped testimonies of at least three different women, certain of whose features are exaggerated, transformed, or largely invented.[6]

With all of that in mind, let us consider his summary of the debate, which reads as follows:

> Many months later, a conference of historians, psychoanalysts, and artists, gathered to reflect on the relation of education to the Holocaust, watched the videotaped testimony of the woman, in an attempt to better understand the era. A lively debate ensued. The testimony was not accurate, historians claimed. The number of chimneys was misrepresented. Historically, only one chimney was blown up, not all four. Since the memory of the testifying woman turned out to be, in this way, fallible, one could not accept—nor give credence to—her whole account of the events. It was utterly important to remain accurate, lest the revisionists in history discredit everything.
>
> A psychoanalyst who had been one of the interviewers of this woman, profoundly disagreed. "The woman was testifying," he insisted, "not to the number of the chimneys blown up, but to something else, more radical, more crucial: the reality of an unimaginable occurrence. One chimney blown up in Auschwitz was as incredible as four. The number mattered less than the fact of the occurrence. The event itself was almost inconceivable. The woman testified to an event that broke the all compelling frame of Auschwitz, where Jewish armed revolts just did not happen, and had no place. She testified to the breakage of a framework. That was historical truth." (BW, 59–60)

From the perspective discussed just a moment ago, whose dramatic quality will inevitably affect the perception of even the most critical reader, the historians as Laub portrays them are bound to appear insensitive, if not obtuse, and their concerns quite trivial. Ignoring all that matters to the psychoanalyst (subsequently identified as Laub himself), they focus exclusively on the number of chimneys destroyed, as though one's first response to an earthquake victim should be to ask what this quake measured on the Richter scale. Moreover, Laub compounds the poor impression they make by having them speak, like the positivistic or objectivistic historiography they are alleged to advocate, in a single voice, or rather, in no real voice at all.[7] For unlike the psychoanalyst, whose speech is quoted, theirs is only reported, as would befit a group none of whose members is capable of thinking independently of the others. To make matters still worse, they claim, according to Laub, that the fallibility of the woman's memory concerning the number of chimneys destroyed during the Auschwitz uprising justifies dismissing her testimony as a whole,[8] and thus they appear to abuse the historical method in a way that is typical of the revisionists or Holocaust deniers themselves.[9] In light of all this, one cannot help but suspect that these anonymous historians collectively constitute, for Laub, little more than a convenient straw man. And since nothing in his essay so much as suggests that they might not be representative of historians in general, it is just as difficult to avoid the suspicion that their portrayal is mainly informed by Laub's own questionable assumptions about history as a discipline.[10]

It is worth remarking as well that, in his rebuttal, the psychoanalyst makes a mistake quite similar to that of his adversaries, despite the attempt to distinguish his argument from theirs by speaking in his own voice and as a solitary defender of the otherwise defenseless woman and by emphasizing another, supposedly more fundamental consideration in terms of which her testimony, regardless of its factual inaccuracy, becomes historically intelligible. Just as the historians find in its single flaw sufficient reason to reject her testimony as a whole, so the psychoanalyst finds in the preoccupation with factual accuracy sufficient reason to reject in its entirety their response to that testimony—and this in the name of an interpretive conclusion of which he states, in a fashion no less dogmatic than their own: "That was historical truth." Thus, we need to recognize not only that Laub introduces this debate in a manner deeply colored by his own response to the woman's testimony but that he conveys the competing claims prompted by her testimony through a rather exaggerated rhetoric of persuasion, a rhetoric that must be taken into account if these claims are to be reliably adjudicated.

At this point, though, I would like to enter into the real substance of the debate, beginning with what I take to be the three main components of Laub's position. My presentation of this position is meant to emphasize its strengths, or at least its critical implications, more fully than I believe is done by the essay itself. The same will hold when I present the position of the historians.

In the first place, then, by insisting that the woman testified to "an event that broke the all compelling frame of Auschwitz," that she testified to "the breakage of a framework," Laub clearly highlights the failure or refusal of the historians to take note of this breakage. And by claiming that "one chimney blown up in Auschwitz was as incredible as four," he no less clearly relates this failure or refusal to their own insistence on factual accuracy.

Yet whether they do so knowingly or not, the historians also rely on a rhetoric of persuasion, and in particular on a stratagem that consists essentially in conflating a factual issue with an issue of interpretation. Thus, they begin by rejecting the woman's testimony because of a factual error in her account of the Auschwitz uprising: she alleges that four chimneys were blown up, when in fact only one was destroyed. Moreover, it appears also to be a matter of "the facts" when one of them, having asserted that her account is "hopelessly misleading in its incompleteness" and even that "she had no idea what was going on," notes that "the revolt [was] put down and all the inmates [were] executed," that "they flung themselves into their death, alone and in desperation" (BW, 61)—as though the witness had not already observed that "of course these men knew that this would probably be the end for them" and that the SS "killed out every man." It is apparently still a question of "the facts," and of an account "hopelessly misleading in its incompleteness" due to the witness's having "no idea what was going on," when the same speaker points out that "the Jewish underground was . . . betrayed by the Polish resistance" (BW, 61)—as though the witness had not already demonstrated an awareness of this in her reference to possible but unforthcoming assistance from "the outside, the others."[11] The factual basis on which the historians reject the woman's testimony thus proves to be rather precarious, both because she actually knows much of what they claim she does not and because, in the case of the chimneys, she makes a mistake not only unexceptional in the annals of eyewitness testimony but against which the discipline of history has at its disposal well-known and reasonably adequate methodological or procedural safeguards (such as the comparison of testimonies, the consideration of the personal history of witnesses, and the evaluation of testimony in the light of other forms of evidence).

We might feel justified, therefore, in suspecting that the objections raised by the historians do not primarily concern "the facts," indeed that, again in the case of the chimneys, the wholesale rejection of the woman's testimony seems almost comically dogmatic precisely because at this point a lone fact has been asked to bear the full weight of an unstated interpretive prejudice. Our suspicion is scarcely allayed, moreover, when from the midst of these objections emerges a statement whose predicate is of a clearly interpretive tenor, namely: "She ascribes importance to *an attempt that, historically, made no difference*" (BW, 61, my emphasis). Granted, to describe the rebellion in this way is, on the face of it, simply to express a view according to which it did not, in the end, seriously disable the machinery of extermination at Auschwitz and hence did not alter the course of genocide. In other words, we do not really know enough about the historians to determine whether this view reflects a particular position regarding, for instance, the Jewish response to persecution in general. What we can say for sure, however, by considering their assessment of this particular event, is that for the historians only a general point of view, that is, a position external and posterior to the Holocaust and encompassing the Holocaust in its "completeness," can insure a correct judgment of what, "historically," is "important," and in so doing provide a foundation for the Right Story. As such, the very framework assumed by the historians, in which an act of resistance to genocide is judged "an attempt that, historically, made no difference," can only beg the question: For *whom*, for *whose* history, did it make no difference? And if we now recall that what Laub here considers to be the real point of the woman's testimony, what he refers to as "the breakage of a framework," is precisely this resistance, this act whereby participants in the uprising violated the norms of Auschwitz, it almost seems as though the historians, having left unexamined their own most basic assumption, could not help but miss or dismiss the point. At the same time, the peremptory dismissiveness exhibited by these self-appointed arbiters of what counts in the grand sweep of history can help us to understand why, as a survivor, Laub so "profoundly disagreed" with them, why, indeed, he may have felt bound to marshal his own resistance by staking a claim to historical truth for those courageous inmates who knew only too well that the odds were against both the success of their rebellion and the possibility of their story ever being told or appreciated.[12]

But this leads directly to a second point, or rather to something like a consideration of the first point from a second perspective. For Laub's disagreement with the historians does not revolve exclusively around the significance of the Auschwitz uprising. What he calls "the breakage of a framework" has to do, in his eyes, not only with the act of resistance to which the woman testifies but at least as much with the testifying itself as just such an act. As he puts it, the woman "is breaking the frame of the concentration camp by and through her very testimony: she is breaking out of Auschwitz even by her very talking" (BW, 62). The analogy so drawn between the two types of resistance implies an alternative framework for the reception of testimony that appears, in Laub's account, to have escaped the attention of the historians.

Thus, on the one hand, emphasizing the performative dimension of testimony gives us to understand testimony as an event in its own right. It reminds us that history, especially when it is traumatic, is not just the past, any more than the past is "history," that the very act of representing the past not only reflects but also affects—concretely, empirically—concerns of the present and future. What matters in the woman's witnessing to the revolt at Auschwitz is therefore not merely what she says but what happens, according to Laub, as she says it. The sudden transformation of her demeanor, the strengthening of her voice, the "intensity, passion and color . . . infused into the narrative"—these, too, are signs to be read, visual and auditory clues to the recovery of speech as an agency whereby the silenced victim becomes a storytelling survivor.[13]

On the other hand, envisioning testimony as a recovery of agency inflects our understanding of the knowledge it conveys. "Knowledge in the testimony," notes Laub, is "not simply a factual given that is reproduced and replicated by the testifier, but a genuine advent" (BW, 62). That is, the knowledge conveyed by testimony may certainly turn out to be of a factual order and hence be useful for documentary or historiographical purposes. Yet even knowledge of this kind emerges solely within a narrative framework on which the significance and the very selection or omission of any "factual given" will depend, and in Laub's view, as I suggested at the outset, this framework requires the reconstruction, in witnessing, of the dialogical relation whose disruption is indissociable from victimization itself, a relation in which she who could once be but an object of cognition becomes its subject as well and in which the advent of this subject changes what is or can be known about the object. The point here, indeed, is that the knowledge to which this transformation affords access constitutes, in a sense, a discovery no less for the witness than for the listener. This is so not only because, given the overwhelming nature of trauma, the survivor tends to take cognizance of her own experience in variably delayed stages,[14] but also because the knowledge to which Laub refers only "happens" when the witness has, herself, a witness. In other words, "knowledge in the testimony" is not embodied in a story that would somehow precede its own narration. It is rather a "genuine advent" insofar as it is *produced* by the act of telling.[15]

Granted, the apparent obliviousness of the historians to this dimension of the woman's testimony may come as no surprise. But we should ask why this is so, and whether Laub's claims concerning testimony as performance might not indirectly call historical objectivism itself into question. Indeed, one can surely make due allowance for the generic differences between testimonial and historical narrative, including, most notably, the difference between the first- and the third-person voice and all that it entails, while recognizing nonetheless that both kinds of narrative require an agent whose function is to impart meaning to "the facts" by integrating them into a story.[16] And it is clearly no less true for the historian than for the witness that knowledge or, more precisely, understanding of the past proves worthy of the name only by going beyond the reproduction of isolated facts to encompass the narrative interrelations through which facts are made to signify. Yet in order to resolve these demands in a manner consistent with historical objectivism, its practitioners typically resort to a subterfuge that consists in imputing their own work to history itself. In other words, they deny or at least disguise their role as subjects of knowledge or understanding and agents of narrative interpretation by promoting the notion that the story of the past is found and not made, that the truth of history lies already embedded in the facts themselves, where it simply awaits re-presentation by the historian.[17] Of this we have just seen an example in the assumption, with respect to the Auschwitz uprising and by extension the Holocaust in its entirety, that there can be or rather is one and only one Right Story. Whether we are tipped off by the conspicuous dogmatism of such a story or by the observation that the Holocaust has in fact given rise to multiple and conflicting stories, detecting the cognitive subterfuge of objectivism should suffice to make us realize that the subject of historical knowledge is inevitably implicated in the representation of its object, that those who frame history can always be found reflected within the very frames they impose. By the same token, it suggests that the historians in Laub's account not only pay no heed to the performative dimension of the woman's testimony but fail to suspect how their view of the Holocaust might itself be motivated because they have not been trained to attend, or have been trained not to attend, to their own narrative "performance."[18]

That the teller of a tale is implicated in what is told or how it is told brings us to a third and final point concerning Laub's position vis-à-vis the historians. The point pertains to the interactive nature of witnessing and specifically to the role played by the listener in the shaping of a survivor's story. What Laub has to say about another portion of the woman's testimony is especially instructive in this respect:

> I figured from the woman's testimony that in Auschwitz she had been a member of what is known as "the Canada commando," a group of inmates chosen to sort out the belongings of those who had been gassed, so that those belongings could be recuperated by the Nazis and sent back to Germany. The testifying woman spoke indeed at length of her work in a commando that would leave each morning, separately from the others, and return every night with various items of clothes and shoes in excellent condition. She emphasized with pride the way in which, upon returning, she would supply these items to her fellow inmates, thus saving the lives of some of them who literally had no shoes to walk in and no clothes to protect them from the frost. She was perking up again as she described these almost breathtaking exploits of rescue. I asked her if she knew of the name of the commando she was serving on. She did not. Does the term "Canada commando" mean anything to her? I followed up. "No," she said, taken aback, as though startled by my question. I asked nothing more about her work. I had probed the limits of her knowledge and decided to back off; to respect, that is, the silence out of which this testimony spoke. We did not talk of the sorting out of the belongings of the dead. She did not think of them as the remainings of the thousands who were gassed. She did not ask herself where they had come from. The presents she brought back to her fellow inmates, the better, newer clothes and shoes, had for her no origin. (BW, 60)[19]

From a historian's perspective, what is startling here is not the question Laub asks of the woman but rather her putative ignorance of the term "Canada commando." This ignorance is arguably even more damning than the error she commits in her account of the uprising, for while it would understandably have been difficult to take in all that happened during such a sudden, surprising, and indeed unprecedented disruption of "life" in Auschwitz, it seems quite implausible that an inmate working for any length of time in the *Effektenlager* would not have learned that, in camp slang, this place was called "Canada," and that the items to be sorted there belonged to victims of mass murder.[20] Then again, as we have seen, a preoccupation with factual accuracy or an indulgence of interpretive preconceptions can quickly skew the reception of testimony. In this instance, it is Laub himself who apparently clings to an agenda and who, in his subsequent commentary, emphasizes what can happen when one overplays the historical card. Not only, it seems, does his query concerning the Canada commando momentarily silence the witness and distract attention from the lifesaving assistance she provided to fellow inmates, from acts of resistance he characterizes as "almost breathtaking exploits of rescue" (and this, presumably, because he knows that the theft of property claimed by the Third Reich was subject to severe punishment, even death). Just as important, his alleged change of tactics appears to be motivated by the realization that the query about the Canada commando focuses on what the woman's testimony has in common with others at the expense of what distinguishes it from them, what makes it *this* woman's testimony.

The general lesson Laub draws from his intervention is that the listener actively contributes, for better or for worse, to the construction of testimonial narrative, that the receiving is analogous to the giving of testimony precisely insofar as it involves a process of selection and omission, attention and inattention, highlighting and overshadowing, for which the listener remains responsible. At the same time, there is no mistaking the particular inflection he imparts to this lesson, whereby the listening to be preferred is a listening inclined to favor the experience of the individual survivor over the collective context of that experience. Of course, it is also one thing to interview a Holocaust survivor and quite another to watch videotaped witnessing or to read written testimony, since the interviewer obviously participates in the telling of a story *as* it is told. But this does not really detract from the point Laub wishes to make, for in the case of videotaped or printed testimony, reception manifests itself elsewhere, that is, in the spoken or written response offered to other viewers or readers. Provided this response does not consist in merely quoting a given testimony, it will unavoidably entail interpretation, and thus reflect as much on those who receive and rephrase it as on the witness. Of the interactive nature of witnessing in its very implication of respondents, the debate between Laub and the historians is itself a telling illustration.

At this juncture, however, I would suggest that a more discerning consideration must be granted to the historians, at least insofar as this is possible on the basis of a text that tells us so little about them and that tends to caricature the perspective of traditional historiography. The most forceful response to Laub's position is to be found, not accidentally, in speech that is quoted rather than reported. Although the speaker is not identified, there is still an individualized voice to which we can attend, instead of the ventrilo-quized choral protestations of a like-minded herd. And while this interven-tion does not provide itemized answers to Laub's principal concerns, it nevertheless implies a position from which those concerns can be genuinely addressed. The following passage, much of which I have already quoted in another vein, poses, I would argue, the challenge of listening more carefully than Laub himself appears to have done:

> "Don't you see," one historian passionately exclaimed, "that the woman's eyewitness account of the uprising that took place at Auschwitz is hopelessly misleading in its incompleteness? She had no idea what was going on. She ascribes importance to an attempt that, historically, made no difference. Not only was the revolt put down and all the inmates executed; the Jewish underground was, furthermore, betrayed by the Polish resistance, which had promised to assist in the rebellion, but failed to do so. When the attempt to break out of the camps began, the Jewish inmates found themselves completely alone. No one joined their ranks. They flung themselves into their death, alone and in desperation." (BW, 61)

In the economy of Laub's essay, this passage serves a purpose ostensibly very different from the one I shall now assign it. Immediately after quoting the historian, Laub admits that, when interviewing this woman, he himself was unaware of the betrayal of the Jewish inmates by the Polish under-ground, but he offers this admission only in order to make the point that, had he known of the betrayal, he would probably not have brought it up since, as his query concerning the Canada commando purportedly shows, to do so might well have "derailed the testimony" or even "suppressed [the woman's] message" (BW, 61). To be sure, the delicate dialogical balance to be struck by the listener is, as we have seen, a problem of crucial impor-tance in the reception of testimony. However, Laub's sustained insistence on listening in a certain manner to the witness seems to have prevented him to some extent from listening to his fellow listeners. Intent on using the intervention just quoted to promote his own framework for reception, he appears oblivious to the ways in which this very framework is called into question by the remarks of the historian. I would like to turn here to the analysis of this contestation as it pertains to Laub's three main arguments, starting with the one discussed most recently.

To begin with, then, it is clear that the historian in question is aware of the interpretive role he or she plays in the reception of testimony. Were this not the case, there would simply have been no debate. But more to the point, the debate took place, as I have indicated, at a conference devoted to Holocaust education, where the whole thrust of his or her intervention had arguably to do with the proper contextualization of the woman's testimony for those still learning to contextualize, with the communication of Holocaust history to other as yet less informed listeners. In this connection, we should also note that the tone in which the historian's remarks were delivered is characterized by Laub as one of "passionate exclamation." Since when do the proponents of a cold, hard, impersonal truth of history indulge in passionate exclamation? Might not this passion suggest that something is at stake here beyond mere disciplinary territoriality? Does it not force us to consider whether the objective ideal of traditional historiography might be a matter not only of cognition but of ethics as well? And if so, where precisely does its ethical motive manifest itself?

I believe we can base a reliable answer to this question on the pedagogical issue just mentioned no less than on the debate devoted to it. Although it is admittedly one thing to speak with fellow educators and another to speak with students, in both cases one bears responsibility toward a multiplicity of listeners. To be sure, this situation of address by no means precludes exchange between just two interlocutors; yet such exchange is always mediated by a "third party," be it in the form of another person witnessing the exchange or, in the absence of any witness, in the form of institutional standards or simply the most basic rules of social conduct. Thus, from the perspective afforded at once by relations between teachers and students and among educators themselves, responsibility must be assumed not only toward "the other" but toward all others, that is, toward the community. And I think it is safe to say that the passionate and exclamatory tone characterizing the response of the historian to the woman's testimony and perhaps especially to Laub's own reception of it derives in turn from the adoption of this perspective not only in regard to colleagues and students as other listeners but also in regard to victims and surviving witnesses other than the testifying woman. Indeed, while suspending the framework of community may be justified to some degree in an interview, for educational or more broadly social purposes any such suspension is dubious at best, since it ensures no hearing to those whose experience and memory differ from the interviewee's and whose stories are probably of equal and possibly of greater collective significance. In contrast, for instance, to the testimony cited by Laub, or more precisely to Laub's embellishment of the woman's silence, other accounts of the Auschwitz uprising, including the one by Filip Müller, a member of the *Sonderkommando* itself, can hardly be said to describe its atmosphere as "jubilant," "dazzling," or "brilliant."[21] One can legitimately ask therefore whether Laub has not so thoroughly conflated the position of the educator and author with that of the interviewer (or rather, as we shall see, the psychoanalyst) as to ascribe an imagined "jubilation" to resisters who, by other accounts, "flung themselves into their death, alone and in desperation"—and whether, in stressing the story of the individual survivor to the detriment of the collective history in which it is embedded, he does not convincingly if inadvertently demonstrate that the successes and failures of listening amount to a good deal more than mere "vicissitudes."

No doubt, the gathering opacity of a text that appears at first glance to be relatively transparent is due in large part to the multiple roles played by Laub, or rather, as I have just suggested, to his failure to distinguish adequately between them at certain moments. The resulting confusion comes into play once again where the performative function of testimony and its relation to knowledge are concerned. Alluding to his own ignorance of the betrayal of the Jewish underground by the Polish resistance, Laub states of the interviewer: "Of course, it is by no means ignorance that I espouse. The listener must be quite well informed if he is to be able to hear—to be able to pick up the clues. Yet knowledge should not hinder or obstruct the listening with foregone conclusions and preconceived dismissals, should not be an obstacle or a foreclosure to new, diverging, unexpected information" (BW, 61). On the face of it, there is nothing here that we have not already encountered or that would have elicited persuasive objections from Laub's adversaries in the debate. But he then goes on to say that "in the process of the testimony to a trauma, as in psychoanalytic practice, in effect, you often do not want to know anything except what the patient tells you, because what is important is the situation of *discovery* of knowledge—its evolution, and its very *happening*" (BW, 62). Whether it is deliberate or not, the very vagueness of the phrase "the process of the testimony to a trauma" clearly neglects to stipulate the framework of that process, thus facilitating an implicit conflation of the witness with the "patient" and hence of the listener with the psychoanalyst. However, if we assume—as the very framework of Laub's essay would entitle us and the framework of the debate itself would have entitled the historians to do—that "the process of the testimony to a trauma" means the interviewing of a Holocaust survivor for a videotape archive, then the comparison of this process with psychoanalytic practice in terms of the advent of knowledge they supposedly have in common serves in fact to highlight their radical dissimilarity as contexts for this advent. It is not only that psychoanalytic practice typically involves a single listener and is bound by rules of confidentiality or privacy, whereas the interview may well include, as in the testimony cited by Laub, more than one listener and is in any case made accessible to the public. What is more, their structural dissimilarity is evidently determined by a fundamental difference of purpose, a difference reflected in turn by the incommensurable values they respectively ascribe to narrative in relation to knowledge.

Thus, in the psychoanalytic "talking cure," the priority granted to knowledge as an event is of a piece with the priority granted to the performative function of storytelling: that is, the process of cognition coincides with a process of narration that literally changes or alters the patient. The therapeutic efficacy of this narrative "working-through" can in fact be gauged by the degree to which it tempers the behavioral reenactment or "acting-out" of trauma, by the degree to which it moves the patient to shed a role scripted by others in order to assume authorship of her or his own story.[22] And this "breakage of a framework," wherein one comes to know oneself as a silenced victim only through one's transformation into a storytelling survivor—this *is* the event or advent, the "happening" of knowledge. Such knowledge remains, however, essentially *intra*subjective. Indeed, if in psychoanalytic practice the objective truth or falsehood of what is discovered through storytelling can be relegated to a secondary status or even bracketed altogether, if as a practitioner "you often do not want to know anything except what the patient tells you," it is because this practice seeks first and foremost to reestablish and reinforce within the patient the very distinction between subject and object on whose basis a cognitive relation to objects other than the self, including other subjects, becomes possible. And it is, furthermore (and among other reasons), because this distinction is for the patient both precarious and evolving that the practice of psychoanalysis or psychotherapy must be shielded from public scrutiny.

The testimonial interview, on the other hand, can be said to "break the framework" of psychoanalysis to the extent that, in keeping at once with its public character and with its documentary and educational purpose, it must presuppose on the part of the narrating witness a relatively unimpaired capacity for objective cognition.[23] This is not to say that, in the interviewing of a Holocaust survivor, the performative should or does simply give way to the constative function of storytelling, or that the haste with which Laub's interlocutors overlook the performative force of the woman's testimony is, after all, excusable (although, as before, we must take into account the tendentious manner in which Laub conveys their reaction). It is rather a question of counteracting Laub's own inclination to tip the scales in favor of performance, to stress the performative at the expense of the constative, to promote a psychoanalytic to the detriment of a historical framework for the reception of testimony—when it is otherwise clear from the debate in which he is engaged that the generic hybridity of testimony requires for its reception that the very tension between such frameworks be maintained.[24] Here again, I will revert to the example of the Canada commando. Simply put: Why would a (competent) psychoanalyst ask his patient for the name of the commando on which she served in Auschwitz? What properly therapeutic purpose could such an inquiry serve, especially when it might, and in this case, according to Laub, actually does entail startling and momentarily silencing the woman just as she is "perking up again"? That Laub nevertheless makes this inquiry attests, as I see it (and as I suspect the historians would have seen it), to his doing so from a position irreducible to that of the psychoanalyst, from the position of a listener who understands that the role of an interviewer for a video archive is to represent other listeners, to listen not only for himself but for those who, like him, want to know and for whom the woman's memory of the Canada commando contributes to a sense of who she was and is relative to the events she recounts. At the same time, I would suggest that, instead of being construed as a sign of disrespect if not a violation of the unspoken taboo against testing the word of a Holocaust survivor, holding the witness accountable to certain objective standards in order to fulfill the responsibility of listening for others might well be considered a way of welcoming the witness herself into the community of these listeners.

Finally, let me return to the issue of historical truth. As we have seen, Laub describes the *Sonderkommando* rebellion that took place at Auschwitz-Birkenau on October 7, 1944, as "an event that broke the all compelling frame of Auschwitz, where Jewish armed revolts just did not happen, and had no place." He then summarizes his response to the historians, who so hastily impugn the credibility of the woman witnessing to this event, by saying: "She testified to the breakage of a framework. That was historical truth." In thus relating the breakage of a framework to historical truth, Laub clearly ascribes such truth both to the rebellion itself in its historical reality and to its witnessing by this woman, whom he portrays, again, as "breaking the frame of the concentration camp by and through her very testimony."[25] There is, moreover, another framework at stake here, which Laub's assertion on behalf of the insurgents and their witness threatens in turn to "break." For as we have also seen, the historians appear to hold a view of the Holocaust that not only leads them to devalue or dismiss this account of resistance but would presumably lead them as well to credit survivor testimony in general primarily if not exclusively insofar as it serves to document a story of collective persecution. What Laub is perhaps too kind or discreet to state explicitly, and which I will thus take it upon myself to point out, is that, by defining the individual overwhelmingly in terms of his or her membership in and conformity to a group, this view can prove to be (re)victimizing in its own right, and most noticeably so when it seeks to silence particular voices that cannot be easily accommodated within its universalizing framework. And what he is doubtless too modest to claim is that to this framework, in which the Auschwitz uprising is characterized as "an attempt that, historically, made no difference," he enacts, as I earlier suggested, his own resistance, posing in effect the simple question: For whom, for whose history, did it make no difference? To put this otherwise, one could say that, like the woman from the Canada commando, Laub is engaged in a rescue operation, contesting a depersonalizing historiography in order to restore the historical truth of what a fellow survivor, Aharon Appelfeld, calls "the individual, with his own face and proper name."[26]

Aside from the question whether Laub has fairly represented the position of the historians, however, one can ask on their behalf (but not only on theirs) if he has met the demands of his own project. As I have already observed, the witness to whom he refers as a single individual may well be a composite figure, whose features are based on the videotaped testimonies of at least three different women. And as I have also remarked, certain of these features are exaggerated, transformed, or invented. In short, despite Laub's promoting an approach to the reception of Holocaust testimony so deeply concerned with the individual survivor, an approach of which one would expect at the very least an attentiveness to the facts pertaining to this or that particular witness and distinguishing witnesses from each other, his "testifying woman" appears to have come into being through a process quite similar to the way in which writers of fiction construct the characters peopling their novels or short stories. True, the three interviews just mentioned were all conducted on the same day (November 7, 1982), and similarities between the witnesses, together with the strain placed on the interviewers themselves in such lengthy and psychologically taxing interactions, could help to explain the creative misremembering that contributes to Laub's portrayal of the "testifying woman."[27] Yet presumably nothing prevented Laub from reviewing the tapes of these interviews prior to drafting and especially to publishing his essay. The inescapable impression one receives, namely, that he failed to do so, seems therefore to suggest a fundamental neglect of the very individuals whose voices he seeks to champion. What is more, although the act of publishing here implies an invitation to collaborative listening and, by extension, to critical dialogue, Laub's readers are deprived of the means required to offer an informed response, that is, of any notational reference identifying the videotape(s) in question (not to mention the conference where the debate took place and, of course, the historians supposedly involved in it). As a result, either these readers are misled or else they discover, through a good deal of detective work, that the evidentiary basis on which a community of respondents must rely to ascertain the truth of the individual survivor has been undermined by what one might call Laub's own mythmaking.[28]

I would point out as well, to conclude my analysis of the debate, that this mythmaking is not entirely unmotivated. In fact, it is by recalling the relational model with which I credited Laub at the very outset that we can begin to ascertain how, in his personal practice of witnessing witnessing, relationality itself is sacrificed to something on the order of what in psychoanalysis would be termed "identification" or "transference."[29] As we have just seen, the failure to grant due consideration to other listeners is of a piece with the failure to respect the identity of the three witnesses, that is, their otherness in regard both to one another and to the image that their immediate addressee is inclined to form of them. Indeed, if it is felt that no verifiable account of "the testimony to a trauma" need be or, as in psychoanalysis, even should be offered to a community of potential respondents, there is obviously no constraint capable of assuring witnesses that the integrity of their testimony will be preserved in whatever account of it is actually offered. Whether we then speak, in the case at hand, of transference or identification, fairly free rein is therefore given to a tendency on the part of the listener to reduce or even surmount the very difference between self and other.

This tendency is at work, for example, when Laub recalls the segment of Serena N.'s testimony pertaining to the Auschwitz uprising. Not only is the witness's statement misquoted and overdramatized, not only is a barely detectable change in her demeanor described as a striking transformation, but a "fixed silence," unattested by the videotape itself, becomes the locus in which Laub imagines a "jubilant" rebellion against the SS—as though it were possible to achieve with the survivor a kind of "communion" in the memory of heroic resistance. The same tendency manifests itself in Laub's recollection of testimony concerning the Canada commando. Whereas the witness (be it Irene W. or Rose A.), referring to the smuggling of goods from the *Effektenlager* for the sake of less fortunate fellow inmates, shows no change in her tone of voice or her demeanor and no sign that she considered her actions especially noteworthy, Laub states that "she was perking up again as she described these almost breathtaking exploits of rescue." More serious still, whereas Irene W. or Rose A. (no less than Serena N.) knew perfectly well that the clothes, food, and other items from which surviving deportees were benefiting belonged to victims of mass murder, Laub claims that she was completely unaware of their provenance. He thus invents another silence, whose function, it seems, is not so much to salvage human agency from a universe of overwhelming victimization as to rescue innocence itself from a world in which even the victims were made to feel permanently compromised by the atrocities committed in their midst. Such innocence, far more "unimaginable," "incredible," or "inconceivable" (BW, 60) than the uprising itself, suggests a wish that certain values or beliefs might survive the Holocaust intact and hence, like the faith in human goodness expressed by Anne Frank only days before her arrest and deportation, could perhaps provide some degree of reassurance when the real testimony of Irene W. or Rose A., in its brittle sobriety and occasional despair, offers none. But the price to be paid is clear, since, in the image of the "testifying woman" to which this fiction contributes, none of the three individuals mentioned here, "with her own face and proper name," none of these witnesses to whom, in their otherness, one is enjoined to listen (as to other listeners and, indeed, to oneself) remains entirely recognizable.

———

As I have tried to show, all of the major issues dividing Laub and the historians derive from a fundamental disagreement about the frame or frames within which testimony is or should be received. What counts as historically significant or truthful; the value attributed respectively to the constative and performative dimensions of testimonial narrative in its relation to knowledge; the precise role assigned to the listener or reader in the interactive process of witnessing—and much else besides, including the competing claims of the community and the individual as well as the relative pressure of the past and the present and future—all of these depend on the conventions, at least as often implicit as explicit, according to which the context of reception is delimited.

I also hope to have shown, however, that what we witness here is not just a disagreement but a deeply polarized polemic, a debate in which both parties practice a listening so highly selective as to yield consequences at once unintended and undesirable, such as the silencing of survivors. No doubt, it is tempting to think that the partisan thrust of this debate reflects the anxiety of historical transmission mentioned in the introduction, to think that, as the last survivors pass from the scene, those concerned with the future reception of their testimony seek a certainty of hearing if only in listening of a certain kind (when they have not already chosen a certain kind as the avenue to all such certainty), and in so doing promote divisive views about the community not only of witnesses but of listeners as well. But be this as it may, the least we can do is to ask what general conclusions might be drawn from the listening impairments just diagnosed, especially insofar as these conclusions bear on the issue of education, whether understood, as it presumably was at the conference where the debate took place, in the formal, institutional sense, or more broadly as the process whereby any listener or reader learns, and relearns, to receive testimony.

To begin with, there is the matter of "objectivity"—and so, inevitably, of "subjectivity"—concepts that, given the ideological polarization so palpable in the debate, might be most easily elucidated through their respective differentiation from the extremes of objectivism and subjectivism. As I suggested a moment ago, it would be a mistake to dismiss Laub's work as a whole, especially his relational model of witnessing, simply on account of shortcomings in his own reception of testimony. This is so, however, not only because the model can serve as a diagnostic tool but also because it presupposes a notion of the self or subject that can facilitate the differentiation just mentioned. Thus, although Laub himself does not make use of the following terminology, it is clear that, in his as in any such model worthy of the name, the subject is understood not as an existent constituted independently of any relations with others of its kind but rather as one whose constitution depends on these relations in the first place. Whether, for further examples, we look to philosophy, where, in Levinas's work, the very singularity of the self emerges from the encounter with and response to an other; to Freudian psychoanalysis, where the ego is born of the id through contact with the external world and above all with parents; or to linguistics, where Benveniste, among others, defines the "I" as inextricable from the "you" (and, since these pronouns are universally available, from third persons as well)—we find that the identity of the self derives from alterity, its sameness from difference, its interiority from an "outside" without which no relation *to* itself—in this instance, no listening to itself or, in keeping with the holism of the model, to others as others—would even prove conceivable. According to this view, in short, the subject, bearing the indelible stamp of that from which it becomes separate, remains in its very separation a fundamentally relational being.

It follows from this that relationality provides the basis of a capacity for "putting oneself in the place of another." The identificatory tendency impelling creation of the "testifying woman" would thus hardly be peculiar to Dori Laub, except in the extent to which it detracts from relationality itself.

Yet everything depends, indeed, on this extent. Where identification means putting oneself in the place of another without leaving one's own, where it fosters an empathy tempered by the awareness of an irreducible difference,[30] where it sustains the relation *between* listener and witness, identification remains in the service of reception, since it is in this relation that, putting themselves in the place of listeners, silenced victims become storytelling survivors (without ceasing to have been silenced victims), and in this relation, therefore, that memory finds the space or "extent" of its articulation. And yet—whether motivated by a desire to rescue survivors from their traumatic past, to reduce tensions aroused in oneself by the witnessing of witnessing, or to make sense of one's own experience by appropriating another's—where identification leads the listener to usurp the place of the witness, to lose sight of what distinguishes them, this space is severely constricted or abolished altogether, and an approach to testimony determined to emphasize the "other" historical truth, the truth of memory, becomes so subjectivistic as to betray that truth no less thoroughly than does historical objectivism itself.

As for objectivism, it should not be difficult to characterize within the limited scope of this discussion, given how familiar we have become with the position often assumed, in the debate with Laub, by the historians.[31] Thus, if in this case subjectivism consists in assimilating the other to the self through an unrestrained identification of the listener with the witness, objectivism, for its part, proceeds, through a radical *dis*identification of the listener with the witness, to deny any sameness of self and other. Either way, of course—by fusion, by exclusion—it is relationality that suffers eclipse. To be more precise, one would have to say that through its denial of relationality—that is, through its opposition of the purely "objective" historian and the merely "subjective" witness—objectivism purports to renounce *all* subjectivity as such for the sake of its "view from nowhere" or its "God's eye view" of history, since only if the historian is divested of his or her particular selfhood can the objectivity of history as a discipline be absolved of its own historicity.

While this position has predictably produced any number of futile arguments between objectivists and their critics,[32] its more serious effect has been to obscure the very basis on which a credible objectivity can be sought, which is, again, the capacity for "putting oneself in the place of another," or as the historian Thomas Haskell has phrased it, the capacity "to achieve some distance from one's own spontaneous perceptions and convictions, to imagine how the world appears in another's eyes, to experimentally adopt perspectives that do not come naturally."[33] Of this capacity, we should note especially that the distance it affords does not involve the self-renunciation behind whose pretense, as in the Right Story of the Holocaust, objectivism gives rein to the indulgence of "one's own spontaneous perceptions and convictions." For "to imagine how the world appears in another's eyes" is to acknowledge the position from which one does so, to acknowledge, in other words, one's self in relation to that other. It is therefore also to recognize, in light of this relation to another or to others, that historical inquiry begins not with an absolute or dehistoricized and hence delusional "detachment" but from a position informed by the this-worldly standards of an evolving community, and that claims to historical knowledge or truth are inevitably constrained by the context in which they are advanced. Rather than deny, like objectivism, its own historicity, and instead of turning a blind eye as well to the intrinsic fallibility of human cognition, the objectivity in question strives to take these into account, founded as it is on a relationality in which awareness of the other and self-awareness are entirely of a piece.[34]

In regard to the "testifying woman," then, or more precisely, to Serena N.'s account of the *Sonderkommando* rebellion at Auschwitz, this objectivity would require us to consider how it was possible and even highly likely, in such chaos and confusion, *not* to know fully what was happening,[35] and to ask in turn how this not knowing might contribute, precisely in conjunction with the historiographical record since established, to a greater understanding of Auschwitz and perhaps more broadly of the Holocaust than any we could derive from mere fact checking. At the same time, it would entail observance of the most elementary methodological precept, namely, that all eyewitness testimony must be evaluated on a comparative basis, and that, just as no historical narrative can rely on the account of a single eyewitness, so no single error committed by an otherwise reliable eyewitness justifies dismissing that witness's testimony in its entirety. And finally, an objectivity cognizant of its debt to the relational subject would force us to consider what is socially, politically, historically, or otherwise at stake in the context of reception, and what our personal investment in a particular mode of reception might be, so that, unlike Laub's historians at their most objectivistic, we might at least avoid the silencing of others entailed by the forgetting of ourselves.

A second point to be made in light of the listening impairments detected in the debate between Laub and the historians has to do with the question of genre, to which I earlier referred in claiming that, as a generic hybrid, testimony requires for its reception a plurality of interpretive frameworks.[36] Strictly speaking, to be sure, all genres are hybrid, since each depends for its generic cohesion on an implicit differentiation from other, especially neighboring, genres. If emphasizing hybridity in this sense does not yet teach us anything about testimony in particular, however, it is worth noting that the interpretation of testimonial discourse, as of any other type, is bound to suffer if it cannot rely on an understanding of the difference constitutive of genre per se. This understanding proves all the more crucial as the conventions associated with a given genre not only govern its production but serve to shape its reception, to establish the very expectations it strives to meet.

For all the talk of "frames" in Laub's essay, it is thus quite remarkable how little attention is actually paid to the framing of videotaped testimony as a genre. The historians (to the extent, once more, that we can rely on Laub's portrayal of them) appear to approach such testimony in complete disregard of its generic specificity, as though it were just another source of historical documentation. And yet, faced with documentation of any kind—be it articles, books, speeches, letters, memos, orders, bills, blueprints, films, photographs, confessions, memoirs, or eyewitness testimony (oral or written)—no self-respecting historian, even or perhaps especially among those of the most objectivistic stripe, would enlist it in support of a narrative reconstruction without first considering its form, its provenance, its intended use, the conditions under which it was produced, and its significance in relation to other available evidence. At the very least, then, through their wholesale rejection of testimony in which it is mistakenly alleged that four chimneys were destroyed during the Auschwitz uprising, the historians miss the opportunity to open a discussion about educating others in the use of eyewitness accounts for the narrative reconstruction of historical events—a discussion in which, moreover, the fallibility of such accounts could give rise to instructive questions regarding the fallibility of historiography itself.

As for Laub, we have seen how strong is his tendency to look at video-taped testimony through the lens of clinical psychotherapy, as though at stake were primarily if not exclusively a "private" relation between the witness and an individual respondent. In addition to the shortcomings I have already emphasized in this approach, it seems fairly obvious that Laub is unable or unwilling to consider the ways in which both testimony and its reception are inflected by the very act of videotaping, by the protocol that governs it, and by the consignment of witnessing so recorded to a publicly accessible archive.

This said, the major features accounting for both the specificity and the hybridity of videotaped testimony as a genre are plain to see. Although the audiovisual recording of thousands of survivors and the creation of a permanent archive to house their testimony attest in themselves to a sense of historical mission, the very sense of history operative in this mission is inextricably bound to a certain understanding of memory. If the Archive serves to "document" the Holocaust, it is not primarily by corroborating and extending what is or can be known from other sources about the collective cataclysm of 1933–45.[37] Nor does its principal documentary value derive solely from preserving the stories of individual lives as they were lived during this cataclysm. Memory here surpasses the mere recollection of events circumscribed by the commonly dated period of the Shoah. For at stake in the stories told by survivors is not only what happened but *how* it is remembered, and the "how" of memory in turn not only has itself a history but suggests accordingly that, as an event, a traumatic historical event whose repercussions have far from diminished with time, the Holocaust must be understood to include its own aftermath.[38]

In this respect, it is worth noting that the creation of what is now called the Fortunoff Video Archive dates from the same era as the release of Claude Lanzmann's film *Shoah*, which "documents" the Holocaust exclusively through testimony (albeit that of perpetrators and bystanders no less than of survivors),[39] as well as the publication of Henry Rousso's *The Vichy Syndrome*, which examines the "history of memory" pertaining to France's "dark years" (1940–44) and is one of the first historical works to emphasize at any length the crucial role played by filmed testimony in representing the war and the Holocaust.[40] As in Lanzmann's film and Rousso's book, so in the Archive memory appears as the mode in which history most tangibly lives on, outlives or survives itself. And for this history, objective historiography is at once necessary, since only against its universalizing background can the particularization of memory be made to stand out, and insufficient, since this particularization can be explained only by factors that do not fall exclusively or even primarily within the purview of such historiography, be they social, psychological, political, cultural, or of still another order. In brief, the "field" in which the Archive is situated requires that its holdings be approached from a consciously interdisciplinary perspective.

Equally important, however, are formal features that, in keeping with the differential nature of genre in general, emerge from a closer comparison of videotaped testimony with what is arguably its nearest neighbor, namely, filmed testimony as it appears, indeed, in *Shoah*. On the one hand, neither the kind of witnessing to be found in the Archive nor the kind presented by Lanzmann can be assured of even a remotely adequate reception if this reception does not demonstrate an awareness of the formal characteristics they share. Thus, in both cases the visual and verbal media constitute a hybrid "text" whose differing modes of signification demand a reading not only in their own right but especially in relation to each other. At the same time, the narration of a first person whose voice is audible (with its accent, its inflections, its rhythm and volume) and whose face and body are visible imparts to such testimony an aura of indexicality[41]—conveys, that is, a tangible remnant of history itself—to which no written testimony can aspire. And finally, the audible and occasionally visible presence of the interviewer(s) lends to the dialogical relation of witnessing a concreteness far removed from what may seem, in written testimony, to be only a disembodied interaction of pronouns.

On the other hand, although, due to the relatively recent development of filmed and videotaped testimony, the distinction between them may remain less pronounced than between other genres, in this case one can point to at least two fundamental differences. First, there is an obvious difference in scope. By this, I mean not so much a difference in length (the viewing time of Lanzmann's film exceeds nine hours, while that of tapes from the Archive is typically ninety minutes) as a difference in breadth: whereas videotaped testimony focuses on the story of an individual survivor, the witnessing of *Shoah* comes from a large number and wide variety of individuals (including, as I have noted, perpetrators and bystanders as well as survivors) and is excerpted and configured in such a way as to create a vast testimonial tableau of the Final Solution. This editorial intervention points in turn to a second fundamental difference, having to do with the staging of testimony. What some might call the "amateurish" quality of tapes from the Archive is the result of an explicit policy: the bareness of the rooms in which such testimony is recorded, the minimal changes in camera angle or framing, the anonymity and discretion of the interviewers, the "open-ended, free-flowing interview process" itself[42]—all of this is designed to leave the initiative to the witness and to concentrate attention on the telling and the tale of victimization and survival. In *Shoah*, by contrast, Lanzmann's directorial control is unmistakable, most notably in the pursuit of a certain reenacting distinct from retelling (be it at an emotional cost to survivors); in the filming, for this purpose, of interviews at sites of atrocity or, failing this, at locations resembling such sites, or even on constructed sets, whose effect on the viewer is reinforced by camera work of some sophistication; and lastly, in the sustained presence of Lanzmann's familiar voice as well as the frequency with which he enters the visual frame.

To be sure, the dual role of director and interviewer and its decisive impact on the work itself, just like the use of historically significant sites to frame the act of witnessing, are not peculiar to Lanzmann but can be found, for example, in Marcel Ophuls's earlier *The Sorrow and the Pity*.[43] Nevertheless, a feature that strikingly distinguishes Lanzmann's film, both from Ophuls's work and especially from the kind of videotaped testimony discussed here, is the drive to elicit from interviewees a reenactment—whether it is Simon Srebnik intoning a ballad he sang in exchange for his life or, in another scene, surrounded by villagers who offer a victim-blaming explanation for the killing of the Jews; the barber Abraham Bomba, asked to imitate cutting the hair of friends about to be gassed; or Henrik Gawkowski, driving a locomotive in Treblinka—a reenactment designed, it seems, to afford immediate access to the experience of atrocity, to enable those who "were not there" to participate in, and hence in some measure to appropriate, the traumatization of those who were.[44] Concerning the reception of Holocaust survivor testimony, few contrasts are more instructive than that between an approach respectful of the distance separating witnesses from their listeners and an approach intent on abolishing that very distance.[45]

Much more undoubtedly remains to be said about the issue of genre in relation to Holocaust survivor testimony. Here I will add only that such testimony should not itself be confused or conflated with a genre. This is not to deny the historical precedence of testimony in its legal acceptation, nor to overlook the role that testimony of this kind has played in the postwar trials of perpetrators, nor to underestimate the contribution that this or similar types of witnessing have made to the factual documentation of the Holocaust. However, if the meaning of a term is really its usage, then we should be prepared to ask why "Holocaust testimony" today not only refers to statements elicited from survivors by courts of law or simply for the historical record, as well as to the chronicles, diaries, journals, and reports produced during the war and the written memoirs and oral history produced after it, but also frequently encompasses other modes of expression to which survivors have had recourse, such as the short story, the novel, and lyric poetry.[46] As though in response to this question, Geoffrey Hartman wisely remarks that "to 'transmit the dreadful experience' we need *all* our memory-institutions: history-writing as well as testimony, testimony as well as art."[47] But it may be that the lines between historiography, testimony, and art are no longer so clearly drawn—and especially that not even all our memory institutions, not even all the genres in which testimony might be housed, have proven or are likely to prove adequate to "transmit the dreadful experience," since the experience itself pertained to the destruction of community and hence could only leave testimony to seek a temporary home in its cultural ruins, to haunt the remnants of genre, just as more generally the Holocaust continues to haunt its own historical aftermath. It is in this vein, indeed, that Ross Chambers, in a chapter of his *Untimely Interventions* devoted to Holocaust testimony, speaks so eloquently of "orphaned memory."[48] In short, no general consideration of genre should remain uninformed by the awareness that testimony exceeds any and all of the shapes it has assumed, because this excess is itself meaningful or significant, because it sheds light on the nature of "that which happened."[49]

The last point I wish to convey differs somewhat in nature from those already discussed but nevertheless has everything to do with the spirit in which we approach them and, for that matter, any of the major issues raised by the debate. It has to do specifically with certainty—or uncertainty. Let me recall that, in an apparent attempt to justify their wholesale rejection of testimony in which it is mistakenly alleged that four chimneys were destroyed during the Auschwitz uprising, the historians conjure up the specter of Holocaust denial, claiming, according to Laub, that "it was utterly important to remain accurate, lest the revisionists in history discredit everything." In order properly to contextualize this remark, I would also recall that, in the years immediately preceding the debate, the so-called "revisionists" or Holocaust deniers began to achieve an unusual degree of public exposure, having shifted their agenda from the disreputable fringes toward the mainstream of political exchange precisely by appropriating the respectable discourse of academic historiography.[50] To be fair to the historians, then, we should recognize how severely the already prevalent anxiety of historical transmission may have been exacerbated by this development, by this resurgence of a denial that, insofar as it seeks to obliterate the very memory of "that which happened," I would not hesitate to characterize as the pursuit of genocide by other means.

However, what the historians fail to recognize in their dogmatism is how easily they themselves fall prey to the deniers. For one of the tactics most frequently employed by Holocaust deniers consists in appealing or feigning to appeal to the assumptions of their adversaries—in this instance, the objectivistic assumption whereby history is found and not made, whereby historical truth simply inheres in facts that "speak for themselves," and whereby, therefore, doubts concerning certain facts or relations between facts can suffice to bring the whole edifice of the Right Story tumbling down. On the basis of such doubts, especially in their effort to reach a public whose members are too young or lack the opportunity or the inclination to familiarize themselves with the complexities of historiography and for whom the notion of the Right Story may seem to make so much common sense, it is mere child's play for deniers to convert the issue of what, to the best of our knowledge, can be said to have happened (not to mention how or why it happened) into the issue of *whether* it happened. And this unfortunately is not all, since, as the debate suggests, the tactic in question can function within a strategy whose larger purpose is to sow division among those who have every reason to practice solidarity with one another (and which in some measure is reminiscent of the strategy implemented by the Nazis through ghetto *Judenräte*, or Jewish Councils): not only do the historians "silence" Serena N., as would their adversaries, but they lead Laub to exhibit in her defense a dismissiveness of factual accuracy that plays no less than their own dogmatism into the hands of Holocaust deniers.

My concern here, though, is not primarily with Holocaust denial or the kind(s) of response that must be made to it but with the cognitive constriction it produces or reinforces in this debate. For the historians focus overwhelmingly on *what* happened, with the all too obvious ambition of "being right." And in pursuing such a narrowly circumscribed certainty, they can easily fail to acknowledge that although "the reconstruction of the most detailed sequences of events related to the extermination of the Jews is progressing apace," as Saul Friedlander puts it, "for some historians at least, an opaqueness remains at the very core of the historical understanding and interpretation of what happened."[51] In other words, the historians in Laub's account can easily avoid the difficult task of considering *how* or *why* what happened happened, and with it a fundamental uncertainty of historical understanding or what Friedlander calls "the unease in historical interpretation," an unease that "*cannot but stem from the noncongruence between intellectual probing and the blocking of intuitive comprehension.*"[52]

To be sure, the debate between Laub and the historians is itself of rather limited scope. But to assume on this basis that it cannot be expected to occasion the "noncongruence" to which Friedlander refers is a mistake, since often enough this noncongruence surfaces precisely in details the mere knowledge of which does little or nothing to meet their challenge to the understanding. Friedlander himself cites a letter in which Walter Benjamin observes that the Viennese gas company had suspended service to its most important customers, the Jews, because these customers, using gas mostly to commit suicide, were not paying their bills.[53] Yet as I have just suggested, such food for thought can be found as well in the debate discussed in these pages, if we are willing to look for it. Consider, then, one last time, the situation of Serena N. (not to mention the thousands of other inmates assigned to the "privileged" Canada commando): to put it simply, her survival depended on how effectively she could contribute to an industrialized process whose goal was her own destruction. These are things we have come to know, perhaps, *too* well, or at least to the point where we are no longer sufficiently surprised and disturbed by them; so that, in conjunction with the emotional and psychological tension, with the "empathic unsettlement" to which Holocaust survivor testimony can give rise,[54] we may wish to foster or renew, in the reception of such testimony, something like a cognitive unease. Of course, this is by no means the only task facing humanistic education about the Holocaust. But I would venture to say that it is one of the most important.

Trauma and Theory

The current interest in Holocaust survivor testimony has been stimulated to no small degree by a resurgence of interest in trauma. This resurgence, extending virtually unabated, it seems, over the past thirty years or so, has carried well beyond psychology to a number of other fields, including not only history, politics, and sociology but literary criticism, philosophy, and visual studies. In these last areas of inquiry, moreover, where concern with issues of a formal nature is particularly pronounced, the relation between trauma and survivor testimony has generally been envisioned as a problem pertaining to the ways in which traumatic experience is represented. And yet this perspective reflects, in addition to a disciplinary orientation, the acknowledgment of an unavoidable question long familiar to survivors who have chosen to bear witness, namely, how to convey an experience that appears to have disabled the very means of its own representation, how to speak of the Holocaust when this event seemingly outstrips anything that can be said about it. Of course, the putative unspeakability of the Holocaust has not prevented these same witnesses from speaking. But this paradox merely underscores the need to consider more closely the central communicative dilemma of survivor testimony. Does this dilemma really derive from the nature of the event itself? Does it reflect the intrapsychic effects of the event? Does the principal problem of testimonial representation have to do with the social disintegration caused by trauma, that is, with the difficulty of finding a language common to victims and nonvictims alike? Does it have to do with the very ability or inability, the willingness or refusal of nonvictims to listen?[1]

No doubt, each of these questions can be answered in the affirmative. But taken together, they may prove most useful by suggesting that the reception of Holocaust survivor testimony (and for that matter, the listening granted to survivors of other traumatic events) will likely depend to a considerable extent on what we understand or think we understand about trauma itself. With this in mind, I propose to examine a theory that has recently gained wide currency in literary studies and related fields, namely, the theory of trauma advanced by Cathy Caruth, which appears to take the notion of unspeakability at face value insofar as it affirms a radical disjunction between traumatic experience and its representation. To be sure, the insistence on such a disjunction is not peculiar to Caruth but can be found, for example, in the work of Shoshana Felman, Dori Laub, Jean-François Lyotard, and Giorgio Agamben.[2] But this merely underscores the prevalence of a theoretical tendency of which Caruth remains, in regard to trauma per se, the most prominent proponent.

In the first part of the discussion that follows, I will focus at some length on the epistemic status of Caruth's theory, largely in comparison with the Freudian theory of trauma on which Caruth bases her views. My critique of Caruth is not a defense of Freud but an attempt to clarify their divergence and to indicate both the epistemic consequences of Caruth's position and the fundamental ways in which Freud's work continues to inform our understanding of trauma. The ultimate aim of this analysis is nevertheless to show how Freud's reflections on trauma carry, in regard to its victims, beyond epistemic concerns to questions of an ethical nature. And it is to certain ethical implications of Caruth's theory, especially as they pertain to the reception of Holocaust survivor testimony, that the second part of the discussion will be devoted.

The theory of trauma for which Caruth has become known is presented in the introduction to a collective volume she edited, *Trauma: Explorations in Memory*, and in her book *Unclaimed Experience: Trauma, Narrative, and History*. Since this theory relies so heavily on Freud's work, however, and especially on *Beyond the Pleasure Principle*, it is to Freud that I turn initially, in order to establish a framework for discussion.

From the beginning of *Beyond the Pleasure Principle*, Freud emphasizes the economic perspective that constitutes, with its topographical and dynamic counterparts, the basic architecture of his metapsychology. In particular, he makes it abundantly clear that the pleasure principle itself, whose status he will reevaluate in this text, is of an economic nature, serving to regulate the quantity of free, mobile, or "unbound" excitation in the mind. Not content, however, to view it only as an economic principle, Freud wishes to consider pleasure (or unpleasure) also as a feeling. Thus, still at the outset and in a manner reminiscent of his groundbreaking but then unpublished *Project for a Scientific Psychology*,[3] he suggests that the conversion of quantity into quality, of stimulus into affect, might depend on the *period* of excitation involved, on a temporal coefficient destined to figure prominently in his theory of trauma.[4] Moreover, having discovered that "the mental reaction to external danger" (*SE*, 18:11 / *GW*, 13:8) opens onto a region "beyond" or rather, as we shall see, *before* the pleasure principle, Freud must, recalling once again the earlier *Project*,[5] invoke the topographical point of view, most notably the notion of a "protective shield" (*SE*, 18:27 / *GW*, 13:26) lying between the external world and the interior of the mental apparatus. Adopting as the standard of "traumatic neurosis" a condition occurring after "severe mechanical concussions, railway disasters and other accidents involving a risk to life" (*SE*, 18:12 / *GW*, 13:9), he stresses the unexpectedness of the traumatic event and its effect on this shield, known more prosaically as the "system *Pcpt.-Cs.*" (perception-consciousness).[6] Simply stated, the function of the system *Pcpt.-Cs.* is to screen external stimuli and to initiate their organization—to initiate, that is, the conversion of unbound into bound energy through its channeling into or investment in mental representations (what is technically termed "cathexis"). But in trauma, according to Freud, this system is suddenly and unexpectedly, without *Angstbereitschaft* or "preparedness for anxiety" (*SE*, 18:31 / *GW*, 13:31), confronted by stimuli that far exceed its protective capacity and that, as internalized yet unbound excitation, can subsequently trigger what strikes the organism as a recurrence or repetition of the trauma itself. Not only is the continuity of experience disrupted, therefore, but the very means with which to represent rather than repeat that disruption are, to some extent, disabled.

The clinical basis of this hypothesis lay, for Freud, in the dreams of those suffering from traumatic neurosis. Indeed, if *Beyond the Pleasure Principle* marks a turning point in psychoanalytic theory, it does so in large part as a response to these dreams, which clinically contested Freud's view of dreams in general. As he remarks, in a passage on which Caruth heavily relies:

> The study of dreams may be considered the most trustworthy method of investigating deep mental processes. Now dreams occurring in traumatic neuroses have the characteristic of repeatedly bringing the patient back into the situation of his accident, a situation from which he wakes up in another fright. This astonishes people far too little. . . . Anyone who accepts it as something self-evident that their dreams should put them back at night into the situation that caused them to fall ill has misunderstood the nature of dreams. (*SE*, 18:13 / *GW*, 13:10–11)

As Freud first claimed in *The Interpretation of Dreams*, published some twenty years before *Beyond the Pleasure Principle*, the nature or, more precisely, the function of dreams consists in so-called "wish-fulfillment," that is, in representationally organizing for expenditure the energy of stimuli that would otherwise interrupt sleep. This organizing is what he calls the "dream-work": it is a dynamic mediation of the conflict between the id and the preconscious ego whereby the censoring agency at their interface insures that the "disturbing impulses" (*SE*, 18:33 / *GW*, 13:33) of the id will manifest themselves only in forms distorted by displacement and condensation.[7] Thus, preventing the interruption of sleep normally requires repression of these impulses *as such* through their figurative representation. In dreams symptomatic of traumatic neurosis or what we would now call post-traumatic stress disorder (PTSD),[8] the dysfunctionality of wish-fulfillment will therefore raise first of all the question of how trauma can be said to disable such representation.

In commenting on the lines just quoted, Caruth outlines her own theory of trauma:

> The returning traumatic dream startles Freud because it cannot be understood in terms of any wish or unconscious meaning, but is, purely and inexplicably, the literal return of the event against the will of the one it inhabits. Indeed, modern analysts as well have remarked on the surprising *literality* and nonsymbolic nature of traumatic dreams and flashbacks, which resist cure to the extent that they remain, precisely, literal. It is this literality and its insistent return which thus constitutes trauma and points toward its enigmatic core: the delay or incompletion in knowing, or even in seeing, an overwhelming occurrence that then remains, in its insistent return, absolutely *true* to the event. (*TEM*, 5)

Caruth seems to make two major claims here—having to do, on the one hand, with the purported literality of traumatic dreams (and flashbacks) and, on the other, with their purported truth—while insisting that the delay in apprehending the event itself is essential to both.[9] Although there is no obvious distinction between these claims, I will argue that the truth in question is of a particular kind. For now, since it appears to bear immediately on the question of figurative representation, I turn to the claim concerning literality.

Let me point out, to begin with, not only that Freud himself never makes such a claim (for reasons I will mention in due course), but that the claim as Caruth states it is, at best, unclear. The very word *literal* remains fundamentally ambiguous, carrying either the sense of "nonfigurative" (but still representational) or that of "actual" or "real" (as when, in a passage quoted in full below, Caruth speaks of "the literal threatening of bodily life"; *UE*, 62). As a result, there is at least potentially a confusion of two perspectives whose distinction is crucial to the understanding, not to mention the treatment, of trauma. Granted, it may appear absurd to read "the literal return of the event" as "the actual return of the event," both because, strictly speaking, no event repeats itself and because at stake is evidently not an event at all but a "returning traumatic dream," that is, a representation. However, this representation owes its traumatic effect, the fright it causes, to the fact that it is experienced by the survivor not as such but rather *as though* it were the real repetition or return of the event. What is missing from the claim concerning literality, then, is this "as though" (or some equivalent thereof), which would serve to distinguish the position of the survivor, for whom—be it a matter of dreams, flashbacks, or other symptoms—the reexperiencing of the event is only too real, from that of the critic or analyst, who must recognize this repetition for the representation it is while also acknowledging its divergence from the strictly figurative. In the absence of such a marker, these positions, as irreducible as one is to the other, can seem to be interchangeable; and this interchangeability can seem in turn to offer the critic or analyst direct access to the experience of the survivor.

Indeed, even as we recognize that, in traumatic dreams, the "literal" return of the event means for the survivor its "real" or "actual" repetition, it would appear to go without saying that the only basis on which the critic or the analyst could ascertain this meaning resides in the account provided by the survivor—in the representation of a predominantly sensory phenomenon in a form that is primarily if not exclusively linguistic and that comprises an important share of narrativity. For the critic or analyst, therefore, not only is access to this reality of the survivor mediated by representation, but it becomes impossible to determine with certainty whether this representation is "literal" in the other sense, that is, cleansed of figuration (and hence also faithful, or in Caruth's even stronger phrasing, "absolutely true to the event"), since one of the terms of literality as a relation between word and object, namely, the event itself, remains inaccessible as such.

It would be trouble enough, then, for the claim that dreams or flashbacks are purely literal (and absolutely true) if the traumatic event were inaccessible only to nonvictims, including the analyst and the critic. Yet according to Caruth's theory, the events that supposedly return in these symptoms also remain by definition inaccessible to victims themselves. As she puts it: "The ability to recover the past is thus closely and paradoxically tied up, in trauma, with the inability to have access to it. . . . Indeed, the literal registration of an event—the capacity to continually, in the flashback, reproduce it in exact detail—appears to be connected, in traumatic experience, precisely with the way it *escapes* full consciousness as it occurs" (*TEM*, 152–53). In other words, there is a direct correlation between literality and unconsciousness: to the extent that the event exceeds the capacity of the protective shield, its "registration" is not mediated by consciousness and hence not altered by integration into a symbolic order. "In trauma," says Caruth, "the outside has gone inside without any mediation" (*UE*, 59).[10] It is for this reason as well that "recovery" of the past is predicated not on conscious recall but on compulsive repetition, that it takes the form of involuntary reenactment rather than willed representation. However, what is recovered in such reenactment is still the inaccessibility of the event itself: "The traumatic reexperiencing of the event thus *carries with it* . . . the impossibility of knowing that first constituted it" (*TEM*, 10). In short, even victims have no way of telling whether their flashbacks "reproduce [the event] in exact detail," no basis on which to determine whether their dreams are "literal" and "absolutely true to the event," since it is to conscious memory itself, which presupposes the distinction between past and present, event and representation, and indeed, victim and survivor, that traumatic experience remains unavailable.

From these considerations, I believe it would be safe to conclude that Caruth's theory of trauma is epistemically unfounded. In other words, there is, as we have just seen, no conceivable subject position from which it is possible to know what supposedly remains, by definition, unknowable—unless, of course, we were to assume, as theorists, a position absolved of *all* cognitive constraints. In that case, a godlike "view from nowhere" would make it possible to occupy two positions at once, that is, to relive the event with the survivor or, better yet, *as* the survivor and to stand at the distance required to certify that this reliving is purely literal (meaning in this instance beyond or before representation) and absolutely true to, because indistinguishable from, the event. Our vision would thus transcend the cognitive impasses created by such a dissociative model of trauma. Indeed, our very disembodiment would afford, as if by magic, unmediated access to other minds, including traumatized ones in which the event itself could be recovered in its originarity. In saying this, I do not mean to imply that there is no truth in Caruth's theory of trauma. But its truth is purely speculative.

No doubt, it is surprising to find in a theory widely associated with deconstruction so strong a reliance on the notion of originarity, whose radical critique was one of the earliest tasks undertaken by deconstruction itself. Just as surprising, however, is the alliance of this theory with clinical psychiatry, since there is no obvious reason why such unbridled speculation should wish to share the road with empiricism. For, if trauma is unavailable to representation and knowledge, as Caruth claims, then anything of an empirical nature she might wish to enlist in support of her theory would appear to be entirely superfluous, while anything contradicting it would ipso facto be disqualified. Why, then, this concern with the clinical?

Since, as we have noted, the inaccessibility of traumatic experience to knowledge undermines the very foundation of the theory that asserts it, it may be that the theory can only steady itself by outsourcing the problem of accessibility to science, and above all, in this instance, to the work of the well-known clinician Bessel van der Kolk, one of the "modern neurobiologists" who affirm "the unerring 'engraving' on the mind, the 'etching into the brain' of an event in trauma" (*TEM*, 153).[11] Although there is indeed an obvious bridge between Caruth and van der Kolk, consisting in the shared view not only that the traumatic event "etches" or "engraves" an exact replica of itself in the psyche but that its return takes the form of reexperiencing rather than remembering, of reenactment rather than representation, nevertheless Caruth has the disadvantage, as a literary critic, of dealing exclusively with representations, in which the event can only be detected by its absence, whereas van der Kolk, as a clinical researcher, focuses on the observable symptoms of its reexperiencing, that is, on what is taken to be, in the person of the victim, its exact psychosomatic replication. What van der Kolk's work can presumably do for Caruth's theory, then, is to confirm the very existence of this replication, or, which amounts to the same, the renewed presence of the event, thereby not only providing the theory with the ontological assurance it lacks but exempting it from the "impossibility of knowing" that the theory itself predicates of traumatic experience.

Whether or not this suffices to explain the appeal of clinical research for Caruth's theory of trauma, however, work such as van der Kolk's offers no solution to the problem lying at the foundation of that theory. It is not only or even primarily that van der Kolk's position has been challenged by others in his field, or that attention has been drawn to shortcomings in the research on which he bases his position.[12] The point is rather that, in any case, the existence of exact internal replications of external traumatic events cannot be proven: on the one hand, because victims themselves are denied cognitive access to them and, on the other, because any access to which nonvictims may lay claim, including the best neuroimaging in the world, is necessarily representational and hence "distorted." In this respect, indeed, it is useless to object that a distinction should be drawn between the verbal representation of a traumatic event and its repetition as a psycho-somatic "performance," since the authenticity of this repetition must still be established through the very knowledge of the "original" event that van der Kolk and Caruth rule out. Yet it may be misleading simply to say that their theory of trauma cannot be proven when, in science, what matters is rather that a theory be susceptible of *dis*proof, that it not be, as Ruth Leys puts it, "*immune to refutation.*"[13] In sum, since any scientific theory worthy of the name must be disconfirmable, the immunity to refutation entailed by the assertion that traumatic experience is unknowable means that the epistemic cornerstone of Caruth's work is also its principal stumbling block.

Moreover, in regard to both the etiology and especially the aftermath of trauma, Caruth's theory can be accused of explanatory inadequacy. To demonstrate this inadequacy, I will resume contrasting her theory with Freud's. As I suggested at the outset, my concern is not to defend Freud, much less to claim that his theory of trauma achieved an explanatory ideal, even in his own eyes. I aim instead to show how a reading of Freud that clearly diverges from Caruth's may contribute to a fuller understanding of trauma. And this will afford the opportunity to revisit a number of questions left in abeyance, beginning (and ending) with the apparent disabling of figurative representation in dreams.

As I earlier observed, Freud never claims that post-traumatic dreams are "literal" in the sense of being *entirely* devoid of figuration. And by no means would he have been inclined to characterize them as "absolutely true to the event," for at least two reasons. First, the simple causal connection thus posited between an external traumatum and its internal replication derives from what he called "projection," and as such is of a piece with the metaphysics that, in *The Psychopathology of Everyday Life*, he proposes to replace with metapsychology.[14] Second, and more to our point, the reexperiencing of a traumatic event cannot become an object of cognition outside of the symbolic order in which matters like truth and falsehood first arise.[15] Of course, Freud does say, in the passage already quoted, that "dreams occurring in traumatic neuroses have the characteristic of repeatedly bringing the patient back into the situation of his accident, a situation from which he wakes up in another fright." Yet what interests him in these dreams is not their representational "faithfulness" to "the situation of [the patient's] accident" but the clues they may provide to the nature of psychic disturbance:

> what *we* seek to understand are the effects produced on the organ of the mind by the breach in the shield against stimuli and by the problems that arise from it. And we still attribute importance to the element of fright. It is caused by lack of any preparedness for anxiety, including lack of hypercathexis of the systems that would be the first to receive the stimulus. (*SE*, 18:31 / *GW*, 13:31)

It may be that Freud overestimates the etiological role of "lack of preparedness for anxiety," which, in current clinical literature, is considered an important factor contributing to PTSD but by no means its sufficient cause.[16] In this respect—and not only in this one, of course—Freud's theory of trauma must be read with as critical an eye as any other. What I wish to emphasize here, however, is that Freud defines affect (in this instance, fright) as an effect of the relation not only between a quantity of stimulus and its duration but between this stimulus and the degree to which the protective shield has been cathected: the "lack of preparedness" resulting in fright is a "lack of hypercathexis of the systems that would be the first to receive the stimulus." To this he adds that the variable receptive capacity of the organism may account at least in part for the specificity of individual traumas: "In the case of quite a number of traumas, the difference between systems that are unprepared and systems that are well prepared through being hypercathected may be a decisive factor in determining the outcome" (*SE*, 18:31–32 / *GW*, 13:32). In short, his emphasis on the economic etiology of trauma helps to account, on the one hand, for the fact that the psychic apparatus is disabled *to a certain degree*, and on the other, for the fact that different degrees of disabling can yield qualitatively different experiences.[17]

Let me now quote Caruth's commentary on Freud, since it is the most effective way to demonstrate how she inflects his position. Referring to the passage just cited, she writes:

> The breach in the mind—the conscious awareness of the threat to life—is not caused by a pure quantity of stimulus, Freud suggests, but by "fright," the lack of preparedness to take in a stimulus that comes too quickly. It is not simply, that is, the literal threatening of bodily life, but the fact that the threat is recognized as such by the mind *one moment too late*. The shock of the mind's

relation to the threat of death is thus not the direct experience of the threat, but precisely the *missing* of this experience, the fact that, not being experienced *in time*, it has not yet been fully known. (*UE*, 62)[18]

In order to gauge this inflection of Freud's view, it is important to remember that, for Freud himself as for his contemporaries, the foremost example of a traumatic stressor was the railway disaster.[19] Thus, despite his interest in the traumatic neuroses resulting from World War I, the type of traumatizing event that most often served him as an empirical reference was that of a single, sudden, and unforeseen accident. Knowing what we now know about trauma, we can recognize the pertinence of this model to many cases but by no means to all. Yet Caruth predicates this temporal schema alone and seemingly at its most extreme of *all* traumatic experience, while subtly disengaging it from the economic considerations on which Freud insists. Indeed, although for Freud as for Caruth the sudden nature of the traumatizing event is such that its assimilation by the organism is necessarily delayed, in Freud's eyes the delay is due not only to that suddenness but also, as we have seen, to the differential relation between the magnitude of the stimulus and the cathexis of the protective shield. In the passage just quoted, however, Caruth ends up discounting the economic or quantitative dimension of trauma to such an extent that even time itself is divorced from its own "quantity," that is, from duration, in the form of a pure moment that can no more be "experienced" by the victim of trauma than it can be integrated into a temporal or historical continuum. From this, one can only infer, as far as the etiology of PTSD is concerned, that the protective shield is totally destroyed (or else suffers no damage whatsoever, which is just as implausible) and that, despite overwhelming evidence to the contrary, the "experience" of trauma is universally the same.

The tendency to divorce the temporal and economic perspectives on trauma is confirmed when Caruth remarks, in a more general vein:

Throughout his work, Freud suggests two modes of trauma that are often placed side by side: the model of castration trauma, which is associated with the theory of repression and return of the repressed, as well as with a system of unconscious symbolic meanings (the basis of the dream theory in its usual interpretation); and the model of traumatic neurosis (or, let us say, accident trauma), which is associated with accident victims and war veterans ... and emerges within psychoanalytic theory, as it does within human experience, as an interruption of the symbolic system and is linked, not to repression, unconsciousness, and symbolization, but rather to a temporal delay, repetition, and literal return. Freud generally placed his examples of the two kinds of trauma side by side ... and admitted, in the *Introductory Lectures on Psychoanalysis* (1916), that he was not sure how to integrate the two: "Traumatic neuroses are not in their essence the same thing as the spontaneous neuroses which we are in the habit of investigating and treating by analysis; nor have we yet succeeded in bringing them in[to] harmony with our views" (*SE*, vol. 16, p. 274). (*UE*, 135n18)[20]

If it were simply the case that Freud operated with two such models, we might be tempted to ask why Caruth's own theory, whose claims about trauma are universal in nature, is based on only one of them. However, Freud's work lends itself to a different reading.

To begin with, Caruth's use of the word *unconsciousness* to characterize the model from which she wishes to distance her own may seem a bit puzzling, since, as we have seen, unconsciousness is a prominent feature of her model of trauma. Of course, she may have in mind the *dynamic* and *systematic* or *topographical* senses of "unconscious" that most often come into play in the theory of repression. But the fact remains that the *descriptive* sense applies to both models. Second, and more telling, even if we were to concede the existence of two models of trauma in Freud, these models could not be distinguished by ascribing "temporal delay" and "repetition" only to accident and war neuroses, since Freud first detected these phenomena as effects of repression in the etiology of hysteria.[21] And what, after all, is the "return of the repressed" if not temporal delay and repetition? Third, where Caruth concludes her quotation from the *Introductory Lectures*, Freud is about to say that "in one respect we may insist that there is a complete agreement between [traumatic and spontaneous neuroses]," namely, a repetition that "shows us the way to what we may call an *economic* view of mental processes" (*SE*, 16:274–75 / *GW*, 11:283–84). Finally, if we are really to consider Freud's views throughout his career, then we should note that in works published after the *Introductory Lectures*, specifically his "Introduction to *Psychoanalysis and the War Neuroses*" (1919) and *Inhibitions, Symptoms and Anxiety* (1926), advances in the study of narcissism enabled Freud to hypothesize a sexual component—in the broad, economic sense of "sexual"—in accident and war neuroses, and thus to move even further toward an integrated model of trauma.[22]

To be sure, Freud recognized different *kinds* of trauma, since his working hypotheses were always constructed on an empirical foundation. What I wish to argue is that his aim was, within an overarching metapsychology, not to dissociate but to integrate the economic and temporal dimensions of trauma—and this in order, among other things, to account for the wide variety of traumatic experience.

As I have suggested, however, we can find an explanatory inadequacy in Caruth's theory in regard not only to the etiology of trauma but also to its aftermath. Consider once again the following sentence: "The shock of the mind's relation to the threat of death is thus not the direct experience of the threat, but precisely the *missing* of this experience, the fact that, not being experienced *in time*, it has not yet been fully known." Whether by design or not, the italicized expression "in time" conveys an instructive ambiguity, since it means *both* that the threat is not experienced "on time," that is, "at the time of" the threat itself, *and* that, thus eluding registration by or through the system *Pcpt.-Cs.*, to which Freud attributes our sense of time,[23] it is experienced "out of time" or in what one could call, for want of a better word, "timelessness." Of course, the failure of the system *Pcpt.-Cs.* to register the threat does not mean that the threat is not registered at all but rather that its registration takes place in another part of the mind. At the same time, it should be noted that Caruth displays remarkably little if any concern about its topographical circumscription.[24] What appears to matter is simply that there be no communication between this "elsewhere" and the system *Pcpt.-Cs.*, so that the reexperiencing of the threat or traumatic event shall remain inaccessible to (waking or nondelusional) consciousness. It can thus safely be said that Caruth's theory of trauma elides what constitutes, in most cases, a necessary if not sufficient cause of post-traumatic suffering, namely, the *conscious* memory of the event (or at least a portion of it).

In other words, Caruth confuses consciousness and assimilation: because the traumatic event cannot be readily integrated into a narrative or other symbolic framework, she mistakenly infers that it cannot have been consciously experienced or be consciously recalled. To be sure, in saying that the threat "has not yet been *fully* known," she seems willing to acknowledge that it may after all be known *in part*. But according to her theory, whatever is known of the threat does not, per definition, "count" as traumatic, and cannot therefore make any difference in its reexperiencing. Once Caruth has posited an absolutely dissociated self at the beginning of traumatic experience, her theory cannot envision any aftermath or survival other than an endless, invariable, and "literal" repetition of the event: "Not having truly known the threat of death in the past, the survivor is forced, continually, to confront it over and over again," she claims, adding that survival itself is "the endless *inherent necessity* of repetition, which ultimately may lead to destruction" (*UE*, 62–63).

To contest this claim is not to deny that dissociation is a fairly common symptom of PTSD but rather to dispute, in addition to its putative universality, the absoluteness with which it is endowed by Caruth, which in effect is challenged even by van der Kolk when he concedes that, between the victim compelled to repeat or reexperience the event and the survivor capable of remembering or representing it, there is "some degree of coconsciousness."[25] To dispute this absoluteness is in turn to question the interpretive validity of a theory of trauma that fails to account for the difference in repetition and hence for the possibility of a survival beyond revictimization.[26]

To see how Freud allows a fuller understanding of the aftermath of trauma, we can begin by noting that repetition is for him not a mechanical process whose only raison d'être lies in its own senseless perpetuation but an organic puzzle whose "solution" must be sought in a psychoanalytically intelligible purpose. It is no accident, of course, that he frames this question in economic terms, since in his eyes it is the differential relation between the cathexis of the protective shield and the stimulus that breaches it, the excess of this stimulus over the capacity of the mental apparatus either to bind or to discharge, that induces what strikes the organism as a repetition of traumatic experience in dreams. And it is this compulsive repetition that leads him to hypothesize a psychic realm "beyond" or before the pleasure principle:

> We may assume . . . that dreams are here helping to carry out another task, which must be accomplished before the dominance of the pleasure principle

can even begin. These dreams are endeavouring to master the stimulus retrospectively, by developing the anxiety whose omission was the cause of the traumatic neurosis. They thus afford us a view of a function of the mental apparatus which, though it does not contradict the pleasure principle, is nevertheless independent of it and seems to be more primitive than the purpose of gaining pleasure and avoiding unpleasure. (*SE*, 18:32 / *GW*, 13:32)

I will not belabor what may be a tendency in Freud's thought to overstate the etiological role of the omission of anxiety. It should nevertheless be noted that, since the system on whose behalf these dreams are supposedly attempting to develop anxiety is the system *Pcpt.-Cs.*, which is designed to protect the organism from *external* stimuli, the development of anxiety (or hypercathexis) is all the more urgent as this system can otherwise scarcely protect *itself* against the traumatizing stimuli now emanating from *within*. In fact, it is this very topographical consideration in conjunction with the repetition compulsion that leads, in *Beyond the Pleasure Principle*, from the theory of trauma to the theory of the instincts by way of an analogy that can help to clarify the attempt at retroactive mastery in question here. For instincts are themselves, says Freud, "the most abundant sources of this internal excitation . . . the representatives of all the forces originating in the interior of the body and transmitted to the mental apparatus" (*SE*, 18:34 / *GW*, 13:35). And if they give rise to "the manifestations of a compulsion to repeat" (*SE*, 18:35 / *GW*, 13:36), it is because, in their very excess, they force the mental apparatus to stagger the dose of what it can neither contain nor expend all at once. Most important of all, the fundamental disequilibrium created by this excess imparts a *direction* to repetition: since the mental apparatus must, for the sake of self-preservation, retain a portion of the instinctual energy invested in it, the succession of such investments impels an ever greater development of the apparatus itself, most notably of the highly systematized cathexis called the ego. In this light, we can see how dreams in traumatic neurosis suggest an analogous process, for not only is the effort to master an internal(ized) stimulus destined to repeat itself, given that the force of that stimulus surpasses the defenses of an ego weakened by trauma, but this recurrent effort is oriented, according to Freud, toward the binding of an ever larger portion of the stimulus to the ego, in order both to strengthen its defenses and to integrate traumatic experience into its established representational schemata. Indeed, only if experience is thus tied to a nexus of symbolic relations can the dream-work then impose the kind of substitution, that is, the figuration through displacement and condensation, required for the "normal" functioning of dreams in accordance with the pleasure principle.

If Freud thus ascribes a hypothetical purpose to the repetition of traumatic experience in dreams, it is nevertheless not in dreams that he envisions the realization of that purpose, nor in his reflections on dreams alone, therefore, that one can gauge the full explanatory force of his theory of trauma. The reason, or rather reasons, for this have to do with the state of sleep. In sleep, the censorship exercised by the ego is already weaker than in waking life and is bound to be further weakened in the aftermath of trauma. As a result, it is even more likely not only that sensory reminiscences of the traumatic event will elude its grasp but that these reminiscences will retain the affective charge from which, in order to prevent the disruption of sleep, the censorship normally insures their divorce.[27] Repetition in traumatic dreams may accordingly "give the appearance," in Freud's words, "of some 'daemonic' force at work" (*SE*, 18:35 / *GW*, 13:36), since in them the return of emotionally charged traces of the event is at least initially more conspicuous than the incremental "recovery" whose purpose it presumably serves.

This impression is reinforced, moreover, by another, equally important feature of sleep, namely, motor paralysis.[28] In Freud's view, the motor activity that characterizes waking life is not only a means by which internally generated stimuli can be discharged. Motor activity is also fundamentally related to the system *Pcpt.-Cs.*, to whose development it contributes, since it is through the body's movement in and action upon the external world that the mental apparatus conducts "reality-testing" and thereby achieves the capacity to distinguish, within perception, between objects that are real (meaning also external or material) and those that are imaginary (internal or psychical).[29] The suspension of this activity will thus entail fairly predictable consequences: on the one hand, the body is not available for the discharge of stimuli, be they affective or ideational or both, that threaten to disrupt sleep, and this threat may even be exacerbated if the body's paralysis is represented in the dream itself (hence recalling, in the case of trauma, a state of fright or helpless terror); on the other hand, the immobilization of the body, combined with a weakened censorship, attenuates or abolishes the distinction between real and imaginary, so that in almost all instances dreamers are unable *not* to believe in the reality of their delusions. It is not surprising, then, that the repetition of traumatic experience in dreams should seem somewhat "demonic," given how the peculiarities of sleep compound the difficulty of detecting in such repetition anything beyond an inexorable revictimization. What is surprising, rather, is that Freud managed to discover in this repetition a sense that can be "translated" into waking life without betraying the interpretation of traumatic dreams.

To follow this translation, we might initially consider how to explain the existence, in waking life, of symptoms such as flashbacks, which, like dreams, are of a hallucinatory or delusional nature and which waking life itself would normally preclude. Of course, Freud could not benefit from the field where we would be inclined to look for an answer to this question, namely, contemporary neuroscience. And although the term *flashback*, invented long after Freud, designates a phenomenon resembling certain symptoms with which he was familiar from the investigation of other psychological disorders, he does not appear to have associated these symptoms with the kind of trauma at issue here. Yet the metapsychological framework in which he thinks about trauma proves nonetheless instructive since, to begin with, it implies that, because the traumatic stimulus exceeds the capacity of the mental apparatus to retain or expend, a portion of it is inevitably communicated to the body (in clinical terms, the "sensorimotor apparatus"), so that, like the mind in dreams, in waking life the organism as a whole must make repeated attempts to bind that stimulus before the pleasure principle, or rather its modification, the reality principle, can regain the upper hand.

Indeed, if there were a traumatic "literality" in Freud, then, by analogy of the soma to the letter (and the psyche to the spirit), it would have to do with this somatization, which is retraumatizing in its own right, since the stimuli that produce it are inescapable. Furthermore, as we have just seen, this repetition tends toward an increase in the proportion of bound to unbound excitation (and hence toward an increased capacity for the organized expenditure of what remains unbound), such that, with all due allowance for the variety of traumas and of factors contributing to any single trauma, the course of PTSD can generally be expected to include, as clinical observation has in fact shown, a gradual alleviation of somatic or psychosomatic symptoms. This is not to say that healing or recovery is a reassuringly linear affair, or that it is ever complete, or even that one can speak of "healing" or "recovery" without qualification. After all, Freud's model of trauma also implies that the traumatized individual can regain a stable sense of self only by accommodating the alteration of self that trauma induces. Thus, we might speak of "recovery" with the understanding that this word does not signify a simple return to pretraumatic existence. But the point is that, unlike Caruth's model, Freud's accounts for the *possibility* (and, in many if not most cases, the actuality) of this post-traumatic alteration or change, the possibility of "life after trauma." And yet even this does not become fully clear unless we translate the sense of repetition still further, that is, into the context of psychotherapy.

Here, repetition takes the form of what Freud calls "acting-out." If acting-out offers a resemblance to traumatic dreams and flashbacks, this resemblance is not to be sought in the direction of strictly sensorimotor phenomena, contrary to what the term itself might lead one to believe. The similarity derives instead—as does, for that matter, the difference—from comparable confusions: just as, in dreams and flashbacks, the imaginary is taken for the real, so patients said to be acting out are those who in their *behavior* unwittingly relive in the present a traumatic event belonging to the past. At the same time, although, like dreams and flashbacks, acting-out can be considered a symptom, it is the only one of the three whose presentation requires an interpersonal or intersubjective context. Within the psychoanalytic situation, in fact, Freud does not distinguish between acting-out and transference, the process whereby features of traumatic experience, most conspicuously those of an affective nature, are transposed to the relation between patient and analyst. Moreover, this transposition explains the ambiguous status of acting-out: as a symptom, it obviously calls for alleviation, but since it is also the means by which the patient's experience becomes present or visible to the analyst, and through the analyst to the patient, "the physician," says Freud, "cannot as a rule spare his patient this phase of the treatment" (*SE*, 18:19/*GW*, 13:17). More clearly than in traumatic dreams or flashbacks, then, repetition in the mode of acting-out appears to be the precondition of its own transformation—the transformation, facilitated by the analyst, into a conscious act of remembrance. What the analyst or therapist can learn from this repetition is employed precisely "to force as much as possible into the channel of memory and to allow as little as possible to emerge as repetition," and so to augment "the ratio between what is remembered and what is reproduced" (*SE*, 18:19/ *GW*, 13:17).[30]

Among the therapeutic desiderata mentioned by Freud is thus a certain "aloofness [*Überlegenheit*]" (*SE*, 18:19/ *GW*, 13:17), that is, a distance taken by the patient from the patient's own past *as past*. This distance also bears the name of "consciousness" or, more precisely, is afforded by the "system *Pcpt.-Cs.*," to which, as I have noted, Freud ascribes both our sense of time and our sense of the difference between "inside" and "outside." It is therefore no accident that, to reestablish the distinction of past from present— and in so doing to differentiate the remembered from the remembering self, the victim from the survivor—conscious remembrance assumes an act of externalization, an act of speech witnessed in an intersubjective context. This is true both within analysis, which Freud more than once characterized as "an exchange of words between the patient and the analyst,"[31] and outside of it, not only from a Freudian perspective but also, for example, in the view of Pierre Janet, with whom, as we know, Freud did not often see eye to eye. "*Memory*," says Janet, "*is the action of telling a story*." That is:

> A situation has not been satisfactorily liquidated, has not been fully assimilated, until we have achieved, not merely an outward reaction through our movements, but also an inward reaction through the words we address to ourselves, through the organisation of the recital of the event to others and to ourselves, and through the putting of this recital in its place as one of the chapters in our personal history.[32]

Or as Freud might phrase it: storytelling is both an act of binding whereby traumatic experience is integrated into the representational framework of the ego, which it simultaneously alters, and an act of discharge whereby the energy that once fueled the compulsive repetition of acting-out is now expended in narrative representation—whereby, in other words, the symptom is replaced by the sign. Of course, Freud's own theory of trauma makes it clear that this integration is a matter of degree, of the variable "ratio" or difference between remembering and repeating, narrating and reliving, and hence that traumatic experience will only yield its story through a multiplicity of tellings. And although, by gradually putting the story "in its place as one of the chapters in our personal history," these tellings restore the possibility of association and comparison, that is, of figuration, one cannot, given the peculiarities of sleep, infer that the figurative capacity regained in waking life will immediately or automatically spare dreamers their traumatic nightmares. Yet unlike Caruth's, Freud's theory establishes in no uncertain terms that survival is not restricted to what trauma has made of its victims but includes what, in colloquy, victims make of their trauma.

The centrality of intersubjectivity to survival suggests that at stake in the theory of trauma are concerns not only of an epistemic but also of an ethical nature. In particular, both recovery, understood as the integration of traumatic experience into the framework of a personal history already altered by that experience, and the reintegration of victims within a broader community, can be seen to depend on the listening of nonvictims, on a reception that is not confined to the mere registration of traumatic narrative but encompasses a response to it. And as I noted in the previous chapter, direct interlocution is not the only mode in which reception takes place. Reception also includes communication between respondents, even in such highly mediated forms as written texts about witnessing or, in the case at hand, a theory of trauma. I turn here to the implications of Caruth's theory for listening to survivor testimony.

Although Caruth is aware of "the implication of the theory of trauma in its own object, or the inextricability of the theory from what it describes" (*UE*, 117), we have observed that her theory assumes, for the subject of knowledge, a position wholly transcendent to its object, which, moreover, it characterizes as unknowable and unrepresentable. Given this absolute disjunction between trauma and representation, it is not obvious how survivors could be expected to communicate their experience, assuming it is theirs to begin with. Indeed, if, as Caruth claims, survival carries with it the impossibility of knowing the traumatic event, it would seem to follow that testimony can do no more than bear witness to its own impossibility. To listen to survivor testimony is thus, Caruth says, "to listen to the impossible," and this, she continues, "is its danger—the danger, as some have put it, of the trauma's 'contagion,' of the traumatization of the ones who listen. But it is also its only possibility for transmission" (*TEM*, 10).

Now, one might infer that the traumatization in question has to do with the affective disturbance that is arguably an integral part of reception— except that this vicarious traumatization is said to constitute reception *in its entirety* (the "only possibility for transmission") and is predicated on the impossibility of representation, which means, most often, speech. One can acknowledge the risk to which empathic listeners expose themselves, therefore, while asking whether surviving witnesses do not run a greater risk, since the exclusion of all symbolic mediation from the communication of their experience logically equates "its only possibility for transmission" with a silencing reenactment. Presumably, listening too, as an activity based on symbolic exchange, would then logically give way to a passive, identificatory "contagion." Here, indeed, Caruth's theory of trauma most clearly exhibits its affinity with a noteworthy tendency in the work of Claude Lanzmann, whose film *Shoah* one can appreciate for the impressive achievement it is and still find objectionable those moments in which the interviewer elicits from certain Holocaust survivors—especially Simon Srebnik and Abraham Bomba—a reenactment that presumably affords viewers, Lanzmann included, a vicarious experience of trauma at the expense of survivors themselves. If, however, to listen to survivors means not only to support their recovery of speech but to respect their singularity, to recognize that their experience, however deeply it may affect us, is not our own, then the kind of reception to which Caruth's theory exposes them should suffice to call the theory itself into question.

Moreover, one may wonder how the status thus granted to reenactment could be reconciled with Caruth's view of the structure of traumatic experience, which clearly implies that *all* transmission is of a mediated nature. Indeed, assuming that this experience is characterized by "the inherent departure, within trauma, from the moment of its first occurrence" (*TEM*, 10–11)—assuming, in other words, that the apprehension and hence the transmission of the event is intrinsically belated or displaced—then for the listener or viewer, at least, reenactment is no less a representation than spoken or written testimony. This includes the moments in Lanzmann's *Shoah* to which I have just referred. In fact, not only is the film itself obviously a representation, but, as we learn elsewhere, the scene in which Bomba breaks down while demonstrating how he cut the hair of friends about to be gassed and in which we can supposedly join him in his retraumatization was entirely staged by Lanzmann.[33] What lies before or beyond representation thus turns out to be doubly representational. The "literal" return of the event is figured twice over. And we can fairly ask, returning to Caruth, why the fiction of a nonrepresentational replication of trauma that is "absolutely true to the event" should retain its privilege when the theory provides no reasoned justification for it.

It may be most expeditious to approach this matter by considering what Caruth has to say about representation, especially of the narrative variety:

> The transformation of the trauma into a narrative memory that allows the story to be verbalized and communicated, to be integrated into one's own, and others', knowledge of the past, may lose both the precision and the force that characterizes traumatic recall. Thus in the story of Janet's patient Irène, her cure is characterized by the fact that she can tell a "slightly different story" to different people: the capacity to remember is also the capacity to elide or distort, and in other cases, as van der Kolk and van der Hart show, may mean the capacity simply to forget. . . . The possibility of integration into memory and the consciousness of history thus raises the question, van der Kolk and van der Hart ultimately observe, "whether it is not a sacrilege of the traumatic experience to play with the reality of the past?" (*TEM*, 153–54)

I would not dispute the possibility that narrative memory may retain less precision and force than traumatic recall, and I see no need to digress for the sake of evaluating Caruth's commentary on Janet, except to note that it conforms to the view she shares with van der Kolk and van der Hart. What interests me here, following the characterization of narrative memory as the ability to tell different stories to different people, is the allegation of certain consequences that this difference could entail, namely: elision, distortion, forgetting, and sacrilege. The pejorative tinge with which narrative memory is thus imbued may indicate an answer to the question raised just a moment ago. Indeed, if we recall that the idea of trauma as an "unerring 'engraving' on the mind" susceptible of exact replication is epistemically unfounded and hence does not convey a knowledge, it may appear instead to reflect a value, that of an original sameness, of a single, inalterable Right Story. This would at least explain how the privileged status of replication can be maintained in the absence of any epistemic justification, since it suggests that the justification was, from the beginning, axiological.

It would also account for the negative evaluation of narrative memory and its transmission, given that no real story could meet the standard of an ideal, invariable template.

My concern, however, is with the implications of this theoretical position for listening to survivor testimony. On the one hand, if truth pertains strictly to the nonrepresentational replication of traumatic experience, the inescapable corollary is that any narrative or other representation of that experience will be suspected of distortion or betrayal. Of course, the indiscriminate doubt into which testimonial interlocution is thus cast would seem to render both the corollary and the claim from which it derives rather suspect in their own right. But this should lead us to ask whether, on the other hand, something else might be awry. For in replication or reenactment, there is no interlocution at all. And in this respect, I would have to question Caruth's statement that "the inherent departure, within trauma, from the moment of its first occurrence, is also a means of passing out of the isolation imposed by the event" (*TEM*, 10–11), if passing out of isolation means finding a listener or listeners. To the extent that, as we have seen, her articulation of this displacement privileges reenactment over representation, displacement can hardly be said to alleviate the survivor's isolation. What it does is to place the survivor's experience into circulation, where, "unclaimed," it can be freely appropriated by others.

Finally, Caruth points to the possible loss of trauma's *"affront to understanding"* (*TEM*, 154) in the transition from traumatic to narrative memory: the assimilation of traumatic experience through the ordering, sense-making mechanisms of narrative may reduce the awareness of trauma as a profound disturbance of those very mechanisms. Or as she puts it: "The danger of speech, of integration into the narration of memory, may lie not in what it cannot understand, but in that it understands too much" (*TEM*, 154). This, as we shall see, was also a concern in Adorno's reflections on art after Auschwitz. But it should already be clear that a greater danger, for survivor testimony and its reception, lies in a theory that defines trauma as intrinsically unspeakable.

THREE

Art after Auschwitz, Again

Anyone proposing to revisit Theodor W. Adorno's statement that "to write poetry after Auschwitz is barbaric" can rightly be expected to explain why it is necessary, or at least worth the trouble, to do so. Of course, in the ever expanding field of critical work on representations of the Holocaust, Adorno remains very much a figure to be reckoned with. Yet his considerable influence seldom if ever manifests itself independently of the famous phrase, which, whether accurately or not, has been cited often enough to produce the numbing effect of a seriously overworked platitude. In thinking about the Holocaust and its representation, why gravitate, then, toward a path already well trodden? And what purpose can it serve here, given that Adorno's reflections on poetry or literature in the post-Holocaust era are not of obvious pertinence to survivor testimony and its reception?

For an answer to the first of these questions, I would refer to Michael Rothberg, who, in a chapter of his important book *Traumatic Realism*, offers a close and thoughtfully contextualized reading of Adorno's statement, together with insightful reflections on its appropriation. As Rothberg points out, it is not only the epigrammatic quality of the phrase but Adorno's own repeated reconsideration of it that helps to explain the frequency of its citation by others; and as he clearly demonstrates, this citation can prove interpretively useful insofar as it affords a metacritical view both of perspectival differences and of historical stages in the aftermath of the Holocaust. Thus, a basic grasp of Adorno's statement proves indispensable for assessing its many inflections, through which we can better understand the legacy of the Holocaust as it pertains to the relation between aesthetics and ethics.[1]

Returning to the second question, however, one can ask whether this framework is appropriate for the study of survivor testimony. Can the art of Samuel Beckett, in particular, by which Adorno is guided in qualifying his initial statement, retain its exemplarity when the focus has shifted from high modernism (or postmodernism, if subverting the very distinction between "high" and "low" were not a hallmark of this -ism) to what we call "testimony" or "witnessing"? It is true that testimony does not respect generic boundaries and can arguably extend to drama, fiction, and poetry. Then again, it is also true that this extension is limited by historical considerations that do not necessarily pertain to art. Yet I would suggest that the relevance of Adorno's work to the subject of this book will only emerge if, to begin with, we carefully consider his understanding of the aesthetic as such and in its ethical implications. To this end, I propose to examine primarily the essay entitled "Commitment" and then, in light of the position developed there and in related texts, to discuss testimonial memoir and above all the situation of address that frames it.[2]

To sharpen even further the focus on giving and receiving testimony, I will subsequently turn to one of the inflections just mentioned, namely, the stance taken by Berel Lang in "The Representation of Evil: Ethical Content as Literary Form," a chapter of his book *Act and Idea in the Nazi Genocide*. As we shall see, the task in reading Lang lies not in determining the sense he imputes to Adorno's statement, which seems abundantly clear in its almost breathtaking literality, but rather in articulating the assumptions underlying his interpretation and the far-reaching consequences it entails. It is a task that should prove worthwhile, however, since Lang explicitly raises the question of genre, thus establishing a context that is not only well suited to the discussion of testimony but can even be said to invite the testing of theoretical claims against the practice of witnessing. In conclusion, I will refer to a noteworthy example of this practice, Charlotte Delbo's *Auschwitz and After*, in an effort to show how this work challenges a position such as Lang's, even as it reframes and enriches what Adorno had to say about art after Auschwitz.

———————

It is at the end of Adorno's essay entitled "Cultural Criticism and Society," drafted in 1949 and published in 1951, that we find the original claim: "to write poetry after Auschwitz is barbaric [*nach Auschwitz ein Gedicht zu schreiben, ist barbarisch*]."[3] In the German, Adorno's statement does not constitute a sentence unto itself but rather summarizes what is called, in the clause immediately preceding it, "the final stage of the dialectic of culture and barbarism."[4] As this phrase suggests, "Cultural Criticism and Society" was written within the framework established by *Dialectic of Enlightenment* (1947), where, with his coauthor Max Horkheimer, Adorno shows at some length how Enlightenment culture, especially in the mode of instrumental reason, can become the means to irrational or barbaric ends.[5] Indeed, it is instrumental reason above all, based on universal quantification and exchangeability and, as such, extended from the domination of nature to the domination of human beings, that explains why, for Adorno (and Horkheimer), the emancipatory potential of Enlightenment has proven inseparable from the possibility of industrialized genocide. As far as poetry is concerned—and by "poetry" it is safe to assume that Adorno means lyric poetry—its "barbaric" character reflects the barbarism of a social formation in which the ubiquity of reification and exchange makes a mockery of individual difference, including that of the lyric voice.[6] The charge of barbarism is arguably directed, therefore, not so much at those who write or wish to write poetry after Auschwitz as at a society in which their verse is no sooner composed than commodified and whose cultural or ideological hegemony is so pervasive as to enlist them as its unwitting collaborators.[7] The peremptoriness of Adorno's pronouncement may in fact have been designed to counteract this mystification, for which the word *barbaric* would not have been too strong, if one considers that "Cultural Criticism and Society" was written less than five years after the liberation of Auschwitz, which Eric Santner has aptly characterized as a "modern industrial apparatus for the elimination of difference."[8]

By the time Adorno publicly reconsidered his statement about poetry after Auschwitz, the world had learned a good deal more about the camp and the Holocaust generally from the many survivors called to witness at the trial of Adolf Eichmann in Jerusalem (1961). This is not to suggest that Adorno's attention was turned to testimony per se, but it doubtless accounts to some extent for what Rothberg calls "the surprising *personal* quality that Adorno's writing exhibits" in the closing pages of *Negative Dialectics*, which appeared in 1966.[9] This quality emerges immediately after his allusion to the earlier statement, which reads: "Perennial suffering has as much right to expression as a tortured man has to scream; hence it may have been wrong to say that after Auschwitz you could no longer write poems."[10] He then observes:

> But it is not wrong to raise the less cultural question whether after Auschwitz you can go on living—especially whether one who escaped by accident, one who by rights should have been killed, may go on living. His mere survival calls for the coldness, the basic principle of bourgeois subjectivity, without which there could have been no Auschwitz; this is the drastic guilt of him who was spared. By way of atonement he will be plagued by dreams such as that he is no longer living at all, that he was sent to the ovens in 1944 and his whole existence since has been imaginary, an emanation of the insane wish of a man killed twenty years earlier.[11]

As much as this passage invites reflection on Adorno's "guilt" in the light of Primo Levi's essay "Shame," if not also a comparison of their respective dreams "after Auschwitz"—and this precisely because of the difference between their fates[12]—what I wish to stress here is the claim, which Adorno makes in reference to himself, that "his mere survival calls for the cold-ness . . . without which there could have been no Auschwitz." A puzzling proposition, no doubt, not only because of the apparent continuum encom-passing this particular bourgeois subject and the perpetrators of the Final Solution but because of the verb "calls for [*bedarf*]." Since the coldness in question is not "called for" in the sense of *enabling* survival—which, ac-cording to Adorno, is purely accidental—it can only represent a moral re-quirement that, to judge by his use of the third person, Adorno imposes upon himself. This in turn would prove less noteworthy if it did not imply that such coldness toward himself makes him complicit in coldness toward others, and in particular that his earlier prohibition on poetry may have concealed a refusal to recognize that "perennial suffering has as much right to expression as a tortured man has to scream." To be sure, he can be said to atone here for his previous position by acknowledging that right, and even to exercise it himself by divulging the nightmares with which he has paid for his survival. But as one can see in the phrasing of his concession, "it *may* have been wrong to say that after Auschwitz you could no longer write poems [*mag falsch gewesen sein, nach Auschwitz ließe kein Gedicht mehr sich schreiben*]," Adorno's thinking about post-Holocaust art remained indissociable from the ethical ambivalence articulated at greater length in "Commitment," to which I now turn.[13]

To judge merely by its date of publication (1962), "Commitment" would constitute an intermediary text, falling between "Cultural Criticism and Society" and *Negative Dialectics* in the course of Adorno's reflections on art after Auschwitz. Yet it is by far the most important of the three, since here, enlisting so-called committed literature as a point of departure or even a touchstone, Adorno attempts a sustained articulation of the relation between ethics and aesthetics. In broaching this text, no less than his others, it is important to keep in mind that the "negative dialectics" of his thinking entails perpetual movement, movement without the prospect of repose in a positive synthesis, and hence that no single one of its propositions can stand alone. This includes the following: "I do not want to soften my statement that it is barbaric to continue to write poetry after Auschwitz" (*NL*, 2:87/*GS*, 11:422). In the explanation that follows, one can detect two principal reasons why Adorno apparently intends to maintain his position. First, he points out that "the so-called artistic rendering of the naked physical pain of those who were beaten down with rifle butts contains, however distantly, the possibility that pleasure can be squeezed from it" (*NL*, 2:88/*GS*, 11:423). Second, he notes that "the aesthetic stylistic principle, and even the chorus' solemn prayer, make the unthinkable appear to have had some meaning; it becomes transfigured, something of its horror removed" (*NL*, 2:88/*GS*, 11:423). In the first instance, Adorno alludes to the immemorial association of art and sensation (*aisthēsis*), and in the second, to the redemptive function it has fulfilled as a sensuous realization of the ideal, as an imposition of meaning on the otherwise meaningless, of form on the formless, or of familiarity on the radically unprecedented. The conjunction of these features is suggested by the seemingly incongruous mention of "the chorus' solemn prayer," for the derivation of pleasure from the spectacle of pain and the understanding of dramatic action as a condition of this pleasure constitute two major components of classical tragedy. Yet what is most noteworthy here is the correlation between aesthetic success and ethical failure: the artistic mediation of experience, whether its purpose be pleasure, understanding, or both, is considered tantamount to moral betrayal, to a renewed obliteration or silencing of victims. When Adorno includes in this betrayal "even the chorus' solemn prayer," he refers not only to its lyrical attraction but also to its formal embodiment of communion, of belief in and appeal to a transcendental source of intelligibility.

As befits the thinker of negative dialectics, however, Adorno also ascribes to art the moral "authority" that he appears to deny it. After repeating his claim that "it is barbaric to continue to write poetry after Auschwitz," he remarks:

> But Hans Magnus Enzensberger's rejoinder also remains true, namely that literature must resist precisely this verdict, that is, be such that it does not surrender to cynicism merely by existing after Auschwitz. It is the situation of literature itself and not simply one's relation to it that is paradoxical. The abundance of real suffering permits no forgetting; Pascal's theological "On ne doit plus dormir" ["Sleeping is no longer permitted"] should be secularized. But that suffering—what Hegel called the awareness of affliction—also demands the continued existence of the very art it forbids; hardly anywhere else does suffering still find its own voice, a consolation that does not immediately betray it. The most significant artists of the period have followed this course. The uncompromising radicalism of their works, the very moments denounced as formalist, endows them with a frightening power that impotent poems about the victims lack. (*NL*, 2:87–88/ *GS*, 11:423)

By now it is clear that Adorno is concerned with the ethical stakes of art in general, for which, despite the allusion to "impotent poems about the victims," poetry still occasionally serves as a synecdochic stand-in. The affirmation of art in this passage focuses primarily on what is elsewhere disparaged, namely, its form: "the most significant artists of the period" are valued for "the uncompromising radicalism of their works, the very moments denounced as formalist." This does not mean that Adorno has suddenly become a proponent of art for art's sake. Rather, he emphasizes those moments "denounced as formalist" because it is at such moments that form in its very conspicuousness draws critical attention to itself, because it is at such moments that art consists, as he puts it, in "dismantling" its own illusion (*NL*, 2:90/*GS*, 11:426).[14] To be sure, even art of the most "uncompromising radicalism" can be said to depend, for its effect, on the very illusion it dismantles, and to this extent it runs the risk of affording an exploitative pleasure, a spurious understanding, or both, and thus would not entirely escape the condemnation of poetry as barbarism. Yet this art is of the kind that suffering not only forbids but also demands, since its own formal self-contestation creates both an antidote to aesthetic pleasure and a disruption of complacent understanding, and in so doing challenges the very norms of the culture that produced the Holocaust. It is in this light that one may interpret Adorno's assertion:

> Kafka's prose and Beckett's plays and his genuinely colossal novel *The Unnamable* have an effect in comparison to which official works of committed art look like children's games—they arouse the anxiety that existentialism only talks about. In dismantling illusion they explode art from the inside, whereas proclaimed commitment only subjugates art from the outside, hence only illusorily. Their implacability compels the change in attitude that committed works only demand. (*NL*, 2:9/*GS*, 11:426)

Adorno's rather derisive reference to committed literature comes nonetheless as somewhat of a surprise here, given not so much the title of the essay ("Commitment") as what he adds immediately after asserting, "I do not want to soften my statement that it is barbaric to continue to write poetry after Auschwitz," namely: "it expresses, negatively, the impulse that animates committed literature" (*NL*, 2:87/*GS*, 11:422). But sharing the impulse of committed literature is about as far as he is prepared to go. In fact, it is a problem at the very heart of this literature that explains, "negatively," Adorno's valorization of form in an artist such as Beckett. For as he repeatedly points out, the literature of commitment tends to reproduce the very world to whose transformation it is declaredly committed. In the case of Jean-Paul Sartre, to cite one of Adorno's two major examples (the other being Bertolt Brecht),[15] the ethicopolitical commitment of literature as it is set forth in *What Is Literature?* (1948) prescribes a purely instrumental use of language, a perfectly transparent prose that can only remain so, and hence can only fulfill its phenomenological task of immediately disclosing the world, if, as Sartre actually recommends, its formal properties "pass unnoticed,"[16] that is, if it succeeds in effacing itself as a historically determined discursive practice. The committed writer thereby engages in what amounts to an act of deception or denial by reinvoking familiar pre-Holocaust discursive norms as though the radical indictment of these norms by the Holocaust had simply never occurred. Clearly, Adorno's explicit concern in this case does not have to do with "the possibility that pleasure can be squeezed" from committed literature—although we should not assume that pleasure has nothing to do with the illusion of representational transparency and the sense of mastery it affords. The main concern here relates rather to what Adorno calls "the aesthetic stylistic principle," that is, the imposition of form where form goes "unnoticed" and "make[s] the unthinkable appear to have had some meaning." In other words, Adorno's indictment of committed literature focuses primarily on its redemptive ambition, on its implicit claim that, through the instrumental or technological mastery of language, through the perfect transparency of its prose, such literature can always "make sense," even of the senseless. In a manner entirely consistent with the movement of negative dialectics, one could therefore rephrase Adorno's famous statement as follows: to write *prose* after Auschwitz is barbaric.

At this point, to be sure, one might feel inclined to object that Adorno's emphasis on the *form* of literary works appears to leave their *content* unexamined, and hence that his effort to articulate the relation between aesthetics and ethics in a historically specific way risks falling victim to its own abstractness. Although this is not an objection to be taken lightly, it may also miss the point if, as seems to be the case, it reflects a tendency to assume that "form" and "content" are either identical each to itself in opposition to the other or else identical to each other, to assume, in other words, that their relation is susceptible only of the modalities of antithesis and synthesis. As we have just seen, it is against this tendency that Adorno thinks when, in the absence of any reference to "content" in the traditional sense of the term and of its relation to form, he argues that the inextricability of aesthetic form from ethical content emerges precisely where art dismantles its own illusion, that is, precisely where form *differs from itself.*

Yet it is also against this tendency that he thinks when he does in fact attend to "content" in its traditional sense. Pursuing his critique of committed literature, Adorno observes:

> One characteristic of such literature is virtually ever-present: whether intentionally or not, it shows humanity blossoming even and indeed precisely in so-called extreme situations. At times, this becomes a dreary metaphysics all the more inclined to affirm the horror of the "boundary situation" as it is supposedly there that the authenticity of the human being manifests itself. In this cozy existential atmosphere the distinction between victim and executioner becomes blurred, since after all they are equally exposed to the possibility of nothingness, something generally, of course, more bearable for the executioner. (*NL*, 2:88–89 / *GS*, 11:424)[17]

In this passage, Adorno obviously focuses on the content of committed works, and particularly on the predominance in them of *situations limites*, of "extreme" or "boundary" situations. If it were only a question of such situations, however, the critical edge of his language would undoubtedly prove much sharper in regard to Beckett than to Sartre. For nowhere in Sartre's fiction is one likely to locate a situation as extreme as what we find in Beckett's *The Unnamable*, where the narrator, having spent the good old days as a head in a jar, is now no more than a disembodied voice. And nothing in Sartre's copious dramaturgical production can compare with the post-apocalyptic paralysis of Beckett's *Endgame*, where a blind cripple and his ailing factotum do battle in a dead language while the former's progenitors waste away in their respective trash cans. Yet it is clearly not Beckett whom Adorno has in mind when speaking of a literature in which the extreme situation "shows humanity blossoming," or of a metaphysics that holds the boundary situation to be the privileged site at which "the authenticity of the human being manifests itself." That Sartre remains the target of this critique suggests that, for Adorno, extreme situations are not merely a matter of content, or more precisely, that their content cannot be assessed independently of the formal framework in which it is conveyed.

The framework on which Adorno chooses to focus in Sartre's work, both in "Commitment" and in "Trying to Understand *Endgame*," written a year earlier, is not that of the novel but of the *pièce à thèse* (drama of ideas)—a term applied equally, for example, to the existentialist play *No Exit* (1944) and to the historically and politically inflected *Dirty Hands* (1948).[18] To judge by the thoroughly conventional and hence familiar or "invisible" aesthetics of Sartre's theater, which, as Adorno points out, made him "acceptable to the culture industry" (*NL*, 2:81 / *GS*, 11:415), the framework of the *pièce à thèse* is entirely in keeping with the effacement of form that *What Is Literature?* requires of the committed work. This is hardly surprising, of course, since no committed work can be expected to convey its ideas if the vehicle on which it must rely breaks down, to represent its "thesis" through the portrayal of an extreme situation if, instead of serving as the transparent means to that end, the symbolic tools at its disposal sooner draw attention to their own defectiveness. Nevertheless, this formal transparency becomes an issue once again when, as a corollary to his claim that committed literature, in its preoccupation with the masterly manipulation of extant forms, tends to replicate the administered world it aspires to change, Adorno indicates that in such literature, here exemplified by Sartre's *pièces à thèse*, the effacement of form also entails an erasure of history. In the plays just mentioned, this erasure is attested by the indistinguishability of their respective "theses": for despite its apparent historical and political concreteness (a concreteness consisting for the most part, however, of stock characters and stereotyped situations), *Dirty Hands* is essentially a dramatization of the choice with which freedom confronts the individual (in this instance, Hugo), and hence is scarcely less "existential" than *No Exit*, in which Garcin, Estelle, and Inès enact the plight of those condemned to freedom in the "hell" of other people. Here, in other words, whatever differences one might wish to point out between the two plays will be of little or no account, since at bottom both serve as the vehicle of a single philosophical "message." And so the question remains how committed literature can "show humanity blossoming" in extreme situations, how it can implicitly assert that in these situations "the authenticity of the human being manifests itself," without presupposing and promoting a purely abstract and ahistorical notion of "humanity" or "authenticity." How can it happen in such literature that "the distinction between victim and executioner becomes blurred," if not because the "dreary metaphysics" of commitment assumes that "they are equally exposed to the possibility of nothingness," that for each, as Adorno also puts it, "it is a matter of choice in and of itself" (*NL*, 2:81 / *GS*, 11:415)?[19] In short, where "philosophy appoints itself the substance of literature"

(*NL*, 2:81 / *GS*, 11:414), and where literary form amounts to no more than an indifferent medium through which the universal is instantiated or particularized—such that, as Adorno points out, "the sentence 'Hell is other people,'" from *No Exit*, "sounds like a quotation from *Being and Nothingness*" (*NL*, 2:81 / *GS*, 11:415)—it can safely be said that commitment, despite or rather because of its redemptive ambition, converts extreme situations into aesthetic abstractions, and in so doing betrays the real suffering with whose alleviation it is centrally concerned.

The contrast between Sartre and Beckett is discussed at greater length in "Trying to Understand *Endgame*," where Adorno begins by conceding that "Beckett's oeuvre has many things in common with Parisian existentialism," being "shot through with reminiscences of the categories of absurdity, situation, and decision or the failure to decide."[20] Having acknowledged this apparent similarity, as a result of which Beckett was, for many years, (mis)read as a philosophical anthropologist, he notes, however, that "whereas in Sartre the form—that of the *pièce à thèse*—is somewhat traditional, by no means daring, and aimed at effect, in Beckett the form overtakes what is expressed and changes it" (*NL*, 1:241 / *GS*, 11:281). This statement about Beckett constitutes the thesis to whose explication is devoted the remainder of a substantial essay that I will further consider here only insofar as it bears on the relation between aesthetics and ethics at issue in "Commitment."

To this end, it may be expedient to revisit the notion of extreme situation. Although, as I have observed, the situation in *Endgame* is more extreme than any to be found in Sartre's theater, it is not because Beckett has simply chosen another form to express an identical content, a different means to achieve the same end. The extremity of *Endgame* lies rather in the very absence of that end: the situation in which Hamm and Clov, Nagg and Nell find themselves does not instantiate an *idea* of humanity, does not point to or signify a transcendental "beyond" capable of conferring upon it a redemptive meaning. In fact, the very possibility of its doing so is treated as a joke:

HAMM: We're not beginning to . . . to . . . mean something?
CLOV: Mean something! You and I, mean something!
[*Brief laugh.*]
Ah that's a good one![21]

This is why, in Adorno's view, "interpretation of *Endgame* cannot pursue the chimerical aim of expressing the play's meaning in a form mediated by philosophy. Understanding it can mean only understanding its unintelligibility, concretely reconstructing the meaning of the fact that it has no meaning" (*NL*, 1:243/*GS*, 11:283).[22] Thus, interpretation, arrested in its trajectory and thrown back upon itself, or rather upon the form(s) that it normally takes for granted, here discovers that all of the major dramatic categories—the unities of time, place, and action no less than character and dialogue—have been parodied, that is, used "in the era of their impossibility" (*NL*, 1:259/*GS*, 11:302), like the remnants of a bygone culture, of a world that has outlived itself. In "reconstructing the meaning of the fact that [the play] has no meaning," then, the interpretation of *Endgame* can no more conclude than can the "action" of the play itself, but must respect its fundamental indeterminacy or uncertainty:

> HAMM [*anguished*]: What's happening, what's happening?
> CLOV: Something is taking its course.[23]

To the extent that this "something" induces at least a certain perplexity in the reader or spectator, moreover, it recalls Adorno's claim that Beckett's plays "arouse the anxiety that existentialism only talks about," that "their implacability compels the change in attitude that committed works only demand." This "change in attitude" entails neither the search for another meaning nor the denial of all meaning but a tolerance for the anxiety aroused by its indefinite suspension. Indeed, while *Endgame* can be said to demonstrate the obsolescence of the dramatic categories just mentioned, the possibility of *dénouement* or resolution is simply missing from it altogether. This is so not only or even primarily because the play itself is of an undecidable genre. It is sooner the case that its genre is undecidable for lack of the collective framework presupposed by tragedy *or* comedy. After Auschwitz, there is no order to whose reestablishment spectators can look for relief from their psychic disturbance, or in which, for that matter, one could stage the plight of an individual hero or heroine of such noble character and quasi-divine stature as to produce, in the first place, the kind of disturbance that Aristotle considered the sine qua non of tragedy. And as for the not uncommon belief in the capacity of Beckett's comedy to redeem a traumatized civilization, it is worth asking whether we still really have, in

Adorno's words, "a place of reconciliation from which one could laugh" (*NL*, 1:257/*GS*, 11:300). In brief, whereas committed literature uncritically enlists the very conventions of the world it seeks and then fails to transform, Beckett's work suggests how the world has already changed by enacting the failure of those conventions.[24]

In so doing, it recalls the paradoxical "situation of literature" after Auschwitz, in which suffering "demands the continued existence of the very art it forbids" and in which the work of art is called upon to maintain the very tension between these ethical imperatives by articulating the inextricability of its content from the dismantling of its form. On this point, Adorno is categorical: what he means by such "dismantling" is neither an effacement of form, as we have seen, nor a preoccupation with form alone, either of which would "resolve" the tension in question. In fact, counterbalancing his critique of committed literature is a critique of works whose "loss of tension" evinces a move "away from representation and intelligible meaning" toward an idle formalism that even "gives legitimacy to the crude demand for commitment" (*NL*, 2:90–91/*GS*, 11:426). It is on this point as well that Adorno's view of the fraught relation between aesthetics and ethics after Auschwitz invites a first "translation" from art to testimony. For as I suggested just a moment ago, the interpretive dilemma posed by *Endgame* in its exemplarity calls into question the very framework within which one would seek in vain to resolve it. And this framework, whatever its character (philosophical, psychological, theological, or other), is necessarily a social construct. The dismantling of form thus testifies to a crisis of community epitomized, in Adorno's view, by Auschwitz, whose repercussions extend to all of the means with which we may seek to represent or interpret the crisis itself.

Thus, for Holocaust survivors who have chosen to bear witness, the fundamental challenge has always consisted in finding the language least poorly suited to the communication of "that which happened"[25] without creating therewith the impression that what happened "made sense." To be sure, this challenge has varied in degree: those who testified in postwar trials, for example, were clearly confined in advance by prevailing legal norms, whereas the kind of testimony with which I am mostly concerned in this book, and which is most closely aligned with memoir, leaves the witness freer from such external constraints (and hence faced, in a sense, with a more daunting task). Of course, this freedom is itself constrained, especially if not only by the claims of historical veracity. However, the mistake would be to think that the Holocaust survivor testimony at issue here is or should or even could be devoid of art. If survivors are to rediscover, in Celan's expression, "an addressable you,"[26] to communicate their experience to those who did not in any way share it, then they must have recourse to forms, from the simplest nouns to the most highly developed generic structures, with which nonvictims are familiar and through which, therefore, that experience can be made intelligible to them. And the construction of this bridge between a world of unprecedented atrocity and one that, without survivor testimony, might still believe itself unscathed, is precisely what we call "figuration." The fact that survivor testimony *also* draws attention to the inadequacy of this figuration, and thereby calls into question the very understanding it is meant to foster, does not amount to a repudiation of art but rather reflects, in the artistry of testimony itself, the ethical tension on which Adorno insists.

It is not only through the question of community, however, that the relation between aesthetics and ethics links art to testimony, but also through a question indissociable from it, namely, that of the self or subject. In "Commitment," Adorno remarks that "Beckett's oeuvre . . . deals with an extremely concrete historical state of affairs: the dismissal [*Abdankung*] of the subject" (*NL*, 2:90/ *GS*, 11:425).[27] This "dismissal" recalls the social reification already mentioned in connection with lyric poetry: the "extremely concrete historical state of affairs" at issue is, precisely, a state of abstractness, the universal sameness and exchangeability to which individuality is sacrificed for the replication of society as a whole. It is thus no accident that this remark precedes a reference not only to Beckett's plays but to "his genuinely colossal novel *The Unnamable*," for as its title suggests, the last volume that, with *Molloy* and *Malone Dies*, constitutes the so-called trilogy of novels extends the depersonalization of previous narrators so far as to make of its own merely an anonymous "I." Yet if *The Unnamable* "deals with" reification by representing it, it also resists reification by undoing representation itself: as Beckett's readers well know, the anonymous "I" concedes at the end of the novel that it "must go on" for having repeatedly failed to say its self, to arrest once and for all its own sameness or identity in a representation, to finish its own story.[28] And this failure to achieve the closure that all of the trilogy's narrators vainly pursue can be seen to derive, at its simplest, from the act of speaking with which each of them is increasingly concerned. Although saying "I" produces an objective representation of the speaking subject, the subject in turn necessarily exceeds that representation insofar as the very saying or utterance of "I" carries it outside of itself, that is, involves it in a situation of address where its identity is defined strictly *in relation to* an other. The real pertinence of *The Unnamable*, in its dismantling of the novel as form, lies in this emphasis on the irreducibility of utterance to statement, of saying to the said, of interlocution to what it frames, be it the novel or, as we shall see, testimonial memoir. Indeed, it is interlocution or the situation of address, understood as the aesthetic site of an ethical resistance to reification and as the space in which the subject or self is inextricably tied to community, that allows here a second "translation" from art to testimony. To be sure, this translation will require us to move from the highly abstract idioms of Beckett's art and Adorno's critical thought to a language offering greater purchase on what many if not most would equate with historical concreteness. But I assume that this is a challenge worth meeting.

It would be best to begin by considering more closely the first person singular pronoun, "I." On the one hand, whenever it is uttered, "I" designates a particular speaker whose identity not only differs from that of others but is intrinsically subject to change. On the other hand, "I" also marks a linguistic function that can be activated by anyone speaking the language of which it is a part and is in this sense universally the same, as attested by its objective definition: "the person who utters the present instance of discourse containing *I*," in Benveniste's words, or in Husserl's, "whatever speaker is designating himself."[29] Simply put, then, to say "I" is to instantiate a relation between individual and community, particular and universal.

However, although saying "I" does indeed imply membership in a community in which anyone can say "I," it is not *to* anyone (or no one)—that is, to a third "person"—that one says "I," but rather to a second, to a "you," whether implicit or explicit, singular or plural. What we call "the first person singular voice" can thus be said to represent the universal possibility of address, of dialogue, and of recognition (a possibility whose material representation will vary, needless to say, from one natural language to the next, as "I" could, for example, just as well be *je* or *Ich*). And of this possibility, which I will here take to be emblematic of social life in general, Nazism deprived its victims, especially the Jews, by prohibiting the universal to *certain* particulars, by eliminating each and every one of these as a potential referent of the "I." Long before "the solution of the Jewish question" came to mean extermination, during the years in which the imposition, by "legal" or other means, of what amounted to social death paved the way for that extermination, Jews became the indistinguishable third persons named "the Jews" insofar as each was denied the universal right to speak or, more precisely, *to be heard* in the first person and hence to state something other than his or her membership in this reified or collectively stereotyped Other. The "space" in which, in principle, any speaker can take the position of the first person and enter into the dialogical relation it entails was transformed by Nazism into a kind of *Lebensraum* to be occupied only by those considered worthy of its identitarian idea of Self or Community (essentially, the *Volksgemeinschaft* embodied or voiced by the *Führer*), an idea whose realization on this earth required the evacuation of all those "others" for whom that space had offered something like a home.[30]

Yet the nature of the first person singular voice may also help to explain in some measure why the effort of surviving victims to reclaim the symbolic space from which they had been excluded could not fail to prove deeply fraught. To begin with, recovering this voice meant finding the attentive listener or listeners to whose scarcity or absence victims might well have become so accustomed as to doubt the very possibility of ever being heard again. Moreover, for those whose doubt did not turn to despair, the situation of address raised certain unavoidable and troublesome questions: For what purpose do I bear witness? To whom precisely do I address myself? For whom do I speak? And while even tentative answers to these questions could determine the kind of testimony to be given (whenever, that is, the kind of testimony to be given had not already, as in law, determined those answers), and in so doing free speech through the very constraint of form, there was no guarantee that the form or the answers that presumably recommended it would put to rest the questions from which they had arisen. What is certain is that any effort to understand the responses to these questions must be mediated by the forms in which survivors have chosen to bear witness, among which, as I have already observed, this discussion will focus primarily on memoir.[31]

Although readers of testimonial memoirs discover sooner or later that not all of those who have written them struggled to survive *in order to* bear witness, this motive is cited more often than any other and as such commands serious attention. However, bearing witness is never sufficient unto itself but always implies a motive of its own, its own "in order to . . ." or "so that. . . ." And in most if not all cases, witnessing is undertaken because, in short, "the world must know."[32] To be sure, this imperative can in turn be variably motivated (beyond or in addition to the purpose of commemorating the dead): the world must know so that the crime will not be replicated by its erasure or forgetting, so that those who lived their lives far from and oblivious to its perpetration may understand the appalling potential of their own species, so that current and future generations can take measures to prevent the recurrence of genocide and all that it entails. The means to all of these ends remains nonetheless the communication of a certain knowledge, the precise nature of which is indissociable from both "the world" to whom it must be communicated and the very mode of its communication. In this regard, it can safely be said that while all testimony, in order to count as such, must respect the historical record, and while it must also, even at its most poetic, rely on that record for its own intelligibility,[33] its scope is never restricted to the objective course of events (with the obvious exception of testimony whose express purpose is juridical or, as in ghetto diaries and chronicles, documentary). Whatever the extent to which it may approach or even overlap with objective historiography, in other words, testimony, and memoir in particular, does not seek to impart a knowledge of the kind derived primarily from what Saul Friedlander calls "systematic historical research, which uncovers the facts in their most precise and most meticulous interconnection."[34] Of course, it should be emphasized that such research is indispensable in its own right. Friedlander goes so far as to insist that "the historian cannot work in any other way, and historical studies have to be pursued along the accepted lines."[35] But this statement about traditional scholarly historiography—whose mold, incidentally, Friedlander's own later work would break[36]—in no way detracts from the critique in whose context it is made, and which shows that, although necessary, traditional historiography is insufficient and even problematic, especially when it comes to an event such as the Holocaust. In particular, the very effort to construct a single and universally valid representation of the facts and their interconnection requires a rigorous discursive standardization that "protects us from the past, thanks to the inevitable paralysis of language."[37] Worse yet, by also requiring exclusive recourse to the impartial perspective of the third person, it tends to divorce cognition from emotion as well as from the ethical implications of the story it tells. Indeed, through a close reading that I cannot reproduce here (and that recalls Adorno's critique of instrumental reason), Friedlander compellingly demonstrates how, in a text that is representative of traditional historiography pertaining to the Holocaust, the "bureaucratic" tone used to describe *both* organizational measures *and* the mass murder to which they led "places each one of us . . . in a situation not unrelated to the detached position of an administrator of extermination."[38]

Since, however, as I have just remarked and as Friedlander also suggests, the form in which a story is told and the addressee it implies are inseparable from the kind of knowledge it conveys, it should be possible to specify this inseparability in memoir by contrasting memoir with historiography. But this will only work if, while acknowledging the historiographical component of memoir, we look for its specificity through a lens other than that of historiography, where the first person will inevitably appear to be merely a deficient alternative to the third insofar as the situated view it affords can never attain to the panorama offered by its counterpart. In fact, the historiographical third person achieves its detachment by suppressing the situation of address, thus creating a place that can be identically occupied by "each one of us" precisely because it belongs to no one—except God—and that risks leaving us all (as some have said of God during the Holocaust) indifferent to history, including what Adorno calls "the abundance of real suffering." By contrast, the first person of testimonial memoir represents not so much a place one might occupy as the site of a tension between the speaker who says "I" and second persons who, as potential first persons, are invited to identify with the speaker and yet simultaneously forbidden to do so, since identification can obliterate the difference between survivor and nonsurvivor and hence renew, in effect, the silence that the survivor seeks to break. The knowledge conveyed by memoir depends, therefore, not only on what is said but on the saying by which it engages us in the interval between identification and estrangement, where it favors a resolution of the resulting tension no more through some spurious sentimental communion with survivors than through indifference to them.

To be sure, memoir *also* imparts knowledge through the tale it tells, a tale that declines to divorce cognition from affect and that furthermore, precisely in this, its "partial" or "subjective" character, lies at least as close to history *wie es eigentlich gewesen*, to history "as it actually happened," as does objective historiography.[39] Then again, as Adorno would lead one to suspect, a tale of seamless formal integrity could betray the experience of its own teller, whether by lending itself to the pleasure of emotional catharsis or lending to that experience a meaning it did not have, or even by so deftly combining these with the suspension of disbelief as to pass the story off as history itself. The situation of address that frames the story nonetheless dismantles this illusion: since the loss of voice can only be narrated by means of its recovery, and since its recovery is also the means by which a victim becomes a survivor, the first person of testimonial memoir undoes the fiction of identity that the pronoun "I" cannot help but foster by marking the difference between the one whose story is narrated and the one who narrates it, between the tale that is told and the telling itself. Needless to say, both the way in which and the degree to which this difference is marked will depend on the individual memoir, as the ensuing discussion of Delbo's *Auschwitz and After* will doubtless suggest. In any case, and contrary to what might be inferred from it, this difference between the tale and its telling, between the story and its frame, does not impugn the story but exceeds it, and in so doing allows the implied inadequacy of testimonial narrative—unlike aesthetic phenomena that rely on our credulity—to point to an event whose reality so far outstripped available means of interpretive representation as to induce an abiding sense of disbelief even in those who most suffered from it. The difference internal to the "I" of memoir registers the shock of trauma itself, and, lest readers be tempted to believe that they really feel a survivor's pain, tempers the knowledge of affliction communicated to them with an anxious and sobering uncertainty.

But who, precisely, are the memoirist's addressees? It is clear that, considered purely as a discursive function, the second person, like the first, can shed no light on the history that led to its specific use in testimonial memoir. At the same time, since the publication of a text makes it available, at least in principle, to everyone, and since publication also forces us to look beyond any given individual, the addressee of testimonial memoir cannot be equated with a real reader or readers. It would thus appear that, situated

neither outside the text, like a real reader, nor inside, like a narratee susceptible of inscription as a character, the testimonial addressee resembles what
narratologists call an "implied reader," immanent to and inferable from the
text as a whole.[40] However, given that the inference of the addressee relies
on the legibility of collective assumptions or expectations, of social norms
or values shared with the addresser (among others), the addressee never
admits of more than a general profile (and can, for that reason, be considered either singular or plural). The dialogical *relation* established through
the situation of address suggests, therefore, that the question of the identity
of the testimonial addressee be approached as a question of historical "subject position" in relation to the survivor. And assuming once again that the
answer to this question is indissociable both from the knowledge conveyed
by memoir and from the very form of memoir, it seems safe to add that the
most likely addressees are those who do not yet know (both what happened
and how survivors experienced it) but in whom the testimonial engagement
of mind *and* heart might be expected to awaken or reawaken a sense of moral
responsibility (to be sure, a distinctly un-Kantian desideratum, if ever there
was one).

The notion of subject position calls to mind the triad of perpetrator,
victim, and bystander, which of course is not exhaustive and to which I refer here primarily for its heuristic potential.[41] At first glance, the least likely
of testimonial addressees would appear to be the victim, or rather, the fellow survivor. After all, do survivors not already know what testimony seeks
to communicate? Yet while Nazi persecution of the Jews in particular focused
on destroying the group as a whole, that is, without regard to differences
between subgroups or individuals, the victims' experience of that persecution could vary widely depending on those very differences, as well as on
when, where, and in what form the persecution occurred, on the influence
of political institutions and sociocultural norms, and on specific familial
and professional circumstances. And this is to say nothing of the qualities
that an individual survivor might bring to the writing of testimony. So it is
certainly not as though survivors have nothing to learn from one another.
Indeed, Primo Levi, for example, remarks in his last completed work, *The
Drowned and the Saved*, that his view of survivor testimony evolved through
"reading the memoirs of others and rereading mine at a distance of years."[42]
Nor is it the case that, in composing testimonial memoirs, survivors might

not write *to* fellow survivors, among others. On the contrary: there is even, as we shall later see, a sense in which the very act of composing a memoir requires the survivor to serve as his or her own first addressee, a sense in which survivors must first register for themselves the story of persecution they wish to convey to readers.

That said, the very idea of former perpetrators as addressees of survivor testimony seems initially almost as counterintuitive, and not only or even primarily because perpetrators know, albeit from a perspective opposed to that of victims, what happened to them. For perpetrators are not likely to be counted among those most psychologically and emotionally inclined to listen to persons whom, at least at one time, they considered unworthy of even living, and they have also amply demonstrated a lack of the moral sense to which testimony appeals. In keeping with the generality of the testimonial addressee, however, it is possible for a published memoir to attract unforeseen readers who suggest to its author that the book was, if unwittingly, written as well or even above all for them. In this respect, it is instructive to consult Levi once again, as he discusses the German translation of *Survival in Auschwitz*:

> One stage of its itinerary was of fundamental importance for me: its translation into German and its publication in West Germany. When, around 1959, I heard that a German publisher (Fischer Bücherei) had acquired the translation rights, I felt overwhelmed by the violent and new emotion of having won a battle. In fact, I had written those pages without a specific recipient in mind. For me, those were things I had inside, that occupied me and that I had to expel: tell them, indeed shout them from the rooftops. But the man who shouts from the rooftops addresses everyone and no one; he clamors in the desert. When I heard of that contract, everything changed and became clear to me: yes, I had written the book in Italian, for Italians, for my children, for those who did not know, those who did not want to know, those who were not yet born, those who, willing or not, had assented to the offense; but its true recipients, those against whom the book was aimed like a gun, were they, the Germans. Now the gun was loaded. (*DS*, 168 / *O*, 2:1124–25)

Although there is much one could say about this remarkable passage, I would like to focus here on the position of "the Germans," observing, to begin with, that if perpetrators are defined as those who actively contributed

to the implementation of the Final Solution, not all Germans are perpetrators in Levi's eyes. In fact, as he points out in the next paragraph, "the
Germans" are "not that handful of high-ranking culprits, but them, the
people," not only "those from among whom the SS militia were recruited"
but "also those others, those who had believed, who not believing had kept
silent, who did not have the frail courage to look into our eyes, throw us a
piece of bread, whisper a human word." Granted, Levi goes on to show that
exceptions could be found in this otherwise "deaf, blind, and dumb" population (*DS*, 168–69/*O*, 2:1125). But the one condition he appears unprepared
to recognize in any of "the Germans" is that of *not knowing* (for which not
wanting to know is no excuse, if only because it presupposes some awareness
of the very thing one wishes to ignore). One can therefore safely conclude
that, in Levi's view, the addressees of the German translation of *Survival in
Auschwitz* were, for the most part and notwithstanding their passivity or
indifference, collaborators.

In the second place, however, Levi's figurative positioning of "the Germans" is ambiguous: on the one hand, he envisions them as "those against
whom the book was aimed like a gun," and on the other, he expects with his
translated memoir to "tie them before a mirror" (*DS*, 168/*O*, 2:1125). At
stake in both cases, of course, is an act of retributive justice, and in the case
of the mirror, that act clearly consists in exposing and hence in shaming.
Yet even there, one suspects that it is not merely a question of "the Germans"
being ashamed of themselves, or rather that this effect will be produced
only if they are still capable of putting themselves in the place of another,
in the place of a third before whose gaze they feel ashamed (a condition
whose historical realization was certainly favored by the fact that Levi's
memoir had already been read, at least in Italy). This in turn would help to
explain the figurative ambiguity of their position insofar as the basis of the
simile "like a gun" lies not in shooting but in "aiming against," that is, in
pointing toward, which is presumably done for the benefit of a third, in the
"presence" of a witness. And what this position further discloses is indeed
Levi's assumption that the norms or values from which one infers the general profile of the testimonial addressee belong no less to "the Germans,"
despite their recent history, than to anyone else, and that it is in the light of
these values that the "true recipients" of *Survival in Auschwitz* will witness
themselves.

Lastly, although Levi's claim that he was "not interested in revenge" might raise a few eyebrows, given the tangible aggressiveness of his remarks, it would be a mistake to think that this aggressiveness toward "the Germans" is incompatible with the "colloquy" through which he approaches his main task, namely, "to understand them" (*DS*, 168/*O*, 2:1125). Indeed, the chapter of *The Drowned and the Saved* under discussion here, entitled "Letters from Germans," concerns for the most part responses from German readers of *Survival in Auschwitz* and Levi's own subsequent responses to them. The point, however, is that, for a survivor whose traumatic experience finds, as we saw earlier, no more telling an emblem than the *denial* of colloquy, to initiate such exchanges is not only to reclaim the first person voice and the recognition it entails but to "welcome back" to the situation of address and, by implication, to the larger community that values it those whose exclusion of the survivor is "mirrored" in the memoir itself. Since, therefore, the "true recipients" of *Survival in Auschwitz* can only rejoin that community by acknowledging their deed, or more precisely, by acknowledging its shamefulness, to imagine that the memoirist's welcoming gesture is one of pure generosity or of purely restorative justice, that it is free of any aggressive or retributive impulse, is to have one's head in the clouds. It is also to underestimate the complexity of the testimonial addressee.

But then where in this complexity are we to locate the bystander, the "one who is present without taking part in what is going on" (*OED*)? It should be noted, first of all, that the way in which this term is used in discussions of the Holocaust may reflect, as in Hilberg's *Perpetrators Victims Bystanders*, a broader and more nuanced definition. In this case, although bystanders may have been physically present as eyewitnesses, they need not have been, since their categorization only requires *some* knowledge of the genocide, whatever its form or the manner in which it was acquired. Bystanders of the Holocaust are thus understood to have been "present" as "knowing contemporaries," and this temporal interpretation of "presence," which makes allowance for eyewitnessing but also exceeds it, explains why the category of bystanders may include not only people physically far removed from the events but institutions such as churches and governments or their representatives. Moreover, to say that bystanders did not take part in what was going on is, in the context of the Holocaust (but not only there), to beg the question, and it reminds us that the line between bystander and collaborator, like the line between collaborator and perpetrator, cannot always be clearly drawn. At the very least, while information pertaining to the genocide could, instead of becoming a spur to action, be met with a distancing reaction of one kind or another, from self-protective denial to the feeling that the concern it undoubtedly demanded was too far-reaching to be accommodated within the daily struggle for one's own survival, these reactions themselves gave the lie to moral neutrality. Yet the ever greater persecution of the Jews also afforded ample opportunity to collaborate in and profit from it, which many found too enticing to pass up, or else to resist, although the overwhelming imbalance of forces meant that far fewer would choose this path. And not least important, the mere possession of reliable information about the genocidal murder of the Jews was enough, where the means to act were available, to make of inaction itself, of just "standing by," an act with serious moral consequences, as was notably the case, for example, in the public reticence of Pope Pius XII or the refusal of the Allies to bomb the rail lines leading to Auschwitz. But finally, however they may have responded to events, what all bystanders shared was the knowledge of actions by others in which bystanders themselves were morally implicated.

Of course, if bystanders are to be included among the addressees of survivor testimony, who according to our working definition not only harbor a sense of moral responsibility but also are supposed not yet to know what happened and how survivors experienced it, then allowance must clearly be made, in the case of bystanders as in that of survivors themselves and of "the Germans" in Levi's sense, for variations of both kind and degree in the knowledge to which they had access. But as I earlier indicated, the triad of perpetrator, victim, and bystander is hardly exhaustive, excluding as it obviously does those who knew nothing as well as children and those not yet born. The working definition may, therefore, be in need of revision. For it almost goes without saying that what testimonial memoirists try to convey depends on a certain *fore*knowledge tacitly ascribed to their addressees, which, like the knowledge of bystanders, admits of different degrees and kinds.

Thus, for example, "Auschwitz" may be expected to evoke a kind of generic concentration camp, or the base camp with its (in)famous gate and chimney, or maybe the entrance tower and gas chambers at Birkenau,

Monowitz and its chemical factory, the adjacent town whose name the camp assumed, or some combination of these. At the same time, for testimonial memoir, having much less to do with history writ large than with how people lived it, such foreknowledge must encompass not only an acquaintance with the general outlines of the Holocaust but, more important, an understanding of the world mediated by the norms whose violation constituted the individual experience of victimization. It follows from the very nature of this experience, however, that what may come to be known from its narration will challenge the understanding it presupposes and will in this sense make of its addressees those who *still* "do not know" (a predicate that could apply to many bystanders and collaborators or perpetrators). This is not to say that the knowledge communicated by testimonial memoir amounts to nothing, but that, as in the relation between saying and the said, where the substantive is exceeded by the verb, the known is here exceeded by the process of coming to know, the story itself by the learning—which is at once an *un*learning—required of its addressee. In short, like the first person of the speaker, the second person of the addressee is the locus of a tension—in this instance, the tension between certain assumptions or expectations, certain norms or values, and the testimonial discourse that calls them into question.

As with the marking of the first person's difference from itself, moreover, the ways and means of this calling into question will necessarily shift from one memoir to the next. It could hardly be otherwise, of course, since in the writing of a memoir, the second person to whom the first addresses itself is initially internal to the writer and bears the stamp of that writer's personal history. For that matter, we all serve the first stage of our linguistic apprenticeship as second persons, being spoken to long before we learn to speak and acquiring speech only by acquiring the ability to listen *to ourselves,* saying "I" in response to an internalized "you." But indeed, in the case of a testimonial memoirist, the voice of the first person can only be recovered in the act of writing if the second person internal to and constitutive of the speaking subject makes itself heard again. This does not mean that the first and second persons come to mirror each other: on the contrary, whereas the second represents an understanding of the world that was shattered by the experience of victimization, the first represents that experience to the second, that is, to the self as it once was or, more likely, as it might still be had what happened not happened. Nor, then, does the internal genesis of the testimonial addressee imply the slightest solipsism, for the understanding just mentioned, far from being idiosyncratic, derives from social norms and shared assumptions and hence allows survivors to put themselves "in the place" of others, including those who, neither perpetrators nor victims nor bystanders, inhabit the world that "must know." Thus, by externalizing the internal "you" through writing, testimonial memoirists clearly accommodate other, comparable second persons. Yet they transpose and generalize the dialogical relation in this way precisely in order to narrate, in the first person, the singular experience of its destruction.

This dissonance, which I have more often called a "tension" and which, in keeping with the relational nature of subjectivity, I have pointed out both within and between the first and second persons, constitutes the frame of testimonial memoir as an "art of survival." Within the frame, this tension is transmitted through the dismantling of certain forms that would otherwise contribute to the intelligibility of experience, as well as through certain forms of dismantling the very assumption of that intelligibility. Thus, at the level of genre, that is, of memoir defined as a first person narration of experienced or witnessed events, distinguishable from autobiography but lending itself in similar fashion to the articulation of temporal continuity,[43] there may be a preponderance of metalepses or temporal shifts, which in themselves are not new to the practice of narrative but are nonetheless used in this context to especially discontinuous or disjunctive effect. The normative boundaries of the genre may also be breached, as, for example, in Delbo's *Auschwitz and After*, where poems are interspersed among short prose texts whose own formal status is frequently undecidable. At the same time, to convey the radically unprecedented character of the Holocaust, the memoirist may, in reference to an event, a place, or a situation, choose a deeply defamiliarizing mode of description; or else, for the organization of the narrative as a whole, for an internal sequence, or even for the construction of a single sentence, resort to a parataxis so pronounced, to a juxtaposition so devoid of connectives as to disarm the principle most fundamental to our interpretation of experience, namely, causality. There is no dearth, either, of lexical disruption, whereby the most common nouns and verbs become semantically deceptive and disorienting, or of such rhetorical devices as irony and euphemism, which underscore precisely what

is not said or said only indirectly. In fact, as Ross Chambers has compellingly demonstrated in reference to the opening pages of Jorge Semprun's
Literature or Life, a rhetoric of indirectness, of indexicality or "pointing to,"
is particularly suited to the dialogical tension in question, since it allows for
the signification of traumatizing phenomena that, if mimetically represented, might either alienate readers or induce in them the presumptuous
impression of reliving events with, or even as, the victim.[44] Aside from
making it clear that the interpretation of testimonial discourse must not
confine its attention to mimetic representation (and aside, then, from spar-
ing us a good deal of talk about the putative "unrepresentability" of traumatic experience), Chambers also shows, in *Untimely Interventions*, how
indexicality, by pointing to something that is "there" without being represented, helps to articulate what is so strikingly spectral or haunting about
the Holocaust, especially for its survivors.[45]

To be sure, reflecting on the art of survival in this way may lead one to
consider the possibility of constructing a discursive typology, whose purpose would presumably be to circumscribe the specificity of Holocaust
survivor testimony or even just testimonial memoir. Yet however instructive such a typology might prove to be, it could not avoid divorcing the
devices or techniques just mentioned from the situation of address whose
tension they transmit and in whose terms alone their use remains intelligible. For that matter, the divorce could not even be effected unless the
typologists had already dissociated themselves from the relation between
first and second persons that frames and informs the writing and reading of
testimonial memoir. The detachment required to typologize its discourse
would thus forsake the very situation constitutive of its specificity.[46] Nevertheless, we can at least thank the internal incoherence of such a project for
making something else quite clear, namely, that testimony as an art of survival begins and ends with the act of communication, with the communicative relation, whose severance is indissociable from victimization. If we
turn to the first person, we note the irreducibility of utterance to statement, of saying to what is said. Turning to the second, as we shall do in
reading the poem of Delbo's that begins "O you who know," we perceive a
challenge to any purported knowledge or understanding that would, so to
speak, place term limits on listening. But in the situation of address and in
all that it informs, one can see at work what Jakobson, after Malinowski,

calls the "phatic" function of language, which establishes, monitors, or re-establishes communication and which, for that very reason, appears wher-ever communication has been threatened, impaired, or disrupted.[47] Indeed, it may be that hardly a word of testimony fails to engage this function, if only in the guise of an implicit question, or rather two: Are you listening? Can you hear?

If we can, then the personal voice we hear will surely be entitled to con-sideration within Adorno's perspective on art after Auschwitz and may even, in being so considered, force us to reconsider that perspective itself. As I earlier indicated, there should be no doubt, to begin with, that testi-monial memoir *is* an art. This is so not only because it relies on certain ar-tistic means of expression but especially, from Adorno's point of view, insofar as it calls the adequacy of those means into question. Yet one could ask whether memoir as an art of survival might not amount to something more or other than a dialectic of appropriation and dismantling. Indeed, it would seem that in the voice of the memoirist we also find a "positive" *poiēsis*, a making or construction, pursued in two different but simultaneous ways: the act of narration performatively (re)constructs the self or subjectivity of the survivor precisely *as* it (re)constructs that survivor's history of deper-sonalization. In this light, one could also ask whether Adorno's insistence on the dismantling of form does not have the effect of arresting dialectics itself, and whether this paralysis does not in turn reflect on his part, to borrow the title of a groundbreaking study of postwar German society, a certain "inability to mourn."[48] At the very least, the question arises as to how the acknowledgment of testimonial *poiēsis* would inflect the double im-perative that defines the ethical "situation of literature" after Auschwitz, according to which, again, suffering "demands the continued existence of the very art it forbids." For let us recall that, in "Cultural Criticism and Society," the choice of (lyric) poetry to represent art in general focuses at-tention on the personal voice in particular, which is considered "barbaric" to the extent that it can lend itself only to the reification of the individual in a culture where that same reification has already paved the way for indus-trialized genocide. However, would one also call "barbaric" the use of the personal voice by the very survivors of that genocide? To be sure, in "Lyric and Society" and especially, as we have seen, in "Commitment," Adorno revises his ethical stance in such a way as to offer a reasonable summary of it in the double imperative just mentioned. Nevertheless, on whose moral authority would one initially "forbid" artistic expression to Holocaust survivors, even if one then concedes that this expression is necessary? For whose sake would one even think of "prohibiting" the use of the personal voice to those so unjustly denied it?

Assuming, as I claimed in my reading of "Commitment," that the artistic representation of suffering may afford a pleasure or a semblance of understanding that is tantamount, in Adorno's eyes, to a betrayal of victims, it is presumably for the sake of victims themselves that such representation would be forbidden to survivors (although, obviously, this begs the question of the relation between the victims who survived and those who did not, to which I will return in a moment). But since the object of the prohibition is the very art that suffering also demands, this art would presumably be created for the sake of those victims. Thus, whereas until now we have been concerned with the rather broadly defined community to which individual survivors address themselves, the problem of subjectivity finally leads us here to consider the much more narrowly defined community of which survivors, having been victims, are actually a part, yet also not a part, precisely because they survived. This ambiguous status is what makes so fraught for them the question: For whom do I speak?

As we know, the Jews were targeted for an accident of birth, regardless of all else. The "community" into which they were forcibly molded by the Nazis thus reflected the obliteration of whatever may have distinguished its individual members from one another. Even for those in whose lives the Jewish heritage had played a relatively minor role, such as Primo Levi, victimization was inseparable from the awareness of being identified as a Jew. And it is not so surprising, given the severity of that victimization, that its individual experience included the internalization of this group identity, in which individuals were entirely dissolved. As Aharon Appelfeld puts it:

> There was no place for the individual, for his pain and despair, in the camps. . . . The individual, or what was left of him, was nullified, and only a barren gaze remained, or, rather, apathy. After the Holocaust as well, there was shame in talking about oneself. . . . To write about the Holocaust is impossible, it's forbidden, people said repeatedly, and you agreed with them, for this was also your own feeling. . . . To write about oneself, about one's personal feelings, seemed selfish and vulgar.[49]

Indeed, even to write about oneself in order also or primarily to speak for those who perished was, in a sense, to betray them, since it required availing oneself of the speech that they had been forever denied. Moreover, the sense of betrayal to which the act of reclaiming the personal voice could give rise was compounded by the phenomenon of survivor guilt, a phenomenon all the more puzzling and intractable in light of the randomness of survival itself—as though, in the face of such randomness, feeling guilty derived from an autonomic effort to restore at least a semblance of moral causality to the world, to affirm retroactively a correlation between responsibility and agency.[50]

Survivor guilt is only puzzling, however, if we assume, like Kant, that responsibility is strictly entailed by agency, or conversely, that the categorical "you must" presupposes an "I am able," in short, that the self-legislating, morally autonomous first person precedes and determines the second and neither bears nor should *feel* any responsibility for the actions of others over whom it has no control. Were this the case, my previous remarks about moral responsibility in the addressee of testimonial memoir would of course turn out to have been quite pointless. But if, as Levinas contends, we discover our responsibility when, as second persons, we are addressed by an other not like us and become first persons or moral agents only in responding to that address, then responsibility produces not only agency but extends from the outset beyond the compass of agency, of actions that are mine and mine alone. Yet the fundamental dissymmetry of what Levinas calls the ethical relation (*l'éthique*), whereby responsibility both precedes and exceeds the ability to fulfill it, does not account solely for the uncanny reversal of causality in survivor guilt. It also helps to explain why, for thousands upon thousands of survivors, the seeming impossibility of speaking of oneself without betraying others did not take precedence, after all, over the obligation to speak *for* those who perished, since only in this way could survivors respond *to* them, breaking the silence imposed on their silencing and reaffirming the relation on which the destructive force of Nazism had been concentrated. To rephrase Adorno's double imperative, one could say that, for survivors of the Holocaust, the silence of the dead compelled the testimony it prohibited.[51]

Needless to say, writing about oneself for the sake of the dead does not preclude doing so for the sake of other survivors. Aside from what survivors have in common, the possibility that one of them may write a testimonial memoir that strikes others as rather unrepresentative of their experience is only a problem if these others fail to see in the discrepancy an invitation to break their own silence.[52] And as I have also suggested, survivors may write about their experience for the sake of their contemporaries or of future generations, or at least for their edification in the name of social justice and peace. But amidst all these considerations, there is one that is notably missing, namely, whether survivors might, regardless of what their fellows have already said, write about themselves for their *own* sake. In a sense, of course, we know that they may well do so, at least to judge by the passage already quoted from *The Drowned and the Saved*, where Levi states concerning *Survival in Auschwitz*: "those were things I had inside, that occupied me and that I had to expel." The question should therefore be formulated more precisely, perhaps as follows: In the act of bearing witness, what is at stake in witnesses' relation to themselves? And at the same time, recalling Appelfeld's observation that "after the Holocaust as well, there was shame in talking about oneself," what does shame have to do with this relation?

Since survivors, too, were once victims, they remain, mutatis mutandis, among those at risk of betrayal when they reclaim the personal voice. Should the word *betrayal* seem too strong here, the relation between survivor and victim certainly allows of other possibilities. For if it is true, as I have claimed, that the survivor is an altered self constructed in the very act of narrating the victimization of its predecessor, then in regard to the victims that survivors once were, testimonial memoir may constitute not so much a betrayal as a parting or leave-taking, as well as a memorial or a testament (derived from the Latin *testis*, "witness"). Or indeed, testimonial memoirists could be said to practice for themselves as individuals what no one else can do for them, even though it is also they who, in a sense, practice it for all of the dead: namely, mourning. But however plausible these characterizations of writing about oneself for one's own sake may be, in none of them can one plausibly claim to find an occasion of shame. Shame must therefore be sought elsewhere, and specifically, I would argue, in the embodied act of telling.

If shame is often associated with the body, it is not only because the body is vulnerable to exposure. After all, psychological or mental phenomena share that vulnerability, even if not to the same degree. However, attitudes and desires, thoughts and beliefs that come into open conflict with social or moral norms and expectations can only constitute a source of shame because they are tied to an *embodied* and hence inescapable self, to a self without alibi, to my self and mine alone. Much has been written concerning the physical degradation to which the victims of Nazism were subjected, especially in the ghettos and camps, and it would be impossible to overestimate either the pain or the shame they were made to suffer as a result.[53] But this treatment was of a piece with the social and psychological warfare waged against them, including segregation and, as I earlier indicated, the prohibition of address (which naturally entailed the impossibility of *re*dress), incarceration, the replacement of names with tattooed numbers, interminable roll calls, forced labor, and so forth—all of it designed to "persuade" victims, by abusing the reversed moral causality discussed a moment ago, that they deserved this treatment, to convert individuals, in their *own* eyes, into life unworthy of life. In fact, the creation of Jewish Councils and Jewish police in the ghettos and of the so-called Special Squads in the death camps were tactics determined by the same strategic goal of making the victims of Nazism feel responsible for their own persecution.[54] Shame did not arise, therefore, solely from abasement of the self but from the sense that the self was the source of that abasement—and not least of all for having once harbored about its own and other selves what turned out to be a most misguided presumption, that is, a belief in something like the dignity of the individual.

To be sure, it would be naïve to think, given what survivors went through, that they only began to speak or write if this belief had been fully restored or else in the expectation of fully restoring it themselves. Even to assume that they were worthy of being heard and that they might find people able and willing to listen was an act of daring, since to reclaim the personal voice and so to commit themselves to a situation of address was to run the risk of being shamed once again by the other's refusal to respond. As Appelfeld remarks:

> "Death to death," I remember hearing a religious Jewish survivor shout in the midst of the liberation camp. I didn't know what he meant. Now it seems to me that he was referring to the indifference that surrounded the survivors and threatened to submerge them in another death—mute silence.[55]

At stake here, clearly enough, is not so much the giving as the receiving of testimony. What shame has to do with witnesses' relation to themselves is a question that can only be answered, *in practice*, by those to whom their testimony is addressed. And the alternative to mute silence is not simply a willingness to face the atrocity of the Holocaust. This alone could lead, after all, to an infatuation with the "extreme situations" in which the "authenticity" of the human being supposedly manifests itself, in which the essence of the self is purportedly revealed in its traumatic violation, and in which one can lose oneself by imaginatively usurping the place of real historical victims—an infatuation whose deafness to those victims rivals that of indifference. To avoid, in Adorno's words, "surrender[ing] to cynicism merely by existing after Auschwitz" requires an awareness of our place in the situation of address that frames the story of atrocity, as second persons engaged by but differentiated from the first, as selves made responsive to and responsible for a tale not our own by the singular voice of its teller.

My reading of Adorno differs substantially from that of a prominent Holocaust scholar, Berel Lang, in his essay "The Representation of Evil: Ethical Content as Literary Form." This difference is, to me, rather puzzling, since, in reading Lang's five wide-ranging books on the Holocaust (among a host of additional authored and edited volumes), I find myself in agreement with his positions on many other issues.[56] My purpose here, however, is not to solve this puzzle but to examine his position on written representations of the Holocaust (including survivor testimony), together with its assumptions and its consequences. The decision to focus on Lang in particular is motivated not only by his emphasis on the issue of genre but especially by his articulating an interpretation of Adorno that, for the sway it has held, demands to be understood.

Adorno looms large from the opening pages of Lang's essay: "When Theodor Adorno refers, in his much-quoted phrase, to the 'barbarism' of writing lyric poetry after Auschwitz (all the more, by implication, for [sic] writing poetry *about* Auschwitz), or when Elie Wiesel asserts that a 'Holocaust literature' is a 'contradiction' in terms, they call into question the moral and aesthetic justification for the very act of writing about the Nazi genocide, whatever the genre or other literary means."[57] In itself, this statement seems unobjectionable enough, even if Adorno's charge of barbarism

was not clearly extended to *all* kinds of writing, any more than it was restricted to writing *about* the Holocaust. However, Lang never explains what
Adorno might have meant by "barbarism," and scarcely acknowledges his
subsequent critical development of the phrase.[58] Indeed, having enlisted, in
addition to Elie Wiesel (whose very prominence in Holocaust literature
complicates the stance attributed to him), two writers of fiction, Leslie
Epstein and Cynthia Ozick, to promote "historical" over "imaginative" writing about the Holocaust, Lang proceeds to dismiss, for his own purposes,
the pertinence of Adorno's crucial self-qualification: "Admittedly, both
these authors—and also Adorno, in respect to his more radical claim—later
qualified these invidious comparisons. But the fact that they were made at
all anticipates the grounds for the thesis posed here" (*AI*, 127). In developing
his thesis, then, Lang will eschew any sustained interaction with Adorno,
preferring to retain, from the dialectic embodied in Adorno's claim that
suffering "demands the continued existence of the very art it forbids," only
one of its "terms," namely, prohibition. The thesis is thus bound to run the
risk of dogmatism, both because Lang chooses to ignore the tension or
movement of Adorno's thinking and because he assumes that the meaning
of "barbarism" should be either self-evident or accepted on authority.

But what, exactly, is this thesis? In brief, it amounts to the claim that, in
representations of the Holocaust, literary form has an ethical content, that
we possess not only the descriptive but the evaluative means with which to
differentiate forms of writing from one another, and that this differentiation will authorize the judgment that "the forms of historical discourse"
are superior to "those of fictional prose or drama or poetry" (*AI*, 123). It is
clear, however, that the thesis cannot even be debated until the means of
differentiation have been determined. And yet that determination depends
in turn on what Lang calls "the grounds for the thesis posed here," and
which, as we shall see, is designed to brook no debate.

The foundation of Lang's whole argument consists in the assumption
that, as far as the Nazi genocide is concerned, "the facts speak for themselves" (*AI*, 116).[59] What speaks perhaps most loudly here is the very fact of
Lang's having then developed an argument on the basis of such an authori-
tarian non sequitur. In any case, we never do find out what the facts are
presumed to say, and this is no accident: for one can only make the facts
speak by establishing relations between them, that is, by integrating them

into a human, all too human and hence fallible interpretation in which their status as "pure" facts is inevitably compromised.[60] Indeed, "the facts speak for themselves" is a proposition that recalls the fundamental and fundamentally theological postulate of universal history, which holds that the story of the past is found and not made, that the meaning of history lies embedded in the facts as such, prior to any representation and, so to speak, untouched by human hands.[61] To be sure, this postulate can serve as a regulative ideal rather than a dogmatic axiom, and whether or to what extent the assumption on which Lang relies can do the same remains to be seen. In the meantime, however, since this assumption provides no means with which to describe or evaluate forms of writing, it can only continue to function at all if it is made immanent to the means that *are* adopted.

Thus, we rediscover facts that "speak for themselves" in the form of historical discourse and literal language, which are, respectively, distinguished from and even opposed to imaginative discourse and figurative language. Moreover, historical discourse and literal language are located at the high end of a moral scale at the bottom of which one predictably finds their counterparts. And by means of these distinctions, to which I will return in a moment, the various genres according to which one may categorize representations of the Holocaust are ascribed a greater or lesser moral value as a function of their proximity to the ideal of facts that "speak for themselves."

But contrary to what one might expect, the highest position on this scale is not necessarily occupied by the objective historiography we have inherited from the nineteenth century. Although the association of this genre with the style of documentary realism may ensure, in Lang's eyes, its ethical superiority to certain kinds of testimony (to say nothing of "art"), he is not unaware, from the work of Hayden White above all, that it is indeed a historically determined form of writing and especially that its emplotment is a trope, an interpretive "turning away" from "the facts themselves."[62] Ranked above historiography, therefore, are the chronicle and the diary, both purportedly plotless and, what is more, both affording the greatest possible temporal proximity between events and their recording. That this very proximity, as well as the systematic manner in which the Nazis deceived their victims, could and did produce factual errors correctable by historical research obviously carries less weight for Lang than the proximity itself. In other words, the idealization of facts has less to do with accuracy than with immediacy and suggests that Lang is looking beyond even universal history to something like reenactment.[63]

Following chronicle, diary, and history, and before "art," one finds memoirs, to which, given their centrality to Holocaust representation, Lang devotes surprisingly little analysis, in part, no doubt, because of their generic hybridity.[64] On the one hand, memoirs cannot claim the temporal immediacy or the plotlessness of diary and chronicle, although they may, like diary and chronicle, contribute to the historiography of the Holocaust. On the other hand, they "indulge," more than historiography does or is willing to admit, in figuration or imagination and even in the critique of historical or literal representation. And yet memoirs are also conventionally distinguished, precisely because of the historical or factual constraint to which they are subject, from fiction. As we shall see, however, Lang's indictment of art ends up cutting across generic boundaries by focusing on aesthetic features that could in principle be found in any of the genres to which he refers but the likelihood of whose real occurrence increases dramatically as one moves from chronicle and diary to memoir and fiction (to say nothing of drama and poetry). In fact, that these features do not in themselves affect the distinction between testimonial memoir and fiction may be another and perhaps the more important reason for which Lang does not dwell on memoir as a genre. But in any case, it is with testimonial memoir in mind that I would like to consider in more detail the indictment of art, and specifically of literature, informed by his reading of Adorno.

Although their articulation is frequently confused, Lang raises three main objections to the artistic representation of the Holocaust, all of which are perhaps less interesting in themselves than for the assumptions underlying them. Thus: "The characteristic use in imaginative writing of figures of speech (such as metaphor or metonymy) and tropes (for example, irony or tragedy) establishes a literary field or space between the writer and his writing and between that writing and what is written 'about.' Without such a space, the relation between language and what it represents would be unmediated; the event or referent *would be* the word" (*AI*, 142). As this statement makes clear, Lang considers linguistic mediation to be solely the province of figurative or imaginative discourse: the literal or historical representation of the Holocaust is, for him, *no representation at all*, but rather "the thing itself." There is no more argument for this than for the

earlier assumption that the facts "speak for themselves," and for good reason, since any argument would have to begin by recognizing literal language
as a mediation susceptible, albeit less conspicuously, to the same "flaws"
here attributed to its figurative counterpart. These are: that figure and
trope are a "turning" from "the thing itself"; that they induce the reader to
follow this turning; and that figurative discourse "purports to add to the
subject something that it would otherwise lack" (*AI*, 143). Moreover, even
though these flaws are stated descriptively, their normative thrust is inescapable. Indeed, given that, for Lang, literal language is not really language
at all, while figurative language is morally suspect, one cannot avoid the
impression that this first general objection (and, as we shall see, the second
and third as well) is motivated by the notion that the Holocaust simply
ought not to be spoken (or written). This is suggested in particular by the flaw
that consists in "adding something," an ethical failure reminiscent of the
transgression to which Revelation attributes rather dire consequences:
"For my part, I give this warning to everyone who is listening to the words
of prophecy in this book: should anyone add to them, God will add to him
the plagues described in this book."[65] In his emphasis on the moral superiority of literal or historical discourse, Lang thus elides discourse itself, and,
as a consequence if not by intention, promotes a quasi-religious view of the
Holocaust.

Lang's second objection to the artistic representation of the Holocaust
is that "the discourse . . . is personalized; the writer obtrudes," and this to
the point that such discourse may even become "emotive" (*AI*, 145). It may
well be, as Ernst van Alphen claims, that "Lang has a strictly romantic view
of art and literature."[66] In any case, it would be difficult to imagine a historical event in regard to which being "emotive" requires less justification
than the Holocaust. Still more telling, however, is the assumption on which
this second objection is essentially based, namely, that the representation
of the Holocaust should reproduce certain features of the event itself. So
Lang remarks: "For a subject which historically combines the features of
impersonality with a challenge to the conception of moral boundaries, the
attempt to personalize it . . . appears at once gratuitous and inconsistent, gratuitous because it individualizes where the subject by its nature is corporate;
inconsistent because it sets limits when the subject itself has denied them"
(*AI*, 144). In what van Alphen terms "a bizarre gesture of collusion,"[67] Lang

implies that the proper response to the Holocaust would consist not so much in representing as in *reenacting*, through the obliteration of the personal voice, the depersonalization that characterized the Nazi genocide. This is all the more serious given a further assumption that he makes about the event: although the Holocaust was incontrovertibly depersonalizing, Lang does not recognize that depersonalization was *personally* experienced by its millions of victims.[68] And as for the claim that the "personalization" of discourse or the "obtrusion" of the writer sets limits inconsistent with "the subject itself," we should observe that, by Lang's own reasoning, it would clearly be inconsistent to respect, in the representation of that subject, the limits that he himself advocates, including most notably the constraints of literal or historical discourse.

Finally, Lang's third objection could be formulated as follows: while imaginative discourse foregrounds both the choice of a particular figurative or tropic possibility among others and the obtrusive writer as the agent of that choice, this particularization is also a generalization insofar as it calls attention to possibilities not chosen. Or as he himself puts it: "The figurative assertion of alternative possibilities . . . suggests a denial of limitation: *no* possibilities are excluded. And although for some literary subjects openness of this sort may be warranted or even desirable, for others it represents a falsification, morally *and* conceptually" (*AI*, 145–46). I will not dwell on the fact that, having condemned figurative representation for imposing limits, Lang now condemns it for failing to do so. What I wish to stress once again is the assumption underlying the objection: for it is essentially the same to say that "the facts speak for themselves" or that their literal representation is no representation at all, that the only truthful and morally appropriate representation of the Holocaust mimics the impersonality of the Nazi genocide itself, and, as in the case at hand, that thanks to a God's eye view of history, there exists a Right Story of the Holocaust of which the many possible figurations amount to little more than cognitive and moral travesties.[69]

As I have noted, "the facts speak for themselves" is not a debatable proposition, since it can be neither proven nor disproven. This is why the argument itself looks like a petitio principii, like begging the question: since the principle embodied in the statement "the facts speak for themselves" cannot bear the burden of proof, it must be presumed in the premises, beginning, as we have seen, with the claim that historical discourse and literal language somehow lie outside the realm of representation. And so it is that, aside from fostering such incoherent notions as what Lang elsewhere calls "nonrepresentational representation,"[70] the structure of his argument can at times make it difficult to tell a premise from a conclusion, an assumption from a consequence, as is perhaps most obviously the case with the idea that a "morally *and* conceptually" adequate representation of the Holocaust would consist in its reenactment. But indeed, far from simply begging the question, Lang's argument constantly shifts the burden of proof between the conceptual and the moral, between its descriptive and normative components: while "the facts speak for themselves" is un(dis)confirmable and hence epistemically unserviceable, it can still function as a disguise for the claim that "the Holocaust ought not to be spoken" or that "we should not represent the Holocaust," which, to be sure, is also un(dis)confirmable but may nevertheless prove more persuasive if it is said to be based on a knowledge of "the facts," which knowledge, however, is in turn discredited by its normative inflection—and so forth. Needless to say, this added confusion is hardly dispelled, nor the circular argument that produces it rendered any less arbitrary, when Lang states that the forms of writing about the Holocaust will ultimately be judged according to which are "the most significant and compelling—the most valuable" (*AI*, 123).[71]

Thus, a perspective on written representations of the Holocaust that would, among other things, devalorize if not condemn the "personalization" of discourse turns out to be based, at least to a very considerable degree, on personal preference, that is, on what Lang finds significant, compelling, valuable (or not). Although this disqualifies his criterion of judgment as a regulative ideal, the extent to which his view or views similar to it have informed the reception of Holocaust literature suggests that the preference underlying it is widely shared. In regard to Lang, therefore, but unlike him, I would not equate "personal" with "gratuitous." But then the further assessment of his position, which, as I earlier observed, respects only one term of Adorno's dialectic, might benefit from our briefly reconsidering, in Adorno's own case, what motivated his initial, seemingly dogmatic stance and what led him to modify it.

Let me recall that, in "Commitment," Adorno expresses reluctance to "soften" his statement about poetry after Auschwitz because he perceives in aesthetic form, and specifically in the pleasure it may yield or the sense it may make of the senseless, a possible betrayal of those who perished in the Holocaust. On this reading, "to write poetry after Auschwitz is barbaric" is a statement motivated by solidarity with the victims of the Third Reich. Let me also recall that in "Cultural Criticism and Society," where the famous phrase originated, the accusation of barbarism is leveled essentially against the social reification that transforms the individual into a commodity (which can be exchanged or, as in the Holocaust, "consumed") and that can make of lyric poets and, for that matter, any artists resorting to the personal voice unwitting collaborators in its reproduction as such. Finally, I will recall that in *Negative Dialectics*, which comes after "Commitment" and in which Adorno concedes that his statement about poetry after Auschwitz "may have been wrong," since "perennial suffering has as much right to expression as a tortured man has to scream," he refers as well to his own survival and to the guilt that induces in him a certain "coldness" toward himself. As I have remarked, this coldness, which implies complicity in coldness toward others, may also have motivated his original statement—or, what amounts to the same, his failure to acknowledge that "perennial suffering has as much right to expression as a tortured man has to scream"— and, to the extent that the figurative value of "coldness" resembles that of "hardness," his subsequent reluctance to "soften" that statement. Yet hardness or coldness toward survivors of the Holocaust and solidarity with its victims are by no means incompatible: what ties them together is the unstated notion that to respect victims is to resemble them, to identify with them through a denial of self, including one's voice—a denial exemplified when, speaking of his survival, Adorno refers to himself in the third person. Of course, this is a recognizable feature of mourning as well as of its pathological extension, melancholy. It can also function as a mechanism of defense, since attending to the personal voice of a camp survivor is likely to be a good deal more upsetting than reading Raul Hilberg's *The Destruction of the European Jews*. For all of these reasons—solidarity with victims, mourning of the dead, self-protection—if not also for others, a perspective from which one looks warily or disfavorably upon artistic representations of the Holocaust can indeed prove quite compelling.

The problem, however, is not only that self-denial tends to elide the difference between survivors and victims and to convert them all into an anonymous or, to use Lang's term, a "corporate" mass, but especially that, raised to the status of a principle, as in "to write poetry after Auschwitz is barbaric," and so extended to other survivors, it favors their revictimization. As we have seen, Adorno tackles this problem dialectically: reification can only be resisted, the traumatic silencing of individuals can only be answered, for the sake of both the dead and the living, if, again, suffering "demands the continued existence of the very art it forbids." What must nonetheless be noted here is that, although Adorno's thinking may eventually have led him to this point in any case, the dialectic appears to have been set in motion or at least explicitly articulated thanks to a dialogue, initiated by the response of a poet, Hans Magnus Enzensberger, to Adorno's condemnation of poetry after Auschwitz. In other words, it was a situation of address in which he was personally called to account that led Adorno to abandon the dogmatism of this condemnation and to develop a view of post-Holocaust aesthetics as the site at which competing ethical imperatives enter into dialectical tension with each other.

Returning to Lang, and considering that he clings to the very dogmatism that Adorno discarded, one cannot help but wonder whether he would be prepared, in a personal encounter with, say, Elie Wiesel or Ruth Kluger, to denounce the "personalization" of discourse about the Holocaust. Or whether he would have been prepared to do so if face to face with Primo Levi or Charlotte Delbo, Jorge Semprun or Jean Améry. Be that as it may, he certainly creates the impression that the writer cannot be trusted to make an intelligent and ethically discriminating choice of figure or trope, as though the mere act of figuration cast its agent onto a slippery slope leading inexorably into a moral abyss where anything goes. And he also gives the impression that the reader cannot be entrusted with the task of critical and morally responsible interpretation, but will, "turned" from the facts, be seduced by the aesthetic attractiveness of figure or trope, abducted by the verbal equivalent of the graven image. Most telling of all, however, may be the absence of any reflection on the situation of address that, especially in testimonial memoir, brings writer and reader together, a situation in which the personal voice, itself a figure, calls upon us, not to turn away from the facts, but to turn toward and face the survivor.

I turn now, in concluding the chapter, to the remarkable articulation of this encounter in Charlotte Delbo's *Auschwitz and After.*

Delbo, a member of the French Resistance arrested on March 2, 1942, and deported from Compiègne in the women's convoy of January 24, 1943, survived twenty-seven months of imprisonment in Auschwitz-Birkenau, Rajsko, and Ravensbrück, and was repatriated by the Red Cross via Sweden at the end of June 1945.[72] Her trilogy of memoirs, *Auschwitz and After*, includes *None of Us Will Return*, *Useless Knowledge*, and *The Measure of Our Days*.[73] Since I am concerned here primarily with the communicative relation between writer and reader or between witness and testimonial addressee, and since this relation so thoroughly informs the initial framing of the trilogy, I plan to focus on the beginning of *None of Us Will Return*. Nevertheless, in order to convey in some measure Delbo's general awareness of the situation of address (no doubt connected to her extensive experience in the theater), I would first point out, for example, that the third volume, which tells initially of repatriation, consists thereafter almost entirely of testimonies attributed to certain of her fellow survivors and addressed to her as "you" (*vous* or *tu*) or even as "Charlotte." As we shall see, this exemplification of listening or reception, this practice of witnessing witnessing is anticipated from the very beginning of *Auschwitz and After*.

By "beginning," I mean first of all the title, *None of Us Will Return*. The referent of its first person plural pronoun "us," for whom Delbo presumably speaks, is anything but a simple matter. On the one hand, few if any readers could be expected to broach this text without some knowledge of Auschwitz and of the role it played in the fate of the Jews, and to none does the text spare such knowledge. On the other hand, one can learn from this text or from other sources that Delbo herself was not Jewish, that she was imprisoned and deported for political reasons, and that her life in the camps was spent primarily in the company of women from her own convoy, whose class and ethnic differences yielded to a solidarity founded on the language and nationality they shared.[74] And in fact, the first person plural pronoun in *None of Us Will Return* most often designates this particular community. But while this determination is not unimportant, it does not necessarily dispose of the question raised by the initial indetermination of the title. For the pronoun *us* (or *we*) does not *always* designate the particular community of which Delbo was a member. It can also denote, for example, a gathering of fifteen thousand women that includes all of the groups imprisoned at Birkenau (*AA*, 31–34 / 1:51–57). Moreover, the masculine *aucun* of *Aucun de nous ne reviendra* clearly indicates that the *nous* should be understood to refer as well to the men incarcerated at Auschwitz. And since, finally, thanks in large part to Adorno's expression "after Auschwitz," the name *Auschwitz* already connoted, long before the publication of this volume, the "concentrationary universe"[75] in its entirety, the *us* could arguably be extended to all those deported to labor, concentration, or death camps.[76]

It may not seem unreasonable to infer from this that the threat of destruction directed at pre-Holocaust groups in their very multiplicity and diversity created an "us" whose sense of community derived from a universal despair of return. However, even if one can speak, in such a case, of "community," the "us" so created can hardly be said to have superseded the groups of which it was composed. To the extent that, as we know, these groups were threatened to different degrees, the acuteness of their despair, and hence the inclusiveness of the *us*, were bound to vary.[77] To this Delbo attests, for example, in a short passage entitled "Dialogue," where a conversation between the narrator and a Jewish compatriot revolves around the greater danger to which the Jewish woman is exposed. In response to the latter's assertion that "for you perhaps there's hope, but for us . . . ," the narrator, failing to convince even herself, nevertheless offers such words of encouragement as "oh, come on, it's the same odds for both of us." The passage concludes with the same pronominal reference to the two interlocutors: "Smoke lingers in the camp weighing upon us and enveloping us in the odor of burning flesh" (*AA*, 15–16 / 1:26–27). But this smoke, earlier evoked by a gesture of the Jewish woman's hand, is precisely what confirms the distinction she emphasizes in saying that "for you perhaps there's hope, but for us . . . ," the distinction literally marked by the contrast between the narrator's *F* (meaning French, superimposed on the red triangle worn by political prisoners) and her own yellow star. In its silence and in the silence of the gesture by which it is evoked, the smoke of the crematoria indicates the crux of this conversation: "Dialogue" centers around the unstated point that the "us" for whom the Jewish woman speaks is defined by the much greater odds of being permanently excluded from speech or dialogue.

Yet the exemplary difference to which "Dialogue" alludes as a matter of who among "us" shall remain to speak could just as well be phrased as a matter of who shall return. And although one might expect the meaning of *us* in *None of Us Will Return* to be simplified at least to some extent by this determinant, the reverse is rather the case insofar as "return" poses its own interpretive challenge, beginning here again with the title itself, which, taken literally, appears to have been belied by the survival of the author who conceived it. Of course, on the one hand, we know that in fact some *did* return, including Delbo herself and forty-eight other women from her convoy. And this "literal" return is not interpretively unimportant, since it can be said to have "cemented" the difference in question, and to have done so, as I suggested in the second section of this chapter, all the more tangibly for survivors who chose to bear witness, as they could proceed only by availing themselves of the speech forever denied to the dead, and as, furthermore, they could not speak *for* the dead without purporting to represent an "us" in which they were no longer included. But on the other hand, we know just as well that, whenever it may have been conceived, "aucun de nous ne reviendra" was retained as a title—a title in which the *inclusion* of survivors among those of whom it is claimed that "none will return" means that the sense of "return" cannot be restricted to biological survival. Indeed, the sense in which survivors did *not* return can be grasped from a different reading of the negation brought to bear on the future tense of the verb (*"aucun . . . ne* reviendra," *"none . . .* will return"): although obviously alive, as the dead are not, survivors retain at least the memory if not the feeling of hopelessness endemic to the camps, to what Delbo calls "a place where time is abolished" (*AA*, 32 / 1:53), that is, where the future is permanently frozen *as such* and consequently forecloses the possibility of a definite *"after* Auschwitz."[78] Moreover, the arrested future conveyed by the prolepsis of the title finds a counterpart at the end of the volume, where the penultimate "None of us will return" is followed, alone on the last page, by the sentence: "None of us was meant to return" (*AA*, 113–14 / 1:182–83). What this coda suggests is that survivors never "left behind" or "got over" their own victimization or their witnessing the victimization of others. In regard to this "past that will not pass,"[79] one could mention the French colloquialism *je n'en reviens pas* ("I can't get over it"), and also the term *revenant* (more common in French than in English), meaning ghost or specter, with which Delbo characterizes herself and her fellow survivors upon repatriation and in so doing imputes to their "return" the sense of a haunting (*AA*, 230–31 / 2:191).[80]

Thus, although in one sense survivors returned, as their less fortunate fellow victims did not, the traumatic experience they carried with them precluded any unambiguous return to the world outside of the camps, precluded anything like full reintegration into the community from which they had been deported. And although one could certainly say that, in the aftermath of the Holocaust, they shared the experience of being "revenants" to the world at large, Delbo makes it clear, at the conclusion of *Useless Knowledge* and throughout *The Measure of Our Days* (albeit especially in its opening section), that the return to "normal life" dispersed their *own* community, converting its members into specters for one another, haunted by the ghost of "us."[81]

Still, as complicated a matter as the referent of "us" in *None of Us Will Return* may appear to be, one might think that it could at least be contrasted with that of an implied "you," with the public to which, as Delbo maintained, "il faut donner à voir,"[82] including most notably such nonvictims as those from whom, in the portions of the trilogy just mentioned, the very return of survivors marks their definitive estrangement. That the Holocaust was *internal* to the community suggests nevertheless that the scope of this "us" may be further extended. What if the "us" should designate, as a whole, the community whose traumatic sundering into an "us" and a "them" precludes its return to an "us as we used to be"? Indeed, what if this "us" that will never return should force us to recognize, in the nostalgia for an "us as we used to be," the longing for a social formation capable of genocide? What if, in short, the "us" of *None of Us Will Return* should include, in the sense of implicating, those who were *not* victims of the Holocaust? It should be clear that asking this question does not entail eliding the crucial distinction between victims and nonvictims (or, among nonvictims, between bystanders and perpetrators). Nor, however, does it entail confining the pertinence of the question to a moment of history safely removed from present concerns—as though the question itself did not continue to haunt us more than sixty years after the Holocaust. Rather, asking the question whether and in what sense the "us" of *None of Us Will Return* could include nonvictims, even those born after the war, means asking how they might read this "us," that is, how their response to a story such as Delbo's might performatively reiterate the question of community. Will they, wishing to respect the singularity of victims' experience or else to lighten the emotional burden of reading about it, so thoroughly distance that experience from their own as to ascribe the "us" to victims alone or (what amounts to the same) consign victims anew to a corporate "them," and hence reenact their exclusion or "concentration"? Will they, from a misplaced sense of solidarity or a desire to purge the affective charge of testimony, so completely assimilate victims' experience to their own as to obliterate the former in the name of the "us," and so reenact the silencing constitutive of the victimized "them"? Or will these readers succeed in maintaining a tension between proximity and distance, between identification and estrangement, a tension that Dominick LaCapra has aptly characterized as "empathic unsettlement"?[83]

Needless to say, I have delineated in only the most general terms some possible responses to the question of community in *Auschwitz and After* (and, by extension, in other Holocaust testimony), and it is a safe bet that the response of most if not all readers would require more extensive and nuanced reflection. Yet my purpose here is simply to suggest how, from the beginning, Delbo problematizes the framing of her memoirs: the tacit agreement on whose basis "we" would assume a stable if still underdetermined identity for the "us" of *None of Us Will Return* (and perhaps look confidently forward to other such facts that "speak for themselves") is breached before it can even begin to function as a guarantee of intelligibility for the narrative itself. And as a result, the identity of the "we," that is, of the implied "you" to whom Delbo addresses herself and whose position we readers occupy, is also and no less forcefully called into question.

But the title *None of Us Will Return* is only one component of this initial framing. Turning the title page, we come upon an epigraph that reads: "Today, I am not sure that what I wrote is true. I am certain it is truthful [*Aujourd'hui, je ne suis pas sûre que ce que j'ai écrit soit vrai. Je suis sûre que c'est véridique*]" (*AA*, 1 / 1:7). The problem of interpretation posed by this epigraph becomes clear when we compare its translation here to that of a virtually identical statement from the opening section of the later but closely related text *Days and Memory*, where the same translator renders *vrai* as "real" and *véridique* as "correspond[ing] to the facts."[84] On the one hand, I would agree that the difference Delbo posits between *vrai* and *véridique* can be most plausibly credited if, as *Days and Memory* suggests, we construe *vrai* as "real," so that the statement "je ne suis pas sûre que ce que j'ai écrit soit vrai" is heard to echo the uncertain sense of reality or, to phrase this more forcefully, the shock of disbelief that pervades Holocaust survivor testimony. On the other hand, the question remains how exactly to define *véridique* (etymologically, "truly said") both in itself and in relation to *vrai* so understood. Although its translation as "corresponding to the facts" is not wrong, it can, like "truthful," be construed in more than one way. If this correspondence is assumed to mean that what is written consists in a mere representation of facts ostensibly independent of any interpretation, then one is bound to expect of the writing itself a certain conformity to the norms of documentary realism, and in Delbo's case, to see that expectation frustrated. But if "corresponding to the facts" means that Delbo's text is "truthful" in the sense I earlier predicated of testimony in general, namely, that it respects the historical record but is not confined to it and, for that matter, does not presume to dictate what qualifies for it, then not only can an uncertain sense of reality or the shock of disbelief *also* be recognized for the historical facts they are but the diction charged with conveying them will inevitably challenge discursive conventions, and not only those of so-called "realism." Indeed, here I would recall my earlier observation that *Auschwitz and After* is a hybridized work combining poems and brief, narratively more or less discontinuous sections of prose—to which I would add that in this poetry and prose, whose formal status can actually quite often seem undecidable, one finds specific features of the lyric, the epic, and drama. Moreover, as we have just gathered from the discussion of the title *None of Us Will Return*, the conventions in question extend to the unstated collective agreement that supports the assumption of textual intelligibility as well as to the very "coming together" (from the Latin *con-venire*) or community of the "us." And like the "us," for the construction of whose meaning readers are held partly responsible, the sense of *véridique* in *Auschwitz and After* cannot be determined in advance but will only emerge only from the reading of this testimony, from a listening to this diction.

Nevertheless, the significance of the epigraph obviously depends as well on the first person singular voice, of which so much has already been said in this chapter. In addition to its presumptive role as spokesperson for the "us" of the title, and notwithstanding its explicitness, the "I" can be said to occupy the position of what in narratology is called the "implied author," correlated with the implied reader (or what I have more often termed the testimonial addressee), of which much has also been said, and distinguished at once from the real author (in this case, the Charlotte Delbo who wrote and published other books) and from the narrator of the text. And as always, the "I" is the site of a tension between particular and universal, since it designates a specific individual in conjunction here with a "today" locatable between the writing of *None of Us Will Return* and its publication, that is, in a definite past, but also lends itself to anyone familiar with the language and can therefore serve as a vehicle of identification, redefining "today" as "now" and converting both the individual's speech and the experience it articulates into mine or yours. The epigraphic "I" thus admittedly presents the formal possibility of an identification so thorough as to constitute, as the foregoing discussion of Adorno would suggest, a "betrayal" of the survivor, and yet, at the very threshold of Delbo's testimony, the epigraph also explicitly stages the situation of address in which this illusion can be dismantled. What makes the epigraph even more noteworthy, however, is that the opening of the testimony itself marks the total, if temporary, eclipse of the "I." Between this eclipse, to which I will return, and the moment when Delbo next stages the situation of address, lies one of the most memorable passages in all of Holocaust survivor testimony, which, although written almost half a century earlier, is also an eloquent rejoinder to Lang's thesis.

This passage—the first section of *None of Us Will Return*—is entitled "Arrivals, Departures." It does not refer to the arrival at Auschwitz of Delbo's own convoy, for the only intervention of the first person (plural) voice more than halfway through the section suffices to indicate that the members of that convoy are already in the camp. This intervention occurs in reference to a mother who slaps her son in order to keep him quiet next to her on the platform. Delbo writes: "She hits her child, and we who know cannot forgive her for it. Yet, were she to smother him with kisses, it would all be the same in the end" (*AA*, 7 / 1:15). Those designated by "we" are thus not only prisoners but also witnesses possessed of knowledge denied to the new arrivals on their way to the gas chamber. In fact, from allusions to a synagogue and a rabbi as well as from a statement made toward the end of the section ("All those Jews have mouths full of gold, and since there are so many of them it all adds up to tons and tons" [*AA*, 9 / 1:18]), it is clear that "Arrivals, Departures" has to do with a convoy of Jews. While the estrangement of survivors to which I earlier called attention is thrown into sharpest relief upon their return to "normal life," the estrangement of these Jews from themselves and from humanity generally is initially brought into focus here by the contrast between a "normal" train station and the terminus to which they are deported (the "station" at Auschwitz, which will, however, as Delbo observes, "remain nameless for them" [*AA*, 5 / 1:12]). I quote the first lines:

People arrive. They look through the crowd of those who are waiting for those who await them. They kiss them and say they are tired from the trip.

People leave. They say good-bye to those who are not leaving and hug the children.

There is a street for people who arrive and a street for people who leave.

There is a café called "Arrivals" and a café called "Departures."

There are people who arrive and people who leave.

But there is a station where those who arrive are also the ones who are leaving
a station where those who arrive have never arrived, where those who left have never come back.

It is the largest station in the world.

This is the station they reach, wherever they come from.

They get here after days and nights
having crossed whole countries
they reach it together with their children, even the little ones who were not to be part of this journey.

They took the children because for this kind of trip you do not leave without them.

Those who had some took gold because they believed gold might come in handy.

All of them took what they loved most because you do not leave your dearest possessions when you set out for distant lands.

They all brought their life along, since what you must take with you above all is your life.

And when they get there
they think they've arrived
in hell
maybe. Yet they did not believe it.

They had no idea you could take a train to hell but since they are there they steel themselves and feel ready to face it
with their children, their wives, their aged parents
with family mementoes and family papers.

They do not know there is no arriving in this station.
They expect the worst—not the unthinkable. (*AA*, 3–4/ 1:9–11)[85]

As promised, I will return to the question concerning the eclipse, in this opening passage, of the epigraphic first person singular by the third person voice. For now, I would like to examine, in both the quoted passage and the remainder of the section, the artistry with which Delbo engages her readers in the experience of these arrivals and their witnesses.

In introducing the passage, I referred to the contrast between a "normal" train station and the station at Auschwitz. Although this characterization of the text is not, strictly speaking, erroneous, it is certainly proleptic or anticipatory, since what it says about the scene described in the first nine lines can only be *inferred* from those or subsequent lines. In the very first part of the passage, in other words, Delbo says nothing about a train station. The procedure she adopts here recalls what Husserl terms the "phenomenological *epokhē*" or "eidetic reduction," which brackets the "natural attitude," that is, the various assumptions we habitually make about, say, an object of perception, in favor of a purely descriptive rendering of that object as it appears to consciousness.[86] In literature, such description has most often been employed as a technique of defamiliarization—and could indeed be considered a mode of what the Russian formalist Viktor Shklovsky called *ostranenie*[87]—a technique whereby the very strangeness of the object arouses in the reader an awareness both of features to which normal perception is at least insufficiently attentive and of the cultural filter(s) to which such perception is attributable. Of course, to be effective this technique requires a moment of *re*familiarization or recognition: I cannot perceive the normal inflection of perception unless at some point I am able to compare what I might have expected with what Delbo actually describes. Maybe, having inferred from the emphasis on arrivals and departures, on crowds and their behavior, and on the streets and cafés, that this is in any case a station of some sort, I further infer from my own experience or from knowledge otherwise acquired that it is much more likely to be for trains than for buses or airplanes. Maybe I rely instead or as well on the lines that follow these. But whatever the inferential process through which I conclude what Delbo never states, namely, that this is a train station, the literary restraint of her description makes it clear how I as a reader must collaborate in and bear responsibility for the act of witnessing.

Yet if Delbo engages her readers by *not* naming what she describes in the first nine lines, she may engage them even more clearly and compellingly by first using the word *station* in reference to the terminus at Auschwitz. Indeed, by euphemistically naming "station" that which, despite its obviously exceptional character, the deportees initially assume it to be, she marks the irreducible discrepancy between their enforced ignorance and the "useless knowledge," shared by her readers with the witnesses in the text (with the "we who know"), that "the station is not a station" but "the end of the line" (*AA*, 4/1:11). In so doing, she enlists these readers, who have just inferred the familiarity of a train station from the strangeness of its description, as witnesses of a development that reverses the direction of such inference insofar as the familiar assumptions to which the deportees so desperately cling concerning their destination gradually succumb to the realization of what this strange "station" really represents. Moreover, although on three occasions Delbo states quite plainly that "they do not know [*ils ne savent pas*],"[88] the discrepancy between their ignorance and our knowledge, between the perception of this "station" as a frightening exception (what Delbo calls "the worst") and its perception as a normalization of atrocity (what she calls "the unthinkable"), is underscored in other, arguably more effective ways.

Thus, she repeatedly alludes to the assumptions just mentioned, which extend from the beginning of deportation to the final "selection," and whose baselessness contributes to the structural irony of her narrative. These assumptions include: that "gold might come in handy"; that it would have been preferable for the formally attired wedding guests "to change into something less dainty" (*AA*, 6/1:14); that courageous and orderly behavior will make a difference (*AA*, 4, 6, 7/1:10, 14, 16); that not all civility is lost since, on the platform, "women and children are made to go first" (and besides, "what can they do to boarding-school girls shepherded by their teacher?" [*AA*, 5, 6/1:12, 14]); and that there will be a "later on" (*AA*, 5/1:13). As these assumptions further suggest, Delbo also makes frequent use of prolepsis, even more pointedly perhaps in the sentence already quoted, "They took the children because for this kind of trip you do not leave without them," where the sense in which parents would have understood "this kind of trip"—as a relocation whose unprecedented and possibly definitive character required them (when they were not already forced) to include their children—is overshadowed by its sense for us, that is, by our anticipation of the doom awaiting them all. And of course, the discrepancy in question is reflected in the semantic dissonance not only of the word *station* but of such others as *arrival*, *departure*, and their lexical correlatives.

Nevertheless, focusing attention on the enforced ignorance of the deportees is only one of the ways in which Delbo emphasizes their radical estrangement from witnesses. Another consists in describing their depersonalization, and this almost exclusively in the impersonal voice of the third person. To be sure, this voice also dominates the description of the "normal" train station. But indeed, aside from the features distinguishing this station from the ramp at Auschwitz—such as the greetings and farewells, the two-way circulation of travelers, and the cafés, all of which render its impersonality or anonymity comfortingly familiar—the dominance of the third person in the opening lines of "Arrivals, Departures" is *total*: not once does Delbo individualize "people," not once do we hear them speak. By contrast, however unrelieved the reference to the Jewish deportees as "they" or "them" may appear in the description of Auschwitz, we nevertheless learn enough about them to be able to perceive what happens as a *process* of depersonalization rather than, as Lang would have it, a *state* of impersonality, and so to have some sense of what is being lost. In fact, Delbo's use of synecdoche alone is enough to contest Lang's whole argument about Holocaust representation. For by singling out from the mass of deportees such individuals as a mother and her son, boarding-school girls, a bride and groom, and "old people who used to get letters from their children in America" (*AA*, 6/ 1:14), this rhetorical figure, far from distancing us or turning us away from what happened, has the effect of bringing it closer and compelling us to face it. Rather than unduly "personalizing" events, furthermore, it reminds us that events were personally experienced and engages us through allusion to that experience. And far from betraying some universal, preestablished, and sacrosanct Story, Delbo's figuration of the deportees as a group through certain of its members suggests that falsification lies precisely in such a mythical narrative, which excludes historical contingency, that is, the wide diversity of individual stories, from the reconstructed history of the Holocaust.[89]

As I have indicated, moreover, the description of depersonalization is not completely entrusted to the third person. In two instances, the deportees seem not to be entirely deprived of speech, even as the attribution of speech can be said to anticipate their silencing. In the first instance, Delbo writes that, having complied with the order to leave their belongings on the platform, "They say: 'We shall see' [*Ils disent 'on verra bien'*]" (*AA*, 4 / 1:11). Clearly, the quotation of these arrivals constitutes a more direct and individualized representation of speech than does the reported discourse of undifferentiated travelers who "say they are tired from the trip" or "say good-bye to those who are not leaving." Yet at the same time, since the *ils* refers without distinction to all of the arrivals, the expression attributed to them (the stock phrase, *on verra bien*) does not resemble "real" individualized speech so much as what the narrator imagines anyone in their position might say. In the second case, a schoolteacher exhorts her pupils: "Be good, children [*Soyons sages, les petites*]." The girls "don't have the slightest desire not to be good" and are already trying their best to behave "as though on a regular Thursday school outing" (*AA*, 6 / 1:14). Aside from the fact that the teacher's exhortation, addressed as much to herself as to her charges, is seen by us in the light (or the shadow) of their imminent annihilation, one could argue that the individual to whom speech is here ascribed has already begun to suffer the depersonalization of a "type" (The Schoolteacher) among others, such as "old people," "intellectuals," and "tailors" (*AA*, 6 / 1:14–15), that is, of a categorized position that others might imaginatively occupy, and hence that, as in the first case, the attribution of speech indicates a step in the direction of silence. This appears all the more plausible given Delbo's use of free indirect discourse, which is closer to quotation than reported discourse but involves nonetheless a loss of voice. Thus, for example, in reference to mothers concerned for their children, the voice of the third person can be said to usurp their own: "At last they have reached their destination, they will be able to take care of them now" (*AA*, 4 / 1:11).

Even these examples are restricted, however, to the group. Immediately on arrival, the deportees are "abstracted" from any situation of address extending beyond it (to whom else would they address themselves, unless it were to the guards, who communicate through "truncheon blows"? [*AA*, 4 / 1:11]). And of course depersonalization is not only a matter of speech, since they also lose everything else that might still differentiate them from one another: their mementoes, their money, their papers, their clothing, their family members, their lives. Depersonalization can even be said to transcend death, as objects stranded on the platform or in the undressing room are appropriated and become haunting indices of their owners' absence: "a band will be dressed in the girls' pleated skirts," "a blockhova will cut homey curtains from the holy vestments worn by the rabbi," "a kapo will masquerade by donning the bridegroom's morning coat and top hat, with her girlfriend wrapped in the bride's veil," and "black Calamata olives and Turkish delight cubes will be sent to ailing German women" (*AA*, 8 / 1:17–18)—to say nothing of what will happen to the gold extracted from the teeth of "all those Jews." Finally, whatever singularity or particularity might yet have been ascribed to this group *as such* is denied by its insertion within an endless series of more or less identical convoys: the abstractness of the third person includes a space and time in which "train after train gets here every day and every night every hour of every day and every night" and "all day and all night / every day and every night the chimneys smoke" (*AA*, 8–9 / 1:18–19).

Of course, the question remains how this opening section of *None of Us Will Return* bears on the epigraphic "I" (and, as we shall see, on the "us" of the title). In drawing attention to the eclipse of the framing first person singular by the third person of the narrative proper, "Arrivals, Departures" invites us to consider the implications of this eclipse for the relation between the witness and both those of whom and those to whom she speaks. So, then, what is to be made of the fact that the narrative frame established by the epigraphic first person is no sooner in place than the third person of the narrative renders the first literally speechless? Does the obliteration of this frame not suggest that trauma can only be "truly said," that testimony can only remain "truthful" to trauma, if testimony formally repeats or reenacts the silencing induced by trauma itself? And if so, what does this reenactment imply concerning the relation of the witness to those whose "departure" she represents?

On the one hand, it is not unreasonable to construe the reenactment of silencing as an identification of the witness with those about to be murdered, especially in light of her own victimization and the ways in which, as we have seen, she is able to imagine and express the assumptions, the feelings, and the thoughts to which anyone in the situation of those about to be murdered would be inclined. But on the other hand, this reenactment is still of a formal or mediated nature: the "I" does not take their place, it is not destroyed or permanently silenced but rather "obliterated" or "eclipsed." In other words, the first person is still *implied* by the third, and it is implied *as* the spokesperson of the "we who know," as a *porte-parole* whose speech and whose knowledge differentiate her irreducibly from those entering the gas chamber. The witness thus appears to articulate the tension between an identification that would universalize the experience of the Jews and an estrangement underscoring the unassimilable singularity of that experience. More fundamentally, one could say that, by speaking implicitly in a first person voice suppressed by the third, the witness performatively reaffirms the very relationality whose destruction constitutes the explicit object of her testimony.

Yet what then of the relation between the witness and her readers? On the face of it, one cannot help but think that the eclipse of the first by the third person would eliminate or at least severely restrict the possibility, mentioned earlier, of readerly identification with the testimonial "I." Indeed, if the obliteration of the "I" formally repeats, in the witness, the silencing of those whose fate she witnesses, if it formally reenacts the severance of any dialogical relation between the witness and the doomed deportees, then it could just as well do so between the witness and her readers. As we have just observed, however, it is precisely the suppression of the first by the third person that favors an identification of the witness with her less fortunate fellow victims. And there is no obvious reason why this suppression would not in turn favor an identification of readers with the witness. In fact, by speaking in the third person, Delbo opens a "space" of symbolic substitution that may be occupied, implicitly, by *any* first person. Or to put this in another way: the very invisibility of the first person singular in "Arrivals, Departures" creates, like the camera in cinematography, an impression of immediacy, the illusion that "you are there" before "the thing itself." But this in turn raises the question whether the lone occurrence of the first person voice in the opening section of *None of Us Will Return*, namely, the plural "we" of "we who know," allows this illusion to be sustained.

Let me recall that the first person momentarily resurfaces in reference to a mother who cuffs her unruly son: "She hits her child, and we who know cannot forgive her for it. Yet, were she to smother him with kisses, it would all be the same in the end." In keeping with what was earlier said regarding the "us" of *None of Us Will Return*, this "we" apparently refers to Delbo and her comrades but could just as well include others, since the grammatical subject is fully identified by its immediate predicate, that is, by the knowledge of extermination common to all prisoners in Birkenau (except, of course, the arriving passengers). Furthermore, although the "we" might be assumed implicitly to address itself to a "you" who does not know, the knowledge of extermination with which this text is broached by most if not all readers having no experience of the camps suggests that the "we" could also address to the "you" an invitation to inclusion or identification. This appears all the more convincing given not only the techniques through which, as I have noted, Delbo enlists her readers as knowing cowitnesses, but also the proximity into which the present tense ("we who *know* [*nous qui savons*]" [*AA*, 7 / 1:15]) brings yesterday and today. Finally, one could argue that the very discrepancy between the ignorance of the doomed and the knowledge of which (or by which) both witnesses and readers are possessed fosters in readers an affective awareness of witness trauma. In other words, readers are more closely bound to the "we who know" as what these witnesses "share" with readers is a threat to their common and constitutive relationality. As a result, the sole intervention of the first person voice in "Arrivals, Departures" seems to support, for Delbo's readers, the possibility of identification initially derived from the epigraphic "I" (if not already from the titular "us") and paradoxically preserved through the eclipse of this "I" by the overwhelmingly predominant third person.

But this intervention is momentary, and identification is no sooner encouraged than challenged. The challenge first concerns primary witnesses: while the narrator speculates that, once the arrivals are gathered naked in the gas chamber, "perhaps then they all understand" (*AA*, 8 / 1:17), the time extending from final imprisonment to extermination occupies a narrative hiatus all the more noticeable as the formerly prevalent present tense yields to the future of an aftermath in which "a band will be dressed in the girls' pleated skirts." At the moment of their total estrangement and destruction, victims in their incommensurable particularity are thus paid the tribute of silence. To be sure, one might feel inclined to see in this silence another identification of witnesses with those now dead. Yet it bears keeping in mind not only that, unlike the dead, the narrating witness regains her speech, but that her silence is articulated or mediated by the very text it disrupts, and functions therefore as an indexical sign of what is not represented. Just as important, it is at this moment that the victims portrayed in "Arrivals, Departures" acquire a knowledge that irrevocably separates them from their surviving witnesses, who become in this respect a "we who *do not know*."

If Delbo thus assigns a limit to the identification of witnesses with the dead, she is certain to impose a limit on the identification of readers with witnesses, with the "we" who, in other respects, "*do* know." It is not only that, like the epigraphic "I," the "we" and the "you" it implies suffer eclipse, and hence that their relation is ostensibly severed, in "Arrivals, Departures." Even more telling, this opening section of *None of Us Will Return* is followed by an untitled poem in which Delbo explicitly restages the situation of address and calls the "you who know" directly into question. The poem reads:

> O you who know
> did you know that hunger makes the eyes sparkle that thirst dims them
> O you who know
> did you know that you can see your mother dead
> and not shed a tear
> O you who know
> did you know that in the morning you long for death
> and in the evening you fear it
> O you who know
> did you know that a day is longer than a year
> a minute longer than a lifetime
> O you who know
> did you know that legs are more vulnerable than eyes
> nerves harder than bones
> the heart firmer than steel
> Did you know that the stones of the road do not weep
> that there is one word only for dread
> only one for anguish
> Did you know that suffering has no limit
> horror no bounds
> Did you know this
> You who know. (*AA*, 11 / 1:21–22)

One way to characterize this poem as a whole would be to say that it consists of a sustained rhetorical question ("did you know") to which the implied answer is negative, given not so much the absence of any question mark as the fact that whatever the "you" may know does not encompass the experiential knowledge on which the poem insists. The limit imposed on the identification of readers with witnesses would then appear to be analogous to the limit assigned to the identification of witnesses with the dead.

Even so, one may wonder whether this limit at which dialogue supposedly ceases is not in turn called into question by the situation of address in which it is rhetorically posited, that is, by the very *saying* of the poem itself. Indeed, while I do not wish to minimize the interrogative dimension of this text, it is patently obvious that the question it asks ("did you know") is framed by an apostrophe ("O you who know"). This vocative or accusative framing of interrogation arguably accounts here for the most rigorous sense in which one can understand the expression "to *call* into *question*." Thus, when the "you who know" is called into question, it means *not* that the limit under discussion configures identification and estrangement in mutual exclusion, but rather that an act of address focusing on the impediment to communication defines the limit as the site of an irresolvable *tension* between interlocutors. When the "you who know" is called into question, it does not mean that the invitation to listen has been rescinded, but instead that those presuming to know are accused of having already failed to answer it. When the "you who know" is called into question, in short, it does not mean that there is thenceforth no "us," but that the "us" only begins when the "you" assumes responsibility for a dialogical relation with survivors whose experience remains incommensurate with its own.

In the end, however, what may prove most striking about this invocation of an ethical responsibility beyond the presumption of knowledge, especially if one imagines Delbo addressing those who would presume, on both cognitive and moral grounds, to proscribe poetry after Auschwitz and, *a fortiori*, poetry *about* Auschwitz, is precisely that it takes the form of a poem. And even though, as I have argued in this chapter, Adorno himself does not really belong among such addressees, one may ask whether the dialectical development of his famous phrase, to the extent that it envisions art in general, including that of the post-Holocaust era, as a mode of cognition, is not surpassed by the artistry of this poem. Granted, I too have ascribed a cognitive function to the situation of address in claiming that this situation can, to use Adorno's term, "dismantle" the aesthetic illusion it frames. Yet I have also stressed its phatic and, in this instance, its "conative" and specifically vocative function, which is oriented toward the addressee and, like the phatic, supports the communicative relation on which cognition relies but does not thereby fall within the cognitive realm. Indeed, "O you who know" may summon us to consider, among other things, matters of truth and falsehood, but is itself neither true nor false. And the question it raises here is how our perspective on art after Auschwitz and, insofar as it, too, is an art, on Holocaust survivor testimony in particular would be transformed if we were to recognize that what is ethically at stake extends beyond the dialectic of representation and its undoing to the fundamental if most often implicit act of address it presupposes. Although I do not presume to know the answer to this question, I suspect that we may begin to approach it when, in receiving testimony, we acknowledge that the "you," as in Delbo's "you who know," is not just the "you," but you. That is, us.

Theory and Testimony

It seems safe to say that no philosophical or theoretical approach to Holocaust survivor testimony can afford to disregard the status of theoretical inquiry itself after Auschwitz. On what grounds, indeed, could theory have earned an exemption from the general indictment expressed in Theodor Adorno's claim that "Auschwitz has irrefutably demonstrated the failure of culture"?[1] To be sure, as he broaches the survival of philosophy in the introduction to *Negative Dialectics*, it is not exactly this issue that Adorno has in mind. When he remarks that "philosophy, which once seemed obsolete, lives on because the moment to realize it was missed,"[2] he is alluding to the failure of the socialist revolution anticipated in the eleventh of Karl Marx's "Theses on Feuerbach," where the former Hegelian asserts that "philosophers have only *interpreted* the world in different ways; the point is to *change* it."[3] Considering this failure, Adorno also ventures to suggest, in reference to the philosophy of Marxism, that "perhaps it was an inadequate interpretation which promised that it would be put into practice."[4] Yet there is a sense in which philosophy *was* realized, a sinister sense acknowledged by Adorno when, in the concluding section of this work, he states that "Auschwitz confirmed the philosopheme of pure identity as death." In other words, the principle of identity governing conceptual thought was enlisted in the service of an ideology whose material fulfillment required the literal extermination of all deviant individuals, making of genocide "the absolute integration."[5] From this, however, it would be absurd to infer that philosophy lives on simply because mass murder has not yet encompassed humanity as a whole. What Adorno indicates is rather that the unprecedented violence of the Holocaust has forced theoretical thought to undertake its own critique. As he puts it, "if thinking is to be true—if it is to be true today, in any case—it must also be a thinking against itself."[6]

This thinking that thinks against itself may certainly appear analogous to the post-Holocaust art that dismantles its own illusion, so much so that, from Adorno's point of view, any thought devoid of self-contestation after Auschwitz could be said to render theory every bit as "barbaric" as poetry. But even Adorno could scarcely have underestimated the challenge of thinking against thinking while remaining true to the mode in which that thinking has been done. Indeed, does theory really qualify to undertake a critique of itself when the only resistance it is sure to encounter will be entirely its own? Can philosophy do justice to particularity, for example, when, philosophically speaking, "particularity" is still a universal? Can it deal with heterogeneous modes of thought or discourse otherwise than by subsuming them under "the heterogeneous"? In short, can it bear to acknowledge the history in which "absolute integration" was actually paralyzing terror, burning bodies, blood, and shit—or will it enlist the idiom of "absolute integration" as what Freud called a "protective shield" against such external stimuli?[7]

For present purposes, these questions can be rolled into one, or rather, two, namely: Does a given theoretical approach to Holocaust survivor testimony succeed, while accommodating the demands of theory, in upholding the singularity of the Holocaust as an historical event as well as the singularity of the survivor's experience and voice? And if not, then what is it up to?

It is in reference to these questions that I propose to situate the discussion that follows, which will focus on Giorgio Agamben's book *Remnants of*

Auschwitz: The Witness and the Archive. Agamben stands out from other scholars who, like him, ascribe an unspeakability to the Holocaust for having proposed a sustained philosophical reflection on Holocaust survivor testimony that is based to a considerable extent on the work of one survivor, Primo Levi. It is perhaps regrettable that Agamben does not draw more on Levi's memoirs, and on *Survival in Auschwitz* in particular, since bringing his philosophical mind to bear on this narrative genre might well have contributed original interdisciplinary insights to the study of Holocaust literature. But *Remnants of Auschwitz* has proven no less challenging or influential for its emphasis on the philosophically more assimilable analytical essays of Levi's late work *The Drowned and the Saved*. After all, it is still a matter, for Agamben as for us, of listening or reading, of witnessing witnessing—a task whose importance for survival was brought home to Levi while he was still in the camp, as he suggests in a well-known passage from *Survival in Auschwitz* on which I will briefly comment in the concluding section of this chapter.

In the preface to *Remnants of Auschwitz*, to which I will have occasion to return, Agamben outlines the framework in which he plans to approach what he calls "the decisive lesson of the century" (*RA*, 14/10). As though echoing a concern with the discrepancy between knowledge and understanding voiced ten years earlier in Saul Friedlander's "The 'Final Solution': On the Unease in Historical Interpretation,"[8] Agamben writes: "The aporia of Auschwitz is, indeed, the very aporia of historical knowledge: a non-coincidence between facts and truth, between verification and comprehension" (*RA*, 12/8). For Agamben, however, this "aporia" does not constitute a source of ongoing and potentially evolving interpretive uncertainty but rather founds a whole theory of witnessing—of witnessing to "a reality that necessarily exceeds its factual elements" (*RA*, 12/8). Indeed, the "aporia of Auschwitz" can be said to mark a gap in history, "an essential lacuna" whose articulation lies in survivor testimony: "the survivors bore witness to something it is impossible to bear witness to" (*RA*, 13/9). Not only does this "something" (which, being a lacuna, is also a nothing) remain inaccessible to language, but since, according to Agamben, its nature is ethical, then just as it defies historical interpretation, so it requires us "to clear away almost all the doctrines that, since Auschwitz, have been advanced in the name of ethics" (*RA*, 13/9). In other words, to see clearly into this nothingness demands, in the first place, a thoroughgoing *tabula rasa*, a perfectly clean slate. Then, to begin remapping this slate "for future cartographers of the new ethical territory," as Agamben proposes to do, will mean "to listen to what is unsaid" (*RA*, 13–14/10).

Agamben begins by emphasizing the distinction between two senses of the word *witness*:

> In Latin there are two words for "witness." The first word, *testis*, from which our word "testimony" derives, etymologically signifies the person who, in a trial or lawsuit between two rival parties, is in the position of a third party (**terstis*). The second word, *superstes*, designates a person who has lived through something, who has experienced an event from beginning to end and can therefore bear witness to it. (*RA*, 17/15)

Lest there remain any confusion about his having just stated that "Primo Levi is a perfect example of the witness [*testimone*]" (*RA*, 16/14), Agamben now adds: "It is obvious that Levi is not a third party; he is a survivor [*superstite*] in every sense" (*RA*, 17/15).[9] And in order to emphasize this categorization, he further specifies that, for the purpose of being a third party, Levi "is not neutral enough" (*RA*, 17/15). What *does* seem obvious, then, is that, among the qualities pertaining to the type of witness of which Levi supposedly represents a perfect example, one must include something like insufficient neutrality. And yet, as we shall see, it is precisely in order to associate Levi with *complete* neutrality that Agamben distinguishes the *superstes* he exemplifies from the ostensibly more neutral *testis*.

Authorized by the need "to clear away almost all the doctrines that, since Auschwitz, have been advanced in the name of ethics," the distinction just discussed foreshadows an attempt to dispel what Agamben perceives as a confusion of ethics and law:

> One of the most common mistakes—which is not only made in discussions of the camp—is the tacit confusion of ethical categories and juridical categories (or, worse, of juridical categories and theological categories, which gives rise to a new theodicy). Almost all the categories that we use in moral and religious judgments are in some way contaminated by law: guilt, responsibility, innocence, judgment, pardon. . . . (*RA*, 18/16)

We should note here a certain disregard of history that recurs throughout Agamben's argument and, indeed, derives from one of its major premises. It is reflected in the lack of any effort to explain how or when this "contamination" might have taken place or to adduce any historical evidence in support of the subsequent claim that "ethics, politics, and religion have been able to define themselves only by seizing terrain from juridical responsibility" (*RA*, 20–21/19). By the same token, we might ask, assuming, as does Agamben, that Auschwitz represents not only "the decisive lesson of the century" but a rupture in or of history, why only ethical doctrines advanced *since* Auschwitz should be "cleared away" and why, having divulged the main features of his "new" post-Holocaust ethics, he will seek confirmation of it by appealing to Spinoza (referring incongruously, given his subject, to "the doctrine of the happy life" [*RA*, 24/22]). What is more, there is no obvious reason why the use in ethics of the categories Agamben mentions should in itself pose an insurmountable problem for thinking about the Holocaust, provided, as always, that the sense in which they are employed be defined as well as possible. But in any case, to continue following his argument will require, as here, that we do our own "clearing away."

Having next averred that "law is solely directed toward judgment, independent of truth and justice" (*RA*, 18/16) and that in law "judgment is in itself the end" (*RA*, 19/17), he adds:

> it is possible that the trials themselves (the twelve famous trials at Nuremberg, and the others that took place within and outside German borders, including the one in Jerusalem in 1961 that ended with the hanging of Eichmann) are responsible for the conceptual confusion that, for decades, has made it impossible to think through Auschwitz. Despite the necessity of the trials and despite their evident insufficiency (they involved only a few hundred people), they helped to spread the idea that the problem of Auschwitz had been overcome. The judgments had been passed, the proofs of guilt definitively established. With the exception of occasional moments of lucidity, it has taken almost half a century to understand that law did not exhaust the problem, but rather that the very problem was so enormous as to call into question law itself, dragging it to its own ruin. (*RA*, 19–20/17–19)

It seems obvious that this last claim is belied by the extensive body of international law developed over the past sixty years, beginning with the United Nations Convention on the Prevention and Punishment of the Crime of Genocide of 1948. Of course, the failure to take such legislation into account is very much in keeping with Agamben's agenda, which aims to exclude from the "new ethical territory" the categories he ascribes solely to law, including those of judgment and responsibility in particular. Yet the disregard of history tells here again on his own argument, all the more so as, in asserting that the postwar trials may have misled people into thinking that the matter of the Nazi genocide had been resolved, he ventures the semblance of a historical explanation for an issue that does not exist. For where, in all the documents pertaining to these trials and their aftermath, in all the commemorative speeches and public debates about the Holocaust, in the voluminous historiographical and other scholarship devoted to it, in the massive corpus of survivor testimony, could one obtain evidence of a belief that, thanks to the trials, "the problem of Auschwitz had been overcome"? To what source could one attribute such naïveté, unless it were some purely imaginary vox populi? And where, exactly, is the "conceptual confusion" to be located? For if, on the one hand, there are those who, like Agamben, hold that judgment belongs to law alone, it does not follow that in the eyes of these individuals such judgment "exhausts" the problem of Auschwitz. And if, on the other hand, there are those who, unlike Agamben, find that judgment is not restricted to law, it is even more obvious that for them no number of trials can "overcome" this problem. The most plausible conclusion to be drawn at this point may well be that, aside from authorizing the tendentious displacement of major conceptual categories, such spurious historical claims serve to disqualify, "with the exception of occasional moments of lucidity," all previous thinking about Auschwitz, and in so doing create the space in which to construct a historical and historically unique raison d'être for the coming theory.

That theory has two major components, based respectively on consecutive essays from Levi's *The Drowned and the Saved* entitled "The Gray Zone" and "Shame." In the first instance, Agamben argues that the "gray zone" of moral ambiguity examined by Levi constitutes the "new ethical territory" with which he himself is concerned. And in the second, he attempts to portray the so-called *Muselmann* or "Muslim"—that is, the type of camp inmate who has reached, physically and mentally, the threshold between life and death—as the only "true" or "complete" witness. Given my interest in whether a theoretical approach to Holocaust survivor testimony respects the singularity or particularity both of the event itself and of the survivor who bears witness to it, in what follows I will analyze Levi's text and Agamben's reading of it, implicitly and, where appropriate, explicitly drawing on historical research or the testimony of other survivors.

As I have already observed, the effort to consign such categories as judgment and responsibility exclusively to law and so to banish them from the "new ethics" is anticipated by the distinction between "witness" in its legal acceptation and "witness" as survivor, into which class Levi falls, in part because he supposedly lacks the neutrality required of a juridical third party. But as I have also remarked, the characterization of Levi as "not neutral enough" fails to preclude his being associated with what Agamben perceives as the complete neutrality of the gray zone, at least insofar as Levi can be said to bear witness to it. For "it seems, in fact, that the only thing that interests him," Agamben claims, "is what makes judgment impossible: the gray zone in which victims become executioners and executioners become victims" (*RA*, 17/15). As he further avers, in a subsequent and somewhat expanded description of this zone:

> The unprecedented discovery made by Levi at Auschwitz concerns an area that is independent of every establishment of responsibility, an area in which Levi succeeded in isolating something like a new ethical element. Levi calls it the "gray zone." It is the zone in which the "long chain of conjunction between victim and executioner" comes loose, where the oppressed becomes oppressor and the executioner in turn appears as victim. A gray, incessant alchemy in which good and evil and, along with them, all the metals of traditional ethics reach their point of fusion. (*RA*, 21/19)

Thus, in the gray zone, according to Agamben, the absolute interchangeability of victim and executioner precludes the ascription of responsibility and renders judgment impossible. "Not that a judgment cannot or must not be made," he adds, but "the decisive point is simply that the two things not be blurred, that law not presume to exhaust the question" (*RA*, 17/15). Rather than clarify matters, however, this statement presumes of Levi the strictly juridical conception of judgment (and responsibility) that Agamben fails to establish independently of him—a conception that also happens to fare rather poorly on an attentive reading of "The Gray Zone."

By "gray zone," Levi means essentially the moral space of collaboration. Although the group occupying this space was obviously not confined to the concentration or death camps, it is on the camps that he focuses for the most part, since, as he puts it, "the Lager . . . can be considered an excellent 'laboratory'":

> the hybrid class of the prisoner-functionary constitutes its armature and at the same time its most disquieting feature. It is a gray zone, poorly defined, where the two camps of masters and servants both diverge and converge. This gray zone possesses an incredibly complicated internal structure and contains within itself enough to confuse our need to judge. (*DS*, 42 / *O*, 2:1002)

Having conceded the possibility of this confusion and acknowledged "the imprudence of issuing hasty moral judgment on such human cases," Levi "lightheartedly absolve[s]" lower-level functionaries before tackling the more difficult issue of those in "commanding positions" (*DS*, 43–45 / *O*, 2:1023–24), most notably the notorious labor *Kapos*, whose power over their charges included the license to kill. Yet far from reserving judgment on the apparent "exchange of roles between oppressor and victim," far from declaring the gray zone a zone of irresponsibility, he concludes his reflections on the *Kapos* with a forceful objection to Liliana Cavani's statement that "We are all victims or murderers," that "in every environment, in every relationship, there is a victim-executioner dynamism more or less clearly expressed and generally lived on an unconscious level." Levi replies:

> I do not know, and it does not much interest me to know, whether in my depths there lurks a murderer, but I do know that I was a guiltless victim and I was not a murderer. I know that the murderers existed, not only in Germany, and still exist, retired or on active duty, and that to confuse them with their victims is a moral disease or an aesthetic affectation or a sinister sign of complicity; above all, it is precious service rendered (intentionally or not) to the negators of truth. (*DS*, 48–49 / *O*, 2:1027)

For Levi, then, the gray zone is not a site where "victims becomes executioners and executioners become victims." What the chiasmic, neutralizing symmetry of Agamben's syntax reflects is a failure or refusal to recognize that the gray zone is framed and thoroughly informed by camp *hierarchy*, that is, by a fundamental dissymmetry entailing multiple kinds of moral ambiguity and unequal degrees of responsibility, or, in terms of the metaphor, many different shades of gray.[10] To confuse the *Kapos*, in whom the

SS induced a murderous identification with the oppressor, with the mass of unprivileged or less privileged prisoners is not only historically misleading but indeed "a sinister sign of complicity," a betrayal of "our need for justice" (*DS*, 49/*O*, 2:1027) in favor of those who say, as Levi puts it: "We, the master race, are your destroyers, but you are no better than we; if we so wish, and we do so wish, we can destroy not only your bodies but also your souls, just as we have destroyed ours" (*DS*, 53–54/*O*, 2:1031).

Agamben does not focus on the *Kapos*; to do so would require attending to the portion of Levi's essay that most directly debunks the conflation of victim and executioner. Instead, he turns to the so-called *Sonderkommandos* or Special Squads, the groups of overwhelmingly Jewish prisoners charged upon pain of immediate death with the general operation of the crematoria, including the maintenance of order among arrivals about to be gassed, the removal of their bodies from the chambers, the collection of clothing and valuables, cremation, and the disposal of ashes. Given the "sensitivity" of their tasks and the risk of "leaks" to the outside world, the Special Squads lived in forced isolation from all other prisoners and were periodically murdered en masse.[11] According to Levi, they were at once "an extreme case of collaboration" (*DS*, 50/*O*, 2:1028) and "National Socialism's most demonic crime," since they not only "impose[d] on others the most atrocious tasks" but represented "an attempt to shift onto others—specifically, the victims—the burden of guilt, so that they were deprived of even the solace of innocence" (*DS*, 53/*O*, 2:1031). For this reason, and because, in Levi's view, it is impossible "to foresee one's own behavior" in such circumstances, he asks "that judgment of [the Special Squads] be suspended" (*DS*, 60/*O*, 2:1037). Here, then, the gray zone may well "confuse our need to judge" and even appear to point toward the "new ethical element" whose "unprecedented discovery" Agamben attributes to Levi.

Yet the scant commentary that Agamben himself devotes to the *Sonderkommandos* seizes almost exclusively on one component of Levi's analysis, concerning an anecdote recounted by Miklos Nyiszli, who worked as a research pathologist for Josef Mengele and physician to the Special Squads:

So, Nyiszli tells how during a "work" pause he attended a soccer game between the SS and the SK (*Sonderkommando*), that is to say, between a group representing the SS on guard at the crematorium and a group representing the Special Squad. Other men of the SS and the rest of the squad are present at the game; they take sides, bet, applaud, urge the players on as if, rather than at the gates of hell, the game were taking place on the village green. (*DS*, 54–55 / *O*, 2:1032)[12]

This episode, which owes its wide dissemination to Levi rather than Nyiszli, is also a center of gravity for critical readings of Agamben, to certain of which I am quite indebted even if my emphasis on the difference between what Agamben and Levi infer from the infamous soccer game is not quite the same as theirs.[13]

At first glance, Agamben seems to concur with Levi's assessment that the creation of the Special Squads was Nazism's "most demonic crime," for he begins his "reading" of the soccer game by remarking that "this match might strike someone as a brief pause of humanity in the middle of an infinite horror. I, like the witnesses, instead view this match, this moment of normalcy, as the true horror of the camp" (*RA*, 26 / 24).[14] Since, furthermore, from his first mention of the gray zone, Agamben's view remains that in this zone "victims become executioners and executioners become victims," it would appear that "the true horror of the camp" has to do, for him, with the moral equivalence of the two "sides," with the discovery of a realm in which responsibility is unassignable and judgment irrelevant. To be sure, one may wonder whether the predication of moral equivalence does not, itself, constitute a moral judgment, according to which either the *Sonderkommandos* were *as* guilty as the SS or the SS itself bore no responsibility. And this is to say nothing of the possibility mentioned by Philippe Mesnard and Claudine Kahan, namely, that the true horror of the camp may have been, not a soccer game, but the gassing of hundreds of thousands of people.[15] Perhaps in part to deflect such considerations, however, Agamben suddenly moves in a different, if not incompatible, direction, locating this horror in its extension beyond Auschwitz, beyond the Holocaust:

For we can perhaps think that the massacres are over—even if here and there they are repeated, not so far away from us. But that match is never over; it continues as if uninterrupted. It is the perfect and eternal cipher of the "gray zone," which knows no time and is in every place. Hence the anguish and shame of the survivors, "the anguish inscribed in everyone of the 'tohu-bohu,' of a deserted and empty universe crushed under the spirit of God but from which the spirit of man is absent; not yet born or already extinguished." But also hence our shame, the shame of those who did not know the camps and yet, without knowing how, are spectators of that match, which repeats itself in every match in our stadiums, in every television broadcast, in the normalcy of everyday life. If we do not succeed in understanding that match, in stopping it, there will never be hope. (*RA*, 26/24)[16]

Readers of Agamben could hardly be blamed for feeling somewhat puzzled at this point. Although the author appears to believe that "understanding that match" is important insofar as it represents the precondition of "stopping it," it also appears that there is no stopping it since the match itself is "the perfect and eternal cipher of the 'gray zone,' which knows no time and is in every place." In fact, the passage as a whole seems designed less to foster understanding than to induce, through "our shame," a rather contrived communion of "those who did not know the camps" with camp survivors. It is thus all the more imperative to read it against the grain of this communion, that is, with a modicum of sobriety.

The passage is most remarkable for its radical decontextualization (and it recalls, in that respect, the statement of Cavani's quoted by Levi). Agamben is not interested primarily, if at all, in the massacres themselves, the real ones, those of the Holocaust, say, or of Bosnia, to which he appears to allude. This is not only because they fall at least to some extent within the purview of law, where responsibility and judgment prevail, and thus lend themselves to an adjudication that might, as he sees it, lead us to believe that the problem of Auschwitz or of Srebrenica has been "overcome." It is also because the historical actuality and specificity of these massacres act as a brake on any attempt to reduce them to a single dehistoricized philosophical form or concept. In fact, in the context of Auschwitz, the same holds for the soccer match itself, as Levi points out: "Nothing of this kind ever took place, nor would it have been conceivable, with other categories of prisoners; but with them, with the 'crematorium ravens,' the SS could enter the field on an equal footing, or almost" (*DS*, 55 / *O*, 2:1032). And it is precisely this context or frame of reference—"other categories of prisoners," and by extension the whole concentrationary universe in which even the Special Squads were on anything but an equal footing with the SS—

that Agamben elides, on the pretext that the soccer match, taking place during a break from "work," not only represents an exception to the norm of "life" in Auschwitz, where the SS committed daily murder with the forced collaboration of Special Squads destined to be gassed in their turn, but as such marks a hiatus or lacuna in history. Thus abstracted from history, the soccer match becomes the cipher of an eternal and ubiquitous gray zone in which the SS and the SK—and for that matter, their spectators as well—are converted, through their functional interchangeability and moral equivalence, into representatives of the species as a whole, into "whatever" humans.[17] It becomes, in other words, the sign of a pure "potentiality"—yet a potentiality endowed with the veneer of actuality once Agamben has conflated the soccer game at Auschwitz with "every match in our stadiums" and thereby suggested that spectators filing through the exits should be able to see in what lies outside those stadiums both the immanence and the imminence of a concentration camp.

What Agamben fails to recognize or chooses to ignore, however, is that, by assimilating an apparent state of exception within Auschwitz to a norm outside of it, he has betrayed the very thrust of Levi's text: "the true horror of the camp" lies not in the pure possibility of violence "in the normalcy of everyday life" but in the actual and, in effect if not in intent, the derisive staging, against the immediate backdrop of mass murder, of the possibility of equality. It is this effect that Levi attempts to convey by imagining anew the voice of the oppressor:

> Behind this armistice one hears satanic laughter: it is consummated, we have succeeded, you no longer are the other race, the anti-race, the prime enemy of the millennial Reich; you are no longer the people who reject idols. We have embraced you, corrupted you, dragged you to the bottom with us. You are like us, you proud people: dirtied with your own blood, as we are. You too, like us and like Cain, have killed the brother. Come, we can play together. (*DS*, 55/*O*, 2:1032–33)

Far from heralding a "new ethics" of moral equivalence or in-difference, this imagined address celebrates the successful enforcement, by the "we," of self-violation in a "you" endowed with but a pretense of agency. Indeed, one can no more imagine the SS and the SK entering upon a level playing field than one can imagine the SK taking the initiative to organize the match.

Here again, Levi stresses the incommensurability of the two groups: the *Befehlnotstand*, the "state of compulsion following an order," often invoked by Nazis at their postwar trials, did not mean for them what it did for their victims, "a rigid either/or, immediate obedience or death" (*DS*, 59–60/*O*, 2:1036). If Levi decides not to pass judgment on the Special Squads, it is not because judgment is impossible but because he judges it to be unfair.[18]

Before broaching the second component of Agamben's theory of testimony, it might be useful to survey the ground already covered. So far, at least, it has been clear that Levi's text does not support Agamben's positing of a "new ethics" from which the notions of judgment and responsibility would be excluded. In fact, the support that Agamben claims to find in Levi derives from a reading whose principal device amounts to something like specious synecdoche, whereby a single notion, phrase, or remark is made to stand for a whole of which it is not truly representative. This device becomes especially conspicuous when it also waxes hyperbolic, as in the mischaracterized "gray zone" that is held to represent a fundamental sociopolitical reality of all post-Holocaust history. Agamben's theoretical reflection thus jeopardizes its own credibility insofar as its universalizing tendency loses sight of the historical specificities on which that reflection is based. Yet it remains to be seen whether this is the case throughout, that is, in relation to what Levi has to say not only about the *Kapos* or *Sonderkommandos* but also about the *Muselmänner* and indeed about testimony itself.

The central chapters of *Remnants of Auschwitz* draw primarily on the essay from Levi's *The Drowned and the Saved* that immediately follows "The Gray Zone," namely, "Shame." And within this essay, the crucial passage for Agamben's purposes concerns the *Muselmänner*, or Muslims. Much has been written, both by survivors and by scholars of the Holocaust, about the etymology of the word *Muselmann*, and especially about the camp inmates it came to designate, including their profound physical degradation, their mental incapacitation and social marginalization, and the anonymity of their death. Simply stated, the *Muselmänner* were those who, in the eyes of other inmates, had come to stand (or lie) at or beyond the limit of the human, those "living dead" produced by the slow murder for which most of the concentration camps were designed.[19] But it is specifically in connection with testimony that Levi first mentions them:

I must repeat: we, the survivors, are not the true witnesses. This is an uncomfortable notion of which I have become conscious little by little, reading the memoirs of others and rereading mine at a distance of years. We survivors are not only an exiguous but also an anomalous minority: we are those who by their prevarications or abilities or good luck did not touch bottom. Those who did so, those who saw the Gorgon, have not returned to tell about it or have returned mute, but they are the "Muslims," the submerged, the complete witnesses, the ones whose deposition would have a general significance. They are the rule, we are the exception. . . .

We who were favored by fate tried, with more or less wisdom, to recount not only our fate but also that of the others, indeed of the drowned; but this was a discourse "on behalf of third parties," the story of things seen at close hand, not experienced personally. The destruction brought to an end, the job completed, was not told by anyone, just as no one ever returned to describe his own death. Even if they had had paper and pen, the drowned would not have testified because their death had begun before that of their body. Weeks and months before being snuffed out, they had already lost the ability to observe, to remember, to compare and express themselves. We speak in their stead, by proxy. (*DS*, 83–84 / *O*, 2:1055–56)[20]

On the basis of this passage, Agamben formulates what he calls "Levi's paradox," to wit, "the *Muselmann* is the complete witness," explaining: "It implies two contradictory propositions: (1) 'the *Muselmann* is the non-human, the one who could never bear witness,' and (2) 'the one who cannot bear witness is the true witness, the absolute witness'" (*RA*, 150 / 140–41).[21] Although I am inclined to examine each of these propositions separately before evaluating the paradox as a whole, in Levi's text, as in Agamben's interpretation, it will quickly become apparent that they can only be discussed together, even if the emphasis must shift between them. What really matters, in any case, are the ways in which we find them connected.

Let me point out, to begin with, that the term "non-human" must be used with caution—and hence will continue to be used here only within quotation marks—not only because Levi himself does not resort to it in speaking of the "Muslims" but because it cannot be dissociated from a moral judgment based on the fear that the "Muslims" evoked, as we shall see, in other inmates.[22] This said, Levi does remark, again, that "their death had begun before that of their body. Weeks and months before being snuffed out, they had already lost the ability to observe, to remember, to compare and express themselves." Thus, what Agamben here calls the "non-human" resembles what he elsewhere calls "bare" or "naked" life, that is, mere biological rather than social existence.[23] And indeed, although Levi does not use these terms either, his emphasis on the loss of expression and hence of the ability to bear witness clearly suggests that the condition of the *Muselmann* included a radical deterioration in relations with others. But if the *Muselmann* can be described as the one who could never bear witness, it does not follow that the one who could never bear witness was necessarily a *Muselmann*. Nor, for that matter, if the inability to bear witness qualifies one as a true witness, does it follow that all true witnesses were *Muselmänner*. In other words, not all of the "drowned" were "Muslims," and this forces us to ask why "Muslims," in particular, were chosen to represent all of the drowned.

In Levi's text, "true" and "complete" are both defined in terms of the relation between rule and exception, and appear to be virtually synonymous. Survivors constitute "an exiguous but also an anomalous minority" and are therefore not the "true" witnesses, these being identified rather with the "Muslims" because their testimony "would have a general significance." However, it is not clear, to begin with, how any testimony could, strictly speaking, be "complete" without including the experience of survivors. Levi seems, of course, to assume that the "Muslims," by reason of the very extremity of their condition, were more representative of the general population of deportees to Auschwitz than any other group. But this, too, begs the question—and not only the question whether, in principle, an extreme can possess "general significance." For how was the condition or the situation of the *Muselmänner* more extreme than that of the *Sonderkommandos* or the hundreds of thousands of Jews gassed on arrival? And why should they occupy the foreground in our iconography of the concentrationary universe? Moreover, as I have just observed, not all the drowned or submerged, not all nonsurvivors, were "Muslims." On the contrary: among those who perished in the Holocaust, the "Muslims" constituted "an exiguous but also an anomalous minority." And presumably, *if* those who returned mute had decided (and been able) to speak, the mere reacquisition of speech would have transformed them to such an extent that, just as "no one ever returned to describe his own death," so, even in reference to their own experience, they too, like Levi, could only have spoken "by proxy." Finally, it should be noted that Agamben, for whose whole reflection on the camps the notion of the exception becoming the rule is otherwise a sine qua non, and who generally, as we have seen, is not the most scrupulous reader of Levi, in this instance so fully endorses Levi's configuration of rule and exception as to suggest that we consider the motivation of that endorsement an issue in its own right.

We may make some headway in the matter by considering the basic epistemic problem that "Levi's paradox" poses for Agamben and then, especially, the manner in which he attempts to solve it. This problem emerges unbidden from a passage devoted to dramatizing the discovery of a "new ethics":

> the atrocious news that the survivors carry from the camp to the land of human beings is precisely that it is possible to lose dignity and decency beyond imagination, that there is still life in the most extreme degradation. And this new knowledge now becomes the touchstone by which to judge and measure all morality and all dignity. The *Muselmann*, who is its most extreme expression, is the guard on the threshold of a new ethics and form of life that begin where dignity ends. And Levi, who bears witness for the drowned, speaking in their stead, is the cartographer of this new *terra ethica*, the implacable land-surveyor of *Muselmannland*. (*RA*, 69/63)

To be sure, this account underscores a problem we have already encountered, namely, Agamben's failure to define a "new ethics" free of judgment, since the knowledge on which such an ethics is supposedly founded here becomes "the touchstone by which to judge and measure all morality and all dignity."

But in addition, this passage raises, through the incoherence of its topographical metaphor, the question of how such knowledge is acquired in the first place. Even though the characterization of the *Muselmann* as a "guard" may seem somewhat less bizarre if we consider, as Dominick LaCapra suggests, that it could stem from the confusion of victim and perpetrator in Agamben's view of the gray zone,[24] we are still left wondering why the *Muselmann* is positioned "on the threshold of a new ethics" when his characterization as "non-human" would indicate that he has already passed that threshold. To put this otherwise: if the gray zone is a zone or threshold of indistinction where the roles of perpetrator and victim are interchangeable, then it is certainly not the same as *Muselmannland* itself, for the simple reason that the *Muselmann* could never be a perpetrator (or a guard). By the same token, it is not clear how Levi can be "the cartographer of this new *terra ethica*," how he can map *Muselmannland* when, by definition, he stands outside of it. In fact, if we recall that, in his preface, Agamben imagines himself paving the way for "future cartographers," it is difficult to avoid the suspicion of a projective identification wherein the *Muselmann* would somehow take Levi by the hand and thereby allow Levi to take Agamben, bringing Levi as Virgil and Agamben as Dante to the gate of a *volkloser Raum* bearing the inscription: "Abandon all dignity ye who enter here." Yet the figure is static: Levi can only enter *Muselmannland* by forsaking, among other things, the means with which to bear witness to it, namely, language itself, and conversely, he can only bear witness to *Muselmannland* by leaving it and betraying, through language, the very knowledge he is supposed to bring back. Hence he must remain to tell "the story of things seen close at hand, not experienced personally." And Agamben cannot even tell this story but must, in claiming that the *Muselmann* "has much to say but cannot speak," rely on Levi, that is, in Agamben's own words, on "the survivor, who can speak but who has nothing interesting to say" (*RA*, 120/111).[25]

The epistemic problem confronting Agamben arises, then, from the fact that the claim according to which the one who cannot bear witness is the true witness relies for its authority on the word of one who *can* and *does* bear witness and who is therefore, by the terms of the paradox—and to put it politely—less than true. Since Agamben cannot abide the implications of this problem for his own theory of testimony, a solution must be sought where the problem originates, that is, in Levi's testimonial relation to the *Muselmann*. And since this relation seems problematic only insofar as the linguistic medium of which Levi avails himself calls into question the very knowledge it is supposed to convey, the solution must consist in or at least involve a negation of language. Enter the mythological Gorgon, the sight of whom turned its beholders to stone and whose pertinence here derives both from the possibility of an unmediated visual encounter and from a potential specularity wherein the Gorgon and the *Muselmann*, the *Muselmann* and Levi, and Levi and Agamben would meet at a "threshold of indistinction." What is more, the very *visibility* to which the figure of the Gorgon directs our attention in the *Muselmann* himself suggests why, for a post-Foucauldian philosopher of biopower, the image of the *Muselmann* would loom much larger than that of Nazism's other victims. In the words of Wolfgang Sofsky, also cited by Agamben:

> The *Muselmann* embodies the anthropological meaning of absolute power in an especially radical form. Power abrogates itself in the act of killing. The death of the other puts an end to the social relationship. But by starving the other, it gains time. It erects a third realm, a limbo between life and death. Like the pile of corpses, the *Muselmänner* document the total triumph of power over the human being. Although still nominally alive, they are nameless hulks. In the configuration of their infirmity, as in organized mass murder, the regime realizes its quintessential self.[26]

Unlike those who were gassed and whose bodies were burned, the *Muselmann* does not suddenly disappear but lingers, offering to the perpetrators, for weeks or months—or even years, given the constantly replenished pool of potential *Muselmänner*—a satisfying reflection of their own power. Of course, it is not from the perspective of the perpetrators and their pleasure that Levi evokes the *Muselmänner*, but rather from the perspective of the *Muselmänner* that he evokes the horror of the Gorgon. And yet it can safely be said that the significance of the Gorgon resides less in its presumed ability to deprive the *Muselmann* of all vision than in the comparable ability of the *Muselmann* to instill horror and fear in those inmates who had not yet succumbed to his condition. Indeed, the *Muselmann* was "powerful" inasmuch as the very sight of him suggested to others the possibility that they, too, might become *Muselmänner*. As Vilo Jurković, a survivor of Auschwitz, attests: " 'The *Muselmann* condition was dreaded by the inmates because no one knew when he might suffer such a fate himself and be a certain candidate for the gas chamber or another kind of death."[27] Or as Agamben puts it: "the *Muselmann* is universally avoided because everyone in the camp recognizes himself in his disfigured face" (*RA*, 52/47). In the *Muselmann*, then, prisoners perceive a frightening potential inherent *in themselves*.

One can thus understand why Agamben would uncritically support Levi's claim that the *Muselmänner* are "the rule," despite their being "an exiguous but also an anomalous minority" among victims of the Holocaust. As a rule within the camp, the "Muslims," who literally embody a state of exception outside of it, not only offer a convenient and conveniently extreme exemplification of modern biopolitics. As representatives of a state of exception that has become a rule, they also testify to a potential "non-humanity" within other humans, indeed within *all* other humans, to which they provide, in their very being, unmediated or eyewitness access. And just as we earlier saw how the "potentiality" of the gray zone can blur the distinction between a soccer match at Auschwitz and "every match in our stadiums," so here the potentiality of the "non-human" appears to insure the epistemic foundation of Agamben's theory of testimony by seamlessly uniting the *Muselmann* and Levi (and, by extension, Agamben and everyone else) in a single vision, or rather, given the effect of the Gorgon, in a single sightlessness: "The Gorgon and he who has seen her and the *Muselmann* and he who bears witness to him are one gaze; they are a single impossibility of seeing" (*RA*, 54/49).[28]

I would argue, however, that the problem has simply been displaced. For one cannot help but infer from the sentence just quoted that, in the relay extending from the Gorgon to the *Muselmann*, from the *Muselmann* to Levi, and from Levi to Agamben, Agamben has dropped the baton. Regarding the rule of sightlessness uniting the *Muselmann* and Levi (and everyone else), in other words, he has, by his very absence from the sentence, declared himself an exception, without then reinscribing the exception as a rule. Like the sovereign of *Homo Sacer*, therefore, he is the only one *not* subject to the law, the one to whom the law applies exclusively through its own suspension. And there is good reason to pursue the resemblance in this case, since nothing is more fearsome for a theorist (from the Greek *thea*, "seeing") than a lack of vision. Of course, he admits, in the voice of a first person plural whose referent, aside from including Agamben himself, remains undetermined, that "we will not understand what Auschwitz is if we do not first understand who or what the *Muselmann* is—if we do not learn to gaze with him upon the Gorgon" (*RA*, 52/47). But this "if" signals a purely potential or suspended blindness—if it does not also anticipate the transcendence of that blindness in a superior or sacred vision, whose promise might console us for the fact that, in the messianic interval, "to bear witness to the *Muselmann*, to attempt to contemplate the impossibility of seeing, is not an easy task" (*RA*, 54/49). In any case, as I have just suggested, Agamben's "solution" to the problem of the relation between Levi and the *Muselmann* leaves the problem of his own relation to Levi quite intact. After all, his theory of testimony is not based on a visual encounter with Levi (even though, without saying as much, he will not shy from staking a claim to the authority of such an encounter, as in the remark: "Levi had this unease about him when I saw him at meetings at the Italian publisher, Einaudi" [*RA*, 16/14–15]). It is based, rather, on a linguistic communication, that is, on precisely the kind of mediation he seeks to evacuate from Levi's witnessing of the *Muselmann*. Agamben must therefore devise a way to transpose the solution in question back to the realm of language. And this he attempts to do, unsurprisingly given the subject of Levi's essay, through a description of shame.

Commenting on Emmanuel Levinas's analysis of shame in *On Escape*, Agamben observes:

> shame is grounded in our being's incapacity to move away and break from itself. If we experience shame in nudity, it is because we cannot hide what we would like to remove from the field of vision; it is because the unrestrainable impulse to flee from oneself is confronted by an equally certain impossibility of evasion. . . .
>
> . . . Here the "I" is thus overcome by its own passivity, its ownmost sensibility; yet this expropriation and desubjectification is also an extreme and irreducible presence of the "I" to itself. It is as if our consciousness collapsed and, seeking to flee in all directions, were simultaneously summoned by an irrefutable order to be present at its own defacement, at the expropriation of what is most its own. In shame, the subject thus has no other content than its own desubjectification; it becomes witness to its own disorder, its own oblivion as a subject. This double movement, which is both subjectification and desubjectification, is shame. (*RA*, 104–6/96–97)

Much could be said about Agamben's relation to Levinas, beginning with the observation that, among "all the doctrines that, since Auschwitz, have been advanced in the name of ethics," Levinas's philosophy would arguably prove the most difficult to "clear away," and that, aside from the commentary just quoted, it is scarcely mentioned in *Remnants of Auschwitz*. *On Escape* itself, while by no means an unimportant text, dates from very early in Levinas's career (1935), when the movement from ontology to ethics as first philosophy was just beginning. And although Agamben's commentary is fair enough, it suggests no awareness of the extent to which this movement, and more specifically, the description of shame—as well as of nausea—may have reflected Levinas's reaction to Heidegger's enthusiastic embrace of Nazism in 1933.[29] For now, however, the point is that, notwithstanding the reference to nudity, which implies the gaze of another, exposure or visibility has been effectively internalized: shame is a relation of the subject to itself, wherein, on the one hand, its only content is desubjectification, that is, bare or naked life, and, on the other, its form is the pure consciousness of that desubjectification. No longer is there any need, therefore, of real *Muselmänner*, of actual beings the sight of whom conjures in their beholders the potential dehumanization intrinsic to them all, for shame alone attests that every subject always already harbors its own "inner *Muselmann*." At one and the same time, then, Agamben confines the relation instantiated by shame to the interiority of the subject and extends that relation ad infinitum, or at least so far as to assert that shame is "truly something like the hidden structure of all subjectivity and consciousness" (*RA*, 128/119).

Nevertheless, even if, for the sake of argument, we were to grant that shame structures all subjectivity and to infer from this that, thanks to their structural homology, Levi and Agamben share a zone of indistinction, it would still remain for Agamben to demonstrate *that this is so*, both in reading Levi and in writing to other readers. In other words, he must show, as a writer, how any reader of Levi would be led to the conclusion that the structure of shame is identical to that of language. Especially telling in this respect, however, is Agamben's dismissiveness of Levi's own attempt to explain the phenomenon of shame. Referring to *The Drowned and the Saved*, Agamben remarks:

> Shame now becomes the dominant sentiment of survivors, and Levi tries to explain why this is so. It is therefore not surprising that, like all attempts at explanations, the chapter of the book entitled "Shame" is ultimately unsatisfying. This is all the more so given that the chapter immediately follows Levi's extraordinary analysis of the "gray zone," which, consciously keeping to the inexplicable, recklessly refuses all explanation. Faced with the *Kapos*, collaborators, "prominent ones" of all kinds, the accursed members of the *Sonderkommando* and even Chaim Rumkowski, the *rex Judaeorum* of the Lodz ghetto, the survivor ended with a *non-liquet*: "I ask that we meditate on the story of 'the crematorium ravens' with pity and rigor, but that judgment of them be suspended." But in his chapter on shame Levi seems hastily to lead his subject back to a sense of guilt: "many (including me) experienced 'shame,' that

is, a feeling of guilt." Immediately afterward, in seeking to discern the roots of this guilt, the very author who had only a little earlier fearlessly ventured into an absolutely unexplored territory of ethics now submits himself to a test of conscience so puerile that it leaves the reader uneasy. The wrongs that emerge (having at times shaken his shoulders impatiently when faced with the requests of younger prisoners, or the episode of the water that he shared with Alberto but denied to Daniele) are, of course, excusable. But here the reader's unease can only be a reflection of the survivor's embarrassment, his incapacity to master shame. (*RA*, 88/81–82)

Since, as we have already seen, the reading of "The Gray Zone" summarized here radically misrepresents that essay, the suspicion it arouses might lead us to think twice about Agamben's judgment of "Shame." To begin with, and despite his insistence on an ethics entirely devoid of it, there certainly is a judgment, not only of the essay itself but also of remembered actions that Levi associates with his "feeling of guilt" (*DS*, 76/*O*, 2:1050), which Agamben simply brushes aside as "excusable." More noteworthy yet may be the judgment of Levi's test of conscience as "puerile," as immature or childish, where we might have expected Agamben to recognize that at least Levi himself takes it seriously, perhaps because, in the extreme situation or state of exception embodied by the concentration camp, such otherwise insignificant actions could in fact have very severe if unintended consequences. For that matter, which reader, exactly, is made to feel uneasy here? And how can responsibility for this unease be ascribed to the survivor's own "incapacity to master shame" unless it is assumed in the first place that the survivor *ought* to master it? Could it be that Levi is indeed concerned with a specific feeling rather than with "the hidden structure of all subjectivity and consciousness"? We will have to return to this last question, in particular, when we look again at Levi's text, instead of focusing primarily on what Agamben has to say about it. But in the near term, what we can gather from the passage just quoted is, on the one hand, that aside from "Levi's paradox," on which his theory of testimony is so dependent and which is derived, precisely, from "Shame," Agamben actually has little else to say about that chapter and, on the other, that, given his disparagement of explanations in general, the coming conversion of shame into a universal structure of language should be met with modest expectations.

Having thus "cleared away" Levi's text, Agamben is free to pursue the analogy between shame, as a universal structure of subjectivity, and language, or rather, as in the title of an article by the linguist on whose work he will rely, subjectivity in language.[30] For it is to Emile Benveniste's influential reflections on "shifters," and in particular on the personal pronouns discussed at some length in the previous chapter, that Agamben here appeals. We would do well therefore to recall briefly the structure of the first person singular pronoun, "I." On the one hand, "I" marks a linguistic function that any speaker can activate and that is therefore universally the same, as Benveniste indicates by defining it in the *third* person: "*I* is 'the individual who utters the present instance of discourse containing the linguistic instance *I*.'"[31] On the other hand, and as the same definition also makes clear, "I" designates, whenever it is uttered, a particular speaker whose identity not only differs from that of others but is itself subject to change and hence is in each case, according to Benveniste, "unique."[32] "There is thus," as he puts it, "a combined double instance in this process: the instance of *I* as referent and the instance of discourse containing *I* as the referee."[33]

Like any text, "The Nature of Pronouns" can be selectively enlisted in support of misleading inferences. Given Agamben's itinerary, one can understand why the following lines figure among the few he cites: "What then is the reality to which *I* or *you* refers? It is solely a 'reality of discourse,' and this is a very strange thing. *I* cannot be defined except in terms of 'locution,' not in terms of objects as a nominal sign is."[34] To judge by this quotation alone, one might think that, for Benveniste, the "I" has no "object," no reality outside of language, and hence that in any of its utterances it is not really an individual but rather language alone that speaks and refers to itself. Yet Benveniste is concerned here precisely to emphasize the distinction between *language* and *discourse*, "this profound difference between language as a system of signs and language assumed into use by the individual,"[35] which, as a careful reading of his text will bear out, encompasses the difference, not between the presence and absence of an object, but between the sameness of the nominal object and the variability or "uniqueness" of its pronominal counterpart. Only by virtue of this difference, indeed, can we account for shifters, for "a group of always available, 'empty' signs that are nonreferential with respect to 'reality' and that become 'full' [that is, referential with respect to reality] as soon as a speaker introduces them into each instance of his discourse."[36] As a fellow linguist, Roman Jakobson, insists: "the sign *I* cannot represent its object without 'being in existential relation' with this object: the word *I* designating the utterer is existentially related to his utterance, and hence functions as an index (cf. Benveniste)."[37]

It is important to keep these considerations in mind when examining Agamben's interpretation of Benveniste, all the more so as his commentary on the lines mentioned just a moment ago will essentially decide the fate of "Levi's paradox." That commentary reads as follows:

> When one looks closely, the passage from language to discourse appears as a paradoxical act that simultaneously implies both subjectification and desubjectification. On the one hand, the psychosomatic individual must fully abolish himself and desubjectify himself as a real individual to become the subject of enunciation and to identify himself with the pure shifter "I," which is absolutely without any substantiality and content other than its mere reference to the instance of discourse. But, once stripped of all extra-linguistic reality and constituted as a subject of enunciation, the subject discovers that he has gained access not so much to a possibility of speaking as to an impossibility of speaking—or, rather, that he has gained access to being always already anticipated by a glossolalic potentiality over which he has neither control nor mastery. Appropriating the formal instruments of enunciation, he is introduced into a language from which, by definition, nothing will allow him to pass into discourse. And yet, in saying "I," "you," "this," "now . . . ," he is expropriated of all referential reality, letting himself be defined solely through the pure and empty relation to the instance of discourse. *The subject of enunciation is composed entirely in and of discourse. But, for this very reason, once the subject is in discourse, he can say nothing; he cannot speak.* (*RA*, 116–17/108)

The first sentence of this passage would lead one to believe that Agamben endorses the distinction between language and discourse and, by extension, their "double instance" in the utterance of "I." In the pages that follow, moreover, there are statements that appear to confirm this impression, as when he states: "The instance in the pure presence of discourse irreparably divides the self-presence of sensations and experiences in the very moment in which it refers them to a unitary center" (RA, 122/114).[38] Here, in the division to which utterance of the ostensibly unifying "I" gives rise, one can read the tension of Benveniste's "double instance," which seems to be reflected as well in Agamben's claim that "every testimony is a field of forces incessantly traversed by currents of subjectification and desubjectification" (RA, 121/112). But in the remainder of the passage just quoted, his commentary is otherwise inflected. To claim that "the psychosomatic individual must fully abolish himself and desubjectify himself as a real individual to become the subject of enunciation" is, I would argue, puzzling at least, since, for Benveniste, this individual *is* the subject of enunciation. No less puzzling is the claim that "to become the subject of enunciation" is "to identify himself with the pure shifter 'I,' which is absolutely without any substantiality and content other than its mere reference to the instance of discourse," since, as we have just seen, enunciation is the conversion of an "empty" shifter into a "full" one, the activation of a universal nonreferential sign for the purpose of referring to a particular speaking subject. The point, however, is that, just as the displacement of shame to the interiority of the subject disposes of all real *Muselmänner*, so the displacement of the subject to a purely intralinguistic realm disposes of all real witnesses. "Stripped of all extra-linguistic reality," "expropriated of all referential reality," "defined solely through the pure and empty relation to the instance of discourse"—the subject, or what remains of it once it has been deprived of any particularizing or differentiating content, is no more than the disembodied witness to that deprivation, to the desubjectification that renders every subject exactly the same as any other.[39]

On the face of it, this sameness would "solve" the epistemic problem arising from Agamben's mediated relation to Levi: the "structure of all subjectivity" now lies within a language that is not only divorced from the extralinguistic world and its history but that essentially abolishes linguistic mediation by emptying subjective experience of all content except a common "impossibility of speaking." The only thing we really need to know about Levi's testimony is what it cannot say.

Moreover, Agamben's view of the subject in language appears to prophesy the fulfillment of "Levi's paradox," since the most salient feature of that subject is the inability to speak, that is, to bear witness, and since this inability supposedly suffices to establish the witness as "true." As often happens when Agamben invokes modal categories, however, especially those of possibility and impossibility, a certain qualification is necessary. In this case, if in the instance of discourse "an impossibility of speaking has . . . come to speech" (*RA*, 117/109), then to state of the subject that "he cannot speak" does not mean that there simply is no speech. It means, rather, that "the one who speaks is not the individual, but language" (*RA*, 117/109). Similarly, to state of the subject that "he can say nothing" does not mean that there is no saying, but that saying itself yields no said. What one might call the remnants of Benveniste thus lie in an enunciation with no subject. Should there subsist any doubt about this, Agamben states not only that "*the subject of testimony is the one who bears witness to a desubjectification*," but that "'to bear witness to a desubjectification' can only mean that there is no subject of testimony" (*RA*, 120–21/112).

At this point, restating a question raised at the beginning of the chapter, I would ask whether Agamben's theory of testimony, while attending to the expectations associated with its "genre," succeeds in upholding the historical singularity of the Holocaust as well as the singularity of the survivor's experience and testimonial voice. And if not, what it might accomplish.

By now, we have become familiar with the universalizing tendency that sees the infamous soccer match at Auschwitz in "every match in our stadiums," that alerts each of us to our own "inner *Muselmann*," that defines shame as "the hidden structure of all subjectivity and consciousness," and that makes of every subject a survivor and, due to the "impossibility of speaking" we all share, not only a witness but a "true" one. Granted, there is no theory without generalization, and no historical event can be understood in isolation from a context that is broader than its own chronological demarcation, since its actuality depends on conditions of possibility that precede and may also succeed it. Yet the cognitive or epistemic value of theoretical thought does not reside in its generalizations alone but rather in their sustained relation to the particular phenomena from which they derive and for which they are supposed, in turn, to account. In *Remnants of Auschwitz*, Agamben assembles from a few selected features of "the camp" a paradigm whose indiscriminate extension beyond the Holocaust proceeds in tandem with a misrepresentation of these features in their historical specificity, as we have seen, perhaps most glaringly, in the case of the gray zone and the *Muselmann*. At the same time, of course, this misrepresentation cannot but call into question the reliability of the paradigm itself and the virtually unbounded interpretive pertinence that is claimed for it.

But if these remarks suggest that *Remnants of Auschwitz* fails to do justice to the historical specificity of the Holocaust, we can still ask whether it does not accomplish something else. As I see it, the book affords above all an important insight into certain designs of National Socialism. In particular, the notion of thresholds or zones of indistinction may represent as well as any other what the perpetrators of the Holocaust *sought* to achieve by blurring, in certain respects, the difference between themselves and their victims and by rendering certain humans more or less indistinguishable from the subhuman image that the perpetrators already harbored of them. Moreover, we know, from Levi and innumerable other sources, that the Nazis sought to achieve a state of affairs in which witnesses would, by definition, be unable to speak. And to a large extent, they succeeded. However, the very existence of a remnant requires us to ask whether it is legitimate to distinguish between testifying survivors and "true," because mute, witnesses. In other words, to conclude our assessment of the relation between Agamben's theory of testimony and the singularity of Levi's experience and testimonial voice, we need to examine the final articulation of "Levi's paradox" in *Remnants of Auschwitz*.

Discussions of *Remnants of Auschwitz* tend to gravitate to these pages, not only because they conclude the book but because they contain something of a surprise ending. The surprise consists both in the quotation of a number of testimonies from former *Muselmänner* (including one woman) and in the brief paragraph that introduces them:

> In the expression "I was a *Muselmann*," Levi's paradox reaches its most extreme formulation. Not only is the *Muselmann* the complete witness; he now speaks and bears witness in the first person. By now it should be clear that this extreme formulation—"I, who speak, was a *Muselmann*, that is, the one who cannot in any sense speak"—not only does not contradict Levi's paradox but, rather, fully verifies it. This is why we leave them—the *Muselmänner*—the last word. (*RA*, 165/154)

The central question raised here could be formulated as follows: How can the speech of a *Muselmann* fully verify a paradox according to which the true and complete witness is the one who cannot speak? What strikes me as the most plausible answer to this question, from Agamben's perspective, would have to rely on his claim that "enunciation . . . refers not to the text of what is stated, but to its taking place; the individual can put language into act only on condition of identifying himself with the very event of saying, and not with what is said in it" (*RA*, 116/108). This saying, divorced from any said, would testify to a pure potentiality or possibility of speech indissociable from its impossibility: as Agamben puts it, "because testimony is the relation between a possibility of speech and its taking place, it can exist only through a relation to an impossibility of speech—that is, only as contingency, as a capacity not to be" (*RA*, 145/135). Thus, regarding the *Muselmänner* he quotes, it is not what they say but the sheer fact of saying it, their speech as remains or remnant, that would bear witness to the impossibility of speech and fully verify Levi's paradox.

The problem with this explanation becomes apparent as soon as we note that the validity of the explanation as a whole depends precisely on what it excludes, that is, "the *text* of what is stated," the content of the expression "I was a *Muselmann*." Indeed, only if the person saying "I" identifies himself or herself as a *Muselmann* is there any need for an explanation in the first place. But to base on this identification the claim that witnessing lies purely in saying, and not in what is said, is at best to create another paradox, or rather, a contradiction. Moreover, it is significant that, in the statement "I was a *Muselmann*," Agamben uses the past tense. Historically, to be sure, it was not impossible, under favorable circumstances, for *Muselmänner* to escape their condition and so to regain, among other things, enough of their speech to state, in effect: "I *am no longer* a *Muselmann*." Yet the past tense poses an additional problem for Agamben's theory insofar as it implies a fundamental difference between the speaker and the *Muselmann*, a difference that belies the most extreme, strictly present-tense formulation of Levi's paradox: "Not only is the *Muselmann* the complete witness; he now speaks and bears witness in the first person." In fact, it is not the *Muselmann* who speaks.[40] The reacquisition of speech means that the relation of these testifying survivors to their former selves is symbolically mediated, and that, as I earlier suggested, they, like other survivors (including Levi), even if to a different degree, can only bear witness to the *Muselmänner* "by proxy."[41]

That this should be the case suggests the possibility of detecting, in Levi's testimonial voice and the experience it attempts to convey, something other than the universal, depersonalizing speechlessness that *Remnants of Auschwitz* claims to find there. For me, this possibility arises as well from wondering whether a thinker as astute as Levi could have been unaware that, in strictly epistemic terms, to state that "we, the survivors, are not the true witnesses," is to call the very truth of the statement into question. To be more precise, I find it highly probable that Levi is concerned here less with making a general statement about truth in testimony than with formulating a specific judgment and expressing the feeling it produces. Moreover, I also believe that he is more interested in problems than solutions, or at least wary of solutions reflecting a failure to assess the difficulty of the problems themselves, and that, not coincidentally, his approach—tentative, exploratory, at times deliberately inconclusive—is in keeping with the essay as a genre, in the tradition inaugurated by Montaigne. Thus, I would like to return to the essay "Shame" to see if there might be another way of listening to Levi.

In considering what Levi offers as examples of his regrettable deeds—his impatient refusal, in most instances, to share vital information with new arrivals and the decision made by him and his friend Alberto not to disclose to another friend, Daniele, a rare source of potable water (*DS*, 78–81/*O*, 2:1051–53)—it is not only a matter of remembering that in the camp these actions or omissions could mean the difference between life and death, but of recognizing that Levi emphasizes the second of them for a very specific reason (unmentioned by Agamben), namely, that Daniele's discovery and exposure of the secret redoubled Levi's sense of shame. As he observes: "Daniele is dead now, but in our meetings as survivors, fraternal, affectionate, the veil of that act of omission, that unshared glass of water, stood between us, transparent, not expressed, but perceptible and 'costly'" (*DS*, 8/*O*, 2:1053). This is not to say that the incident of the unshared water alone plays a decisive role in Levi's reflections on shame; but it does direct our attention to what he calls an "us-ism" (*DS*, 80/*O*, 2:1053), the egotism of Primo and Alberto practiced at Daniele's expense, and introduces remarks of a more general nature on the ethical relation between self and other.

Thus, pondering the state of the survivor, Levi asks himself:

Are you ashamed because you are alive in place of another? And in particular, of a man more generous, more sensitive, more useful, wiser, worthier of living than you? You cannot block out such feelings: you examine yourself, you review your memories, hoping to find them all, and that none of them are masked or disguised. No, you find no obvious transgressions, you did not usurp anyone's place, you did not beat anyone (but would you have had the strength to do so?), you did not accept positions (but none were offered to you . . .), you did not steal anyone's bread; nevertheless you cannot exclude it. It is no more than a supposition, indeed the shadow of a suspicion: that each man is his brother's Cain, that each one of us (but this time I say "us" in a much vaster, indeed, universal sense) has usurped his neighbor's place and lived in his stead. It is a supposition, but it gnaws at us; it has nestled deeply like a woodworm; although unseen from the outside, it gnaws and rasps. (*DS*, 81–82 / *O*, 2:1054)

In light of the regrettable deeds just discussed, to claim that memory yields "no obvious transgressions" can certainly appear to involve Levi in self-contradiction (although another apparent contradiction is easily dispelled, since presumably the "positions" to which he refers were positions of political power, like those of the *Kapos*, and not of the kind he himself obtained, thanks to his professional training, in the Chemical Kommando, whose not unimportant privileges were nevertheless largely material).[42] It may be that he wishes to distinguish acts of omission from acts of commission and considers the latter to have played a more decisive role than the former in determining who survived and who did not. Or it may be that we find here a dissonance or opacity produced by the mutual interference of the two moral codes he mentions, "the code of that time" (of the camps) and "today's code" (*DS*, 81 / *O*, 2:1054). What seems clear, in any case, is that, according to the supposition or suspicion formulated in an effort to explain the phenomenon of shame, shame itself does not have exclusively or perhaps even primarily to do, in Levi's eyes, with one's deeds.

A more serious problem arises, however, from the formulation of this supposition: "that each man is his brother's Cain, that each one of us (but this time I say 'us' in a much vaster, indeed, universal sense) has usurped his neighbor's place and lived in his stead." Does not the universal scope of the supposition threaten to obscure the shame of Holocaust survivors in its specificity? Maybe so. Yet as we shall see, the problem does not really lie in this feature, or at least not in this feature alone. Here as in many other instances, the purpose in whose service Levi enlists his universalizing impulse is clearly pedagogical: like the myth of the Gorgon, the story of Cain and Abel is familiar to readers having no experience of the Nazi genocide and thus can function as a cultural means by which to foster understanding within an inclusive "us" without obliterating the differences that also inform this "us." In fact, the pedagogical thrust of the passage is unusually emphatic, given that the use of the second person singular (*tu*/you) invites individual readers to put themselves in the place of Levi, where their identification with the survivor must nevertheless be tempered by the acknowledgment of difference if they are to avoid a usurpation analogous to the one that is substantively at issue. But as I have suggested, it is elsewhere—to be exact, in another kind of usurpation—that we will find what is centrally at stake in Levi's supposition.

Thus, if each man is his brother's Cain—that is, if everyone is like Cain in relation to everyone else—then, strictly speaking, each man is also his brother's Abel. It is therefore not so much the universal compass of the supposition as the implied interchangeability or "usurpability" of Cain and Abel that poses a challenge to interpretation. For how is one to read this statement, made by the very author who, in the essay preceding "Shame," denounces the confusion of victim and murderer? Of course, we should not confuse Levi's position with that of Agamben, who, like Cavani, fails to distinguish between a certain human potential and its actualization, and also fails to recognize that the actualization of this potential in the gray zone of Auschwitz entailed crucial differences in the distribution of roles. The fact remains that, in "The Gray Zone," Levi describes himself as "a guiltless victim," and then avows, in "Shame," that he "might have usurped, that is, in fact, killed" (*DS*, 82 / *O*, 2:1055). Yet on the obvious assumption that the guiltless victim is not also a real murderer, we ask at whom the accusation is leveled if not at one who killed, at it were, "by proxy," one whose sense of responsibility extends to the deeds of others, one whose mere witnessing of murder was, itself, shaming. This, at least, is what Levi's concluding remarks would lead one to believe:

> The ocean of pain, past and present, surrounded us, and its level rose from
> year to year until it almost submerged us. It was useless to close one's eyes or

turn one's back to it because it was all around, in every direction, all the way to the horizon. It was not possible for us nor did we want to become islands; the just among us, neither more nor less numerous than in any other human group, felt remorse, shame, and pain for the misdeeds that others and not they had committed, and in which they felt involved, because they sensed that what had happened around them and in their presence, and in them, was irrevocable. Never again could it be cleansed; it would prove that man, the human species—we, in short—had the potential to construct an infinite enormity of pain, and that pain is the only force created from nothing, without cost and without effort. It is enough not to see, not to listen, not to act. (*DS*, 86/*O*, 2:1057–58)

As I suggested in the previous chapter, a sense of responsibility exceeding the scope of one's own moral agency can only pertain to a subject that is intrinsically relational, a self whose autonomy is produced by the heteronomy of its ethical involvement with others. There too I stated that this sense is (re)discovered when, as second persons, we are addressed by an other or others not like us and to whom our response constitutes us in turn as first persons. What this means here is that Levi's sense of responsibility, or rather, the shame emerging from a historically unprecedented discrepancy between this sense and the compass of personal agency, is essentially associated not only with survival but with witnessing—that is, with a response to the drowned—and hence that, as we shall see, there is more than one way to read the word *true* in the statement "we, the survivors, are not the true witnesses."

Immediately preceding this statement lies a discussion of his testimonial status in unmistakably moral terms. Levi first alludes to a religious friend who visited him shortly after his return from imprisonment:

He told me that my having survived could not be the work of chance, of an accumulation of fortunate circumstances (as I did then and still do maintain) but rather of Providence. I bore the mark, I was an elect; I, the nonbeliever, and even less of a believer after the season of Auschwitz, was a person touched by Grace, a saved man. And why me? It is impossible to know, he answered. Perhaps because I had to write, and by writing bear witness: Wasn't I in fact then, in 1946, writing a book about my imprisonment?

Such an opinion seemed monstrous to me. It pained me as when one touches an exposed nerve, and kindled the doubt I spoke of before: I might be alive in the place of another, at the expense of another. (*DS*, 82 / *O*, 2:1054–55)

The "monstrosity" of this opinion has to do, however, not only with the possibility that Levi "might be alive in the place of another, at the expense of another," nor only with his friend's religious propensity to fabricate purpose from chance. It has to do above all with the notion that bearing witness could retroactively justify his survival. As he puts it, in a somewhat more subdued manner: "the thought that this testifying of mine could by itself gain for me the privilege of surviving and living for many years without serious problems troubles me because I cannot see any proportion between the privilege and its outcome" (*DS*, 83 / *O*, 2:1055). Indeed, the task of responding to the silent address of the drowned so far surpasses the means available to the first person voice as to indicate that this voice may ring truest precisely in exposing that inadequacy or "injustice." Nowhere is this exposure more striking than in the lines occupying the center of the discussion in question, in which Levi's evaluative idiom suggests that we seek in a moral sooner than an epistemic register the meaning of the word *true* when used in reference to witnesses:

> The "saved" of the Lager were not the best, those predestined to do good, the bearers of a message: what I had seen and lived through proved the exact contrary. Mostly the worst survived, the selfish, the violent, the insensitive, the collaborators of the "gray zone," the spies. It was not a certain rule (there were none, nor are there certain rules in human matters), but it was nevertheless a rule. I felt innocent, yes, but enrolled among the saved and therefore in permanent search of a justification in my own eyes and those of others. The worst survived, that is, the fittest; the best all died. (*DS*, 82 / *O*, 2:1055)

Here, we might check our impulse to dismiss what Levi says because it implies that he himself was among "the worst." In other words, we might bracket the intellectualistic assumption that the central issue is a matter of truth and falsehood. Then we could venture to listen otherwise, both to Levi and to ourselves, if only in order to ask whether our intellectualistic assumption or impulse does not serve to shield us against what is arguably not so much a statement *about* shame, and even less a disquisition on "the hidden structure of all subjectivity and consciousness," as an *expression* of shame, the *demonstration* of a particular survivor's feeling of guilt in the very way in which, as a witness, he speaks of it.[43]

I do not claim nor would I wish to claim that this hypothesis provides the "key" to reading "Shame," since I believe that, in principle and in keeping with both the essay as a genre and the complexity of Levi's writing, the interpretation of this text should remain exploratory and open to revision. The hypothesis nonetheless sheds some light on the inflection of Levi's language, especially as it concerns the survivor and his testimony. Consider, for example, that, in asking himself whether he might be alive in place of another, he imagines that other to be "worthier of living"—an evaluation that Levi would find "monstrous" if applied to him. Or again: even if, "logically," the notion that "each man is his brother's Cain" implies that each is also his Abel, it is only to Cain that Levi refers. And the inclusion of "collaborators of the 'gray zone'" among "the worst" only reinforces the pervasive sense that, even in the eyes of those who in reality did not qualify for this subgroup, survival amounted somehow to a kind of collaboration or betrayal.

But this brings us back, finally, to the word *true* in Levi's claim that "we, the survivors, are not the true witnesses" and raises anew the question whether that word should not be understood primarily in a moral rather than an epistemic sense—or more precisely, whether the claim as a whole should not be reconsidered in light of Levi's correlative claim concerning the "Muslims" or, in general, the drowned. This correlative claim is most succinctly and accurately formulated, I would argue, as a conditional or counterfactual proposition: *If* the drowned had survived, *then* they would be the true witnesses. Yet since the drowned did not survive, "just as no one ever returned to describe his own death," their "true" witnessing is not even a human (or "inhuman") potential but a pure fiction. And the fictitious character of this standard by which Levi judges his own testimony and that of other survivors explains why, experimentally substituting likely synonyms for "not true," we end up with such presumably unintended and in any case wholly untenable claims as that survivor testimony is intrinsically false, or unfaithful, or both. Recalling that Levi equates "true" with "complete," however, we can perceive the moral sense to which I have alluded by focusing on the act of positing this standard, of which any and all survivor testimony will necessarily fall short and in regard to which, therefore, it contracts an unpayable debt, leaving the witness, as Levi remarks, "in permanent search of a justification in my own eyes and those of others." In other words—and once again—the manner in which Levi frames his view of "true" witnessing appears to be itself a manifestation of shame, if not also of remorse. After all, it is often in remorse that we say, or think, "if only."

Were there any further need to disconfirm Agamben's contention that "the only thing that interests [Levi] is what makes judgment impossible," one could thus rely as much on "Shame" as on "The Gray Zone," since "Shame" has essentially to do, as we have just observed, with how survivors judge themselves. Yet the reading I have proposed, which emphasizes both what Levi says and what he does, both the said and the saying of his testimony, suggests at least one further implication of the essay. For if I am not mistaken in claiming that the standard of "true" or "complete" witnessing should be stated as a counterfactual, then we can infer from its very counterfactuality that *in fact* it is above all the witnessing of the drowned that is *in*complete. The debt mentioned just a moment ago is accordingly not the survivor's own but must be *assumed*, and it is for this reason that the suspicion of being alive in place of another is here indissociable from the felt obligation to testify in place of another. Responsibility, for the Holocaust survivor who bears witness, thus means not only responding *to* but responding *for* the drowned. It means speaking as a delegate, and delegating to us the task of listening.

In the chapter of *Survival in Auschwitz* entitled "Our Nights," Levi relates the dream of what he calls "the unlistened-to story":

> This is my sister here, with some unidentifiable friend and many other people. They are all listening to me and it is this very story that I am telling: the whistle of three notes, the hard bed, my neighbor whom I would like to move, but whom I am afraid to wake as he is stronger than me. I also speak diffusely of our hunger and of the lice-control, and of the Kapo who hit me on the nose and then sent me to wash myself as I was bleeding. It is an intense pleasure, physical, inexpressible, to be at home, among friendly people and to have so many things to recount: but I cannot help noticing that my listeners do not follow me. In fact, they are completely indifferent: they speak confusedly of other things among themselves, as if I was not there. My sister looks at me, gets up and goes away without a word.[44]

Levi then recalls not only that he has had this dream before but that his friend Alberto and many if not all of their fellow inmates have had one very much like it. He asks: "Why does it happen? Why is the pain of every day translated so constantly into our dreams, in the ever-repeated scene of the unlistened-to story?"[45]

Not long before, Levi had related another story. When he reached through his barracks window for an icicle to quench his thirst, "at once," he says, "a large, heavy guard prowling outside brutally snatched it away from me. *'Warum?'* I asked him in my poor German. *'Hier ist kein Warum'* (there is no why here), he replied, pushing me inside with a shove."[46] One might think that this tale, in which the guard grants no hearing to the prisoner, suggests at least a tentative answer to Levi's question about the dream. For it almost goes without saying that those who, like Levi, were considered by the Nazis to be *unlebenswertes Leben*, or life unworthy of life, were thereby also considered unworthy of being listened to, indeed that the sense of this unworthiness was integral to the social death inflicted on them, to what Levi calls "the demolition of a man." In view of the treatment to which camp inmates were daily subjected, neither the recurrence nor the prevalence of the dream of the unlistened-to story seems quite so puzzling.

Yet there are at least two features of the dream as Levi recounts it that give us food for thought. First, the scene staged by this dream is not from life *in* Auschwitz but rather from life *after* Auschwitz. Its anticipatory quality may well account for the intense emotions it arouses, which Levi the inmate was normally too numb or exhausted to feel—emotions such as "a desolating grief" within the dream and "anguish" upon awakening.[47] At the same time, this orientation toward the future appears to indicate that, for the survivor, life after Auschwitz may somehow recall life in the camp, that liberation may lead to another kind of silencing, which, despite the absence of gates, guard towers, and barbed wire, will be no less formidable in its own way.

The second feature to which I would draw attention is that it is neither a guard nor even a hostile civilian who refuses to listen, but his very own sister and other "friendly people." Of course, we know when Levi wrote *Survival in Auschwitz* and can, without questioning his trustworthiness as a witness, allow for the possibility that his account of the dream may have been colored—attenuated or exaggerated—by the very future it supposedly portends, that is, by his experience after liberation. But precisely this remains troubling too, since it suggests that the second silencing could well have been more than a dream, and that even "friendly" listeners might not hear a thing.

FIVE

The Survivor as Other

As the ethically charged encounter with an other who is not like me, the reception of Holocaust survivor testimony almost inevitably leads us to discuss the work of Emmanuel Levinas, arguably the twentieth century's foremost philosopher of ethics in the Continental context. Of course, there are additional, equally compelling reasons to pursue this discussion, such as Levinas's thematization of the ethical relation as a situation of address or even as testimony and the role that the Holocaust played in his thought no less than in his life. Here, expanding on a notion put forward in chapter 3, namely, that testimonial memoir amounts to an *art* of survival, I would like first to reconsider, precisely in its implications for his approach to testimony, Levinas's view that the ethical relation as he understands it is essentially at odds with artistic representation. No doubt, this announcement will recall the tension between ethics and aesthetics in Adorno's reflections on art "after Auschwitz." But it would be premature to assume either that Adorno and Levinas see eye to eye on this issue or, on the contrary, that their views diverge so widely as to promise no intersections. For that matter, my concern is not to compare them or somehow to "reconcile" ethics and aesthetics in Levinas's thought. The point is rather to ask whether the aesthetic is not, to coin a phrase, "always already" internal to the ethical relation itself, and how this intrication may affect, from a Levinasian perspective, the reception of Holocaust survivor testimony.

As we shall see, however, the substance of the issue cannot be divorced from the form in which it is stated. In other words, it will be a question, from the outset, of the status of philosophical discourse, whose universalizing or generalizing tendency makes it difficult to accommodate the particularity or singularity not only of "the other"—proverbially, "the stranger, the widow, and the orphan"[1]—but of other discourses resistant to that tendency. Even as we examine, in the next three sections of this chapter, Levinas's philosophy of testimony in light of the relation between the aesthetic and the ethical, therefore, we will have to take into account the implications of this relation for the idiom in which both the relation itself and the philosophy to which it pertains are represented.

In the interest of the heterogeneity toward which the whole of Levinasian ethics is inclined, a subsequent section will be devoted to reading a very different idiom, that is, the testimonial discourse of Jorge Semprun's memoir *Literature or Life*, whose opening chapter, "The Gaze," proves to be all the more thought-provoking in regard to that ethics as Levinas thematizes the ethical relation not only as a situation of address but also as a face-to-face encounter. Finally, both the analysis of Levinas and the reading of Semprun will lead us, in the concluding section of this chapter, to reflect on the possibility that Levinas's work might be read *as* testimony. This, needless to say, does not entail dismissing its formal specificity, since that specificity constitutes, as I have just indicated, a substantive matter in its own right. It suggests rather that philosophy, like memoir, may be found among those forms that Holocaust survivor testimony, in its generic hybridity, indeed in its generic homelessness, has come to inhabit or to haunt. To be sure, respecting the form of philosophical language means that the road to this hypothesis may feel, much of the time, like a detour. But as we shall also see, the question of indirectness is a central motif of Levinas's thinking and informs the "art" of his discourse.

In the most overtly autobiographical text he ever wrote, entitled "Signature," Levinas says that his life was "dominated by the presentiment and the memory of the Nazi horror."[2] While this comes as no surprise to those familiar with Levinas's biography, the statement is nonetheless striking in its abrupt appearance as a paragraph unto itself, after a curriculum vitae extending from childhood in Eastern Europe to a professorship at the Sorbonne and before a much lengthier section in which he retraces his philosophical itinerary up to 1976. It is as though, in its isolation, Levinas's statement indirectly asserted the pointlessness or even the moral dubiousness of any attempt to integrate the Nazi horror into a narrative and as though, in its terseness, it also implied that language can only approach the magnitude of that horror in proportion to the stringency of its means. Yet no less striking is how swiftly Levinas moves from this solemn declaration to the scholarly observation that "Husserl brought a method to philosophy,"[3] thereby framing the intellectual evolution to whose summary "Signature" is largely devoted and during which *what* language says, the "said" produced by its "saying," including narrative (most often referred to, however, as "history" or "memory"), is subjected to an explicit and sustained ethical critique. Thus, although at this point we dare venture no more than a hypothesis, it may well be that the scruples one can only infer from Levinas's pronouncement concerning the effect of the Holocaust on his life are expounded at length in his work, leading one to suspect that the signature of the Shoah might actually be more legible in the highly abstract discourse of his philosophical oeuvre than in his elliptical autobiographical allusions.[4] Levinas encourages such a view by citing, as the epigraph of his text, this "conversation overheard in the métro":

> "The language that tries to be direct and names events fails to be straightforward [*manque de droiture*]. Events induce it to be prudent and make compromises. Commitment agglomerates men, unbeknownst to them, into parties. Their speech is transformed into politics. The language of the committed is encoded."
>
> "Who speaks clearly about current events? Who speaks from his heart about men? Who shows them his face [*visage*]?"
>
> "The one who uses the words 'substance,' 'accident,' 'subject,' 'object,' and other abstractions."[5]

Perhaps it is only in Paris that one can hope to overhear conversations of this kind. For that matter, who knows whether it was real or imagined, or even—given the presence of such terms as *droiture* and *visage*, which are central to Levinas's idiom—whether Levinas was one, or both, of the inter-locutors? Be that as it may (and although the discourse disparaged here is ostensibly political rather than narrative), its quotation at the threshold of "Signature" clearly suggests that, for Levinas, only the indirect language of philosophy can be trusted to speak straightforwardly or uprightly, even about "current events" (from which, in 1976 or even 2013, excluding the Shoah, with its long "afterlife," would only beg the question). In short, while the testimonial dimension of Levinas's philosophy must, for the time being, remain hypothetical, we might at least expect that, as an object of philosophical inquiry, testimony, in which one presumably "speaks from his heart about men" and "shows them his face," will engage the heart of Levinasian ethics.

It remains nevertheless to be determined which of Levinas's texts will provide the most useful guidance. One might be initially inclined to choose the first two sections of chapter 5, "Subjectivity and Infinity," of his second major philosophical treatise, *Otherwise than Being or Beyond Essence* (1974; *OB*, 131–52/167–94). What we find there, however, is the somewhat less focused version of an article published in 1972 under the title "Truth of Disclosure and Truth of Testimony." As indicated by the editors of Levinas's *Basic Philo-sophical Writings*, where it appears in English translation, "Truth of Disclo-sure and Truth of Testimony" can be read, despite its earlier publication, as a "summary" of the first two sections of "Subjectivity and Infinity," since the article presents Levinas's thinking on the subject of testimony more dis-cretely and succinctly than does the chapter.[6] Of course, it is important to keep the later version of this text in mind, if only because of its contextualiza-tion in *Otherwise than Being*. Yet the earlier version in its very conciseness may serve as a better point of departure, especially as it also offers, through its title, an immediate entry into the argument that Levinas will employ.

From this title, one can safely infer that Levinas intends to posit two kinds of truth, the truth of "disclosure [*dévoilement*]" and the truth of "testi-mony [*témoignage*]" (TD, 97/101). Granted, in a philosophy that systemati-cally associates truth with disclosure and disclosure in turn with the phenomenological ontology it seeks to exceed, one may well wonder what other kind of truth could be ascribed to testimony. The opening pages of this essay are even devoted to advancing the claim that truth as disclosure—

that is, as the manifestation of being to a subjectivity equated with consciousness—has dominated philosophical thought from Aristotle to Husserl and Heidegger. "The truth correlative to being . . . ," writes Levinas, "remains, within the thought that issued from Greece, the foundation of every notion of truth" (TD, 99/102). Just as important for Levinas's argument, however, is the claim that, in equating it with a disclosive consciousness, Western ontology has conceived of subjectivity as no more than the vehicle of being's self-manifestation. Or as he puts it, the truth of disclosure is a truth "in which the subject, a pure welcome reserved for the nudity of disclosed being, effaces itself *before* that which manifests itself, and in which effort, inventiveness, and genius are all just the means, ways, and detours by which being is dis-covered, by which its phases come together and its structures are secured" (TD, 99/102).

With this understanding of subjectivity, moreover, Levinas associates a certain form of testimony:

> Testimony—the confession of some knowledge or of an experience by a
> subject—can be conceived only in relation to the disclosed being which
> remains the norm; it brings forth only indirect truths about being, or about
> the relations man has with being. These truths are evidently inferior,
> secondhand, and uncontrollable, distorted by the very fact of their transmission:
> the "subjectivity that effaces itself" in circulating information is capable of
> bad faith and lying. The critique of testimony—by whatever method (the
> proliferation and comparison of testimonies, investigation into the credibility
> of the witness, etc.)—is necessary to draw out the truth (since the *question* is
> suppressed). (TD, 100/103)

The "question" to which Levinas refers here presumably pertains to a conception of subjectivity irreducible to the one presupposed by this form of testimony. When we suppress the question, it seems, testimony can assume no role other or greater than that of handmaiden to, say, a system of law or an objective historiography that remain dependent upon the "subjectivity that effaces itself" and hence upon truth as disclosure. The direction in which we might seek the "other" subjectivity is nevertheless indicated by the one that ensures this truth. For the irony of disclosure is such that being is made manifest only through a subjectivity that does *not* manifest itself, and the characterization of this self-effacement, which is still ostensibly an ontological structure, in terms that are not, as one would expect, purely descriptive but rather evaluative—and not as humility but on the contrary as what enables "bad faith and lying"—clearly suggests by implied contrast that the "other" subjectivity is not only "otherwise than being" but has precisely to do with the Good, in which it shows its face. To be sure, this characterization does not constitute a demonstration or even an argument. And the biggest mistake one could make here would be to infer that the showing of the face must amount to a disclosure in its own right, since this inference would simply return the face itself to the economy of phenomenal being it is supposed to exceed.[7] Even so, to the extent that it parallels the distinction between truth as disclosure and truth as testimony (in the other sense of "truth" yet to be determined), the discrimination of an ontological from an ethical subjectivity gives us a firmer footing on which to proceed.

As it happens, Levinas's assessment of the testimony informed by truth as disclosure is not always quite so disparaging. Yet the most remarkable feature of his very next paragraph, given what he has elsewhere to say about art, is undoubtedly the definition of art itself as a mode of disclosure:

> In its most elevated meaning, testimony can doubtless be understood as the schematization of the abstract concept of being in the concreteness of the subject. Art would testify to the truth according to such a schematism. But once again, the structure of discovery reappears in the schema. The disclosure of being governs testimony. The *concreteness of the subject* in which *being* is schematized and which is studied by the critic or the historian or the philosopher of art, is placed on the side of being. *Before* being, the *subject of knowledge* effaces itself. (TD, 100/103)[8]

Referring to the relation between the aesthetic and the ethical, Jill Robbins rightly points out that "Levinas cannot be said to hold a stable view on the matter," as "assertions about the work of art in his earlier writings—from the forties and fifties—are mostly negative, while in key texts from the sixties and the seventies . . . a more positive appreciation emerges."[9] Nevertheless, from *Existence and Existents* (1947) and "Reality and Its Shadow" (1948), the only text concerned entirely with aesthetics as such, to the collection entitled *Proper Names* (1976),[10] and including reflections in Levinas's first major work, *Totality and Infinity* (1961) as well as in *Otherwise than Being* and *On Maurice Blanchot* (1975),[11] there is to my knowledge no text aside from the one under discussion here in which he associates art with disclosure or phenomenality. The *dis*sociation of art from disclosure would thus otherwise represent a constant in his view of art. Granted, as Robbins further observes, one could choose to see in the instability of Levinas's position the source of a "tension . . . operative *within* each of his texts about art" rather than of "a transformation of his view."[12] In that case, we might surmise that the definition of art as a mode of disclosure in the passage just quoted would constitute but one term of an ambiguity whose counterpart lies elsewhere in the same text—and that the same ambiguity would surface in other texts if only we looked hard enough. Yet as we shall see, disclosure does not at all pertain to the tension in question and here remains, I would argue, an anomaly, although by no means an unmotivated one.[13] For in the early stages of an argument so clearly predicated on the distinction between disclosure and testimony, ontology and ethics, the most efficient way to dispose of issues raised by a dimension of experience that this distinction may not be able to accommodate is precisely to associate it with the term at whose expense the argument is conducted. In order to ascertain exactly what those issues are, of course, we need to consider at some length the view of art that Levinas attempts to articulate. And it is for this purpose that I turn now to the text that figures most often in discussions of his aesthetics, "Reality and Its Shadow," and to its contemporary, *Existence and Existents*.

That art is not to be confused with disclosure is made abundantly clear from the outset: "To put it in theological terms . . . art does not belong to the order of revelation."[14] Yet neither, in its entirety, does being, which "is not only itself" but "escapes itself" (RS, 6/778). In fact, art, whose "most elementary procedure . . . consists in substituting for the object its image" (RS, 3/774), can be said to originate, according to Levinas, in a feature of being itself: "Reality would not be only what it is, what it is disclosed to be in truth, but would be also its double, its shadow, its image" (RS, 6/778). It is important therefore to follow him closely when he proposes as schematizations of this feature both a person and a thing:

> Being is not only itself, it escapes itself. Here is a person who is what he is; but he does not make us forget, does not absorb, cover over entirely the objects he holds and the way he holds them, his gestures, limbs, gaze, thought, skin, which escape from under the identity of his substance, itself like a torn sack unable to contain them. Thus a person bears on his face, alongside of its being with which he coincides, its own caricature, its picturesqueness. The picturesque

is always to some extent a caricature. Here is a familiar everyday thing, perfectly adapted to the hand that is accustomed to it, but its qualities, colour, form, and position at the same time remain as it were behind its being, like the "old garments" of a soul that has withdrawn from that thing, like a "still life." And yet all this is the person and is the thing. There is then a duality in this person, this thing, a duality in its being. It is what it is and it is a stranger to itself, and there is a relationship between these two moments. We will say that the thing is itself and is its image. And that this relationship between the thing and its image is resemblance. (RS, 6/778)

As we shall see, the duality in being is indissociable from a certain duality in its apprehension: the "experience" of the image lies in sensation, to be distinguished from perception, which discloses the thing in its selfsameness. But it is precisely this matter of "reception" that Levinas's schematizations help to articulate.

Let me begin with the thing he chooses to describe, which, despite being "familiar" and "everyday," is not just any old thing but one that is "perfectly adapted to the hand that is accustomed to it," and hence, if not a tool in the conventional sense, at least a thing whose being is normally defined by its use. The pertinence of his choice becomes clear when we consider that, for Levinas, this use locates the thing among those objects of which he notes, in *Existence and Existents*, that they are habitually "caught up in the current of practice where their alterity is hardly noticeable."[15] In other words, just as being enlists the "subjectivity that effaces itself" as the instrument of its own disclosure or manifestation, so this subjectivity employs the thing of which Levinas speaks as the invisible means with which to constitute or maintain its everyday practical world. This, of course, is not to say that the thing cannot appear as an object within that world, but rather that its very exteriority "refers to interiority" (*EE*, 53/85), that its objectivity remains subordinated to the subject(s) whose pursuits delimit the world. And thus although, in a statement closely resembling one already quoted from "Reality and Its Shadow," Levinas insists that "the elementary function of art . . . is to furnish an image of an object in place of the object itself" (*EE*, 52/83), he also explains that this substitution involves a decontextualization whereby the object is wholly "extracted" from the world that frames its objective existence. What this means in the case at hand is not only that, emerging from its customary concealment, the object or thing assumes "the exteriority of a thing in itself" (*EE*, 53/85), but that it does so precisely for a subject whose awareness of the loss of world enables it to see in the image that the thing's own "qualities, colour, form, and position . . . remain as it were behind its being, like the 'old garments' of a soul that has withdrawn from that thing, like a 'still life.'" Indeed, only a subject for whom the thing is normally an extension of the hand, and the hand itself an extension of the gaze, could see how, in its very familiarity, the useful thing when broken or simply removed from the world of means and ends becomes a useless "stranger to itself."[16] Such strangeness, or what Levinas calls the "exoticism" of the aesthetic, can even extend so far as to endow the externalized thing with a "soul" of its own: "the exotic reality of art, which, no longer objective, does not refer to our interiority, appears in turn to contain an interiority" (*EE*, 55/88–89).[17] At the same time, the dimension into which the thing turned image draws the gaze that apprehends it does not leave the gaze intact but rather induces in it a reversal of its own transformation: whereas the externalized thing acquires, as image, a semblance of interiority, the image as an estrangement of the gaze "turns the subjectivity of the subject . . . inside out" (*EE*, 61/100). Both the nature and the implications of this extroversion can be more fully grasped, however, if we turn from the being of the thing to that of the person.

In considering the description of this person, one may already be inclined to isolate from its other components the gaze in particular, if only because the gaze is so readily associated with the face, which Levinas evokes to summarize the person's duality: "Thus a person bears on his face, alongside of its being with which he coincides, its own caricature, its picturesqueness." We should note all the same that the duality it shares with the face pertains to the other features as well, since, in addition to showing that the person "is what he is," not only his gaze but "the objects he holds and the way he holds them, his gestures, limbs . . . thought, skin" are found to "escape from under the identity of his substance, itself like a torn sack unable to contain them." Like them, therefore, the gaze itself can become an image. But as something apprehended by a gaze rather than a gaze that apprehends, it can no longer see. To the extent that the gaze attests in a privileged manner to the interiority of the subject, then, its image attests in turn to the extroversion or evacuation of that interiority, and, as though to underscore Levinas's claim that "every artwork is in the end a statue" (RS,

8/782), deprives the person in question of both sight and soul. Yet we should also observe that the gaze here becomes an image *for another gaze* (our own), and that Levinas's schematization of being in the form of a person is essentially a way in which to figure the reception of the aesthetic. The question it raises has accordingly to do with those features of the schematized person, including but not only his gaze, that ensure the pertinence of the figuration itself.

Now it is impossible to overstate the importance of this question for Levinas's thought, since what emerges from the effort just to formulate it more or less coherently is his fundamental and enduring ambivalence concerning the aesthetic, an ambivalence that, notwithstanding the secondary status to which his philosophy appears to relegate this dimension of experience, informs that philosophy in its entirety and can indeed be discovered, if not always so readily, in any number of texts other than "Reality and Its Shadow" and *Existence and Existents*, on which I will nonetheless focus a while longer. In fact, the question of the aesthetic runs so deep in Levinas's work, and is continually restated in so many ways, that it can safely be said to determine in large part, as I will later argue, the "aesthetics" of his philosophical idiom. We must limit the number of instantiations to be considered, however, which means choosing those that will do the most justice to his thinking about the relation between aesthetics and ethics while leading us back to the discussion of testimony. I thus propose to examine, in the following order and in reference, again, to Levinas's schematization, the nature of sensation (or sensibility), the significance of what he calls the *il y a* or *there is*, and the decisive role of temporality.

When Levinas ventures the tautological definition of the person as one "who is what he is," subsequently mentioning "the identity of his substance" and, in connection with his face, "its being with which he coincides," he refers to a world that is governed by the principle of identity or sameness and that, as we earlier remarked, is first constituted through the disclosure or manifestation of being to subjectivity. In the light that suffuses this world, the subject or ego disposes, in regard to its object, of an interval or distance sufficient for the object to appear to it as such; and this interval, which is essential to perception, makes of perception, and above all vision, the phenomenological model for other operations of consciousness or cognition (such as the formation of conceptual abstractions like "being"). Considered in its active sense, then, consciousness can be understood as the imposition of form. To this it should be added that, in the phenomenal world, the subject can certainly be objectified, like the person portrayed by Levinas, but, as in the act of objectification that he invites us to share by saying "here is a person," exhibits a fundamental intersubjectivity whose most familiar philosophical articulation at the time lay in the Heideggerian notion of *Miteinandersein* (or *Mitsein*, for short), being-with-one-another (or being-with).[18] Even so, for Levinas, being-with, in which the other with whom I find myself is envisioned as an alter ego, as another subject like me—and who, instead of facing me, faces with me in the same direction—does not afford access to the ethical, precisely because it conceals the alterity of the other. It is consequently in the undoing of sameness, or of the perceptual disclosure it presupposes, that we could expect to find an opening to ethics in the Levinasian sense.

This undoing of perception is sensation. And sensation is "the aesthetic element" (RS, 5/776). In *Existence and Existents*, Levinas explains:

> Instead of arriving at the object, intention gets lost in the sensation itself, and it is this wandering about in sensation, in *aisthēsis*, that produces the esthetic effect. Sensation is not the way that leads to an object but the obstacle that keeps one from it; but it is not of the subjective order either. Sensation is not the material of perception. In art, it figures as a new element. Or better, it returns to the impersonality of the *element*. (*EE*, 53/85–86)

Recalling the person Levinas describes, we find that this failure to "arrive" at the object can be conveyed in another, no doubt compatible but arguably more instructive way, since agency is there ascribed to the features that "escape from under the identity of his substance, itself like a torn sack unable to contain them"—since, in other words, it is the person as image or the image of the person that, exceeding his objective form, moves toward the subject (our gaze) and converts the interval of perception into the disempowering proximity of sensation. Granted, in "Reality and Its Shadow" (if not in *Existence and Existents*), the passivity thus imputed to the aesthetic subject, which Levinas will later view as an essential characteristic of the ethical subject as well, appears in a very disparaging light, as we shall see in a moment. But this simply confirms the earlier-noted tensions in his thought, as well as the evolution to which they gave rise. What must be emphasized here is rather the resemblance between his schematization of the person's image in "Reality and Its Shadow" and his description, in any number of subsequent texts, of the (other's) face in the ethical encounter. Thus, to cite but one example, from "The Trace of the Other" (1963), where Levinas refers to the "epiphany" or nonphenomenal appearance of the face:

> Its life consists in undoing the form in which every entity, when it enters into immanence, that is, when it exposes itself as a theme, is already dissimulated.
>
> The other who manifests himself in the face as it were breaks through his own plastic essence. . . . His presence consists in *divesting* himself of the form that nonetheless manifests him. His manifestation is a surplus over the inevitable paralysis of manifestation.[19]

To judge from this passage, there is little if anything to distinguish the epiphany of the face from the image of Levinas's schematized person: for like the epiphany, the image undoes or divests itself of objective form, breaking through the plasticity of the object; like it, the image reveals what is dissimulated by manifestation; and like the epiphany, the image is a surplus or excess attesting to an alterity other than the otherness of the alter ego. Indeed, it would be a mistake to think, as it is nevertheless very tempting to do, that their resemblance is probably a mere semblance and might thus be dispelled by a heftier importation of Levinas's later philosophy, or simply by a shift of emphasis in the reading of this passage such that the life of the epiphany would stand in contrast to the lifelessness of the image, its implied movement to the immobility of the schematization, a gaze that looks back to one that sees nothing. For this would be to assume, in effect, that Levinas's thought is entirely encompassed by the very economy of same and other whose undoing it seeks to articulate, and in particular to dismiss his ambivalence about the aesthetic just as one had picked up its thread. I prefer therefore to follow this thread through what Levinas calls, as in the passage on sensation just quoted from *Existence and Existents*, the "element."

For its fuller discussion of the matter, I turn briefly to *Totality and Infinity*, where the element is described almost entirely in conjunction with "enjoyment" (*jouissance*), itself a mode (or mood) of sensibility. Whether it is a matter of air, light, water, or some other medium, the element is precisely that which "envelops or contains without being able to be contained or enveloped," a "content without form" with which Levinas chooses to convey our "adequate relation" through the expression: "bathing in the element" (*TI*, 131–32/104–5). No doubt, the polysemic resonance of this figure could be explored at length (to say nothing of its allusion to the opening pages of Maurice Blanchot's *Thomas the Obscure*).[20] But for present purposes, I would simply note that it suggests, on the one hand, a certain permeability of the membrane separating inside from outside, hence a tactile proximity of the body to water analogous to the visual proximity of the gaze to the image, and, on the other hand, a suspension or at least an alleviation of gravity, that is, of both weight and seriousness. It may be especially in this second respect that the element conjures enjoyment, which admittedly "embraces all relations with things" (*TI*, 133/106) but also lies beyond the Heideggerian world of care (*Sorge*), "the world as a set of implements forming a system and suspended on the care of an existence anxious for its being" (*TI*, 134/107), and nowhere more so than in art, which is, compared to such a world, "lightness and grace," and which, as "an appeasement . . . beyond the invitations to comprehend and act" (RS, 12/787), allows us, as we have already seen, to get lost in sensation. At the same time as Levinas is concerned to distinguish enjoyment from care, however, he insists on its distinctive egoism: "In enjoyment I am absolutely for myself. Egoist without reference to others, I am alone without solitude, innocently egoist and alone." Should the "without reference to others" prove insufficiently emphatic, as also the "alone without solitude" (alone without reference to an other who is elsewhere)—that is, in case this egoism might still be confused with that of a self apart from or even opposed to other selves in the being-with of same and other—Levinas immediately adds: "Not against others, not 'as for me'—but entirely deaf to others, outside of all communication and all refusal to communicate—without ears, like a hungry stomach [*ventre affamé*]" (*TI*, 134/107).[21] In other words, enjoyment allows of no relations with others for the simple reason that no such relations are possible where egoism consists in the abandonment of the ego itself. And in the enjoyment of art, where, according to "Reality and Its Shadow," "there is no longer a oneself, but rather a sort of passage from oneself to anonymity" (RS, 4/775), one may also find, despite the absence of self, a sort of passage from being "innocently egoist" to a state of "irresponsibility"—or worse, as Levinas makes clear by trading a merely alimentary for a gastronomic simile: "There is something wicked and egoist and cowardly in artistic enjoyment. There are times when one can be ashamed of it, as of feasting during a plague" (RS, 12/787).[22]

Yet what Levinas refers to here is what he himself calls "the most common and ordinary experience of aesthetic enjoyment," where "art, essentially disengaged, constitutes, in a world of initiative and responsibility, a dimension of evasion" (RS, 12/787). The judgment he passes on or against artistic enjoyment thus relies on the (re)framing of art by the very world of which art is supposed to be a radical disruption (it being understood that, at this stage in his thinking, "a world of initiative and responsibility" is essentially the same as the world of manifestation, comprehension, and action, and in any case assumes a relatively autonomous ego).[23] Indeed, only this (re)framing, this re-placement of art within a world reliant on instrumentality, can explain a pronouncement so thoroughly inappropriate when applied to other kinds of enjoyment, especially those tied most closely to the preservation of a self capable of initiative and responsibility: it would be surprising, to say the least, were Levinas to characterize the daily satisfaction we obtain from eating, drinking, and sleeping as "wicked and egoist and cowardly." Then again, at issue here may be not so much *aesthetic* enjoyment as aesthetic *enjoyment*. For there is nothing in *aisthēsis* itself or in Levinas's description of it to indicate that sensation or sensibility is always or uniformly enjoyable.[24] That art should involve "something inhuman and monstrous" (RS, 11/786), that it should induce a "passage from oneself to anonymity" or a return to "the impersonality of the element"—this clearly suggests that aesthetic experience extends beyond enjoyment, and if "bathing in the element" can yield the highly pleasurable "oceanic" feeling of which Freud speaks,[25] it may just as well lead to the terror of drowning. "Frightening,"[26] of course, is not the only word Levinas uses to convey the impression made by what he invites us to think of as the dark or nocturnal side of the element, the so-called *il y a* or *there is*. In fact, it is more often of "horror" that he speaks in reference to our apprehension of it. But these terms alone, so starkly contrasting with *enjoyment* or *enjoyable*, are enough to suggest that we have not lost the thread of Levinas's ambivalence toward the aesthetic. And it is certainly noteworthy that, in *Totality and Infinity*, the description of the element in conjunction with enjoyment concludes on a somewhat foreboding note, having precisely to do with the *there is*, and that this development, when reprised some fifty pages later, then moves from the *there is* to the face.[27]

For a description of the *there is*, however, Levinas himself refers us to *Existence and Existents*.

Since the *there is* is by definition indefinable, it is not surprising that, in order to "define" it nevertheless, Levinas should resort to a number of strategies. The first of these consists in turning the language of ontology back upon itself, beginning with the term "being in general." Simply put, what the qualifying "in general" requires us to think is being devoid of particular beings, devoid of any and all entities disclosed or disclosable as such by the subject. That there should remain, after this sweeping negation, something like being in general is then taken to mean that somewhere in the economy of being there is a weakness or failure of negation. Given further that, as in the "nothingness" of Sartre's *Being and Nothingness*, the phenomenal subject *is* negation—in other words, the "empty space" or interval of nonbeing whereby, effacing itself, subjectivity discloses being—it would seem to follow that the failure of negation is attributable to this subject. Yet Levinas makes it clear that being in general or "existence without existents" exceeds nothingness only because it also precedes and conditions the constitution or what he calls the "hypostasis" of the subject that brings negation to the economy of being.[28] More to the point here, one cannot ascribe the failure of negation to the phenomenal subject for the simple reason that this subject is undone by the *there is*. Or, as Levinas observes: "The *there is* transcends interiority as well as exteriority and does not even make it possible to distinguish them" (*EE*, 57/94). Indeed, as vague as all this may sound—and *should* sound—it is precisely what we have already encountered in the transformation of perception into sensation, where the interval between subject and object becomes a proximity of the image to a gaze that, deprived of the distance required to disclose, comprehend, and act, is captivated or, to borrow Blanchot's term, "fascinated."[29] Hence a second discursive strategy adopted by Levinas, which supplements the otherwise monotonous description of the *there is* as at once a nothingness and an indeterminate something or as the presence of an absence, and which appeals figuratively to sensory experience, either visual, as in "a swarming of points" or "a density of the void," or auditory, as in a "murmur of silence" or a "rustling" (*EE*, 59, 63, 63–64, 65/96, 104, 109).

But as in Blanchot—and in a manner whose pertinence to Levinas's thought could hardly be exaggerated given the phenomenological tradition from which he emerged, with its reliance on a metaphorics of vision and especially of the light that makes it possible—the *there is* is here most consistently thematized as "the night." And it is perhaps especially in this thematization that we discover a fundamental and decisive dissymmetry in being. For the night as Levinas understands it is not the symmetrical counterpart of the day, the mere absence of light in a phenomenal world otherwise unaltered: "There is a nocturnal space, but it is no longer empty space, the transparency that both separates us from things and gives us access to them, by which they are given. Darkness fills it like a content; it is full, but full of the nothingness of everything" (*EE*, 58/95). The alterity of this darkness with respect to the phenomenal same and other of the day and *its* night—an alterity that will lead Blanchot to speak of "the *other* night"—is such that it may even announce itself in plain daylight, as Levinas well knew when reflecting many years later on Blanchot's story "The Madness of the Day," and as he already suggests here: "One can also speak of different forms of night that occur right in the daytime. Illuminated objects can appear to us as though in twilight shapes" (*EE*, 59/97).[30] And it is in keeping with this nocturnal otherness that, approaching the *there is* from yet another angle, he singles out from its possible effects a common everyday experience.

Distinguishing this experience both from the consciousness or wakefulness of the day and from the unconsciousness or sleep of its counterpart, Levinas writes, under the heading "Insomnia":

The impossibility of rending the invading, unavoidable, and anonymous rustling of existence manifests itself particularly at certain times when sleep evades our appeal. One watches on when there is nothing to watch and despite the absence of any reason for remaining watchful. The bare fact of presence is oppressive; one is held by being, held to be. One is detached from any object, any content, yet there is presence. This presence that arises behind nothingness is neither *a being*, nor consciousness functioning in a void, but the universal fact of the *there is*, which encompasses both things and consciousness.

The distinction between the attention turned to objects, whether they be internal or external, and the vigilance absorbed in the rustling of unavoidable being, goes further. The ego is swept away by the fatality of being. There is no longer any outside or any inside. Vigilance is absolutely devoid of objects. This does not amount to saying that it is an experience of nothingness, but that it is as anonymous as the night itself. Attention presupposes the freedom of the ego that directs it; the vigilance of insomnia that keeps our eyes open has no subject. It is the very return of presence into the void left by absence—not the return of *some thing*, but of a presence; it is the reawakening of the *there is* in the heart of negation. It is an indefectibility of being where the work of being never lets up; it is its very insomnia. (*EE*, 65/109–10)

There is a seemingly counterintuitive but nonetheless inescapable resemblance between insomnia as Levinas evokes it here and the aesthetic experience discussed earlier. Indeed, in "Reality and Its Shadow," he describes this experience in terms virtually identical to those in which he conveys insomnia: "It is a mode of being to which applies neither the form of consciousness, since the I is there stripped of its prerogative to assume, of its power, nor the form of unconsciousness, since the whole situation and all its articulations are, in a dark light, present" (RS, 4/775). Moreover, not only is the term "participation," borrowed from Lucien Lévy-Bruhl,[31] associated with insomnia or vigilance in *Existence and Existents* (*EE*, 60/99) and with aesthetic experience—including the enjoyable variety—in "Reality and Its Shadow" (RS, 4/774–75), but in both instances Levinas highlights the features of passivity (or fatality) and impersonality or anonymity. Yet the questions to which this gives rise are plain to see. For how then does one explain the difference between enjoyment and insomnia, or what, as I have pointed out, Levinas often calls "horror" ("The rustling of the *there is* is horror" [*EE*, 60/98])? Are these, after all, merely the terms of a symmetrical relation reflecting his ambivalence in matters aesthetic? And if so, what becomes of the fundamental dissymmetry of the *there is* with respect to the phenomenal world, which Levinas takes such trouble to thematize in "the night"? The answer, I would argue, lies in the temporality of the aesthetic.

In "Reality and Its Shadow," Levinas introduces rhythm, in addition to plasticity, as a basic feature of the aesthetic, meaning by this "not so much an inner law of the poetic order as the way the poetic order affects us" (RS, 4/774). The importance of rhythm for his thinking supposedly derives, in other words, not from temporal structuration but from its potentially mesmerizing effect, akin to participation where, as in the primitive religions studied by Lévy-Bruhl, the boundaries between the self and the external world, including other selves, are seemingly dissolved in mystical ecstasy.

Of course, one should exercise all due caution when speaking of such dis-
solution, no less than when weighing a statement such as that, in the *there
is*, there is "no subject," for these expressions openly resort to the negation
whose failure they are supposed to convey, and thus, instead of pointing to
a subjectivity irreducibly other than and arguably more fundamental than
that of the phenomenal world, misleadingly suggest that the only alternative to the phenomenal subject is its own negation. Caution of the sort is
called for especially where the difference between kinds of subjectivity is at
stake, as in this passage, in which, contrasting the aesthetic with a phenomenal subject to which he imparts a decidedly ethical inflection, Levinas
speaks of works of art as

> closed wholes disengaged from reality and whose elements call for one another
> like the syllables of a verse, but do so only insofar as they impose themselves
> on us. *But they impose themselves on us without our assuming them.* Or rather, our
> consenting to them is inverted into a participation. Their entry into us is one
> with our entry into them. Rhythm represents a unique situation where we
> cannot speak of consent, assumption, initiative, or freedom, because the
> subject is caught up and carried away by it. The subject is part of its own
> representation. (RS, 4/774–75)

Although the definition of works of art as "closed wholes" is certainly open
to debate, what must be stressed here is that, from the perspective implied
by this quotation, their putative "disengagement" has already been (re)
framed by what we have seen Levinas call "a world of initiative and responsibility." Were this not the case, "our consenting to them" would clearly be
impossible, just as it would be impossible to describe that consent in the
terms earlier cited, such as "irresponsibility" and "evasion." In short, and at
the unavoidable risk of tautology, it must be acknowledged that the inversion of consent into participation is voluntary: it presupposes and remains
enframed by the phenomenal subject and its world. The result, as we shall
see, is that rhythm cannot be divorced from temporality after all.

In the phenomenal world, subjectivity can ensure the disclosure, manifestation, or presentation of being in its identity only within the temporal
mode of identity, that is, within a synchronic present. As Levinas puts it in
his essay on testimony: "Since being, by its essence, appears, consciousness
is consciousness of . . . , whereby all that might escape presentation, all that

might signify beyond the synthesis of the present, presents itself, is put together, and synchronized" (TD, 101/104). To be sure, despite advances made toward his later ethics in texts of the same era as "Reality and Its Shadow"—namely, *Existence and Existents* and *Time and the Other*[32]—there is in "Reality and Its Shadow" little indication of Levinas's subsequent view that synchrony as such is ethically suspect insofar as it forecloses access to the time of the other or, which amounts to the same, insofar as it immobilizes time itself.[33] In fact, as we have noted—and odd as it must strike those who have come to Levinas through his mature work—the world of which synchrony is a constitutive feature serves in this essay as the touchstone of the ethical. And yet it is also for its "stoppage of time" (RS, 8/782), for its immobilization of the instant, which otherwise, although synchronic, would be evanescent, that Levinas levels what may be his strongest accusation against the aesthetic, associating it with idolatry. What could motivate this negative judgment of one synchrony or rhythm in light of another if not the sense that, by its existence alone, art testifies to a weakness of the negation that powers the dialectic of time and that thus insures the evanescence of the instant?[34] And how could the phenomenal subject produce the "bad" synchrony of art if that subject itself were not produced by a temporality of which its own present is not the governing principle? How else, if not by what Levinas calls the *entretemps* or the "meanwhile"?

The "stoppage of time" imputed to the work of art is qualified when Levinas immediately adds, still in reference to time, that the aesthetic is "rather its delay behind itself" (RS, 8/782). Moreover, this qualification reflects an effort to substantiate what he has already said about the image: "To say that an image is a shadow of being would in turn be only to use a metaphor, if we did not show *where* the hither side we are speaking of is situated" (RS, 8/781). As we have seen, however, the image is, for him, indissociable from a duality in being, and specifically from the "relationship between the thing and its image" that he calls "resemblance." Indeed, it is in the course of articulating this resemblance in the schematized thing that Levinas remarks of those features pertaining to its image that they "remain as it were behind its being." His emphasis on the "meanwhile" as time's own "delay behind itself" makes it clear, therefore, that the "meanwhile" denotes the temporality of resemblance, or rather resemblance *as* temporality. And what the French term *entre-temps* or "between time(s)" makes equally clear is that, like being in general, whose persistence beyond the negation of all beings attests to its having preceded their constitution, this temporality must be thought as a relation on the "hither side" of the terms to which it gives rise, as a difference from which temporal sameness or identity in the form of the instant or the present emerges through repetition or re-semblance alone. The notion of the *entretemps* thus evokes first of all, to use another of Levinas's terms otherwise employed exclusively in connection with the ethical, the "diachrony" of the aesthetic, which, in its dissymmetrical relation to the synchrony of the phenomenal world, can only prove disruptive or arrhythmic. As Levinas plainly states: "The *there is* lacks rhythm" (*EE*, 66/111). Like the *there is* as a night that will never become day, furthermore, the "meanwhile" is "a future forever to come" (RS, 9/782), the shadow of time. And like the experience of the night, that is, like insomnia, the experience of the "meanwhile," where "the power of freedom congeals into impotence," where "this present, impotent to force the future, is fate itself" (RS, 9/783), is not a matter of consent.

Fortunately, however, this analysis itself need not be prolonged indefinitely but can lead back to issues left in abeyance and eventually allow us to resume the discussion of testimony. Thus, with the "meanwhile" in mind, I would mention one last strategy to which, in *Existence and Existents*, Levinas resorts for the evocation of existence without existents, which consists in drawing from tragedy, especially that of Shakespeare, exemplifications of the *there is* as a *haunting*. "Hamlet recoils before the 'not to be' because he has a foreboding of the return of being ('to dye, to sleepe, to sleepe, perchance to Dreame'). In *Macbeth*, the apparition of Banquo's ghost is also a decisive experience of the 'no exit' of existence, its phantom return through the fissures where one had driven it out" (*EE*, 62/101).[35] In sum, says Levinas, "this return of presence in negation, this impossibility of escaping from an anonymous and incorruptible existence, constitutes the ultimate depths of Shakespearean tragedy" (*EE*, 61/100–101). Of course, Levinas is well known for his literary references, which, in my view, are seldom if ever allowed either to problematize the particular point they are intended to illustrate or to disturb in any way the general framework within which they are ventured.[36] I do not plan to pursue this metacritical line of thought here, as I am concerned for now just to clarify the reasons for which the experience of the *there is* would lead Levinas to Shakespeare or the tragic. To judge from the statements just quoted, there are at least two of these. On the one hand, since the *there is* precedes the constitution of the self or subject, it can only appear by returning; and although on returning it can appear to the subject in the guise of a self-identical being, it can just as well appear as the shadow or indeed the shade, the revenant, the ghost that it is. On the other hand, since the principle of identity established by the subject does not govern the *there is* from which the subject itself derives, neither the subject nor the world over which it presides is ever free or "quit" of the *there is*. It is for both of these reasons, but especially the second, that Levinas makes a second reference to the tragic, in which Racine's *Phaedra* is less important in itself than in the commentary it elicits from the philosopher:

> Horror carries out the condemnation to perpetual reality, the "no exits" of existence.
>
> The sky, the whole universe is full of my ancestors.
>
> Where may I hide? Let me flee to infernal night!
>
> But how? There my father holds the urn of doom.
>
> Phaedra discovers the impossibility of death, the eternal responsibility of her being in a full universe in which her existence, an unbreakable commitment, is no longer in any way private. (*EE*, 62/102)[37]

To any reader reasonably familiar with Levinas's work as a whole, the description of Phaedra's discovery, if encountered in another text or simply out of context, would immediately be taken to refer to the ethical, and especially to the infinity of responsibility and the exposure of the self to the other. For that matter, it could be so understood in this context as well. Yet it also and obviously pertains to what Levinas defines as the fundamental experience of the aesthetic and suggests that, beginning with the motif of haunting, we might pursue the relation between the aesthetic and the ethical beyond the somewhat formal analogy earlier drawn in the discussion of sensation.[38]

Let me briefly recall this analogy, if only because it allows us to make of form itself a substantive issue. The point, then, as we saw, is that what the image of Levinas's schematized person and the epiphany of the other's face both offer to sensation exceeds the objective form imposed by perception, and in so doing reveals an alterity that manifestation or disclosure can only dissimulate. As I pointed out in reference to the image, however, Levinas's description ascribes agency to the image itself instead of to the gaze that apprehends it, which, on the contrary, is disempowered when the distance of perception yields to the proximity of sensation. This would be the moment to rephrase that claim in an important way, in order to underscore what the experience of the aesthetic and the ethical encounter of the other have in common for the subject involved in them. For in both cases, what takes place should be thought of as the undoing of agency as such, since the other who approaches in the aesthetic no less than in the ethical realm is precisely *not*, according to Levinas, another subject endowed with the agency of which the first just happens to have been dispossessed. In other words, there recurs in the aesthetic as in the ethical a passivity that Levinas will characterize as "an-archic" because, without being or having a determinable origin in its own right, it belies the originarity of the phenomenal subject, lying on the "hither" side of that subject and of the distinction it initiates between activity and passivity. For that subject, furthermore, accustomed as it is to its freedom, initiative, and power, the recurrence of "this passivity more passive still than the passivity conjoined with action" is a serious matter, since what returns is, as Levinas repeatedly insists, "the passivity of a trauma" (*OB*, 115, 111/146, 141). Indeed, there would appear to be a fairly strict correlation between the degree to which ethical and aesthetic experience overlap and the degree to which, with the exception of the erotic,[39] the *aisthēsis* in question is of the distinctly unpleasant kind—a correlation borne out even on the level of terminology: the encounter of ethical as of aesthetic alterity is an "exposure" likely to induce "insomnia"; the "invasion" of the night finds its ethical counterpart in one's being "hostage" to the other; and, as the example of Phaedra amply demonstrates, there is in the "horror" of the *there is* a very tangible sense of "persecution."[40] This intersection or, better, this intrication of the ethical and the aesthetic in the matter of trauma suggests that the undoing of form in which we discovered their formal analogy has to do with the very substance of subjectivity. It also helps to clarify Levinas's ambivalence about art—and, in some measure at least, to dispel the confusion this ambivalence inevitably creates in the minds of his readers—by tracing *within* the aesthetic the distinction between an experience of suffering that aligns it with what R. Clifton Spargo has aptly termed Levinas's "revaluation of unpleasure as the very sign of ethics" and Levinas's view of "the most common and ordinary experience of aesthetic enjoyment," which is supposedly inimical to the ethical relation but somehow continues to haunt it.[41] At this point, nonetheless, the question arises whether the dissymmetrical distinction within aesthetics can shed any light on the dissymmetry in Levinasian ethics.

This question affords us still another opportunity to consider Levinas's schematized person, who, as we have observed, "does not make us forget, does not absorb, cover over entirely" the features that, exceeding "the identity of his substance," combine to form a "caricature" of his face. Although this caricature or exaggeration clearly has to do with the excess of the person's image relative to his objective form, the comic impression it implies, were it even of the sort to elicit genial rather than derisive laughter, can seem rather incongruous in the quoted passage, especially when contrasted to the tinge of melancholy evoked by the features of the schematized thing, "like the 'old garments' of a soul that has withdrawn from that thing." Indeed, when Levinas later insists that *"every image is already a caricature"* (RS, 9/783), the meaning imputed to the word *caricature* derives primarily from the immobilization of time that he associates with the tragic. In the very next sentence, he adds: "But this caricature turns into something tragic" (RS, 9/783). If we now inquire where the tragic is to be found in his schematization of the person, however, the answer is not as readily forthcoming as one might expect. Yet comments by Robbins may well point the way:

> But there is something about the analogy that Levinas proposes—reality is to image as face (*face*, not yet *visage*) is to caricature—that, especially from the vantage point of *Totality and Infinity*, gives pause. The face, as Levinas will define it, is never reducible to its plastic image: it gives itself as form *and* also exceeds the form. To *miss* the way in which the face also exceeds its form, to have an image of the face, *to image* a face, is to turn it into a caricature, frozen, petrified, a mask. The whole possibility, indeed, the very temptation, of violence is inscribed in the face's presentation as form or image. . . . In short, the analogy suggests that no aesthetic approach to the face could also be ethical. There is no *ethical* image of the face; there is no ethical image.[42]

Robbins here accurately renders Levinas's thinking about the possibility of violence in the presentation of the face and also, at its most extreme, his view that the aesthetic and the ethical are incompatible. The analogy she draws from "Reality and Its Shadow" is indisputable as well. As we have seen, however, the face of the schematized person is the locus both of ontological self-coincidence or identity, that is, of objective form, *and* of its excess or alterity in the image, whereas in the central statement of the passage just quoted, "image" is equated with the very form—"frozen, petrified"—that it exceeds. I would argue, therefore, that this statement should be rephrased, since "to *miss* the way in which the face also exceeds its form" is precisely *not* "to have an image of the face" but rather to *miss that image itself*—which is further to say that, far from being incompatible, the ethical and the aesthetic are absolutely inseparable. Robbins, who is well aware of the tensions in Levinas's thought, also provides a clue to the necessity of this restatement, which should lead us in turn to the place of the tragic in the schematized person and an answer to the question concerning ethical dissymmetry.

I take it that, although from a strictly grammatical point of view the verbal component of "to have an image of the face" is both active and transitive, the apposition and italicization of "*to image* a face" is meant not only to convey a more immediate transitivity but to emphasize the *act* of a phenomenal subject. If so, it makes a certain sense to (re)define the image in the terms established by this subject, that is, as a form exhibiting the identity imposed on all beings by the disclosive "subjectivity that effaces itself." But as I have argued at considerable length, what Levinas regards as the fundamental experience of the aesthetic—the horror of the *there is*, the insomnia of the (other) night, the passivity of fascination—*precedes* (and exceeds) the advent of this subject and is in no way governed by its initiative or freedom, its power or its will. In fact, if the caricature of the schematized person's face can be said to turn tragic, it is not only because the caricature evokes that person's mortality, but also and especially because, like a corpse, the face in its resemblance "already bears in itself its own phantom, it presages its return" (*EE*, 61/100) *for* the gaze of one whom the inevitability of the other's death and its "return" in memory leave entirely powerless. For Levinas to conceive of this return or "re-presentation" as an act of the subject it disempowers is thus to reverse the genesis of that subject, to make of an effect the cause of its own cause. It is also to convert the aesthetic in general, from which the phenomenal subject emerges, into that subject's own work, and hence into an art that, modeled necessarily on disclosure, is no less necessarily confined to the most conventional mimesis. And to define the image of the other's face as a self-identical form attributable to the phenomenal subject is, finally, to make that subjectivity responsible for the mortality conjured up by the image: it is, in short, and if only symbolically, to transmute mortality into murder.

That the ethical relation according to Levinas, in which one's responsibility for the other precedes and exceeds one's ability to assume it, finds its basis in such a reversal is a rather large claim, whose fuller substantiation must await the last section of this chapter. For now, I wish to focus on the most immediate and noteworthy aesthetic consequence of the relation, to which Levinas alludes at the end of "Reality and Its Shadow." Assuming once again that art is ethically suspect insofar as it consigns alterity to the identity of form, Levinas advocates a "philosophical criticism" that "integrates the inhuman work of the artist into the human world" (RS, 12/788). Of course, this criticism sounds rather suspect since, as we have seen, (re)framing art within the world of disclosure has the very effect that Levinas would ostensibly like to dispel. In addition, given the limited scope of his essay, he admits that "we cannot here broach the 'logic' of the philosophical exegesis of art" (RS, 13/789). It is instructive nevertheless to consider that, in order to do so, as Levinas remarks in his concluding sentence, "one would have to introduce the perspective of the relation with the other, without which being could not be told in its reality, that is, in its time"—and that, from the aesthetic point of view, the task resides in this: "the immobile statue has to be put in movement and made to speak" (RS, 13/788). Thus, the philosophical critique of art, informed by the notion of ethical alterity, seeks to salvage the reality of being from its shadow, to rescue its time from the nightmarish "meanwhile," to reclaim the human figure from the death-like plasticity of the statue by translating the image into words, the visual into the verbal (as the necessity of being's being "told" [*dit*] already indicates). The ethical motive of this aesthetic translation or transformation is not difficult to detect, for, as I earlier noted, phenomenology or phenomenological ontology has always relied on "sight" as its privileged access to truth—to truth understood, precisely, as disclosure. Like much of Western thought, it therefore runs the risk, in Levinas's eyes, of idolatry, whereas "hearing" apparently allows us to avoid that risk altogether, while incurring no others of its like or magnitude.

Yet this is clearly not the case, and Levinas knows it. What remains unsaid and perhaps unthought in "Reality and Its Shadow" and other texts of its era is therefore not that language is prone to its own plasticity, of which

Levinas demonstrates an awareness in discussing narrative discourse (RS, 10/784), but that this plasticity can take hold of philosophical discourse as well, can freeze or petrify a proposition no less than a story, can synchronize both "A is A" and "Once upon a time." Before undertaking the critique of art, then, philosophy must attend to its own aesthetic, lest the ethical alterity to which it strives to be true fall hostage to its representation. This critique can be seen at work, moreover, when, in *Totality and Infinity*, for example, Levinas no sooner thematizes the other as a face than the face itself is translated as "expression" or "language" (*TI*, 181–82/157) or when, in *Otherwise than Being*, he thematizes the relation to that other as a saying whose resulting said, like a statue "put in movement and made to speak," must in turn be "unsaid" (*OB*, 155/198). But the fact that every utterance produces a statement requiring the utterance of a differing restatement means that the critique internal to philosophy, or what Levinas calls "skepticism"—which, significantly for our purposes, he characterizes as the "shadow" or "ghost" (*revenant*) of philosophy (*OB*, 168, 171 / 213, 218)—is, in principle, endless. Indeed, as he plainly argues toward the end of *Otherwise than Being* (165–71/210–18), it is the discursive embodiment of ethical infinity.[43] Its endlessness is also arguably the reason for which the philosophical critique of art never became a major concern of his, since the aesthetic turns out to be inextricable from the ethical perspective in which critique takes philosophy itself as its object.

As it happens, however, the critique foreseen at the end of "Reality and Its Shadow" is already practiced in the body of the essay, at least in the schematizations with whose discussion we began this long excursus and which now lead us back to testimony. Since we are concerned at this point only with the schematized person, let me recall having left off with the idea that the schematization is essentially a way to figure aesthetic reception and that the pertinence of this figuration depends on certain features of the person, including but not only his gaze. Let me recall as well that, from among these features, the analyses of sensation, the *there is*, and the temporality of resemblance eventually drew attention to the "caricature" the person "bears on his face, alongside of its being with which he coincides," that is, to what aesthetically exceeds this self-coincidence or identity, the image of mortality and, as such, the haunting harbinger or memory of a death with ethical implications for the survivor whose gaze apprehends it. I turn here to this gaze, or rather, to the situation of address that frames it, in order to see whether or how the schematized person's own gaze reflects an effort to fulfill the responsibility of critique as Levinas states it: "the immobile statue has to be put in movement and made to speak."

I previously described the framework of Levinas's schematizations in terms of *Mitsein* or being-with, as a situation in which the author and his reader(s) face in the same direction and the schematized person is objectified by their gaze. This description remains valid to the extent that the person is considered *as* an object, as a being that coincides with or is identical to itself. For that matter, it may also serve in the case of his image insofar as this image, just like the object, is represented, in its absence, by a written text. In both cases, the schematized person is presumably dispossessed of any real gaze, of eyes that actually see. Yet if the framework so understood is not exactly wrong, it is certainly insufficient and quite possibly misleading. To begin with, Levinas introduces his schematization with the statement: "Here is a person," where *here* and the other indexicals it implies, such as *now, I,* and *you,* define an instance of discourse or situation of address in which interlocutors *face each other* (at least initially). This is not to say that the framework in question exhibits the im-mediacy that Levinas predicates of the ethical encounter. But neither should one assume that it is of a mediated nature because the material absence of the interlocutors to each other and to the object of their discourse necessitates the medium of writing. In fact, it matters not at all whether Levinas's invitation to imagine the person he portrays is written or spoken. For let us imagine a situation in which the philosopher and his interlocutor(s) *are* together and in the presence of the object. Since Levinas obviously intends for this object—this person—to serve as an example (of being), what concerns him is not the person in his own right, seen from every angle and with all of his features, but only the "version" most likely to achieve the purpose of exemplification. It is not enough, therefore, to show him; Levinas must also talk about him, and must do so in a certain way. Or rather, it is not even necessary to show him, since his exemplary status lies exclusively in the image conjured by his description. The mediated nature of this face-to-face thus has nothing to do with writing as a substance distinct from speech, but derives instead from a necessary reliance on language per se. The second point to be made here (the first being, again, that the framework of Levinas's schematization is fundamentally dialogical), which I will formulate as a question, is this: If, on the one hand, such presumably direct interlocution is mediated by the "aboutness" of language, so that the relation between first and second persons "passes through" the third, and if, on the other hand, reversing the direction of Levinas's schematization, which proceeds from the general to the particular, we move from the particular instance of discourse that frames this schematization to the general terms in which he speaks of the ethical encounter—can it not be said, very much against the grain of Levinas's own thinking, that this encounter is never immediate or direct but always born of the indirectness of signification itself?

Of course, according to the logic of figuration at issue here, the answer to this question and even the plausibility of the question itself will depend on what can additionally be said about the schematized person, and especially about his gaze. In this respect, we might do well to ask why, in the first place, one would think that he has none, that he is blind. Presumably, it is because "he" is not a person at all but a representation. Yet it should also be recognized that this representation, while mediated by Levinas's description, is otherwise a product of our imagination, and hence that how we "see" the represented person's gaze reflects the quality of our own "vision." Does this mean that we, too, are blind? And if so, in what sense? Perhaps, first, insofar as this very figuration escapes us, so that, like Gyges, or like the "subjectivity that effaces itself," we see without being seen, or rather see without seeing ourselves being seen. Perhaps as well, then, to the extent that, in order to avoid the gaze that looks back at us from within, we project its deprivation onto another. Perhaps, finally, when we assume, in our literal-mindedness, that it is indeed a matter of vision, without pausing to consider that we only see blindness in the represented person if our own gaze immobilizes him, be it as an object or an image.

What most concerns Levinas, however, is neither the object nor the image, but their relation, their "resemblance." What most concerns him is that "being is not only itself," that in this very proposition the copula *is* identifies being as difference, and that this difference, this relation preceding the constitution of its own terms, is nevertheless itself not a matter of being but of time. The purpose of the schematization is therefore not only or even primarily to illustrate the nature of these terms, but through them to suggest, from "the perspective of the relation with the other," that the otherness of the person lies as well in a relationality that cannot be shown but only signified. Its purpose, in thus "making the statue speak," is to alert our gaze to its otherness by requiring us to *listen*.[44]

―――――――――――

In light of all this, it might be helpful to reread the passage from "Truth of Disclosure and Truth of Testimony" in which Levinas defines art as a schematization of being that testifies to the first of these truths:

> In its most elevated meaning, testimony can doubtless be understood as the schematization of the abstract concept of being in the concreteness of the subject. Art would testify to the truth according to such a schematism. But once again, the structure of discovery reappears in the schema. The disclosure of being governs testimony. The *concreteness of the subject* in which *being* is schematized and which is studied by the critic or the historian or the philosopher of art, is placed on the side of being. *Before* being, the *subject of knowledge* effaces itself. (TD, 100/103)

Now if the aforegoing reflections do not render this statement any less puzzling, at least for the moment, they may still be of use in explaining *why* it is puzzling (their next and more important purpose being, of course, to inform the critique of Levinas's philosophy of testimony). Again, nowhere in the other texts we have examined nor, to my knowledge, in any texts other than these does Levinas associate art with disclosure. On the contrary: either art is associated with the *there is*, which precedes the world of disclosure and returns to haunt it in radically estranging or defamiliarizing ways— and which too, in its arrhythmia and traumatizing sensibility, is indissociable from the ethical—or else art is (re)framed within the world of disclosure but precisely not *as* disclosure, since it does not directly present being but indirectly re-presents it, and is for that reason both devoid of intrinsic cognitive value and potentially deceitful, that is, ethically suspect. In short, by defining art as disclosure, Levinas locates it exactly where it does *not* belong in the economy of being. What is more, this anomalous move dates from the later years of his career, when, although by no means divesting himself entirely of the ambivalence about art already discussed in these pages, he nevertheless appears to consider in a more positive light its intersection with his understanding of ethics.[45]

Most striking of all, however, is that Levinas acknowledges even in earlier years an aesthetic "model" other than the classical and conventionally mimetic one to which he tends for the most part to refer and whose otherness poses an even greater challenge to the idea of art as disclosure. Thus, in "Reality and Its Shadow," he concedes that in "modern literature" (among whose antecedents he includes "Shakespeare, the Molière of *Don Juan*, Goethe, Dostoyevsky" [RS, 13/789]), the philosophical critique of art he has in mind is already incorporated into the work of art itself. And in *Existence and Existents*, he actually describes at some length an art that openly resists its subjection to phenomenal subjectivity and its integration into the world of disclosure, an art unmistakably and not accidentally resembling the kind of which Adorno states, as we saw in Chapter 3, that it "dismantles" its own illusion:

> Thus we can understand the quest of modern painting and poetry, which attempt to preserve the exoticism of artistic reality, to banish from it that soul to which visible forms are subjected, and to remove from represented objects their servile function as expressions. Whence the hostility toward the subject, which makes painting into literature; the preoccupation with the pure and simple play of colors and lines offered to sensation, for which the represented reality counts in its own right and not through the soul it envelops; the correspondence between objects, between their facets and surfaces, foreign to the coherence of the world; and the care taken to merge the various planes of reality by introducing a real object in the midst of painted objects or their remains. There is in all of this the intention to present reality as it is in itself and after the world has come to an end.
>
> The explorations of modern painting in their protest against realism come from this sense of the end of the world and of the destruction of representation it makes possible. The meaning of the liberties that the painter takes with nature is not correctly appreciated when they are taken to proceed from the creative imagination or the subjectivity of the artist. This subjectivity can only be sincere if, precisely, it no longer claims to be vision. As paradoxical as it may seem, painting is a struggle with vision. It seeks to extract from the light beings that are otherwise integrated into a whole. To look is to be able to describe curves, to sketch out wholes whose elements are mutually integrated, horizons in which the particular appears by abdicating its particularity. In contemporary painting, things no longer count as elements of a universal order that the gaze embraces as a perspective. On all sides fissures appear in the continuity of the universe. The particular stands out in the nakedness of its being. (*EE*, 55–56/89–90)[46]

What Adorno terms the "dismantling" of illusion seems to find a counterpart here in what one might call "unworlding," whereby art contests not only its own conventions but also, outside of art, those that determine particular beings as mere functions of the synchronic universe into which they are integrated. This unworlding is no more a purely formal matter in Levinas than is dismantling in Adorno: as dissimilar as these thinkers may appear in other respects, they both recognize in art—and do so in a similar manner—the potential to resist reification. And for Levinas, one could scarcely imagine an aesthetic more attuned to ethical alterity than the one summarized in his last sentence: "The particular stands out in the nakedness of its being."

This, at any rate, should suffice to underscore, by contrast, the puzzling character of his definition of art as disclosure in "Truth of Disclosure and Truth of Testimony." It may also suggest, after all, a solution of sorts, or at least a clearer sense of what could motivate this anomaly, namely, the need to maintain the distinction between disclosure and testimony not, as I earlier proposed, by *associating* but rather by *identifying* a dimension of experience that exceeds this distinction with the term at whose expense the argument is pursued. For as we have seen, even where Levinas attempts to relegate art to an associate or secondary status within the economy of disclosure, as a mere representation affording "the most common and ordinary experience of aesthetic enjoyment," his more fundamental understanding of the aesthetic, rooted in the *there is*, returns to haunt if not actually to undermine that effort. Better, then, to have done with the aesthetic altogether by conflating it with the phenomenal.

And yet there is no obvious reason to expect that the definition of art as disclosure will forestall this problem, to which, on the contrary, we should remain attentive when he reframes the question of testimony:

> The truth of testimony is certainly irreplaceable everywhere the subject is
> not just the instance that welcomes the manifestation of being but also the
> exclusive sphere of "subjective experiences," the enclosed and private domain
> that opens itself to universality and inspection only through the story that the
> subject makes of these. But do saying and testimony contribute only a means
> of communication and intersubjective control to the experience of subjective
> being? (TD, 100/104).

Presumably, this is the very question that, as I earlier noted, Levinas finds "suppressed" by the conception of testimony as disclosure—a question alluding not only to another kind of testimony but, in the first place, to another experience of subjectivity. However, the manner in which he here introduces the question indicates *both* an effort to maintain the distinction between the truth of disclosure and the truth of testimony *and* an implicit recognition that neither testimony nor its subject can be accommodated by this distinction. The result is an ambiguous statement indeed: on the one hand, Levinas refers to a subject that is *not* the subject of disclosure ("not just the instance that welcomes the manifestation of being") and the truth of whose testimony is qualified by an adjective reserved exclusively, in his work, for the ethical subject, to wit, "irreplaceable"; on the other hand, the distancing quotation marks surrounding "subjective experiences" and their characterization as "the enclosed and private domain that opens itself to universality and inspection" suggest that at issue is the very testimony of which he has already stated that it can be conceived "only in relation to the disclosed being which remains the norm." Were there any doubt about this, it would be dispelled by his equating such testimony with a "story," which for him—notwithstanding the multiple temporalities engaged by storytelling, the radical transformations of narrative discourse during the twentieth century, and the sophisticated aesthetic awareness of which we know Levinas to be capable—means a closed, static whole, a synchronic said. As he broaches the "other" truth, then, Levinas carries with him conceptions of subjectivity and testimony whose ambiguity is bound to resurface in the exposition of that truth.

Referring to consciousness as a "structure of the psychism," he prefaces this exposition by asking another question no less rhetorical than its predecessor: "Is not calling into question such a structure of the psychism to hint at a role for testimony—and for saying itself—that would be more directly 'veritative' than the one they play when transmitting or communicating ontological experiences?" (TD, 101/104). Still, neither the rhetorical nature of this question nor the rather contrived term "veritative" should be allowed to cloud our view of the shift here announced from an ontological to an ethical register. Given in particular that, as far as the ethical relation is concerned, "more direct" means, for Levinas, *better*, it seems safe to say that the truth of testimony in its "more directly 'veritative'" role will reside not in disclosure but rather in something like faithfulness to the sincerity of the relation. In order to understand this truth, however, it is first necessary to understand this relation and its saying.

In the ethical relation as Levinas describes it in "Truth of Disclosure and Truth of Testimony" (101–2/105–6) and countless other texts published before and after, I encounter an other who is unlike me in a number of respects. Arguably the most fundamental of these is temporal: the time of the other, or diachrony, disrupts the rhythm of my existence, the synchronic present in which, like and with other subjects, I go about the business of preserving myself in being, remembering the past and anticipating the future as mere modes of that present. Diachrony is thus not to be understood as the evanescence of the present or as a succession of presents but rather as a temporality without presence: its only sameness or identity consists in the repetition of difference, whereby a past that was never present returns in a future that never will be. This time is nonetheless far from a purely formal structure, since it effects the return of a substantial relation, compared by Levinas to "a sensibility coming back perhaps to the for-the-other of maternity, on the hither side of being; to maternity, which is the very gestation of the other in the same, of the other in the same that would be the psyche itself" (TD, 102/105). In other words, the other I face in the ethical encounter is not only another person but a recurrence of the very relationality, the otherness or difference, of which my own self is born. And the consequences of this dissymmetry are undoubtedly among the most "Levinasian" features of Levinas's thought. On the one hand, insofar as my self is born of this "other in the same," of this "for-the-other" that Levinas also calls "responsibility," responsibility will always exceed my freedom or power to assume it. This, indeed, points to the infinity of the relation whereby I am responsible not only for the other I encounter but, in principle, for *all* others. On the other hand, since responsibility is, as it were, "imposed" rather than chosen, and hence does not derive from a reciprocity to which I would consent as a free and autonomous self, I find myself responsible for an other who is not responsible for me. In fact, the ethical effect of this dissymmetry constitutes the principal and possibly the only difference between ethical alterity and the *there is*: my "election" by the other elicits my singularity or "unicity" from what, as we have observed, is otherwise an anonymous or impersonal existence—a point to which I will return momentarily.

Yet by far the most important feature or, more precisely, the most important synonym of ethical relationality for present purposes is "substitution."[47] This central Levinasian concept has proven and was bound to prove controversial for historical reasons, to which I will also return in a moment. Here I wish to stress that in the for-the-other already mentioned lies, according to Levinas, "*the very possibility of giving*," which at its most material can be understood as "tearing-away-from-oneself-for-the-other in giving-to-the-other-the-bread-from-one's-mouth," but can also appear as the "giving of a sign," as "signifyingness" (*signifiance*), "signification," or "Saying" (TD, 102–3/105–7).[48] To this it must be added that, since the past of the "other in the same" was never present and thus remains immemorial for the conscious subject, whose sameness resides first of all in its interiority, the other who disruptively returns to the world established by that subject will inevitably appear to come from the outside—and hence that, in the ethical encounter, saying is not initially my own but rather summons me to respond *to* the other and to do so through substitution *for* the other.[49] In both instances, however, saying is testimony: my response is "a sign given to the other . . . a sign given of this giving of a sign—the pure transparency of a confession—testimony," while "Saying, before stating a Said—and even the Saying of a Said—is the approach of the other and already testimony" (TD, 103/107).[50]

That said, saying as testimony cannot be further articulated independently of the questions raised here by and about the language of philosophy itself. Indeed, in their very abstractness or generality, the statements just quoted leave us wondering, for example, *to what* saying is supposed to bear witness. What, in other words, is testimony *about*? The answer, too, is abstract: "There is no testimony but that of the Infinite [*Il n'y a de témoignage que de l'Infini*]" (TD, 104/107). In addition, the French *de* and the English "of" are sufficiently equivocal to imply that the Infinite is both the object and the subject of testimony, at once that to which witness is borne and the one who bears it. This equivocation evokes in turn two equally disquieting and by no means incompatible possibilities, namely: that Levinas's philosophy of testimony, for all its talk of "the other," amounts to an exercise in discursive solipsism, and that the alterity in question is of a religious otherworldliness such as to obscure history and its victims, including "those who were closest among the six million assassinated by the National Socialists" and "the millions on millions of all confessions and all nations, victims of the same hatred of the other man, the same anti-semitism," to whose memory *Otherwise than Being* is so movingly dedicated. This is obviously not to say that such consequences are *intended*, and yet, since Levinas chooses an idiom that so easily lends itself to them, it will not do, either, simply to wish them away. It may thus be wisest to reserve judgment until the concluding section of this chapter, where we will presumably be better equipped to hear in the generality or abstractness of that language the singular inflection of his voice.

But it is precisely in regard to subjective singularity that a second and no less daunting question arises. For assuming, with Levinas, that the Infinite still testifies *through* us, who among us gives voice to its testimony? Who truly speaks and, in so doing, also bears witness to the "other" subjectivity within? As I remarked just a moment ago, what supposedly differentiates ethical alterity from the anonymous or impersonal otherness of the *there is* is that the former singularizes me by making me uniquely responsible. In order to secure this differentiation—and yet at the same time, it seems, to suggest that its terms are not always clearly distinguishable—Levinas resorts, as with the *il y a*, to the third person pronoun *il*, coupled with the Latin demonstrative *ille* ("that"), to form the word *illeity* (*illéité*). Illeity can be understood in a number of ways: as the Infinite in the finite, for example, as transcendence in immanence, or as the universal in the particular. In this last formulation especially, *illeity* could be grouped with indexicals, whose universal function consists in referring to a particular instance of discourse, and which include demonstratives such as *this* or *that* as well as *here*, *now*, and the personal pronouns. Thus, *illeity* could also be understood as the third person in the first (or the second).[51]

Now it is arguably in these terms that we can most instructively schematize or exemplify the problem of singularity posed here by the idiom of philosophy. Like Descartes's "cogito, ergo sum," the statement "I am responsible" qualifies as a philosophical proposition only if it is universally true, if "I" is implicitly quoted or mentioned rather than used, if it means "the person who utters the present instance of discourse containing *I*" or "whatever speaker is designating himself,"[52] and the statement accordingly reads *not* "I am responsible" but "The 'I'—that is, every 'I'—is responsible." In other words, the ethical responsibility that particularizes me as a subject is stated in a universalizing language that must, in effect, deny my singularity by ascribing the same responsibility to all subjects. The third person of illeity, which purportedly supersedes that of the *il y a* and which remains in tension with the first, is in turn superseded by the ideal and exclusive third, the universal subject that speaks the truth of disclosure to, and of, everyone. Irreplaceability is itself replaced by interchangeability, recalling the reification of the individual that so preoccupied Adorno in his reflections on culture after Auschwitz. More serious still, in the very notion of substitution, Levinas's ever greater insistence on both the absolute alterity of the other and the uniqueness of the responsibility it imposes on me effects a meeting of extremes, a confusion of same and other that renders substitution itself not only cognitively but ethically untenable against the background of an event—the Holocaust—in which the roles of perpetrator and victim demand to be carefully discriminated, and for which the ascription of universal responsibility would be thoroughly irresponsible. Indeed, one can and should ask whether Levinas's obsession with the absolutely other does not lead him perilously close to a kind of "participation" when he declares, most notably, that subjectivity is "responsibility for the very persecution it suffers," that "in the trauma of persecution," to be a subject is "to pass from the outrage undergone to the responsibility for the persecutor and, in this sense, from suffering to expiation for the other" (*OB*, 195n26, 111 / 156n26, 141). Does this mean that survivors of Auschwitz should bear witness to the Infinite by atoning for the crimes of the SS?

Presumably not—but the apparent naïveté of the query merely highlights the precariousness of an ethics that remains at so far a remove from history. In this light, and given the relational nature of Levinasian subjectivity, a third and equally fundamental question is raised, namely: Who is "the other"? Who summons me to respond, commands me to listen, to witness witnessing? Who qualifies as this other?

There is, to be sure, a sense in which any subject qualifies as the other, a sense in which illeity yields to the universal third but in which substitution is constrained by "the comparison of incomparables," so that, "as a subject incomparable with the Other, I am approached as an other like others, that is, 'for myself'" (*OB*, 158/201). This is the sense of what Levinas calls "justice": "Justice is necessary, that is, comparison, coexistence, contemporaneousness, assembling, order, thematization, the visibility of faces, and thus intentionality and intellect, and in intentionality and intellect the intelligibility of a system, and thence also a copresence on an equal footing as before a court of justice" (*OB*, 157/200). Yet if illeity inscribes the very possibility of justice within the ethical relation, for Levinas it is perfectly clear that the ethical relation comes first and that in its radical dissymmetry I am never the other. The answer to the question of the other must therefore be sought elsewhere, beginning presumably with the thematizations to which he so often has recourse: the stranger, the widow, and the orphan, as mentioned at the outset, but also the weak, the poor, even the enemy (*EE*, 95/162), and, especially in *Otherwise than Being*, the neighbor (*le prochain*). As Levinas never tires of repeating, the language of philosophy poses a problem here as well, since in the thematization of the other the alterity of the other is obliterated by the sameness of the thematization itself: the category of "the stranger" excludes precisely what would differentiate one stranger from another, or for that matter, a stranger from a widow. Furthermore, one could say that the thematizations chosen by Levinas constitute an issue in their own right insofar as they reinforce the distance between the philosophical and the historical other. The stranger, the widow, and the orphan are at a safe—in their case, biblical—remove from us, as are, in their generality, the weak and the poor. Even the neighbor and the enemy seem abstract, or at least as remote respectively from such lesser abstractions as the Palestinian and the Nazi as is the exemplification in the "as simple as 'hello' [*simple comme bonjour*]" (TD, 103/107) of an ethical relation more often described as traumatic. At the same time, one cannot help but wonder whether there is room in this array for the survivor, to whom Levinas only occasionally refers and then in a tone lying somewhere between the dismissive and the disparaging, as though to suggest that survivors as such have little if anything to show for themselves aside from the shame of living on.[53]

It seems obvious, however, that no remark of Levinas's in regard to survivors or survival could fail to allude, whether intentionally or not, to Levinas himself (a point to which, again, I will return in the last section of the chapter), and that the ways in which he chooses to thematize the other as well as his very decision to speak and, in so doing, to inflect the generalizing language of philosophy can be (re)framed as signs of the singularity of his thought. To read them as such is not to identify Levinas with what he says but to listen to what he says in relation to its saying, as he says in *Otherwise than Being*:

> I still interrupt the ultimate discourse in which all discourses are stated, in saying it to the one who listens to it and who is situated outside of the Said that the discourse says, outside of all that it includes. This is true of the discourse in which I am engaged at this very moment [*Ce qui est vrai du discours que je suis en*

train de tenir en ce moment même]. This reference to an interlocutor
permanently breaks through the text that the discourse purports to weave in
thematizing and enveloping all things. In totalizing being, discourse as
Discourse thus belies the very claim to totalize. This reversion is like the one
brought out by the refutation of skepticism. In writing, of course, saying
becomes a pure said, a simultaneity of saying and its conditions. A book is
interrupted discourse catching up with its own breaks. But books have their
fate; they belong to a world they do not encompass but that they recognize in
being written and printed, in getting prefaced and foreworded. They are
interrupted and call for other books and in the end are interpreted in a saying
distinct from the said. (*OB*, 170–71/216–17)

What may appear initially most remarkable about this philosophical reflection on the language of philosophy is at once the tacit admission and the
explicit contradiction of Levinas's own phonocentrism, that is, his tendency
to favor speech over writing in accordance with the immediacy that, for
him, characterizes the ethical relation. To judge by this passage, and as I
earlier claimed in reference to the situation of address in "Reality and Its
Shadow," what matters is not the distinction between speech and writing
but language or signification per se, and especially interlocution. Yet the
point of central importance to the passage has to do not only with interlocution as a thematization of the ethical relation but as it is practiced in the
sentence "This is true of the discourse in which I am engaged at this very
moment."[54] Granted, this sentence, like the one that precedes it and those
that follow, is a said, a statement that can be read, quoted, and discussed independently of its utterance. But unlike the others, it openly enacts or
performs the saying without which there would be no said (and in so doing
contests the very possibility of a pure said). To be convinced of this, one has
only to compare the first two sentences by substituting in each case "the
'I'" for "I": whereas "the 'I' still interrupts the ultimate discourse in which
all discourses are stated" does not betray but rather confirms the sense of
interlocution as a thematization of universal validity, in "this is true of the
discourse in which the 'I' is engaged at this very moment," the universality
of "the 'I'" clearly clashes with the particularity of the indexical "at this
very moment." And from this, there is much to be learned about saying, the
said, and testimony.

To begin with, it is hardly accidental, given what we know of the ethical
relation according to Levinas, that in this instance of discourse the most

obvious disruption of the said is temporal in nature. Indeed, although "at this very moment" may carry the same *sense* for both writer and reader, it does not have the same *referent*, that is, does not refer to the same moment. The synchrony of the said is thus disrupted by the diachrony of saying, all the more plainly so as by the time the reader realizes that "I" here designates a particular first person, that first person, dissimulated until now by the universal third of the said, has already passed, leaving only "I" as his trace and indicating that he can only return as such because he is intrinsically a relational being. Moreover, that this person only "appears" through an unanticipated recurrence attests to an essential dissymmetry between particularity as the instantiation of a relation in which I am always, first, a second person, and particularity in the form of an alter ego whom I may take the initiative to engage in dialogue, in an exchange of words from positions that are themselves exchangeable. In other words, the other who gives me a sign is not only a person, the singular *ille* of illeity, but its universal *il* as well, the very giving of the sign, the surplus of relationality, capable of eliciting from me in turn the other-in-the-same that precedes and conditions my self-sameness or ipseity. What such dissymmetry suggests, finally, is that, although saying is dissimulated by the said it produces, the said always bears the trace of the saying without which it would not be possible, and hence that every said exceeds itself or is, simply put, intrinsically ambiguous. This is true of what I am saying at this very moment. And presumably, it is also true of testimony.

We may well wonder, then, why Levinas insists at times on so sharp a distinction between saying and the said, on a saying either antecedent to the said, as in "Saying, before stating a Said—and even the Saying of a Said," or independent of it, as in "Saying without the Said" (TD, 105/109)—and why, accordingly, he so sharply distinguishes the truth of testimony as he understands it from the truth of disclosure. One way to approach this question is to translate Levinas's language into more narrowly linguistic terms. What I have in mind is not so much a distinction analogous to that between saying and the said, namely, the distinction between utterance and statement, for we have already discussed the basis of this analogy in the corresponding notions of diachrony and synchrony. Rather, since saying has to do with a dissymmetrical situation of address focused on the addressee, I would suggest that it can be instructively compared to what Roman Jakobson calls the "conative" function, which "finds its purest grammatical expression in the vocative and imperative."[55] In Levinas's work, the imperative is most often exemplified by the commandment "Thou shall not kill," while the vocative is most often conveyed by the addressee's exemplary response to the "accusative" nature of the ethical encounter, that is, "Here I am." Furthermore, since saying does command response, it can also be compared to what, as we saw in Chapter 3, Jakobson names the "phatic" function,[56] which serves not to communicate but to establish or reestablish communication, as in the question "Are you listening?" or the commandment "Listen!" Motivating these comparisons, however, is not only a dissymmetry in the situation of address but the fact that all of the functions and categories they invoke pertain to utterances that are *not* subject to truth conditions. One does not inquire, concerning a commandment or a question, whether it is "true," since its role within language cannot be evaluated according to the cognitive criteria governing descriptive propositions (the linguistic modality of disclosure). To the extent that these criteria serve to establish the universal validity of such propositions independently of any interlocution, exemplifications of saying that draw on the grammatical or linguistic forms just mentioned—the imperative and the vocative, the conative and the phatic—can be said not only to emphasize, by contrast, the singular situation of address in which saying is anchored, but also to suggest a role for saying and for testimony "more directly 'veritative' than the one they play when transmitting or communicating ontological experiences."

Of course, one could object that they remain exemplifications, illustrations whose value in a philosophical text is determined by the degree to which they conform to the notion of saying in its descriptive generality. Or, to phrase this otherwise, one could say that they are, in essence, quotations whose function as such requires abstraction from the very context on which their irreducibility to truth as disclosure is predicated. Thus, to quote the commandment "Thou shall not kill" is not the same as to command "Thou shall not kill," since it replaces a singular with a universal situation of address, in which the positions of addresser and addressee can be occupied by anyone and in which this symmetry or interchangeability means, for Levinas, that nothing is ethically at stake. Whether such propositions be considered exemplifications or quotations, therefore, they do not appear to escape "the truth correlative to being."[57]

Yet this awareness amounts to an unsaying of the said insofar as it attests to the saying that the said necessarily presupposes and that is in this sense "before" or "without" any said. At the same time, it is important to recognize the paradoxical belatedness of this attestation and the temporal reversal that accounts for it: for just as the face of the other that precedes disclosure can appear only in an image exceeding disclosure, thus giving the impression that otherness succeeds the establishment of identity, so "testimony" to the precedence and independence of saying in relation to the said that silences or betrays it can lie only in a subsequent unsaying of the said. In this, moreover, the ethical stakes could not be higher:

> Thematization [is] certainly indispensable—for the meaning itself to take shape—a sophism inevitably committed wherever philosophy arises—but [is also] a betrayal that the philosopher must reduce. A reduction that must continually be undertaken because of the trace of sincerity that the words themselves bear. A testimony borne by every saying as sincerity, even when it is the Saying of a Said that the Said dissimulates; but a dissimulation that saying always seeks to unsay [*dédire*]—which is its ultimate veracity. In the game that activates the cultural keyboard of language, sincerity and testimony signify through the very ambiguity of every said, through the greeting it offers to the other. (TD, 107/110).

To define the ultimate veracity of saying as the *un*saying of the said is to locate the ethical itself in an aesthetic of dismantling. Not only is this aesthetic inseparable from the ethical relation, therefore, but if, as Levinas claims, "sincerity and testimony signify through the very ambiguity of every said," then on the one hand, sincerity cannot simply be equated with straightforwardness (*droiture*) and opposed to indirectness, since it signifies precisely in its detour through the said, and on the other, the truth of testimony cannot simply be divorced from the truth of disclosure, since it is through disclosure or the art it governs that truth *as* sincerity must pass. Despite its abstraction and its overwhelming concern with the ethical, Levinas's philosophy of testimony implies an aesthetic in which mimesis or representation is rendered ambiguous by the indexicality it presupposes and that, like the index, points to what is not represented.

It is, I shall argue, an aesthetic of this kind that we discover in the initial framing of Jorge Semprun's testimonial memoir, *Literature or Life* (*L'écriture ou la vie*), to which I turn, as though at Levinas's suggestion, to interrupt the discourse of philosophy with that of literature. In order to prove genuinely interruptive, of course, Semprun's text must not be viewed in the way in which, as I see it, Levinas himself tends to view literature, that is, as a source of particular examples for the illustration of general theses, whose particularity thus remains subordinate to the overarching sameness of philosophy. Rather, his memoir should be approached as the enactment of an interlocution that would not only resist its quotation by Levinas but is capable of altering our reception of Levinas's philosophy. In its irreducible particularity, *Literature or Life* should also bring us a better understanding of the questions earlier raised concerning what testimony is about and who gives and receives it.

At first glance, Semprun's memoir may appear simply to reprise a topos that dates from the earliest days of testimonial literature. The beginning of *Literature or Life* stages a scene of reception whose attendant anxiety informs the very telling of the story, and in so doing clearly recalls the dream of the unlistened-to story in Primo Levi's *Survival in Auschwitz*, discussed at the end of the previous chapter, as well as the tale of Moshe the Beadle in Elie Wiesel's *Night*. In Wiesel's text, Moshe, having miraculously survived deportation and mass murder, returns to the village of Sighet to warn his fellow Jews of what awaits them, only to be rebuffed at every turn: "People refused not only to believe his stories, but even to listen to them."[58] The twelve-year-old Elie, with whom Moshe otherwise enjoys a privileged relationship for having acted as the boy's master in their secret discussions of Kabbalah, represents no real exception to this rule since, as Wiesel points out, "I did not believe him myself."[59] As a character within the story, the young Wiesel can thus be said not only to figure the group responsible for silencing Moshe but to *pre*figure for the narrator of that story—that is, for the older Wiesel, who, like Moshe, is a surviving witness—the possibility of an audience no less disbelieving or indifferent than Moshe's own.

The anxiety of reception to which Wiesel testifies is articulated somewhat differently by Levi, who, as we have seen, recounts a recurring dream he had while incarcerated, the gist of which was familiar to many if not all of his fellow inmates at Auschwitz-Monowitz. In this dream, Levi has survived Auschwitz and returned home, but, while describing camp life to his sister and other, unidentified listeners, he seems no sooner to have gained than lost their attention: "I cannot help noticing that my listeners do not follow me. In fact, they are completely indifferent: they speak confusedly of other things among themselves, as if I was not there. My sister looks at me, gets up and goes away without a word."[60] Here, in the time of the story itself (yet due, of course, to the peculiar temporality of dreams), the character is already cast or forecast as a narrator, while the recurrence of the dream and its prevalence among the prisoners suggest that the anxiety of reception may prove indissociable from survival, susceptible perhaps of being assuaged in some measure but never entirely dispelled.

However, since I wish to compare Levi's and Wiesel's texts with Semprun's and cannot do justice here to any of them in their full complexity, what I would emphasize is simply this: both Wiesel and Levi articulate a narrative configuration in which the attention of those who come to occupy the position of their virtual addressee, of the "you" or second person implied by their use of the first person or "I," is focused on other actual addressees within the story itself, with respect to whom the second person comes simultaneously to occupy the position of the third. To read Levi or Wiesel is therefore not only to read, as second person, the first person account of their experience as victims and survivors of the Holocaust, but to read, as third person, other second persons and hence comparatively to read oneself as a member of the same community.

To be sure, the pluralism of witnessing witnessing is a potential inherent in any testimonial interaction. Nevertheless, whereas in *Night* and *Survival in Auschwitz* the question of reception is raised by the response to a tale of atrocity, in *Literature or Life* it arises before a single word has been uttered. Semprun's memoir opens with a chapter entitled "The Gaze," whose own beginning passage is worth quoting in its entirety:

> They stand amazed before me, and suddenly, in that terror-stricken gaze, I see myself—in their horror.
>
> For two years, I had lived without a face. No mirrors, in Buchenwald. I saw my body, its increasing emaciation, once a week, in the shower. Faceless, that absurd body. Sometimes I gently touched the jutting bones of the eye sockets, the hollow of a cheek. I could have gotten myself a mirror, I suppose. You could find anything on the camp's black market in exchange for bread, tobacco, margarine. Even tenderness, on occasion.
>
> But I wasn't interested in such niceties.
>
> I watched my body grow more and more vague beneath the weekly shower. Wasted but alive: the blood still circulated, nothing to fear. It would be

enough, that thinned down but available body, fit for a much dreamed of—although most unlikely—survival.

The proof, moreover: here I am.

They stare at me, wild-eyed with panic.

It can't be because of my close-cropped hair. Young recruits and country boys, among others, innocently wear short hair. It's no big deal. A shaved head never bothered anyone. Nothing frightening about it. My outfit, then? A curious one, I admit: mismatched cast-offs. But my boots are Russian, of soft leather. Across my chest hangs a German submachine gun, an obvious sign of authority these days. Authority isn't alarming; on the whole, it's even reassuring. My thinness? They must have seen worse by now. If they're following the Allied armies' drive into Germany this spring, they've already seen worse. Other camps, living corpses . . .

The stubble on my head, my worn and ill-assorted clothing—such particulars can be startling, intriguing. But these men aren't startled or intrigued. What I read in their eyes is fear.

It must be my gaze, I conclude, that they find so riveting. It's the horror of my gaze that I see reflected in their own. And if their eyes are a mirror, then mine must look like those of a madman. (*LL*, 3–4/13–14)

As in the case of Levi and Wiesel, the reader of Semprun's text witnesses, as a third person, the encounter of the survivor with others also in a position to witness his witnessing—except that, again, the survivor has yet to address a single word to those who stand before him (subsequently identified as "three officers, in British uniforms" [*LL*, 4/14]). What the passage accomplishes is to sharpen the focus of the gaze to which it refers at the outset. In its second half, the narrator conveys a testing of hypotheses from which it emerges that the self he initially saw in the officers' gaze ("I see myself") has in fact to do neither with his used and mismatched clothing nor with his virtually shaven head nor even with his severely emaciated body but rather with the horror of his own gaze. And this conclusion appears all the more pointed as the first half of the passage emphasizes the part of his body to which he himself had previously had no visual, but only tactile, access, namely, his face.

Equally important, the way in which these interlocking gazes seem to immobilize time itself is entirely in keeping with the historical context of the encounter: "It's April 12, 1945, the day after the liberation of Buchenwald," Semprun remarks—only to add, in reference to "the starving inhabitants of the Little Camp, the Jewish survivors of Auschwitz," that "Death is still a thing of the present" (*LL*, 13/25). This day can thus be said to pertain to an *entretemps* or "meanwhile," to a moment between the Holocaust and its aftermath, a moment suspended between past and future in which, while the killing appears to have stopped, the dying certainly has not. Moreover, the suspense of this moment is reinforced by the space of the encounter: although Semprun does not come across these officers at the gate to the camp but in or near the forest that lies outside of it (the *Buchenwald* or beech forest), the site represents a threshold at which inhabitants of radically heterogeneous worlds confront one another, at which a recently liberated inmate and messenger of death meets the eyes of men not only "from *before*" but "from the *outside*, emissaries of life" (*LL*, 14/26–27), with whom he has little but this paralyzed gaze in common.

The question remains, however, what the special significance of this encounter might prove to be for the giving and receiving of testimony. In referring to Levi and Wiesel, I have indicated how in each case the story includes an account of witnessing with more or less obvious implications for the telling and hearing of the story as a whole. In the scene staged by Semprun, one of the possible effects of witnessing seems paradoxically to precede its own cause inasmuch as the survivor sees fear in the officers' eyes before, he, the survivor, has even opened his mouth. As Ross Chambers has observed in an insightful reading of these pages, the opening scene of *Literature or Life* ends up focusing our attention on the response of the survivor: "How should the survivor respond to that fright? For Semprun, this becomes the defining question of aftermath, and the key problem of bearing witness. How to give an account of the experience that has left so readable a trace of horror? But also, how to do so in such a way as to counter the fright that makes strangers to Buchenwald inclined to shun both the survivor and the survivor's tale?"[61] And how, furthermore, can the response of the survivor help us to understand this opening scene as a framework for the relation between the writer and the readers of *Literature or Life*?

Finally addressing one of the officers, Semprun adopts, according to Chambers, "a tactics of indirection, more specifically of indexicality; that is, of representation through figuration":[62]

He stares at me, bewildered by fright.

"What's the matter?" I ask irritably, and doubtless harshly. "You're surprised to find the woods so quiet?"

He looks around at the trees encircling us. The other men do the same. Listening. No, it's not the silence. They hadn't noticed anything, hadn't heard the silence. I'm what's scaring them, obviously, and nothing else.

"No birds left," I continue, pursuing my idea. "They say the smoke from the crematory drove them away. Never any birds in this forest. . . ."

They listen closely, straining to understand.

"The smell of burned flesh, that's what did it!"

They wince, glance at one another. In almost palpable distress. A sort of gasp, a heave of revulsion. (*LL*, 5/15–16)

In this passage, the survivor shifts the officers' attention away from his gaze, to which he attributes the fright or horror he perceives in their own, toward the silence of the forest; that is, he verbally displaces the reception of his testimony from a visual to an auditory register. He then ascribes this silence, which they had not yet heard, to the absence of birds, itself the effect of smoke from the crematory or, more precisely, its smell, which they can only try to imagine. Thus, he proposes a series of signs that point to or figure, without purporting or promising to re-present, the horror of the camp and even suggest by their example that his gaze might itself be taken as such a sign, might become, as Chambers phrases it, "*readable* rather than threatening or frightful."[63] Admittedly, things do not appear to turn out this way for the three officers, who now "avoid looking at me," says Semprun. "'The crematory shut down yesterday,' I tell them. 'No more smoke over the countryside, ever again. Maybe the birds will come back!'" (*LL*, 10/22). Nevertheless, the officers do not recover from the initial shock of meeting the survivor's gaze, at least to judge by the subsequent and quite conclusive statement: "They're speechless, unable to face me" (*LL*, 14/27). But this outcome is not readable merely as a matter of the empirical contingency with which any witnessing survivor must reckon or of the fallibility of the "tactics" that Semprun adopts. Nor is it enough here to point out that this tactic of indirection has, after all, gained for the survivor more of a hearing than the officers' terror-stricken gaze would have led him to expect. What we need to consider, as I have suggested, is how the survivor's response to the officers might help to explain the framework established for Semprun's encounter with the readers of *Literature or Life*.

I would begin by noting that the tactical indirection or figuration so explicitly employed by the survivor in relation to the three officers *already* defines Semprun's approach to his readers in the opening passage of the memoir. That is, not only does Semprun, like Levi and Wiesel, position his readers as third persons witnessing, along with the narrator, another scene of witnessing (and thereby spare them being put "on the spot"), but a displacement analogous if not identical to the one mentioned a moment ago is operative from the very outset: just as the language of the survivor shifts the officers' attention from his own gaze to an ambient silence that remains in principle accessible to them but that signifies in turn a smell they are in no position to perceive, so the discourse of the narrator focuses the attention of his addressee on a purely visual phenomenon—the gaze—that no reader can directly witness. That these displacements are not identical testifies to the irreducible historical difference between the two instances of witnessing. That they are nonetheless analogous means, to quote Chambers again, that "like the officers, we are not direct survivors of Buchenwald and have not lived its *vécu* of death, but are situated . . . as creatures of aftermath."[64]

Precisely for this reason, however—precisely because we come, like the officers, "from the *outside*," having no direct or unmediated access to the Holocaust and specifically to the experience of its survivors—I would argue that discursive indirection can be employed not only to counter our horror but also to counter the illusion that the survivor's horror is our own. Indeed, it may be the tangibility of this illusion that explains at least in part the otherwise puzzling irritation or harshness of tone with which the survivor asks one officer: "'What's the matter?' . . . 'You're surprised to find the woods so quiet?'" While the survivor has just made a genuine effort to read in the officers' gaze the trace of atrocities he himself has witnessed, the officers, by contrast, do not construe the horror of the survivor's gaze as such a trace or sign but appear instead to reflect or mirror it, as though believing themselves to be in the immediate presence of its cause and hence appropriating or, to use the term borrowed by Levinas from Lévy-Bruhl, "participating" in the survivor's experience.

Similarly, the survivor can employ such figuration in order to avoid repelling those to whom he addresses his testimony, or to state this in positive terms, to draw them toward the experience he wishes to convey—but can also do so in order to establish an appropriate distance between his experience and their own and thus counteract or even forestall the kind of identification expressed in the officers' terror-stricken gaze. If therefore, as Chambers says, Semprun "does not launch into a description of the horrors of the camp,"[65] either with the officers or with his readers, it is not only to refrain thereby from exacerbating the fright of those witnessing his witnessing but to deny them even the momentary delusion, so easily fostered or abetted by a literal(ist) representation, that they, too, "were there." In the case of the officers, as I have observed, this tactical decision ultimately proves to be of limited efficacy, since the initial shock of identification yields to a no less excessive estrangement in which they avert their gaze altogether. In the case of Semprun's readers, however, toward whom he adopts a language subordinating representation to signification from the very beginning of *Literature or Life*, the relation to the witness is founded on a tension between proximity and distance or identification and estrangement, a tension indissociable from the only community available at once to the survivor and to the "creatures of aftermath."

Yet what is most noteworthy about the initial framing of Semprun's memoir lies in the position of the survivor. From a Levinasian perspective, to be sure, one could say that the survivor here represents an other disruptive of the same insofar as the officers represent a world whose zealous pursuit of the *status quo ante* is arrested by the discovery, in Semprun's gaze, of an unprecedented historical and moral catastrophe. But in an apparent reversal of the ethical relation, it is also this other, the survivor, who finds himself summoned, as it were, to respond to and take responsibility for these emissaries of the same. Indeed, Semprun's rhetoric of indexicality or indirection reflects his insistence on responding to the officers with a gaze that, unlike theirs, is neither "horrified" nor "stunned, almost hostile, and certainly suspicious," but "fraternal" (*LL*, 14, 16/ 27, 29).

This gaze seems to have originated in the look Semprun received from his former professor, Maurice Halbwachs, as Halbwachs lay dying in Buchenwald: "Dying," Semprun says, "he smiled, gazing at me like a brother" (*LL*, 23/38). Semprun nevertheless enlarges its scope to encompass a community of inmates and indicates repeatedly that the conjunction of fraternity and death was not fortuitous but essential. Thus, in his summation, he states in no uncertain terms: "Death was the substance of our brotherhood, the key to our destiny, the sign of our membership in the community of the living. Together we lived that experience of death, that compassion. . . . All we who were going to die had chosen the fraternity of this death through a love of freedom" (*LL*, 24/39). Needless to say, one may question the inclusiveness of this "we," as well as Semprun's entitlement to act as its spokesperson,[66] just as one may ask whether, under the circumstances, this uplifting affirmation of fraternity in death does not sound a rather incongruous note, all the more so as it is explicitly associated by Semprun with the Heideggerian notion of *Mitsein zum Tode* (being-with-toward-death). This may have to do, however, with "the youthfulness of Semprun's good-student persona and his enthusiasm for philosophical ideas"[67]—and with the fact that it was only after the war, when the young Semprun used Heidegger's term in conversation with someone who recognized it, that he learned of the philosopher's involvement with Nazism (*LL*, 91/124). In any case, it also goes without saying that these words were spoken, or rather written, by one who survived the "experience of death" constitutive of the community in question and who no longer belonged to that community except to the extent that the community persisted in or as memory. This is precisely what accounts for the specificity of his position: by the time Semprun encounters the officers just outside of the camp, he has himself already encountered within it an other or others to whom and for whom he must respond by translating or transposing the remembered gaze of their community to a world unacquainted with the experience that informs it. His responsiveness to the officers *is* this transposition.

But the position of the survivor can be further specified if we consider how Semprun is led to a fuller understanding of the officers' initial reaction:

> I'm struck by the idea, if one can call it an idea . . . struck by the sudden overwhelming feeling, in any case, that I have not escaped death, but passed through it. Rather: that it has passed through me. That I have, in a way, lived through it. That I have come back from it the way you return from a voyage that has transformed and—perhaps—transfigured you.
>
> I have abruptly understood that these soldiers are right to be afraid, to avoid looking into my eyes. Because I have not really survived death. I have not avoided it. I have not escaped it. I have, instead, crossed through it, from one end to the other. I have wandered along its paths, losing and finding my way in this immense land streaming with absence. All things considered, I am a ghost.
>
> Frightening things, ghosts. (*LL*, 14–15/27)

Recalling our earlier discussion of Levinas, especially concerning the ghost-liness of the *there is*, the survivor appears to the soldiers as what remains beyond the fullest negation of being, or rather, since this appearance is con-centrated entirely in his eyes, as what remains of the gaze when the distance from which it confidently governs the phenomenal world gives way to the invasive proximity of the image. The horror these officers see in Semprun's eyes is that of an insomniac (or, as he says, a madman), in whom the free-dom to open or close the eyes has yielded to an inability not to look. And the horror they evince in looking at him is not attributable solely to encounter-ing this hostage gaze but also and even primarily to recognizing themselves in it. For if, by definition, a ghost returns—and here, Semprun advisedly uses the word *revenant* (rather than *specter*, for example)[68]—if it is in the nature of a ghost to haunt, this is because it pertains to an internal other-ness of which the conscious self is the forgetting and which that self can encounter, therefore, only in the recurrence of an apparently external other. Indeed, without presuming to answer the question about the "identity" of the other in Levinas's philosophy of testimony, I would suggest that the sur-vivor sheds a new light on the exemplary figures to whom he does refer inso-far as all of them can be said to survive the forgetting of the very relationality to which they disruptively testify. And yet, it is also the case that from all of these figures—from "the stranger, the widow, and the orphan," the weak, the poor, the neighbor—the responsibility assumed at once toward those whose memory he carries and toward those to whom he communicates it certainly appears to differentiate the survivor, to make him (or her) not only other than the other of the same but other than the other, who, in the ethi-cal relation according to Levinas, bears no responsibility whatsoever.

At the same time, Semprun's understanding of the officers' fright af-fords a fuller view of what is involved in transposing the fraternal gaze of which he had been the focus. For like this gaze, his projection of it upon the three men is properly imaginative, drawing on the capacity for a substitu-tion constrained by the very difference that motivates it. To be more precise: while the survivor retains his irreducible otherness in regard to the men he encounters, his ability to put himself imaginatively in their place attests to the perspective of a third wherein dissymmetry allows of and even calls for comparison. The responsibility that Semprun takes on vis-à-vis the officers is thus not only a responsibility *for* the other but a responsibility *before* others. As Levinas puts it, "The *thou* is posited in front of a *we*" (*TI*, 213/188), or, in his definition of fraternity, "The relation with the face in fraternity, where the Other in turn appears in solidarity with all the others, constitutes the social order, the reference of every dialogue to the third party by which the *We* . . . encompasses the face-to-face relation" (*TI*, 280/257). So understood, fraternity is reflected in the very framework of the passage just quoted, where the survivor's imaginative projection with respect to his interlocutors is addressed to Semprun's readers *as* third persons.

One may wonder nevertheless whether Semprun, or rather my commentary on him, helps in any way to clarify the matter of what testimony is about. Does such concern with the framing of a testimonial memoir not come at the expense of the story it tells? For as I have pointed out elsewhere in this volume, Holocaust survivors cannot dispense with narrative and other conventions familiar to potential readers if they are to convey an experience with which most if not all of those readers are unfamiliar. To dismiss their stories as betrayals of their experience is merely to expose one's own unexamined assumptions (not to mention the presumptuousness of the judgment itself), such as that the Holocaust is intrinsically unrepresentable, or that it marks an absolute hiatus in history, rendering all previous forms of historical representation obsolete, or that in its very absoluteness it is of a quasi-sacred order and hence ought not to be represented. In Levinas's case, the tacit ascription of superiority to testimony as Saying is reflected in the definition of its counterpart as "the confession of some knowledge or of an experience by a subject" whose truths are "inferior, secondhand, and uncontrollable" in relation to the disclosive norm by which they are judged and by which such testimony is confined to a strictly documentary role, whether for juridical or historiographical purposes. And to suggest, like Levinas, that "transmitting or communicating ontological experiences" through "the story that the subject makes of these" does not fully deserve to be called testimony is to beg the question whether all testimony, at least by survivors of the Holocaust and other traumatic events, does not preeminently concern "the experience of subjective being," that is, matters of life and death. Indeed, if "the other" is not to become a mere word, then we must recognize to begin with that what it designates is indissociable from the body, including the body of a survivor's story. The story of Jorge Semprun is not that of Charlotte Delbo, the tale told by Elie Wiesel is not what

Primo Levi relates. These names are not only, as is said in the foreword to *Proper Names*, "the names of persons whose *saying* signifies a face,"[69] they are also the names of persons whose face shows itself in *what* they say.

No doubt. But as we have also observed, what they say has essentially to do with their having been denied saying itself, with the experience of a subject considered, by those with the say, unworthy of interlocution, unworthy of social as well as biological life. What their stories are centrally about, each in its own way, is the possibility of its telling, or rather, of its being heard. Pondering his own testimony, Semprun remarks:

> All you have to do is begin. The reality is there, waiting. And the words as well. . . .
>
> In short, you can always say everything. The "ineffable" you hear so much about is only an alibi. Or a sign of laziness. You can always say everything: language contains everything. . . .
>
> You can tell all about this experience. You have merely to think about it. And set to it. And have the time, of course, and the courage, for a boundless and probably never-ending account, illuminated (as well as enclosed, naturally) by that possibility of going on forever. Even if you wind up repeating yourself. Even if you remain caught up in it, prolonging death, if necessary—reviving it endlessly in the nooks and crannies of the story. Even if you become no more than the language of this death, and live at its expense, fatally.
>
> But can people hear everything, imagine everything? Will they be able to understand? Will they have the necessary patience, passion, compassion, and fortitude? I begin to doubt it, in that first moment, that first meeting with men from *before*, from the *outside*, emissaries of life—when I see the stunned, almost hostile, and certainly suspicious look in the eyes of the three officers.
>
> They're speechless, unable to face me. (*LL*, 13–14/25–27)[70]

Needless to say, this doubt did not prevent Semprun from embarking on his own "boundless and probably never-ending account," beginning with *The Long Voyage* (*Le grand voyage*) of 1963 and including, more recently, *What A Beautiful Sunday!* (*Quel beau dimanche!*; 1980), *Literature or Life* (*L'écriture ou la vie*; 1994), and *A Necessary Death* (*Le mort qu'il faut*; 2001). But the encounter with the officers described in "The Gaze" seems to have motivated the rhetoric of indirection by which, paradoxically, he turns readers to face him and invites them to speak in response. I would argue as well that Semprun's characterization of the putative ineffability of the Holocaust as an alibi is directed less at fellow survivors than at those to whom witnesses address themselves. In this light, the routinely repeated claim that the traumatic experience of Holocaust survivors is unrepresentable or unspeakable appears to stand in for a refusal to listen. Of course, this is not to say that those who make the attempt to listen can ever claim success, for it can hardly be a matter of success where listening itself is interminable.

These reflections on Semprun remind us that in the testimonial encounter with the other I am always initially a second person, one who is called upon to hear, and that only in response to my interpellation as such do I become a first person who listens (or not) and speaks. Not only Levinas's ethical philosophy but his philosophy of testimony as well can be said to originate in a sustained act of listening to which the philosophy bears witness less through its thematizations than through the endless critique of thematization it both proposes and undertakes. The interminability to which Semprun refers may, in this respect, lend a different and more instructive sense to Levinas's statement "There is no testimony but that of the Infinite." For although "the Infinite" may suggest an otherworldly transcendence, it does not have to be understood in this way, any more than the statement must be taken as a solipsistic credo. Rather, "the Infinite" can be read as the in-finite, as the in-finitude or nonfiniteness of testimonial interlocution, as the unsaying that, for both witnesses and those who witness them, attests to the ineliminable excess of any Saying over the Said it produces. For Levinas, this excess or surplus can mean "more," as in the economic or ontological excess of the *there is* over being and nothingness, or "better," as in the ethical illeity at once beyond and within the I-Thou relation.[71] And although what I have called the singular inflection of his voice may certainly be sought in other directions, including, at the most general level, his deep engagement with Judaism and his transformation of the phenomenology through which he came into his own as a philosopher, I would like to approach it here by way of the connection he articulates between the Infinite and survival.

In *Totality and Infinity*, Levinas, concerned to mark a temporal distinction between the two terms of his title, aligns the time of totality with history and even characterizes historians, albeit in a sense that is obviously distinct from the one in which I have used it here, as "survivors":

The being that thinks seems at first to present itself, to a gaze that conceives it, as integrated into a whole. In reality, it is only so integrated once it is dead. Life permits it an as-for-me, a leave of absence, a postponement, which is precisely interiority. Totalization is accomplished only in history—in the history of historiographers, that is, among the survivors. It rests on the affirmation and the conviction that the chronological order of the history of the historians outlines the plot of being in itself, analogous to nature. The time of universal history remains as the ontological ground in which particular existences are lost, are computed, and in which at least their essences are summed up. Birth and death as punctual moments, and the interval that separates them, are lodged in this universal time of the historian, who is a survivor. (*TI*, 55/26)

Clearly, historians are here considered survivors only in the sense that they stand temporally outside of the events whose narrative reconstruction they undertake. Yet this exteriority would be of little concern to the philosopher did it not entail reframing interiority so as to integrate it into a universal history where the punctual delineation of the individual's birth, life, and death mirrors the closure of the totality itself. For Levinas, the very form of traditional narrative historiography is of a piece with what one could call, in the language of *Otherwise than Being*, the reduction of diachrony to synchrony. This is why, furthermore, he wishes to forestall the notion that the time of infinity amounts to "the eternity of the soul," that is, an extension of synchrony before birth and beyond death:

But if the refusal to be purely and simply integrated into history indicated, according to the time of the survivor, the continuation of life after death or an existence prior to its beginning, beginning and end would in no way have marked a separation that could be characterized as radical and a dimension that would be interiority. For this would still be to insert interiority into the time of history, as though perenniality throughout a time common to the plurality—the totality—dominated the fact of separation. (*TI*, 57/28)

It seems safe to infer from this that the temporality of the Infinite must be sought in separation. And the most expeditious approach to their connection arguably lies in Levinas's somewhat idiosyncratic but nonetheless far-reaching interpretation of the Cartesian *cogito*.

What intrigues Levinas about Descartes—indeed, what constitutes for him, in the example of the *cogito*, the intrigue of subjectivity—is not only, as has often been said, that the thinking being in its finitude discovers within itself, in the idea of the Infinite, more than it can think, nor yet that its separation lies paradoxically in its relation to this exteriority that exceeds it, but that the same relation produces the *cogito* by means of a temporal reversal. As he explains:

> The *cogito* . . . attests to separation. The being infinitely surpassing its own idea in us—God in Cartesian terminology—subtends the evidence of the *cogito*, according to the third *Meditation*. But the discovery of this metaphysical relation in the *cogito* constitutes chronologically only the second step taken by the philosopher. That there could be a chronological order distinct from the "logical" order, that there could be several moments in the process, that there is a process—this is separation. By virtue of time, indeed, being is not *yet*—which does not make it the same as nothingness, but maintains it at a distance from itself. It is not all at once. Even its cause, older than itself, is still to come. The cause of being is thought or known by its effect *as though* it were posterior to its effect. We speak lightly of the possibility of this "as though," which is taken to indicate an illusion. But this illusion is not gratuitous; it constitutes a positive event. The posteriority of the anterior—a logically absurd inversion—is only produced, one would say, by memory or by thought. But the "improbable" phenomenon of memory or of thought must precisely be interpreted as a revolution in being. Thus already theoretical thought—but by virtue of a still more profound structure that sustains it, the psychism—articulates separation. Separation is not reflected in thought, but produced by it. For in it the *After* or the *Effect* conditions the *Before* or the *Cause*: the Before *appears* and is simply welcomed. (*TI*, 54/24–25)

Although it had not yet been coined at the time, Derrida's term "différance" could certainly be invoked to describe this "distance from itself," the difference through whose repetition the subject achieves its sameness or identity.[72] More important here nevertheless is the inversion effected by this repetition, or rather the ambiguity it fosters in turn: for while the *cogito* cannot but posit itself as the origin of a chronology based on its own temporal identity or synchrony, the infinite within its finitude also enables or compels it to recognize, as Levinas's argument makes clear, that this chronology reverses and transforms the "logic" of a time in which the past is never present and the future is forever "still to come." Most important, however, is Levinas's ascription of this ambiguity to memory as well as to thought: on the one hand, he claims that "the posteriority of the anterior—a logically absurd inversion—is only produced . . . by memory" (or thought); on the other hand, his commentary on Descartes no less forcefully implies that, like the *cogito*, like thought, memory is produced by the inversion to which the repetition of difference gives rise. This, as we shall see, is of crucial significance not only for his view of survival but also for the testimonial status of his ethical philosophy.

Having already aligned history with totality, Levinas further insists on the distinction between totality and infinity by opposing memory to history. But here again, as I have just suggested, the role of memory is thoroughly ambiguous:

> Memory retrieves and reverses and suspends what is already accomplished in birth—in nature. Fecundity escapes the punctual instant of death. Through memory, I ground myself after the event, retroactively: I assume today what, in the absolute past of the origin, had no subject to receive it and weighed therefore like fate. Through memory, I assume and call back into question. Memory realizes impossibility: memory, after the event, assumes the passivity of the past and masters it. Memory as an inversion of historical time is the essence of interiority. (*TI*, 56/26–27)

To a surprising degree, Levinas here anticipates the perspective of *Otherwise than Being*, where memory, like history, will be considered a mode of synchronization available to the conscious subject. This is foretold in the sense not only that memory, which "retrieves" and "masters" the past, appears to enact rather than be produced by the reversal of historical time, but that I can exercise it as a faculty by which to "ground myself" and "assume" a past that was not formerly present to me. Yet the concluding claim that "memory as an inversion of historical time is the essence of interiority" plainly maintains the distinction between history and memory, totality and infinity, echoing the otherwise somewhat incongruous statement that "fecundity escapes the punctual instant of death." What precisely is meant in this context by fecundity as a "triumph over death" is subsequently explained as follows:

> This triumph is not a new *possibility* offered after the end of all possibility—but a resurrection in the son in whom the rupture of death is embodied. Death—suffocation in the impossibility of the possible—opens a passage toward

descent. Fecundity is still a personal relation, though it not be given to the "I" as a possibility. (*TI*, 56–57/27–28)

To be sure, the influence of Christianity is quite pronounced here, and will become even more so in *Otherwise than Being*, albeit more in a sacrificial than a resurrectional mode.[73] For present purposes, however, I would emphasize what fecundity (rather obviously assimilated to paternity) has in common with maternity, namely, that both figure an other-in-the-same, an interpersonal or intersubjective relation that precedes and exceeds the autonomous self and opens, in the most tangible fashion, onto a past that this self cannot possibly remember and a future that will never be its own. Indeed, it is precisely in order to distinguish the kind of memory implied by this relation from memory as active remembrance or conscious recollection that Levinas stresses the matter of possibility: to say that fecundity is not "given to the 'I' as a possibility" does not mean that fecundity itself is impossible but rather that it is not subject to the power or will of the "I," that in the relation to the other the "I" returns instead to the "passivity of the past," to a past that "had no subject to receive it and weighed therefore like fate." Here again, Levinas anticipates *Otherwise than Being*, in which the "impossibility" of the ethical relation is of a piece with its immemoriality.

The point nevertheless, for us, is that I survive myself in the embodied other, or more precisely, in the other as embodied memory. Levinas insists that this embodiment is by no means strictly biological, for although fecundity, whether maternal or paternal, may serve as a readily intelligible "model" of the ethical relation, memory itself is fundamentally embodied in the sense that it pertains, regardless of any kinship, to a *positioned* subject, one in whom, moreover, its manifestation lies in the "recurrence" of sensation, that is, in what we have come to understand as the image. But the question that immediately arises, focusing our attention yet again on the language of philosophy (and much else, no doubt), is this: If the "I" survives itself—survives its self—in the other as embodied memory, is it not also the case that in the "I" as embodied memory the other itself survives? If so, then how does a relation on which philosophy thus inveterately imposes its own symmetrical syntax become as radically dissymmetrical as Levinas claims it to be? How is it that a statement from Dostoyevsky's *The Brothers Karamazov*, underscoring once more the appeal of Christian motifs, became, as his

biographer puts it, Levinas's *citation fétiche*, to wit: "Each of us is guilty before everyone for everyone, and I more than the others" (*OB*, 146/186)?[74]
Should we not take seriously, here in particular, Levinas's suggestion that
"all philosophical thought is based on prephilosophical experiences,"[75] and
give at least some consideration, with regard to him, to Nietzsche's claim
that "every great philosophy so far has been . . . the personal confession of
its author and a kind of involuntary and unconscious memoir"?[76] In short,
the question standing at the crux of this entire discussion concerns whether
or to what extent the responsibility that constitutes the singularity of the
subject in Levinas's ethical philosophy testifies to Levinas's own singular
response to surviving the Holocaust.

In this respect, it is worth noting that the reversal of historical time in
which Levinas sees the advent of memory is analogous to the causal inversion informing his view of ethical responsibility. Just as the *cogito* belatedly
posits itself as the origin of its own origin, so the ethical subject assumes
responsibility for what precedes it, *as though* it were the cause of its own
cause. It may be useful as well to recall Levinas's assessment of this "as
though": "We speak lightly of the possibility of this 'as though,' which is
taken to indicate an illusion. But this illusion is not gratuitous; it constitutes a positive event." In other words, from the point of view of the *cogito*,
"the posteriority of the anterior" is logically impossible; yet it is precisely
from this impossibility, from the fiction of the "as though," that the fact of
the *cogito* emerges. Similarly, although it may seem absurd to hold the ethical subject responsible for what preexists its own advent, therein above all
lies the responsibility Levinas ascribes to that subject. If this ascription still
strains belief, it may be helpful, finally, to consider what is plainly at stake
here. On the one hand, Levinas knows perfectly well and openly recognizes
that responsibility for the immemorial past does not derive from deeds that
one could not have committed. Rather, it originates in the relationality
whereby I am not only implicated in the deeds of others but also receive
before I can give, and whereby therefore I am constitutionally indebted. To
put it simply, responsibility is, from this angle, the *feeling* of guilt, a feeling
exacerbated, as we know, in the case of survivors, as Levinas suggests in a
statement all the more striking for its reliance on the "as though": "The
face is a trace of itself, given over to my responsibility and in regard to
which I am wanting and at fault, as though I were responsible for its mor-

tality and guilty for surviving" (*OB*, 91/115). On the other hand, it would be foolish to dismiss survivor guilt as "irrational," since it testifies to an attempt at narrative rationalization. As Susan Brison has pointed out, retroactive self-blame for trauma caused by others may well reflect an effort to impart some reassuring moral intelligibility to a world in which suffering is inflicted seemingly at random—as for an accident of birth.[77] In this light, one could find it difficult to distinguish self-blame from what Levinas calls "election."

Of course, Levinas is not the only one to have evinced a feeling of guilt for surviving the Holocaust. But he *is* the only one to have written *Otherwise than Being*. And in that work—dedicated, as we have seen, to the memory of all those millions victimized by "the same hatred of the other man, the same anti-semitism"—we might further inquire if the embodiment of this memory is to be found only in the narrative of self-blame that the ethical relation appears to allegorize or if instead it should also be sought in the ceaselessly repeated and increasingly exaggerated *telling* of the story, that is, in Levinasian terms, in the endless and ever more hyperbolic resaying of the said. One could easily ascertain this inflation through a studied juxtaposition of *Totality and Infinity*, where "alterity is only possible starting from *me*" (*TI*, 40/10) and the description of the dissymmetry to which I am subjected in the ethical encounter remains relatively sober, with *Otherwise than Being*, where I am only possible starting from an other for whom the burden of my responsibility can never find a saying forceful enough to convey it. But one can also judge the lengths to which Levinas is prepared to go from *Otherwise than Being* alone, where, in the section aptly entitled "Saying as Exposure to the Other," saying itself is characterized as one's being "without clothing, without a shell to protect oneself, stripped to the core as in an inspiration of air," as "exposing oneself to outrage, to insults and wounding," as a "denuding beyond the skin, to the wounds one dies from, denuding to death" (*OB*, 49/63). What these few from among hundreds of examples clearly suggest is not, as Levinas claims, that the putative immemoriality of the other renders it inaccessible to memory but that, within the implied narrative of self-blame, its memory is further embodied both in the thematization of the ethical relation as corporal persecution and trauma and in the relentless challenging of discursive limits.

If, however, I refer to this implicit narrative of self-blame, this thematization of the relation to the other as persecution and trauma, and this transgressive approach to limits as embodiments of memory, it is because in these respects Levinas's philosophy remembers the Holocaust by repeating it, by "acting out." In other words, Levinas's philosophy, and his philosophy of testimony in particular, can itself be considered a *kind* of testimony insofar as the ethical relation at its core is an allegory of post-traumatic memory. And here, once again, the relation between the ethical and the aesthetic in its fundamental sense as *aisthēsis*, as sensation, as embodied experience, is inescapable. Indeed, as the examples just cited indicate plainly enough, the discursive replication of traumatic experience in the ethical encounter of the other goes so far as to foster, in the survivor, a *resemblance* to the victim, as though responsibility *for* the victim, while unassumable in its infinity, nonetheless compelled an effort to fulfill it by being as much as possible *like* a victim. Moreover, even though the approach of this effort to its own fulfillment remains at best asymptotic, one reaches a point in Levinas's thought where the victimization of the survivor is so severe as to require the explicit recognition that the *il y a* is inextricable from illeity, that the *there is* persists in the experience of the ethical:

> But the absurdity of the *there is*, as a modality of the one-for-the-other, as suffered, *signifies*. The insignificance of its objective insistence, recommencing behind every negation, overwhelming me like a fated subjection to all the otherness to which I am subject, is the surplus of nonsense over sense, through which, for the *Self*, expiation is possible—the very expiation that the oneself signifies. The *there is* is the whole weight of the alterity borne by a subjectivity that does not found it. (*OB*, 164/208–9)

Yet it is not only as a "fated subjection" that the *there is* signifies. For at the point in question, where the survivor achieves, through an expiation bordering on expiration, such extraordinary proximity to the victim, the victim, who takes the survivor hostage, who persecutes and traumatizes, bears in turn a striking resemblance to the perpetrator—and the singularizing force of illeity verges on the vagueness, on the impersonality or anonymity of the *il y a*. No wonder, then, that we earlier encountered some difficulty in determining, from Levinas's philosophy of testimony, who speaks and who listens, since the reenactment of trauma in the account of the ethical relation blurs the very distinctions on which, according to Levinas's own thinking, an ethically informed justice would have to insist. No wonder, either, that some difficulty arose from the statement "There is no testimony but that of the Infinite." For where interlocutors are confused, what we hear through them is not a pure saying but "the mute and anonymous murmuring of the *there is*" (*OB*, 3/3).

Having just characterized the testimonial dimension of Levinas's philosophy as a discursive repetition or acting-out of trauma, however, I cannot very well conclude without asking whether this philosophy might *also* articulate, in some sense or to some degree, a mode of remembrance other than repetition, or a working-through of trauma, and whether therefore it might dispose of the transformative means to distinguish more clearly between the victim and the testifying survivor. For this purpose, I will refer to a partly autobiographical text in which Levinas himself "interrupts" the discourse of philosophy. In the last chapter of *Proper Names*, entitled "Nameless" and published in 1966, he observes:

> Over a quarter of a century ago, our lives were interrupted, and doubtless history itself. There was no longer any measure to contain monstrosities. When one has that tumor in the memory, twenty years can do nothing to change it. Soon death will no doubt cancel the unjustified privilege of having survived six million deaths. But if, during this stay of grace, life's occupations and diversions are filling life once more, if all the depreciated (or antediluvian) values are being restored, and all the words we thought belonged to dead languages are reappearing in newspapers and books, and many lost rights are again finding institutions and public force to protect them—nothing has been able to fill, or even cover over, the gaping pit. We still turn back to it from our daily occupations almost as frequently, and the vertigo that grips us at the edge is always the same.[78]

It would be difficult to find, at least in Levinas's own work, a more striking illustration of the *entretemps* or "meanwhile," the time of the *there is*, than this incessant recurrence of vertigo, not time itself but its image, "dead time" (*TI*, 58/29), time outliving itself in the person of the survivor. The same could be said of his reference to memory, which evokes, not a remembered image, but the image of memory itself as tumoral or cancerous, beset by a growth it cannot contain, a hypermnesia matched only by the hyperbolic sense of responsibility it entails. And this excess, at once aesthetic and ethical, has clearly to do not only with the magnitude of the Holocaust but with the burden that collapsed institutions let fall on individuals alone. For "what was unique between 1940 and 1945," says Levinas, "was the abandonment," and the realization that "settled, established humanity can at any moment be exposed to the dangerous situation of its morality residing entirely in its 'heart of hearts,' its dignity completely at the mercy of a subjective voice, no longer reflected or confirmed by any objective order."[79] Indeed, the emphasis on unique responsibility that so overwhelms, in his philosophy, any reliance on community can be said itself to reflect the uniqueness of this abandonment:

> One always dies alone, and everywhere the hapless know despair. And among
> the hapless and forlorn, the victims of injustice are everywhere and always
> the most hapless and forlorn. But who will say the loneliness of the victims
> who died in a world put in question by Hitler's triumphs, in which lies
> were not even necessary to Evil, certain of its excellence? Who will say the
> loneliness of those who thought themselves dying at the same time as
> Justice, at a time when judgments between good and evil found no criterion
> but in the hidden recesses of subjective conscience, with no sign from
> without?[80]

It is tempting to see Levinas's own answer to this question in what he construes as the exemplary response to interpellation by the other in the ethical relation, namely: Here I am. At the very least, one could say that no word more eloquently conveys the historical weight of this loneliness than the central term of his ethical philosophy, *separation*.

Yet, to return to our question, one may ask whether, in the very saying of this said, in the situation of address itself, there is not a reaffirmation of community, and even in the evocation of post-traumatic memory, a remembrance that distances the surviving witness from the event and its victims. For although, at the end of his more personal reminiscence, Levinas compares memory to a "gaping pit" at whose edge "the vertigo that grips us . . . is always the same"—words that admittedly, for anyone familiar with the Holocaust, are bound to conjure up the image of mass executions and burials[81]—nevertheless he does not describe these operations or their victims but, like Semprun, points to them, leaving the emptiness to be filled, if at all, by our imagination. As in the "conversation overheard in the métro" quoted at the beginning of this chapter, Levinas eschews "the language that tries to be direct and names events" and that in so doing "fails to be straightforward" because its codification of the world suppresses the interlocution of those who inhabit it. And again like Semprun, Levinas does not just address his readers implicitly as second persons but positions them also as thirds, *before* whom he gazes into the pit and *to* whose witnessing his own is thus indirectly but no less sincerely proposed.

At the same time, it will escape no one's attention how the scene so evoked differs from those we have already discussed in the work not only of Semprun but also of Levi and Wiesel. For what *Literature or Life, Survival in Auschwitz*, and *Night* all stage for their readers, *within* the framework of the stories they tell, is the encounter of a survivor with potential interlocutors (as disappointing as these encounters turn out to be), whereas the witnessing figure of Levinas, forever returning to his vertigo at the edge of a gaping pit, appears to stand alone.[82] This by itself, of course, does not authorize us to conclude that Levinas remains at an early stage in the evolving post-traumatic apportionment of social isolation and reconnection, any more than the presentation of this scene to his readers entitles us to infer the contrary. The point is rather that the uncertainty thus induced by his memoirlike "Nameless" does allow us to consider how Levinas's singularity is reflected in his choosing to speak or to write, for the most part, in the language of philosophy. To be sure, the choice of an idiom is always overdetermined, dependent on a multiplicity of factors extending beyond the scope of this study, factors at once characterological and familial, cultural and historical—to say nothing of chance. Yet we can still focus on the nature of the choice itself and observe that, whereas Semprun, the storyteller, points to the universality of the testimonial situation of address by telling a particular tale, Levinas, the philosopher, points to the particularity of that situation by leaving "empty," that is, universally available, the place of the addressee. And what the scene in question suggests above all is that "the one who uses the words 'substance,' 'accident,' 'subject,' 'object,' and other abstractions" is not, himself, in the saying of these words, abstract. Indeed, the very way in which Levinas speaks, in the abstract, of survival alone, points to Levinas himself as *this* survivor.

That we end up here after so many detours should come by now as no surprise: to paraphrase a proverb cited by Levinas, we could say that this survivor "writes straight with crooked lines."[83] And that to hear him or, for that matter, any survivor of the Holocaust requires us to listen—not "absolutely," but certainly in some measure—otherwise.

Conclusion

The perspective of this book as a whole is informed by the notion that at stake in the interaction we call "witnessing" is a fundamental and indispensable tension between its participants. Even though in most cases there is no face-to-face encounter with survivors but rather one that is mediated by a recording of some kind, so that we can at best, and largely unbeknownst to survivors themselves, act as the trustees of their testimony by ensuring its continued reception, we are presumably always concerned, whether as listeners, readers, or viewers, with their reconstruction of a sense of self and community. Thus, whatever specific social, political, historical or other purposes this trusteeship may serve, receiving testimony is first of all an ethical exigency that tests our ability to empathize. At the same time, this exigency entails a constraint, at least insofar as it contraindicates the confusion of empathy with an identification that would blur the distinction between survivors and ourselves. Indeed, although it is generally assumed that what witnesses have had most to fear is public indifference or hostility, I would stress that, however it may be motivated, the overidentification with survivors or the appropriation of their experience as our own can prove just as silencing, perhaps even more so if we consider that it can leave them, or others who witness such a response, with the impression of having initially been deceived by outward signs of solicitude and solidarity. As we have already seen more than once in this volume, the witnesses of witnessing are required to maintain a balance of empathy and reserve, to tolerate a tension between identification and estrangement, to recognize and respect the irreducible otherness of survivors while, in effect, welcoming them back into the larger community.

To be sure, we may wonder whether this exigency should not be reframed as the moment approaches when the last Holocaust survivors will have disappeared and it will no longer be possible for the exercise of a tempered empathy to do them any good. But there is more than one way to answer this question.

The first thing that may come to mind, at least for those familiar with the development of Holocaust studies over the past thirty years, is the advent not so much of a shift in emphasis as of a new focus of attention, that is, the children of survivors, to whom the transmission of their parents' experience has been nothing if not problematic and whose own witnessing requires from us an adaptive transposition of what we learn from the reception of survivor testimony itself.

At a broader level, we may draw on an apprenticeship in witnessing the witnessing of Holocaust survivors in order to listen better to survivors of subsequent genocides, not to mention survivors of other, especially man-made traumatic events, from military combat to sexual assault, from terrorist attack to torture—notwithstanding the predictable outcry, from certain quarters, protesting comparison of the Holocaust with anything else before or since. In this respect, I will not belabor the obvious, namely, that incomparability can only be established through comparison and that, furthermore, it rings a bit hollow as a prize for competitive suffering. Nor, however, would I deny for a moment that comparison has frequently been abused with a view to the very misappropriation against which I have argued in these pages. The point is that attunement to the difference between ourselves and survivors of the Holocaust should encompass the difference between one Holocaust survivor and another and as such can facilitate, in principle, efforts to understand the survivors of other traumas. Needless to say, this facilitation does not promise facility. It demands instead a serious work of translation in which the difference between survivors, as well as the tension that informs our witnessing of their witnessing, must be navigated anew, and of which the only thing we can state with certainty is that it will change the translators themselves.

Yet listening to Holocaust survivors or, more precisely, responding to them in colloquy with other listeners also amounts to a *practice* of community, all the more noteworthy as at issue in it is the future of what the Holocaust itself proved to be so destructible. Precisely here, however, we should first recall that the relationality constitutive of community is no less constitutive of the individuals it comprises: the tension I have underscored *between* interlocutors is inseparable from a tension *within* them. Much, indeed, depends on this tension. Concerning the interaction of intellect and affect, for example, we have repeatedly observed what happens when a theory of trauma or its representation pursues its own conceptual elaboration at the expense of the imaginative effort required to put oneself in the place of a survivor and feel what it might be like to hear the theorist say, in essence: "I know all about what you went through. But you yourself cannot speak of it." Of course, the silencing effect of the theory such a statement reflects may seem, by now, perfectly obvious. Less obvious but equally significant is its failure to appeal, for the understanding of trauma or the reception of testimony, to imagination and affect as fundamental modes of cognition. That these alone, unconstrained by an objectifying intellect, can lead in turn to as thorough a usurpation and silencing of the survivor as does the intellect in isolation, and that in so doing they inevitably forfeit their own cognitive value, merely reinforces the importance of the interaction itself. In this instance, then, what I have called a "tension" within the individual suggests that the reception of Holocaust survivor testimony entails an education of *both* the heart and the mind.

Presumably, the distance that this tension allows us to take from ourselves could give us pause before making a claim to the effect that the Holocaust, or trauma of any kind, is "unspeakable." We could stop to consider how, in a concrete situation of address, it might be heard by a Holocaust survivor and whether, among other translations, by no means the least plausible might sound like this: "I don't want to listen." At the same time, we could ask about the implications, regarding other respondents to a survivor's testimony, of the claim so translated, which can boast of no plausibility whatsoever as an invitation for those respondents to speak. This is why I raised just a moment ago the issue I will reformulate here by pointing out that the way in which we receive the testimony of Holocaust survivors is inseparable from the way in which we practice, with one another, a present and future community. Of this point we admittedly have, in the case at hand, where the claim that trauma is unspeakable tends to silence both testifying survivors and their witnesses, what could at best be called a demonstration by default. But if the point itself is valid, then we are clearly not relieved of the responsibility to listen even to those whose dogmatism discourages its fulfillment. On the contrary: the widespread and virtually canonical affirmation of unspeakability is itself a reaction to trauma, which must be sounded as attentively as any other if our listening is to be worth anything at all. This, as the preceding remarks suggest and as those with the patience to read this volume well know, has not precluded my responding to it with feeling.

What these readers also know, however, is not to expect from me, in reference to the reception of Holocaust survivor testimony, the last word. For it is against the last word that I have argued throughout this book, not least of all by emphasizing time and again the situation of address on whose openness a pluralistic community must rely. With any luck, the book may simply help to invigorate and sustain the discussion from which it has already benefited so much.

I. FRAMES OF RECEPTION

1. Chapters 2 and 3, respectively, in Shoshana Felman and Dori Laub, *Testimony: Crises of Witnessing in Literature, Psychoanalysis, and History* (New York: Routledge, 1992).

2. See BW, esp. 57–59, 69, and 70–72, and "An Event Without a Witness," esp. 75–76 and 85, where Laub discusses the witness, the listener, and their interaction. In these pages, at least, the concern for other listeners is, as I say, suggested rather than explicitly addressed as a general issue in the reception of testimony. In other words, it can be inferred from Laub's participation in the activities of the Archive (including the conference at which the debate discussed in this chapter took place), from the decision to publish his reflections, and from his interactive or relational model of witnessing.

It should be noted that to the earlier version of this chapter, entitled "Between History and Psychoanalysis: A Case Study in the Reception of Holocaust Survivor Testimony," published in *History & Memory* 20, no. 1 (Spring/Summer 2008): 7–47, Laub responded in "On Holocaust Testimony and Its 'Reception' Within Its Own Frame, as a Process in Its Own Right," *History & Memory* 21, no. 1 (Spring/Summer 2009): 127–50. There, Laub considers it misleading to infer, as he puts it, "that I advocate a concern for a community of listeners . . . a notion which I do not entertain anywhere in my writings but can be found in Geoffrey Hartman's work" (ibid., 149n.18; for Hartman, see *The Longest Shadow: In the Aftermath of the Holocaust* [Bloomington: Indiana University Press, 1996], esp. 136, 144, 151–56). Not only do I find the inference to be sound, however, but elsewhere Laub does indeed explicitly voice this concern: see, e.g., with Marjorie Allard, "History, Memory, and Truth," in *The Holocaust and History: The Known, the Unknown, the Disputed, and the Reexamined*, ed. Michael Berenbaum and Abraham J. Peck (Bloomington: Indiana University Press, in association with the United States Holocaust Memorial Museum, 1998), 811–12; and "From Speechlessness to Narrative: The Cases of

Holocaust Historians and of Psychiatrically Hospitalized Survivors," *Literature and Medicine* 24, no. 2 (Fall 2005): 262–64.

3. In his response to "Between History and Psychoanalysis," Laub disputes my use of the term *case study* because, he says, it "would imply that my report of the debate is about specific people or a specific historical situation (which it is not)" ("On Holocaust Testimony," 129). This claim—that his report is *not* "about specific people or a specific historical situation"—is not only untenable but somewhat puzzling, given that he himself goes to considerable lengths to prove that it *is* about specific people and a specific situation (see, for the witness(es), 128–33 and 144–45 nn. 3 and 4, and for the historians, 134–35 and 146–47n.9). I will return to these specificities. For now, let me just add that the term *case study* does double duty here, referring both to Laub's text on reception and to my own study of that text—and that, contrary to his assertion that I disregard his own reflections on witnessing (137), these not only serve as a touchstone of my critique but are explicitly evoked on pp. 8 and 28–29 (herein pp. 8–9 and 29).

4. The uprising to which Laub refers took place on October 7, 1944, in Auschwitz-Birkenau. It was led by members of the *Sonderkommandos* or Special Squads, who worked in the crematoria, and its purpose was to destroy the crematoria (including the gas chambers) while allowing as many prisoners as possible to escape from the camp. In the literature on this subject, see esp. Ber Mark, *The Scrolls of Auschwitz*, trans. Sharon Neemani (Tel Aviv: Am Oved, 1985), but also Martin Gilbert, *The Holocaust: A History of the Jews of Europe During the Second World War* (New York: Henry Holt, 1985), 743–47; Danuta Czech, *Auschwitz Chronicle: 1939–1945*, trans. Barbara Harshav, Martha Humphreys, and Stephen Shearier (New York: Henry Holt, 1990), 725–26; Hermann Langbein, *Against All Hope: Resistance in the Nazi Concentration Camps 1938–1945*, trans. Harry Zohn (New York: Paragon House, 1994), 284–88; and Barbara Jarosz, "Organizations of the Camp Resistance Movement and Their Activities," in *Auschwitz: Nazi Death Camp*, ed. Franciszek Piper and Teresa Świebocka (Ośý wieçim: The Auschwitz-Birkenau State Museum, 1996), esp. 232–34.

5. See http://www.library.yale.edu/testimonies/catalog/index.html, where the other interviewer is identified as Eva Kantor.

6. I am indebted to the staff of the Archive for identifying the "core" testimony in question as T-179, Serena N., Fortunoff Video Archive for Holocaust Testimonies, Yale University Library. Of all the interviews with female survivors conducted by Laub prior to the latest of the conferences cited below (n. 10), this is indeed the only one in which the four chimneys and their alleged destruction are mentioned. In reference to the uprising, it runs as follows (beginning at 55:52):

SN: All of a sudden we saw the gates open and . . .
DL: You saw . . .

sn: The men, we saw the gates, yes, the gates open, men running from there and all the four crematoria at one time blew up. And of course these men knew that this would probably be the end for them, but they thought that perhaps they might prolong the fight a little bit if the outside, the others will help. But there was no chance. Instantly they descended, you know, the Germans, the SS, with machine guns and everything. They killed out every man. Two SS died in that incident.

If not already for the inaccuracy of his quotation, one might wish to characterize Laub's rendering of this testimony as something more than an "inflection" for two additional reasons. First, Serena N. is hardly the timid, self-effacing person Laub portrays her as being, but rather a lively, engaging, and confident woman (he may be confusing her with her aunt, Rose A. [T-183, FVA], who states: "And one crematorium blew, and another" [1:06:00ff.]). Hence there is no apparent post-traumatic numbness to be contrasted with "a sudden intensity, passion and color" in her account of the uprising—and for that matter, no "sudden intensity, passion and color" since, in giving this account, she evinces at most a slight change in demeanor (she looks more quickly from one interviewer to the other, and a certain sense of drama is detectable in her face and breath). Second, the account is followed, at least on my viewings, by no such prolonged or "fixed" silence as that in which Laub invents a soundtrack of rebellion. I will return to the composite nature of the testifying woman.

7. At various points in this chapter, I will touch upon the feature of objectivism most pertinent to the debate and, in its context, most obviously open to contestation, namely, the position (figuratively, the voice) of the historian, which purportedly lies outside of history itself and from which one can serenely observe "the facts" while disclaiming responsibility for their interpretation. (See, in this connection, Roland Barthes, "Historical Discourse," trans. Peter Wexler, in *Introduction to Structuralism*, ed. Michael Lane [New York: Basic Books, 1970], 148–49.) However, my own critical perspective in regard to historical objectivism does not entail an endorsement of the position assumed by Laub.

8. It is not entirely clear what "her whole account of the events" is supposed to mean. At first glance, "events" would seem to refer to the uprising alone. Yet what I have quoted above (n. 6) virtually exhausts Serena N.'s testimony on this score, leaving little or nothing to be dismissed in addition. For this reason, and because of their ostensible extremism, I incline to the view that the historians found her wanting as an eyewitness to *any* event or circumstance of collective significance.

9. See Susan Rubin Suleiman, "Do Facts Matter in Holocaust Memoirs?" in *Crises of Memory and the Second World War* (Cambridge: Harvard University Press, 2006), 167–68.

10. As with the testimony he discusses, so here Laub provides no reference to the conference or to the historians who allegedly participated in it. To judge

from his anecdotal remarks (concerning a moment "many months later," that is, later than November 7, 1982, when Serena N.'s testimony was recorded, and "a conference . . . on the relation of education to the Holocaust") as well as from information available on the Archive's website (http://www.library.yale .edu/testimonies/publications/conferences.html), the conference in question probably took place on November 5–6, 1983, and was entitled "The Educational and Research Uses of the Yale Video Archive" (although there are two other possibilities, "Education and the Holocaust: New Responsibilities and Cooperative Ventures," October 28–29, 1984, and "Challenges to Education," November 17–18, 1985). Despite numerous queries and close examination of the conference programs, I have been unable to determine, in any of the three cases, who exactly Laub's "historians" might have been.

I would further note that in "Bearing Witness" Laub debates more than one historian, whereas in his response he refers to "the debate with the historian" ("On Holocaust Testimony," 134). This he must presumably do because, having consulted the program for the conference of November 5–6, 1983, while drafting his response, he discovered that only one of the participants could qualify as a historian, namely, Raul Hilberg (who was, and insisted on being identified as, a political scientist). To Laub's question, "Why did Trezise not raise the question whether Hilberg, whose skepticism regarding testimony is well known, could have been the historian referred to in my essay when seeing his name on the conference schedule?"—to say nothing of his careless insinuation that "it seems Trezise did not look very hard" (147n.9)—there are two answers. First, Laub repeatedly refers, again, to the "historians" (plural), even though Hilberg was the lone de facto historian whose name appeared on the program. And second, in a letter dated July 3, 2006, I asked Hilberg if he would share his recollections of the conference with me. In his reply of July 7, 2006, which his wife has kindly granted me permission to paraphrase, he said that he did indeed attend the conference but had no memory of a debate about the witness to whom Laub refers. Thus, not only does the question concerning the identity of these historians remain open, but one cannot help but wonder how it is that no one save Dori Laub seems to have any memory of the debate itself (see, again, 147n.9: "It is interesting to note that of the thirteen conference participants I was able to contact, not a single one could remember that specific conference or panel").

That said, I focus on the debate precisely because, as Laub himself says, "it cast such a bright light on two diametrically opposed ways of listening to survivors" (134). Moreover, in the thirteen additional chapters or articles of his own that Laub cites (147n.10, 148 nn. 14 and 15, 149n.24), I see little or nothing, as far as historiography is concerned, that would indicate a fundamental change of attitude. This includes the text cited above (n. 2), "From Speechlessness to Narrative," where the traditional historiography to which he refers

(254) does not obviously differ from what one would imagine to be the practice of his opponents in the debate. (A portion of this text [254–55] was previously published in "Kann die Psychoanalyse dazu beitragen, den Völkermord historisch besser zu verstehen?" *Psyche: Zeitschrift für Psychoanalyse und ihre Anwendungen* 57, no. 9/10 [2003]: 946–47. Here, Laub also refers in briefer but otherwise identical fashion to the historians he debated [948].)

11. See testimony cited in n. 6, above. Given their fixation on the number of chimneys destroyed, one may also wonder why none of the historians points out that three rather than two members of the SS perished during the rebellion.

12. It is unfortunate—and puzzling—that Laub believes I was *attacking* him when "using my identity as a survivor as an explanation for the stance I took in the debate with the historians" ("On Holocaust Testimony," 149n.18). In referring to his status as a survivor, I am actually making a point about cognition, namely, that experience, to the extent that it enables one to put oneself in the place of another, entails an objectivity that objectivism itself cannot grasp. For this point, I am indebted in some measure to Laub's own reflections on the relational self. That said, the qualification "as a survivor" is not meant to imply that he did not *also* respond to the historians as a psychoanalyst.

13. I am indebted to Susan Brison's analysis of this transformation in *Aftermath: Violence and the Remaking of a Self* (Princeton: Princeton University Press, 2002), esp. 56–57, 68, 71–73 (Brison refers to Laub's insightful statement that survivors "did not only need to survive so that they could tell their story; they also needed to tell their story in order to survive" [Laub, "An Event Without a Witness," 78; Brison, *Aftermath*, 68]). Of course, it must be asked how seriously we are to take Laub's claim concerning the performative dimension of testimony when, as I have observed (n. 6, above), his account of what happens when Serena N. speaks of the revolt seems so exaggerated. The matter is hardly resolved when he modifies his account, relocating the supposed transformation of her demeanor to a moment some two minutes later, where she mentions the positive effect of the rebellion on prisoner morale (but where, unlike Laub, I still see no sign that "something has radically changed in her emotional experience of her testimony" ["On Holocaust Testimony," 129]). Whether or not any such transformation takes place at this point, however, the problem is that, in "Bearing Witness," Laub ascribes the performative force of Serena's testimony to the coincidence of analogous rebellions: it is, according to him, precisely *as* she narrates the uprising of the Auschwitz *Sonderkommandos* that Serena enacts one of her own, "breaking out of Auschwitz even by her very talking" (BW, 62). Now that the alleged transformation has been displaced, one cannot help but wonder how the rigorous relation between narration and enactment, between the constative and performative dimensions of testimony, is supposed to remain intact. That said, it may be that this particular

testimony does not provide the strongest support for his claim, which in its generality is often enough borne out by the study of trauma and testimony to deserve consideration in any analysis of reception, and perhaps especially where performativity is at risk of being ignored altogether.

14. This notion of delay has been associated with post-traumatic psychology at least since Freud. Although, beginning with the *Project for a Scientific Psychology* (1895), Freud already conceived of *Nachträglichkeit* (deferred action) as an important feature of mental functioning, it looms even larger when, in *Beyond the Pleasure Principle* (1920), he focuses on the partial disabling, in traumatic experience and its aftermath, of binding, the process whereby stimuli are organized for expenditure through their investment in representations. Trauma exposes the organism to stimuli so far exceeding its organizational capacity as to impose a staggered "dosage" of expenditure, thus rendering deferral or delay much more conspicuous. See Sigmund Freud, *Beyond the Pleasure Principle*, in *SE*, vol. 18 (1955), 7–64; *Jenseits des Lustprinzips*, in *GW*, vol. 13 (1940), 60. This and related issues are discussed at greater length in Chapter 2.

15. Laub clearly does himself a disservice, however, when, just a few pages earlier, he claims that "the trauma survivor who is bearing witness has no prior knowledge, no comprehension and no memory of what happened" (BW, 58). This is a statement bound to elicit questions reflecting the naïveté of the statement itself, questions such as: On what basis, then, does the survivor bear witness? To what—if not to whatever is known, comprehended, or remembered—does the survivor testify? How does the witness having "no prior knowledge, no comprehension and no memory of what happened" even know that he or she is a survivor? Underlying this claim (as well as the characterization of the Holocaust as "an event without a witness") is undoubtedly the idea, which Laub shares to one degree or another with Jean-François Lyotard, Cathy Caruth, and Giorgio Agamben, that trauma is an absolute to whose experience victims themselves have no access. To enumerate and discuss here the reasons for which this idea is untenable would take us too far afield (but see Chapters 2 and 4 of this volume). Suffice it to say that Laub's hyperbole might prove less objectionable were it accompanied by an analytical account of specific psychic mechanisms triggered by trauma ("From Speechlessness to Narrative" takes a modest step in this direction, qualifying the hyperbole to some extent and referring to certain dissociative phenomena [257]).

Still, it is important to clarify here the sense in which I understand Laub's claim that "knowledge in the testimony" is a "genuine advent." To make this claim is not, I would argue, to say that prior to this advent, prior to the advent of *this* knowledge, the survivor knows (or comprehends, or remembers) nothing, but rather that "in the testimony," in the externalizing or expressive relation to a listener, the survivor "discovers" herself (including what she knows, comprehends, and remembers), comes to know herself as though for the first time precisely by becoming another, indeed, that this ongoing transformation may even explain the "recovery" of apparently misunderstood or forgotten experience. See, in this connection, Laub, "On Holocaust Testimony," 140–41.

16. I do not mean to suggest that the ambition of all testimonial narrative is or should be a seamless story. Not only would this appear suspect—as though the means with which we make sense of experience had been left entirely intact by an unprecedented historical trauma—but it is rather clearly the case, in witnessing to this trauma, that narrative "failure" of one kind or another can be and often is itself significant. However, in videotaped testimony (as opposed, for example, to written memoirs), a quite pronounced narrative linearity is required if the witness, the interviewer(s), and the viewers are not to become disoriented.

17. See Louis O. Mink's remarkable essay "Narrative Form as a Cognitive Instrument," in *The Writing of History: Literary Form and Historical Understanding*, ed. Robert H. Canary and Henry Kozicki (Madison: University of Wisconsin Press, 1978), esp. 134–38.

18. Thus, to extend an earlier remark (n. 7), the objectivistic historian would be positioned outside of history in both senses of the term, that is, in the sense of event *and* of narrative, or, according to the distinction used by Hegel and familiar to philosophers of history, of the *res gestae* and the *historia rerum gestarum* (G. W. F. Hegel, *The Philosophy of History*, trans. J. Sibree [New York: Dover, 1956; Mineola, N.Y.: Dover, 2004], 60).

19. Beyond the questions already raised by Laub's "inflection" of Serena N.'s testimony concerning the uprising (n. 6), the identity of the "testifying woman" becomes even more problematic here. To begin with, Serena refers to goods smuggled *for* rather than *by* her, and in doing so shows no change of demeanor. More important, she is not startled by Laub's question, but momentarily hesitates before going on to explain the meaning of "Canada." Most important of all, she knows—and knew—perfectly well that everything to be sorted in Canada came from the victims of mass murder (see T-179, 42:00–50:00). In my own puzzlement, I returned to the only testimonies that, as far as I could determine, might be confused with hers, namely, those of Irene W., her sister (T-65, FVA), and of Rose A., their aunt, already mentioned (n. 6), both of whom served with Serena in the Canada commando. Both Irene and Rose recall having smuggled goods from Canada for the sake of fellow inmates, but in neither case do I detect, accompanying this recollection, any change of demeanor. When asked the name of the commando, Irene does not hesitate to provide it, and as for Rose, after a moment of confusion due to her having misunderstood Laub to be inquiring about the *Sonderkommando* (composed exclusively of men), and after Laub then repeats the word "Canada" (contrary to the claim that he "decided to back off"), she not only recognizes it but begins to explain its usage. Finally, like Serena, both Irene and Rose know—and

knew—that what they were assigned to sort belonged to murder victims (for Irene W., see T-65, 1:27:00–1:31:00; for Rose A., T-183, 1:02:00–1:05:30 and 1:27:00ff.).

These considerations strike me as unavoidable if we are to grasp the extent to which and the possible reasons for which Laub misrepresents the witnesses to whom he claims to listen so carefully (a misrepresentation to which I will return). Even more than in the case of Serena N.'s testimony about the uprising, what Laub attributes to the "testifying woman" in connection with the Canada commando tends to undermine his approach to reception by suggesting that the very guideline he is in the process of establishing, and according to which one ought not to listen only for what one wants or expects to hear, may be selectively observed. In his response, he acknowledges "(mis)remembering" but is not deterred, on the one hand, from continuing to speak of "Serena's silence about her experience inside the *Kanada* commando" and, on the other, from turning his inaccuracy to account by claiming that it "in essence consists of replacing the manifest text with its latent meaning" ("On Holocaust Testimony," 132–33).

20. The possibility that such an inmate might not have learned both the name and the function of the commando was in fact extremely remote, for a number of reasons, not the least of which were the communication between inmates and the physical proximity of Canada (in Auschwitz-Birkenau) to Crematorium IV (which lay in plain view just the other side of a barbed wire fence and which, incidentally, due to unforeseen developments at variance with the insurrectionist plan, was where the rebellion actually started).

21. See Filip Müller, *Eyewitness Auschwitz: Three Years in the Gas Chambers*, trans. Susanne Flatauer (Chicago: Ivan R. Dee, 1999), esp. 153–60. Some accounts do suggest such an atmosphere, e.g., the testimony of Zofia Kasakiewicz (who, like Serena N., was working in Canada), quoted by Mark, *The Scrolls of Auschwitz*, 145. Much, no doubt, depends on the situation of the eyewitness at the moment of the rebellion as well as on whether the mood of remembrance derives strictly from that moment or is colored by its horrific aftermath. In any case, Laub's imported exuberance oversimplifies the ambiance of the uprising.

22. For the distinction between acting-out and working-through, see Sigmund Freud, "Remembering, Repeating and Working-Through," in *SE*, vol. 12 (1958), 145–56; "Erinnen, Wiederholen und Durcharbeiten," in *GW*, vol. 10 (1946), 125–36.

23. "[T]he survivor whose story is filmed is not seeking personal help; he is called upon to bear witness. By being interviewed, he is entering history. He is doing his share in remembering. That such interviews are conducted because of the subject's involvement with the Holocaust gives the interview the character less of a personal and more of a social and historical event" (Martin S. Bergmann, "Reflections on the Psychological and Social Function of Remembering

the Holocaust," in *Generations of the Holocaust*, ed. Martin S. Bergmann and Milton E. Jucovy [New York: Columbia University Press, 1990], 320).

24. See Hartman, *The Longest Shadow*, 136.

25. It may appear incongruous to ascribe truth to the woman's "performance" since, strictly speaking, the function of performative language is to do rather than to tell (the truth, for example). But the truth in question is actually being claimed for the assertion that this testimony does have performative force or efficacy.

26. Aharon Appelfeld, *Beyond Despair*, trans. Jeffrey M. Green (New York: Fromm International, 1994), 22.

27. Information concerning this date, the relationship among the three witnesses, and the identity of the interviewers can be obtained from three sources combined: the videotapes themselves, the time-coded finding aids that accompany them (both being available only at the Archive, at least until 2013), and the website (http://www.library.yale.edu/testimonies).

28. Laub says: "It is more than likely that when writing my essay I disguised the identity of all protagonists involved and changed minor details not relevant to the point I was trying to make in order to protect the privacy of everybody involved, as is customary in psychoanalytic reporting of clinical vignettes," adding that "I refuse to be the judge in this ethical dilemma between confidentiality and transparency" ("On Holocaust Testimony," 129 and 145n.5). Aside from the fact that this practice confuses psychoanalysis with the videotaped interviewing of a Holocaust survivor, there is no such "ethical dilemma" here, since among the rules of the publicly accessible archive that Laub himself co-founded and to which witnesses give their informed consent is the *requirement* that any citation include the full first and abbreviated last name of the witness in question.

A related issue arises through the ambiguity of the verb *to refer* as Laub uses it when stating that "my essay refers exclusively to the testimony of Serena N." and that "I never referred to the testimonies of Rose A. and Irene W. in my essay" (128). On the one hand, I would qualify this statement by noting that he never refers to *any* of them *by name*. On the other hand, Laub is clearly concerned here (128–33) to contest my assertion that the "testifying woman" is a composite figure. And he is right to point out (128) that I initially characterized this as a "fact" ("Between History and Psychoanalysis," 11) when it should more modestly and accurately be called a hypothesis. Yet this hypothesis is not, as he protests, "a figment of [Trezise's] own imagination" (128) but rather a carefully considered explanation of the multiple discrepancies between this woman and those on whose videotaped testimonies her character appears to be based. To propose such a hypothesis does not require a lot of imagination—a good deal less, in any case, than would be needed to believe that Laub created the "testifying woman" out of whole cloth. In the end, of course, our disagreement on this matter and even on the general demeanor of the three witnesses in question is such that only third parties having viewed the videotaped testimonies could decide which of us offers the stronger argument. My point, however, is this: nowhere in "Between History and Psychoanalysis" or in these pages do I claim that the author of "Bearing Witness" deliberately distorted or falsified the testimony of Holocaust survivors. Indeed, Laub would be the first to recognize, I take it, that (counter)transference is largely unconscious, and that listening to oneself can only facilitate listening to another insofar as it brings (counter)transference to light. It is thus all the more puzzling why he apparently did not avail himself of the opportunity to visit the archive before publishing his essay, since the inescapable discrepancies between the videotapes and his memory of them could have yielded a groundbreaking and highly instructive exemplification of transference as it is unwittingly practiced in the reception of Holocaust survivor testimony.

29. I see identification and transference essentially as modes of appropriation and cannot do justice here to their psychoanalytic complexity. See, e.g., J. Laplanche and J.-B. Pontalis, *The Language of Psychoanalysis*, trans. Donald Nicholson-Smith (New York: Norton, 1973), 205–8 and 455–62. For the use of the notion of transference in the analysis of Holocaust historiography, see Saul Friedlander, *Memory, History, and the Extermination of the Jews of Europe* (Bloomington: Indiana University Press, 1993), and Dominick LaCapra (who extends the use of this and related psychoanalytic notions to the study of film, literature, and testimony), *Representing the Holocaust: History, Theory, Trauma* (Ithaca: Cornell University Press, 1994), *History and Memory after Auschwitz* (Ithaca: Cornell University Press, 1998), and *Writing History, Writing Trauma* (Baltimore: Johns Hopkins University Press, 2001).

30. On empathy, see LaCapra, *Writing History*, 39–42. As LaCapra notes, empathy as he understands it can be compared to what Kaja Silverman, in *The Threshold of the Visible World* (New York: Routledge, 1996), calls "heteropathic identification," in which "emotional response comes with respect for the other and the realization that the experience of the other is not one's own" (LaCapra, *Writing History*, 40).

31. For general characterizations of historical objectivism, see, e.g., Peter Novick, *That Noble Dream: The "Objectivity Question" and the American Historical Profession* (Cambridge: Cambridge University Press, 1988), 1–2; Michael Shermer and Alex Grobman, *Denying History: Who Says the Holocaust Never Happened and Why Do They Say It?* (Berkeley: University of California Press, 2000), 21–23; and LaCapra, *Writing History*, 2–7. All three authors raise the question of where precisely the line should be drawn between objectivity and objectivism, and Thomas Haskell has persuasively argued that Novick confuses the two ("Objectivity Is Not Neutrality: Rhetoric Versus Practice in Peter Novick's *That Noble Dream*," in *History and Theory: Contemporary Readings*,

ed. Brian Fay, Philip Pomper, and Richard T. Vann [Oxford: Blackwell, 1998], 299–319).

32. Among these critics are, of course, the so-called constructivists, for whom, in their most extreme (Nietzschean) inspiration, there are no facts, only interpretations. Thus, e.g., Hayden White has asserted: "One must face the fact that when it comes to apprehending the historical record, there are no grounds to be found in the historical record itself for preferring one way of construing its meaning over another" ("The Politics of Historical Interpretation: Discipline and De-Sublimation," in *The Content of the Form* [Baltimore: Johns Hopkins University Press, 1987], 75; first published in *Critical Inquiry* 9, no. 1 [1982]). (Worth noting here is that White's own interpretation is called a "fact," which one supposedly "must face.") It thus comes as somewhat of a surprise to see him concede, ten years later, that "in the case of an emplotment of the events of the Third Reich in a 'comic' or 'pastoral' mode, we would be eminently justified in appealing to 'the facts' in order to dismiss it from the lists of 'competing narratives'" ("Historical Emplotment and the Problem of Truth," in *Probing the Limits of Representation: Nazism and the "Final Solution,"* ed. Saul Friedlander [Cambridge: Harvard University Press, 1992], 40). To be sure, those inclined to view this statement as a genuine departure from White's constructivism might wish to consider whether the quotation marks framing "the facts" do not suggest that he is hedging his bets. But be that as it may, he then goes on to suggest that comedy or pastoral could themselves be "set forth in a pointedly ironic way" and so make "a metacritical comment, not so much on the facts as on versions of the facts emplotted in a comic or pastoral way" (40). Perhaps, indeed, ironic pastoral would prove to be an effective mode in which to convey both the delusional and the morally repellent nature of something like "Aryan paradise." However, as White concedes to Saul Friedlander, such representations risk an aestheticization of genocidal ideology that is itself morally repellent. And from the cognitive point of view, it is not enough to assert that "surely it would be beside the point to dismiss *this* kind of narrative from the competition on the basis of its infidelity to the facts" (40). What must be added is that "infidelity to the facts" can only be "beside the point" once the facts have been established *and communicated*. The kind of narrative White has in mind yields at most a second-order cognition: a comic or pastoral misrepresentation of the Third Reich can be "pointedly ironic" *only* for those who already know—and this becomes more rather than less problematic as the Holocaust recedes in memory.

33. Haskell, "Objectivity Is Not Neutrality," 301. As the very title of Haskell's essay suggests, this is not a capacity to be neutrally or indiscriminately employed. In the context of the Holocaust, it raises the crucial question—whose discussion far exceeds the framework of this chapter—whether or to what extent one should, if only as a thought experiment in the name of historical

understanding, "put oneself in the place of" a perpetrator, as in Jonathan Littell's *The Kindly Ones*, trans. Charlotte Mandell (New York: HarperCollins, 2009); *Les bienveillantes* (Paris: Gallimard, 2006). On this text and the controversy surrounding it, see Susan Rubin Suleiman, "When the Perpetrator Becomes a Reliable Witness of the Holocaust: On Jonathan Littell's *Les bienveillantes*," *New German Critique*, no. 106 (Winter 2009): 1–19.

34. On contextualism and fallibilism, see Chris Lorenz, "Historical Knowledge and Historical Reality: A Plea for 'Internal Realism,'" in *History and Theory*, ed. Fay, Pomper, and Vann, 350.

35. In fact, it seems obvious that the value of Serena N.'s testimony *as eyewitnessing* might have become genuinely suspect had she demonstrated a full knowledge of those very things (concerning the Polish resistance, for example) for ignorance of which the historians reproach her.

36. Harking back to the phraseology of his title ("On Holocaust Testimony and Its 'Reception' Within Its Own Frame, as a Process in Its Own Right"), Laub states in conclusion that "testimony has its own frame within which its analysis can proceed" (142). No effort is made to explain the constitution of this boundary separating an inside from an outside, one's own from another's, although the word "analysis" might suggest that for Laub it replicates the frame of psychotherapy. Be that as it may, the statement reflects a reaction to my having promoted an understanding of testimony as a generic hybrid, an understanding that, according to Laub, "perpetuates the very fragmentation inherent in the Holocaust experience itself and undermines the struggle to contain the massive destructiveness at the core of this experience" (142). What I actually say here (and in "Between History and Psychoanalysis," 31) is that "as a generic hybrid, testimony requires for its reception a plurality of interpretive frameworks." In other words, my claim that testimony has no preestablished framework supports as inclusive and integrated a hearing as possible for survivors and their testimony. Laub himself insists: "It is our task to engage the multitude of interpretive voices already existing and . . . to integrate them in a joint endeavor to understand the Holocaust" (142).

37. See esp. James E. Young, "Holocaust Video and Cinemagraphic Testimony: Documenting the Witness," in *Writing and Rewriting the Holocaust: Narrative and the Consequences of Interpretation* (Bloomington: Indiana University Press, 1988), 157–71, and Geoffrey Hartman, "Learning from Survivors: The Yale Testimony Project," in *The Longest Shadow*, 133–50. In this connection, essential reading also includes Lawrence Langer's *Holocaust Testimonies: The Ruins of Memory* (New Haven: Yale University Press, 1991), based entirely on material from the Fortunoff Video Archive, and Annette Wieviorka's *The Era of the Witness*, trans. Jared Stark (Ithaca: Cornell University Press, 2006), esp. 130–35 and 143–44, where Wieviorka delineates the position of professional historians, herself included, in regard to survivor testimony.

38. Marianne Hirsch's notion of "postmemory" has played a crucial role in the articulation of this aftermath. See *Family Frames: Photography, Narrative, and Postmemory* (Cambridge: Harvard University Press, 1997).

39. The eminent Holocaust historian Raul Hilberg also plays an important role in *Shoah.* I place "documents" in quotation marks for the same reason here as in the previous paragraph. See, in this connection, Claude Lanzmann, "The Obscenity of Understanding: An Evening with Claude Lanzmann," in *Trauma: Explorations in Memory*, ed. Cathy Caruth (Baltimore: Johns Hopkins University Press, 1995), 211.

40. The Fortunoff Video Archive for Holocaust Testimonies, so named in 1987, originated in a project dating from 1979 (see http://www.library.yale.edu /testimonies/about/history.html); *Shoah* was released in 1985; and Rousso's book was published in 1987 (Henry Rousso, *The Vichy Syndrome: History and Memory in France since 1944*, trans. Arthur Goldhammer [Cambridge: Harvard University Press, 1991]; *Le syndrome de Vichy: De 1944 à nos jours* [Paris: Editions du Seuil, 1987]).

41. The features of the witness's body, face, and voice function as signs insofar as they point to the person she once was and, by extension, to the time, place, and circumstances of her victimization. Yet these features are also percepts, or qualities apprehended by the senses, which, as such, render the witness "present." That she should be both present and absent, that she should embody a certain contiguity to that which is not and, in this case, cannot be directly shown—this no doubt helps to explain the ambiguity or ghostliness of survival itself. And to speak, as I do here, of an "aura" is not to qualify but to emphasize indexicality, a mode of communication at once less tangible than showing and more so than telling. Indexicality figures prominently in Ross Chambers's seminal work on testimony, *Untimely Interventions: AIDS Writing, Testimonial, and the Rhetoric of Haunting* (Ann Arbor: University of Michigan Press, 2004).

42. Quoted from the website, http://www.library.yale.edu/testimonies /about/concept.html.

43. One of the most noteworthy instances of "siting" in *The Sorrow and the Pity* (1969) is the interview (conducted by one of the producers, André Harris) with Christian de la Mazière, a former member of the SS Division Charlemagne, at Sigmaringen, which Rousso aptly terms "the Mecca of collaborators in exile" (*The Vichy Syndrome*, 101). Of course, this is not a site of atrocity, and there is nothing to suggest the kind of reenactment pursued by Lanzmann (who, incidentally, is interviewed in Ophuls's later film, *Hotel Terminus* [1988]).

44. For the English text of the film, see Claude Lanzmann, *Shoah: The Complete Text of the Acclaimed Holocaust Film* (New York: Da Capo Press, 1995). An early critical response came from Nora Levin, "Some Reservations about Lanzmann's *Shoah*," *Sh'ma: A Journal of Jewish Responsibility*, April 18, 1986,

91–93. See also Dominick LaCapra, "Lanzmann's *Shoah*: 'Here There Is No Why,'" in *History and Memory after Auschwitz*, 95–138. I return to this issue, above all, in Chapter 2.

45. It should be remembered here that Laub's own appropriative tendency shows up in his written account of videotaped interviews and not in the interviews themselves.

46. Concerning the boundary between Holocaust "testimony" and Holocaust "literature," see, e.g., Charlotte Delbo's *Auschwitz and After*, trans. Rosette C. Lamont (New Haven: Yale University Press, 1995), which her French publisher, Editions de Minuit, includes in a series called "Documents" but which for the most part owes the enormous influence it has achieved among scholars and students to its remarkable "literary" qualities. I discuss these at some length in the last section of Chapter 3.

47. Hartman, *The Longest Shadow*, 155.

48. Chambers, "Orphaned Memories, Phantom Pain: Toward a Hauntology of Discourse," in *Untimely Interventions*, 189–243.

49. Paul Celan's expression (in German, *was geschah*), from his "Speech on the Occasion of Receiving the Literature Prize of the Free Hanseatic City of Bremen," in *Collected Prose*, trans. Rosmarie Waldrop (Riverdale-on-Hudson, N.Y.: The Sheep Meadow Press, 1986), 34 (trans. mod.); *Gesammelte Werke*, ed. Beda Allemann and Stefan Reichert (Frankfurt am Main: Suhrkamp, 1983), 3:186.

50. I refer in particular to the Institute for Historical Review, founded in 1978, and to its *Journal of Historical Review*. In France, the Faurisson Affair dates from the same period. See Pierre Vidal-Naquet, *Assassins of Memory: Essays on the Denial of the Holocaust*, trans. Jeffrey Mehlman (New York: Columbia University Press, 1992). The appropriation of academic discourse began with the term *revisionism* itself. See, e.g., Deborah Lipstadt, *Denying the Holocaust: The Growing Assault on Truth and Memory* (New York: Free Press, 1993), 20–21. On denial generally, see also Lipstadt; Shermer and Grobman, *Denying History*; and Kenneth S. Stern, *Holocaust Denial* (New York: American Jewish Committee, 1993).

51. Friedlander, *Memory, History*, 103.

52. Ibid., 111 (author's emphasis).

53. Ibid., 132–33.

54. LaCapra, *Writing History*, 41.

2. TRAUMA AND THEORY

1. I propose a broad discussion of the "unspeakability" of the Holocaust in "Unspeakable," *The Yale Journal of Criticism* 14, no. 1 (2001): 39–66.

2. Regarding Agamben, see Chapter 4 of this volume, and in connection with Caruth, Debarati Sanyal, "A Soccer Match in Auschwitz: Passing Culpability in

Holocaust Criticism," *Representations* 79 (Summer 2002): 1–27, esp. 10–12. For Lyotard, see *The Differend*, trans. Georges Van Den Abbeele (Minneapolis: University of Minnesota Press, 1988), esp. 56–58, as well as Karyn Ball, "Ex/propriating Survivor Experience, or Auschwitz 'after' Lyotard," in *Witness and Memory: The Discourse of Trauma*, ed. Ana Douglass and Thomas A. Vogler (New York: Routledge, 2003), 249–73; Sven-Erik Rose, "Auschwitz as Hermeneutic Rupture, Differend, and Image *malgré tout*: Jameson, Lyotard, Didi-Huberman," in *Visualizing the Holocaust: Documents, Aesthetics, Memory*, ed. David Bathrick, Brad Prager, and Michael D. Richardson (Rochester, N.Y.: Camden House, 2008), 114–37; and Trezise, "Unspeakable," 52–55. Concerning Laub, see *Testimony*, e.g., 80–82, where the disjunction between trauma and representation informs the problematic notion of the Holocaust as "an event without a witness." In Felman's contributions to *Testimony*, this disjunction comes into play in discussions of the same notion (e.g., 194, 211) as well as of the missing of experience (e.g., 168, 199, 268) and the impossibility of witnessing or historical narrative (e.g., 160, 193, 200–201). On Felman, see LaCapra, *Representing the Holocaust*, 116–25, and Sanyal, "A Soccer Match in Auschwitz," 12–20.

3. Sigmund Freud, *Project for a Scientific Psychology*, in *The Standard Edition of the Complete Psychological Works of Sigmund Freud*, trans. and ed. James Strachey, vol. 1 (London: Hogarth, 1966; London: Vintage, 2001), 310/*Entwurf einer Psychologie*, in *Aus den Anfängen der Psychoanalyse*, ed. Marie Bonaparte, Anna Freud, and Ernst Kris (London: Imago, 1950), 395. The *Project* was written in 1895 but not published until 1950.

4. Sigmund Freud, *Beyond the Pleasure Principle*, in *The Standard Edition of the Complete Psychological Works of Sigmund Freud*, ed. and trans. James Strachey, vol. 18 (London: Hogarth, 1955; London: Vintage, 2001), 7–8 (see also 63)/*Jenseits des Lustprinzips*, in *Gesammelte Werke*, ed. Anna Freud et al., vol. 13 (London: Imago, 1940), 3–4 and 69.

5. *SE*, 1:304/*Aus den Anfängen der Psychoanalyse*, 388–89.

6. *SE*, 18:24/*GW*, 13:23; but see also 25–32/24–32.

7. See Sigmund Freud, *The Interpretation of Dreams*, in *SE*, esp. vol. 4 (1955), 122–33 and 277–309/*Die Traumdeutung*, in *GW*, vols. 2 and 3 (1942), 127–38 and 283–310. The first edition of *Die Traumdeutung* was published in 1900, and *Jenseits des Lustprinzips* appeared in 1920.

8. The American Psychiatric Association added the category of Posttraumatic Stress Disorder to the third edition of its *Diagnostic and Statistical Manual of Mental Disorders*, or *DSM*, published in 1980. The entry has since been modified in the revised edition of *DSM-III* (1987), in *DSM-IV* (1994), and in *DSM-IV-TR* (Text Revision) (Washington, D.C.: American Psychiatric Association, 2000). On the history of trauma in psychiatry, see, among others, Judith Herman, *Trauma and Recovery* (New York: Basic Books, 1992), 7–32; Bessel

A. van der Kolk, Lars Weisaeth, and Onno van der Hart, "History of Trauma in Psychiatry," in *Traumatic Stress: The Effects of Overwhelming Experience on Mind, Body, and Society*, ed. Bessel A. van der Kolk, Alexander C. McFarlane, and Lars Weisaeth (New York: The Guilford Press, 1996), 47–74; and Roger Luckhurst, *The Trauma Question* (London: Routledge, 2008), 19–76.

9. For a concise explanation of *Nachträglichkeit* ("deferred action") in Freud's work, see Laplanche and Pontalis, *The Language of Psychoanalysis*, 111–14.

10. Even if we bracket for a moment the primitive causation described here, clinicians, among others, would readily point out that such a total absence of mediation is strictly impossible. Caruth confuses what is registered with its registration, the event with the brain.

11. The reader desiring a general acquaintance with van der Kolk's work could consult Bessel A. van der Kolk and Onno van der Hart, "The Intrusive Past: The Flexibility of Memory and the Engraving of Trauma," in *TEM*, 158–82; and Bessel A. van der Kolk and Alexander C. McFarlane, "The Black Hole of Trauma," Bessel A. van der Kolk, "The Body Keeps the Score: Approaches to the Psychobiology of Posttraumatic Stress Disorder," Bessel A. van der Kolk, "Trauma and Memory," and Bessel A. van der Kolk, Onno van der Hart, and Charles R. Marmar, "Dissociation and Information Processing in Post-traumatic Stress Disorder," in *Traumatic Stress*, ed. van der Kolk, McFarlane, and Weisaeth, 3–23, 214–41, 279–302, and 303–27, respectively.

12. See Ruth Leys, "The Science of the Literal: The Neurobiology of Trauma," in *Trauma: A Genealogy* (Chicago: University of Chicago Press, 2000), 229–65. Of particular note here is an experiment whose results supposedly confirmed the literal or nonsymbolic nature of traumatic memory. Using positron emission tomography, van der Kolk and colleagues discovered that the provocation of traumatic memories led to increased activity in the amygdala (the seat of emotion) and the right visual cortex, while Broca's area (involved with speech) "turned off." But there are several problems with this experiment or its conceptualization. To begin with, the patients, all suffering from PTSD, were asked to write detailed narratives of their experiences, which were then read back to them. The symptom provocation thus relied on a verbal, that is, a *symbolic* stimulus. What is more, as Leys points out, not only was the patient "automatically silenced by being placed in the position of an auditor of his or her own story," but the neuroimaging method itself "required the employment of a thermoplastic mask to minimize the patient's head movements . . . as well as the use of cannulae inserted into the nose for the gas inflow and an overlying face mask attached to a vacuum. All this made it contraindicated if not impossible for the patient to speak during the experiment" (260–61)—to say nothing of how the very design of the experiment may have been retraumatizing. Finally, as Leys also observes (249–50), van der Kolk assumes, rather astonishingly, that visual images are intrinsically nonsymbolic.

See also Leys, *Trauma*, 261n.41, for further information on the experiment and, for a brief summary, van der Kolk, "The Body Keeps the Score" and "Trauma and Memory," in *Traumatic Stress*, ed. van der Kolk, McFarlane, and Weisaeth, 233 and 293, respectively.

13. Leys, *Trauma*, 253 (author's emphasis). See Karl Popper on falsifiability in *The Logic of Scientific Discovery* (New York: Routledge, 2002), e.g., 17–20. I am grateful to Mark Johnson for mentioning this connection.

14. Sigmund Freud, *The Psychopathology of Everyday Life*, in *SE*, vol. 6 (1960), 259/*Zur Psychopathologie des Alltagslebens*, in *GW*, vol. 4 (1941), 288. Freud here makes an unambiguously pejorative use of the term *metaphysics*, associating it, for example, with superstition and myth. See also *Beyond the Pleasure Principle*, where he ascribes to projection the role of externalizing internal stimuli so that the protective shield can be brought to bear against them (*SE*, 18:29/*GW*, 13:29).

15. One could add a third reason for which he would have rejected Caruth's position, namely, his repudiation of the analogy between trauma and infection. See Josef Breuer and Sigmund Freud, *Studies on Hysteria*, in *SE*, vol. 2 (1955), 290–91/*Studien über Hysterie*, in *GW*, vol. 1 (1952), 294–95, and also Leys, *Trauma*, 271–72.

16. Freud's emphasis on what might more intelligibly be termed "anticipatory anxiety" is nevertheless understandable, given that he viewed railway accidents as the prototypical traumatic stressors. Even now, when the extraordinarily extended and diversified field of traumatic stress studies assigns a less prominent role to this anxiety, it is associated with "time-limited events such as an aircraft accident or a rape, which are characterized by the unpreparedness of the victim and the high intensity" (Alexander C. McFarlane and Giovanni de Girolamo, "The Nature of Traumatic Stressors and the Epidemiology of Posttraumatic Reactions," in *Traumatic Stress*, ed. van der Kolk, McFarlane, and Weisaeth, 132). For a more extensive consideration of anxiety, including its anticipatory mode, see Sigmund Freud, *Inhibitions, Symptoms and Anxiety*, in *SE*, vol. 20 (1959), 87–172, as well as the editor's introduction (77–86)/*Hemmung, Symptom und Angst*, in *GW*, vol. 14 (1948), 111–205.

17. Although I would not claim that it is due to his influence, nevertheless I think it can safely be said that Freud thus anticipated the significant emphasis, in current research, on variations in individual premorbid vulnerability to traumatic stress, especially in light of characterological, developmental, and sociocultural factors.

18. We should not overlook the internal self-contradiction here: on the one hand, the "breach in the mind" is a "*conscious* awareness of the threat to life," while on the other, the "shock of the mind's relation to the threat of death" is "*not* the direct experience of the threat, but precisely the missing of this experience" (my emphasis). This contradiction seems to reflect the untenable

position of the otherworldly theorists already described (46), whose consciousness can miraculously experience its own absence.

Referring to the passage as a whole, it may be instructive to consider a certain rhetoric of persuasion at work. Thus, in the first sentence Caruth says that "the breach in the mind . . . is not caused by a pure quantity of stimulus": that is, instead of "not only . . . but also," she says "not . . . but," which, although ambiguous, suggests that trauma might be ascribed largely if not entirely to a temporal dysfunction in consciousness. The second sentence may appear to sound a note of caution in its "not simply . . . but," yet it sustains the possibility of this attribution by explicitly distinguishing between the corporeal and the mental. When we reach the third sentence, the "not . . . but" has been reinstated and any mention of the body omitted, so that trauma is reduced to a pure lapse in the temporality of consciousness.

19. See Luckhurst, *The Trauma Question*, 20–26.

20. For the German original, see *Vorlesungen zur Einführung in die Psychoanalyse*, in *GW*, vol. 11 (1944), 283–84.

21. See, e.g., the *Project*, in *SE*, 1:356–59 / *Entwurf*, in *Aus den Anfängen der Psychoanalyse*, *GW*, 1:435–38. The two models are starkly opposed in Caruth's reading of *Moses and Monotheism*. See *UE*, esp. 10–24 and 67–72; Freud, *Moses and Monotheism*, in *SE*, 23:1–137 / *Der Mann Moses und die monotheistische Religion*, in *GW*, 16:101–246; and Leys's commentary on Caruth's reading in *Trauma*, 283–92.

22. *SE*, vol. 17 (1958), 205–10 / "Einleitung zu *Zur Psychoanalyse der Kriegsneurosen*," in *GW*, vol. 12 (1947), 321–24, and *SE*, vol. 20, esp. 129–30 / *GW*, 14:159–60.

23. *SE*, 18:28 / *GW*, 13:27–28.

24. Indeed, it is simply a mystery where the "event" is supposed to reside while awaiting its reenactment. That Caruth avoids this question altogether is somewhat less mysterious, however, since to consider the replication of a traumatic event in topographical terms requires, on the one hand, recognizing the mediated nature of the replication itself, and on the other, reconciling dissociation with Freud's metapsychology.

25. Bessel van der kolk, Onno van der Hart, and Charles R. Marmar, "Dissociation and Information Processing in Posttraumatic Stress Disorder," in *Traumatic Stress*, ed. van der Kolk, McFarlane, and Weisaeth, 317.

26. The absoluteness of dissociation in Caruth's theory precludes undertaking the difficult but undoubtedly instructive task of reconsidering the relation between dissociation and repression in Freud's own thinking about trauma. To be sure, it was not long after the publication of *Studies on Hysteria* (1895), in which a general endorsement was granted to Pierre Janet's dissociative model (*SE*, 2:12 / *GW*, 1:91), that Freud abandoned dissociation as a diagnostic or interpretive paradigm in favor of repression (or more precisely, in

favor of the defenses that include repression). But it is also well known that, at the end of his career, in *An Outline of Psychoanalysis* (written in 1938 and published posthumously in 1940), he returned to a form of dissociation in *Ichspaltung* or "splitting of the ego" (see *SE*, vol. 23 [1964], 202–4, as well as "Splitting of the Ego in the Process of Defence," 275–78 / *Abriss der Psychoanalyse* and "Die Ichspaltung im Abwehrvorgang," in *GW*, vol. 17 [1941], 133–35 and 57–62). One can scarcely become acquainted with Freud's theory of trauma without also becoming aware of the ways in which it implicitly reprises the question of the relation between dissociation and repression. Do dissociation and repression coincide at all *as* mechanisms of defense, and if so, to what extent? How, in light of the descriptive, dynamic, and systematic or topographical senses of the word *unconscious*, would one characterize the effects of these mechanisms? And considering that they may assume more than one mode or else operate conjointly with other such mechanisms, might it be the case, for example, that hysterical conversion and post-traumatic somatization occupy analogous positions in the etiology of the neuroses? Although I cannot pursue these issues here, they point to what is most thought-provoking in Freud's reflections on trauma and should not be foreclosed.

27. On affect in dreams, see *The Interpretation of Dreams*, in *SE*, vol. 5 (1953), 460–87 / *GW*, 2/3: 462–92.

28. See, for example, *The Interpretation of Dreams*, in *SE*, 4:335–38 / *GW*, 2/3: 341–44. Freud had already discussed this, however, in the *Project* (*SE*, 1:337 / *Aus den Anfängen der Psychoanalyse*, 421).

29. On the connection between motility and reality testing, see esp. "A Metapsychological Supplement to the Theory of Dreams," in *SE*, vol. 14 (1957), 232–34 / "Metapsychologische Ergänzung zur Traumlehre," in *GW*, vol. 10 (1946), 423–25, and *The Ego and the Id*, in *SE*, vol. 19 (1961), 25–26 / *Das Ich und das Es*, in *GW*, 13:253–54.

30. The transformative process in question is what Freud calls "working-through" (*Durcharbeiten* or *Durcharbeitung*). See "Remembering, Repeating and Working-Through," in *SE*, vol. 12 (1958), 147–56 / "Erinnern, Wiederholen und Durcharbeiten," in *GW*, 10:125–36. Although usage varies, I choose to hyphenate "acting-out" (*Agieren*), both to distinguish the noun from the verb and to underscore the relation to "working-through." On this relation, see also "Acting-Out and Working-Through," the conclusion of LaCapra's *Representing the Holocaust*.

31. *Introductory Lectures on Psycho-Analysis*, in *SE*, vol. 15 (1963), 17 / *GW*, 11:9.

32. Pierre Janet, *Psychological Healing: A Historical and Clinical Study*, trans. Eden Paul and Cedar Paul (New York: Macmillan, 1925), 1:661–62, emphasis in original. Oddly enough, this statement may more accurately reflect Freud's than Janet's position. In this connection, see Leys, *Trauma*, 105–19.

33. Marc Chevrie and Hervé Le Roux, "Site and Speech: An Interview with Claude Lanzmann about *Shoah*," in *Claude Lanzmann's "Shoah": Key Essays*, ed. Stuart Liebman (New York: Oxford University Press, 2007), 41.

3. ART AFTER AUSCHWITZ, AGAIN

1. Michael Rothberg, *Traumatic Realism: The Demands of Holocaust Representation* (Minneapolis: University of Minnesota Press, 2000), 19–58.

2. Theodor W. Adorno, "Commitment," in *NL*, 2:76–94; "Engagement," in *Noten zur Literatur III, GS*, 11:409–30. For reasons of economy and because it is less closely tied to the question of Auschwitz, I do not discuss Adorno's *Aesthetic Theory* (which was still in progress when he died and which he planned to dedicate to Beckett) but will refer to it, where appropriate, in notes. In the framework of this chapter, it is most useful for its occasional rephrasing, expansion, or clarification of earlier statements about Beckett (see below, nn. 22 and 24) and for its short discussions of Paul Celan (*Aesthetic Theory*, trans. Robert Hullot-Kentor [Minneapolis: University of Minnesota Press, 1997], 219 and 321–22 / *Ästhetische Theorie*, in *GS*, 7:325 and 475–77)—discussions that render even more implausible the unsubstantiated claim that Adorno, when declaring the "barbarity" of poetry after Auschwitz, had Celan's "Todesfuge" in mind. On this claim, see, e.g., John Felstiner, *Paul Celan: Poet, Survivor, Jew* (New Haven: Yale University Press, 1995), 139 and 189.

3. Theodor W. Adorno, "Cultural Criticism and Society," in *Prisms*, trans. Samuel and Shierry Weber (Cambridge: MIT Press, 1981), 34 / "Kulturkritik und Gesellschaft," in *Prismen, GS*, 10.1:30.

4. Ibid. The sentence reads: "Kulturkritik findet sich der letzten Stufe der Dialektik von Kultur und Barbarei gegenüber: nach Auschwitz ein Gedicht zu schreiben, ist barbarisch, und das frißt auch die Erkenntnis an, die ausspricht, warum es unmöglich ward, heute Gedichte zu schreiben."

5. Max Horkheimer and Theodor W. Adorno, *Dialectic of Enlightenment: Philosophical Fragments*, ed. Gunzelin Schmid Noerr, trans. Edmond Jephcott (Stanford, Calif.: Stanford University Press, 2002) / *Dialektik der Aufklärung: Philosophische Fragmente, GS*, 3:19–234.

6. Adorno's emphasis on lyric, notably in "On Lyric Poetry and Society" (1957; see *NL*, 1:37–54 / "Rede über Lyrik und Gesellschaft," in *Noten zur Literatur I, GS*, 11:49–68), reflects his preoccupation with what is called, in "Commitment," the "dismissal [*Abdankung*]" of the subject or, in plainer language, the erosion of individuality by contemporary forms of political and social organization in conjunction with the culture industry. To my knowledge, however, Adorno does not ask himself whether the "barbarity" of poetry after Auschwitz might not depend at least to some degree on who, specifically, is writing it.

7. See Rothberg, *Traumatic Realism*, 38–40, where consideration of "On Lyric Poetry and Society" helps to explain the transition from "Cultural Criticism and Society" to "Commitment."

8. Eric Santner, *Stranded Objects: Mourning, Memory, and Film in Postwar Germany* (Ithaca: Cornell University Press, 1990), 9.

9. Rothberg, *Traumatic Realism*, 47 (emphasis in original).

10. Theodor W. Adorno, *Negative Dialectics*, trans. E. B. Ashton (New York: Continuum, 1973), 362 / *Negative Dialektik, GS*, 6:355.

11. Ibid., 362–63/6:355–56.

12. In this connection, the most important question is arguably why belief in the randomness of survival, which in principle would make considerations of agency irrelevant, does not preclude but rather, as in many other cases, is accompanied by the seemingly incompatible belief in a moral causality that implicates the survivor, whether evidence of that belief take the form of shame, guilt (as a feeling, needless to say, and not a sense of objective culpability), or some other "punishment," such as nightmares. As I suggest, it would also be interesting to ponder the difference between Adorno's dream, in which the survivor with no direct experience of the camps encounters only what to this day stands out most in the popular imagination, that is, the crematoria, and the dream described by Levi at the very end of *The Reawakening*, in which a "peaceful relaxed environment" gives way, in a mood of unmistakable and mounting anguish, to the realization that this setting was all deception, that he is back in the *Lager* and hears "the dawn command of Auschwitz, a foreign word, feared and expected: get up, *'Wstawàch'*" (Primo Levi, *The Reawakening*, trans. Stuart Woolf [London: The Bodley Head, 1965; New York: Macmillan, 1993], 207–8). What the dreams notably share, however, is the sense that only the camp is real.

13. It should be emphasized nonetheless that this ambivalence marks a departure from the severity of "Cultural Criticism and Society" and already informs an important text of 1959, "What Does Coming to Terms with the Past Mean?" (trans. Timothy Bahti and Geoffrey Hartman, in *Bitburg in Moral and Political Perspective*, ed. Geoffrey Hartman [Bloomington: Indiana University Press, 1986], 115–29/"Was bedeutet: Aufarbeitung der Vergangenheit," in *Eingriffe: Neun kritische Modelle, GS*, 10.2:555–72). "Coming to terms" (*Aufarbeitung*) is closely related to Freudian "working-through" (*Durcharbeitung*) in that both involve a *"turn toward the subject*: reinforcement of a person's self-consciousness and, with that, of a sense of self" (ibid., 128/10.2:571). This "turn toward the subject [*Wendung aufs Subjekt*]" is practiced, I would argue, in the very passage just quoted from *Negative Dialectics*, where Adorno acknowledges that his "coldness"—including, as I have suggested, the coldness characterizing his condemnation of poetry after Auschwitz—derives from "the drastic guilt of him who was spared." But it is not only in the doubt thus coming to surround

this condemnation that we can perceive the effect of Adorno's self-reflection. In the text of 1959 itself, he states:

> I once heard the story of a woman who, after attending a performance of the dramatization of *The Diary of Anne Frank*, said in a shaken voice: "Yes, but really, at least *that* girl ought to have been allowed to live." Surely, even this was to be welcomed as a first step toward insight. But the individual case, which stands for and illuminates the frightful whole, became at the same time (by virtue of its individualization) an alibi for the whole that the woman forgot. The confounded thing about such observations remains that one wouldn't therefore wish to counsel against performances of the Anne Frank play or the like, since their effect indeed feeds into the potential for improvement—whatever one's objections and however much it seems to be a sacrilege against the dignity of the dead. (Ibid., 127/10.2:570)

The writer of these lines certainly distances himself from the author of "Cultural Criticism and Society," who in all probability would have rejected the play out of hand. This is not to say that the extremism of Adorno's earlier view disappears altogether (in fact, it is in *Negative Dialectics* that he declares: "All post-Auschwitz culture, including its urgent critique, is garbage" [367/GS, 6:359]). However, working through or coming to terms with the past is never complete in any case and always leaves a residue of unresolved experience. For that matter, its function is not so much to "master" the past as to shift the position of the self in relation to it. Thus the point is that, beginning in the late fifties, the tendency giving rise to Adorno's more drastic pronouncements is increasingly constrained by other considerations, as when objections to the dramatization of Anne Frank's diary must be tempered by the recognition of its potential contribution to greater individual or collective self-awareness. What I have called "ethical ambivalence" points to a dynamic tension that, despite and beyond any arresting aporia, propels Adorno's attempt to think through aesthetics after Auschwitz. I am grateful to Dominick LaCapra for suggesting to me the pertinence of "What Does Coming to Terms with the Past Mean?" in this connection.

14. "Dismantling" stands for the German *Demontage*.

15. In addressing both committed literature and Adorno's discussion of it, I will focus only on Sartre, since he provides such a ready and instructive contrast to Beckett and since including Brecht as well would carry us too far from the central concerns of this chapter. For Adorno's assessment of Brecht, see esp. *NL*, 2: 82–87/*GS*, 11:415–22.

16. Jean-Paul Sartre, *What Is Literature?* trans. Bernard Frechtman, in *"What Is Literature?" and Other Essays* (Cambridge: Harvard University Press, 1988): "One is not a writer for having chosen to say certain things, but for hav-

ing chosen to say them in a certain way. And, to be sure, the style makes the value of the prose. But it should pass unnoticed" (39).

17. Translation modified. Adorno alludes to Karl Jaspers's notion of *Grenz-situation*, which became a commonplace of existential philosophy. See Jaspers, *Philosophy*, trans. E. B. Ashton (Chicago: University of Chicago Press, 1970), 2:177. Cited by Adorno, "Trying to Understand *Endgame*," in *NL*, 1:252 / "Versuch, das Endspiel zu verstehen," in *Noten zur Literatur II, GS*, 11:294.

18. Jean-Paul Sartre, *No Exit*, trans. Stuart Gilbert, and *Dirty Hands*, trans. Lionel Abel, both in *"No Exit" and Three Other Plays* (New York: Vintage International, 1989).

19. It is for this thoroughly ahistorical, idealistic conception of freedom, unaffected even by the reality of torture and genocide, that Herbert Marcuse, Adorno's colleague at the Frankfurt School, took Sartre to task in "Existentialism: Remarks on Jean-Paul Sartre's *L'Être et le Néant*," *Philosophy and Phenomenological Research* 8, no. 3 (March 1948): 309–36, reprinted with revisions as "Sartre's Existentialism," in *Studies in Critical Philosophy* (Boston: Beacon, 1973), 157–90.

20. Theodor Adorno, "Trying to Understand *Endgame*," in *NL*, 1: 241 / "Versuch, das Endspiel zu verstehen," in *Noten zur Literatur II, GS*, 11:281.

21. Samuel Beckett, *Endgame*, vol. 3 of *Samuel Beckett: The Grove Centenary Edition*, ed. Paul Auster (New York: Grove Press, 2006), 3:114–15.

22. Or, as Adorno puts it in *Aesthetic Theory*: "Beckett's plays are absurd not because of the absence of any meaning, for then they would be simply irrelevant, but because they put meaning on trial; they unfold its history" (153 / *GS*, 7:230).

23. Beckett, *Endgame*, 100.

24. Adorno expands on the issue of genre in an instructive way when he remarks, in *Aesthetic Theory*: "Although Beckett's plays can no longer be taken for tragic or comic, they are not therefore, as would suit academic aesthetics, hybrids on the order of tragicomedy. On the contrary, Beckett's plays pass historical judgment over these categories as such. . . . In accord with the tendency of modern art to make its own categories thematic through self-reflection, plays like *Godot* and *Endgame*—in the scene in which the protagonists decide to laugh—are more the tragic presentation of comedy's fate than they are comic; in the actors' forced laughter, the spectator's mirth vanishes" (340 / *GS*, 7:505).

25. Paul Celan's expression (in German, *was geschah*), from his "Speech on the Occasion of Receiving the Literature Prize of the Free Hanseatic City of Bremen," 34 (trans. modified) / *Gesammelte Werke*, 3:186.

26. Ibid., 35/3:186 (given the importance, in what follows, of the situation of address, I have modified the published translation, rendering *ansprechbar* [*ein ansprechbares Du*] as "addressable" rather than "approachable").

27. I alter the published translation—which renders both *Abdankung* and *Demontage* as "dismantling"—in order to avoid confusion and because, at least on my reading of Adorno, there is an appreciable difference between them: whereas *Demontage* suggests a process in which the work of art has recourse to what remains of a dis-integrated form in order to convey its obsolescence, *Abdankung* indicates a "getting rid of," even if this entails, in the case of the subject, simulacra of individuality that are tolerated in compensation for the loss of individuality itself.

28. Samuel Beckett, *The Unnamable*, vol. 2 of *Samuel Beckett: The Grove Centenary Edition*, ed. Paul Auster (New York: Grove Press, 2006), 2:407.

29. Emile Benveniste, "The Nature of Pronouns," in *Problems in General Linguistics*, trans. Mary Elizabeth Meek (Coral Gables, Fla.: University of Miami Press, 1971), 218 (trans. modified; see "La nature des pronoms," in *Problèmes de linguistique générale*, vol. 1 [Paris: Gallimard, 1966], 252); Edmund Husserl, *Logical Investigations*, trans. J. N. Findlay (New York: Humanities Press, 1970), 1:315.

30. Although I focus here on the first person singular, the same can clearly be said, from a political point of view, about the plural. For the Nazis to allow "the Jews" to say "we" would be to admit of a dialogue between the Jews and themselves, addressed explicitly or implicitly as "you." And of course they did this, even in the late years of the war, as in the appointment of leaders to represent or speak for the Jewish ghetto communities vis-à-vis Nazi authorities. But they did it, as we know, in order better to organize these communities for deportation and extermination. Furthermore, it is clear that the cohesion of the *Volksgemeinschaft* depended not only on the constitution of an external and equally identitarian Other ("the Jews") but also on the concentration and elimination of *internal* others considered *unlebenswertes Leben* ("life unworthy of life"), as in the extensive T4 euthanasia program, where techniques of killing were devised and tested that would later serve the SS well in Operation Reinhard, the "final solution" that established death camps in Bełżec, Sobibór, and Treblinka in addition to Chełmno, Auschwitz, and Majdanek. Thus, while in no way jeopardizing the distinction between the perpetrators and their principal victims, one can see, assuming a relational view of the self (individual or collective), that the annihilation of the other on whom one's own identity depends is, in a sense, suicidal. As Jean-Luc Nancy puts it: "the logic of Nazi Germany was not only that of the extermination of the other, of the subhuman deemed exterior to the communion of blood and soil, but also, effectively, the logic of sacrifice aimed at all those in the 'Aryan' community who did not satisfy the criteria of *pure* immanence, so much so that—it being obviously impossible to set a limit on such criteria—the suicide of the German nation itself might have represented a plausible extrapolation of the process: moreover, it would not be false to say that this really took place, with regard to certain as-

pects of the spiritual reality of this nation" (*The Inoperative Community*, ed. Peter Connor, trans. Peter Connor et al. [Minneapolis: University of Minnesota Press, 1991], 12).

31. According to the working definition I will adopt in what follows, a memoir is a first person narrative pertaining to a segment of the author's life in which he or she witnessed events of general or historical significance. Unlike autobiography, which encompasses the whole of an individual's life up to the time of writing, memoir covers primarily if not exclusively the segment in question. Unlike the diary or journal, it is written from a perspective that clearly postdates the demarcated series of events to which it refers. Unlike memoirs (plural), its author need not have played—and in the case of Holocaust survivor testimony very seldom played—an important public role in those events.

32. It was only after writing this that I came upon Michael Berenbaum's *The World Must Know: The History of the Holocaust as Told in the United States Holocaust Memorial Museum* (Boston: Little, Brown and Company, 1993).

33. This is strikingly so, for example, in Dan Pagis's poem "Europe, Late," perhaps especially in its last lines, where the ironic "heavenly" recalls not only the smoke from the crematoria but, at Bełżec, Sobibór, and Treblinka, the narrow corridor leading to the annihilation sector, euphemistically named *der Himmelsweg* ("way to heaven")—and where the poetic voice is brutally cut off:

You'll see, madame,
that everything will be all right,
just heavenly—you wait and see.
No it could never happen here,
don't worry so—you'll see—it could

(Dan Pagis, *Points of Departure*, trans. Stephen Mitchell [Philadelphia: The Jewish Publication Society of America, 1981], 23).

34. Saul Friedlander, *Reflections of Nazism: An Essay on Kitsch and Death*, trans. Thomas Weyr (New York: Harper & Row, 1984; rpt. Bloomington: Indiana University Press, 1993), 89.

35. Ibid., 92.

36. I refer to Friedlander's two-volume history of the Holocaust, *Nazi Germany and the Jews: The Years of Persecution, 1933–1939* (New York: Harper-Collins, 1997) and *The Years of Extermination: Nazi Germany and the Jews, 1939–1945* (New York: HarperCollins, 2007), and in particular to his innovative use of the stories of individual victims in an effort to meet the challenge of establishing, as he puts it, "a historical account of the Holocaust in which the policies of the perpetrators, the attitudes of surrounding society, and the world of the victims could be addressed within an integrated framework" (*Nazi Germany and the Jews*, 1).

37. Friedlander, *Reflections of Nazism*, 89.

38. Ibid., 91. Friedlander quotes and comments on a passage from Martin Broszat, "Hitler and the Genesis of the 'Final Solution,'" *Yad Vashem Studies* 13 (1979): 93–94.

39. The phrase *wie es eigentlich gewesen*, associated with the historian Leopold von Ranke, is used here in reference to the historiography discussed by Friedlander, which in fact bears less resemblance to the historiography envisioned by Ranke than to a writing of history heavily influenced by positivism.

40. For a succinct description of the implied reader, together with further references, see Gerald Prince, *A Dictionary of Narratology*, rev. ed. (Lincoln: University of Nebraska Press, 2003), 43.

41. See especially Raul Hilberg, *Perpetrators Victims Bystanders: The Jewish Catastrophe, 1933–1945* (New York: HarperCollins, 1992).

42. *DS*, 83 / *O*, 2:1056. At this point, to be sure, Levi's view is that "we, the survivors, are not the true witnesses" (ibid.). But as I argue in the next chapter, this is a statement that calls for careful interpretation.

43. See above, n. 31.

44. Ross Chambers, "Memory, Genre, Truth: Lucie Aubrac, Jorge Semprun, François Maspero and the *devoir de mémoire*," *Contemporary French Civilization* 30, no. 1 (Winter/Spring 2006): 1–27. I return to Semprun's text in Chapter 5.

45. It is important to note, however, that what is "there" is not really there, is not, that is, a presence that happens to be absent but could just as well become present again. Rather, indexicality or haunting is indissociable from the loss of these possibilities.

46. At one point in his important sociological study *L'expérience concentrationnaire: Essai sur le maintien de l'identité sociale* (Paris: Métailié, 1990), Michael Pollack discusses, in reference to survivors and the forms of their testimony, the methodological problem of sampling (a problem all the more vexing as survivors of the camps are already a minority and as the mere fact of surviving may appear to call the representativity of their experience into question). He then observes:

> One is startled, of course, by the "cynicism" of these remarks, whose psychologically or morally unacceptable character culminates in the use of the term "selection," employed here in the idiom of sampling technique whereas one could just as well read it in terms of mass murder and genocide.
>
> But this apparent cynicism only systematizes, by making it more obvious, the process of studying "scientifically," that is, coldly and at a distance, matters that arouse the most extreme emotional reactions and that are ordinarily met with the "heat" of revolt, denunciation, or indignation. By its ex-

treme character, such an object reveals the essence of any scientific approach, which is . . . to impose "detachment" where the object under study calls spontaneously for an extreme "involvement." (181–82, my translation)

No doubt, Pollack is to be credited with at least acknowledging this problem of "method," similar if not identical to the one Friedlander underscores in traditional historiography. And it is surely the case in mainstream social science, as in traditional historiography, that a considerable degree of detachment is more or less unavoidable. What gives pause in the passage just cited, however, is, on the one hand, the apparent and clearly erroneous assumption that the only alternative to "science" is heated emotion or "an extreme 'involvement'" devoid of cognitive value, and on the other, the lack of any stated awareness that complete detachment in regard to an "object" such as Holocaust survivor testimony may well, or rather certainly does, render science itself cognitively deficient.

47. Roman Jakobson, "Linguistics and Poetics," in *Selected Writings*, vol. 3, *Poetry of Grammar and Grammar of Poetry*, ed. Stephen Rudy (The Hague: Mouton, 1981), 24.

48. Alexander and Margarete Mitscherlich, *The Inability to Mourn: Principles of Collective Behavior*, trans. Beverley R. Placzek (New York: Grove Press, 1975). Of course, given the resemblance of mourning (*Trauerarbeit*) and working-through (*Durcharbeitung*) in Freudian thought, as well as the connection between working-through and "coming to terms" (*Aufarbeitung*), one could say that Adorno's essay "What Does Coming to Terms with the Past Mean?" also has much to do with an inability to mourn in postwar German society. As for Adorno himself, I speak of a *certain* such inability because I believe it important to keep in mind that his position did evolve, that it did after all evince a kind of working-through (see n. 13, above).

49. Appelfeld, *Beyond Despair*, x.

50. On the subject of self-blame, see Susan J. Brison, *Aftermath: Violence and the Remaking of a Self* (Princeton: Princeton University Press, 2002), 73–77.

51. I discuss Levinas's thought at length and in a more critical vein in Chapter 5.

52. In this connection, I would note the rather unusual and very interesting case of Paul Steinberg, whose memoir was written in part as a response to the unflattering portrait painted of him, under the name Henri, in Primo Levi's *Survival in Auschwitz*, trans. Stuart Woolf (New York: Macmillan, 1993), 98–100 (originally published under the title *If This Is a Man* [New York: Orion, 1959]). See Paul Steinberg, *Speak You Also: A Survivor's Reckoning*, trans. Linda Coverdale with Bill Ford (New York: Henry Holt, 2000).

53. See, e.g., Terrence Des Pres, "Excremental Assault," in *The Survivor* (Oxford: Oxford University Press, 1976), 51–71.

54. See the chapter entitled "The Gray Zone" in *The Drowned and the Saved*, where Levi speaks of the Special Squads forced to work in the crematoria (and composed almost exclusively of Jewish men) as "National Socialism's most demonic crime," an attempt "to shift onto others—specifically, the victims—the burden of guilt, so that they were deprived of even the solace of innocence" (53). The Special Squads are discussed at greater length in Chapter 4 of this volume. In a similar vein, Robert Antelme observes, in reference to the group of prisoners to which he belonged: "We are becoming very ugly to behold. For this the fault lies with us. It's because we are a human pestilence" (*The Human Race*, trans. Jeffrey Haight and Annie Mahler [Marlboro, Vt.: The Marlboro Press, 1992], 76).

55. Appelfeld, *Beyond Despair*, x.

56. Berel Lang, *Act and Idea in the Nazi Genocide* (Chicago: University of Chicago Press, 1990; rpt. Syracuse: Syracuse University Press, 2003); *The Future of the Holocaust: Between History and Memory* (Ithaca: Cornell University Press, 1999); *Holocaust Representation: Art Within the Limits of History and Ethics* (Baltimore: Johns Hopkins University Press, 2000); *Post-Holocaust: Interpretation, Misinterpretation, and the Claims of History* (Bloomington: Indiana University Press, 2005); *Philosophical Witnessing: The Holocaust as Presence* (Waltham, Mass.: Brandeis University Press, 2009).

57. Lang, "The Representation of Evil: Ethical Content as Literary Form," *AI*, 124–25.

58. See *AI*, 125n.8. Lang here refers to (but does not quote) "Commitment" and quotes briefly from *Negative Dialectics*. There is no mention of "Cultural Criticism and Society" nor any discussion of Adorno's intellectual itinerary.

59. I quote from the last page of the previous chapter, "Jabès and the Measure of History," but the assumption informs "The Representation of Evil" in its entirety and becomes, if anything, even more insistent in *Holocaust Representation*, where Lang restates a number of times the views to which I take exception below.

60. This is not to say that there are no facts but only that there are none situated, as Lang would have it, outside of representation. Nor, however, does it mean that all putative facts are mere interpretations subject to no evidentiary constraints (see my objection to Hayden White, Chapter 1, n. 32. Unfortunately, in "The Importance of Holocaust *Mis*representation" (chapter 5 in *Holocaust Representation*), Lang's defense of historical realism against certain constructivist historians leads nowhere, based as it is on a simplistic opposition of fact and interpretation.

61. On universal history, see Louis O. Mink, "Narrative Form as a Cognitive Instrument," in *The Writing of History: Literary Form and Historical Understanding*, ed. Robert H. Canary and Henry Kozicki (Madison: University of Wisconsin Press, 1978), 134–38. As I suggest in Chapter 1, this appears to be the position of the historians in the debate described by Dori Laub.

62. Just before citing White, Lang acknowledges that "the strong distinction asserted between historical and figurative or imaginative discourse runs against the current of much contemporary literary theory and historiography" (*AI*, 122n.7). Later in the essay, his argument against this current is based on a mere appeal to fact, or more precisely, on the mere *possibility* of a represented fact lying outside of representation: "It may be true that there are no 'bare'—that is, without the means of representation—historical facts; and it may also be that there is no writing (historical or imaginative) that does not in principle engender what has been referred to here as figurative space. But neither of these possibilities denies the possibility of representation that stands in a direct relation to its object—in effect, if not in principle, immediate and unaltered. It is *this* possibility that stands at the crux of the distinction between historical and figurative discourse" (*AI*, 156). The rest of the time, however, Lang assumes this "possibility" to be an actuality, that is, a fact. Hence the circularity of his argument. Hence also a kind of structural irony that appears to escape him, the "fact" responsible for the distinction between historical and imaginative discourse being, itself, purely imaginary. (In other words, there is no such possibility, since mediation is constitutive of all representation.)

63. On chronicle and diary, see *AI*, 127–31, and also Young, "On Rereading Holocaust Diaries and Memoirs," in *Writing and Rewriting the Holocaust*, 15–39, where, among other things, the author convincingly argues that the registration of facts at the time of the Holocaust itself was already mediated by preexisting interpretive paradigms, generic structures, etc.

Worth noting here is another irony (in addition to the one mentioned above, n. 62), namely, that Lang and Cathy Caruth, although beholden to radically different, even opposed intellectual traditions as far as the theory of language is concerned, end up making similar if not identical claims in regard to the disabling of representation by traumatic experience. In both cases, the failure to sustain the description of trauma as unrepresentable exposes the normative bias that that description serves to screen. In *Holocaust Representation*, Lang concedes that "nobody would argue that the 'best' representation or image of the Holocaust would be to reproduce it accurately, to the last detail—that is, to recreate the Holocaust itself," but then adds, as though to clarify matters: "The value of historical nonrepresentational representation is exactly here, in its representation of the events that occurred without mediation but also without bringing the events themselves once again to life" (13).

64. On memoir, see *AI*, 130–31.

65. Revelation 22:18.

66. Ernst van Alphen, *Caught by History: Holocaust Effects in Contemporary Art, Literature, and Theory* (Stanford: Stanford University Press, 1997), 30.

67. Ibid.

68. "Lang conflates the perspective of the perpetrators with that of the victims of the Holocaust. Impersonality and abstractness indeed did characterize the Nazi genocide: it relied completely on a radical and total denial of individuality. But that does not mean that the victims experienced themselves as abstract or impersonal. However damaged their experiences of their subjectivity and their situation might have been, it is not the same thing to claim that they resolved their experiences in abstraction. Unwittingly, [Lang's] argument risks yielding to the pressure of Nazi ideology" (ibid., 30).

69. Here again, it is worth underscoring the parallel with Caruth: to define the Holocaust or trauma generally as that which cannot or should not be represented is necessarily to imply that its representation, including survivor testimony, entails falsification or profanation.

70. Lang, *Holocaust Representation*, 13.

71. Similarly, Lang states further on that "documentary and historical writings about the genocide have been more adequate and more compelling—in sum, more *valuable*—than the imaginative writings about that subject" (*AI*, 140).

72. For further biographical information, see Charlotte Delbo, *Convoy to Auschwitz: Women of the French Resistance*, trans. Carol Cosman (Boston: Northeastern University Press, 1997), 3–13 and 74–76, *Le convoi du 24 janvier* (Paris: Minuit, 1965), 9–14 and 100–102, and Lawrence Langer, introduction to Delbo, *Auschwitz and After*, ix–xviii.

73. According to Langer (introduction, x), the first volume of *Auschwitz and After* was written in 1946 but withheld from publication until Delbo felt it had stood the test of time, and portions of the second volume were composed in 1946 and 1947. I would also refer the reader to a number of more sustained readings of Delbo: Ross Chambers, "Orphaned Memories, Phantom Pain: Toward a Hauntology of Discourse," in *Untimely Interventions*, 189–243; Lawrence Langer, "Charlotte Delbo and a Heart of Ashes," in *The Age of Atrocity: Death in Modern Literature* (Boston: Beacon Press, 1978), 201–44; Michael Rothberg, "Unbearable Witness: Charlotte Delbo's Traumatic Timescapes," in *Traumatic Realism*, 141–77; and Nicole Thatcher, *Charlotte Delbo: Une voix singulière* (Paris: L'Harmattan, 2003). See also the recent collection edited by David Caron and Sharon Marquart, *Les revenantes: Charlotte Delbo, la voix d'une communauté à jamais déportée* (Toulouse: Presses universitaires du Mirail, 2011).

74. As Delbo points out, this solidarity was also based on bonds formed between members of her convoy during their previous imprisonment at Romainville. See *Convoy to Auschwitz*, 9 / *Le convoi du 24 janvier*, 17.

75. The term was coined by David Rousset, *L'univers concentrationnaire* (Paris: Editions du Pavois, 1946), translated as *The Other Kingdom*, trans. Ramon Guthrie (New York: Reynal and Hitchcock, 1947).

76. This extension may seem too large, since there were significant disparities between and within camps, and yet too small, since victims of the Holocaust did not by any means include only those deported to camps (on the contrary, the mobile killing operations of 1941–43 accounted for more than one million deaths among Jews alone; see Raul Hilberg, *The Destruction of the European Jews*, 3rd ed. [New Haven: Yale University Press, 2003], 1:275–408). My delimitation of the "us" in this instance is based on Delbo's own thematics of return, which presupposes departure, that is, deportation.

77. It would take us too far afield to discuss in any detail the invidious stratification or hierarchization of prisoner populations in the camps. Suffice it to say that this was one of many ways in which the SS sought to destroy existing communities and prevent the formation of new ones as bases of resistance.

78. This future is evoked as well by Primo Levi, who remarks that, in camp slang, *"morgen früh"* ("tomorrow morning") meant "never" (*Survival in Auschwitz*, 133).

79. "Die Vergangenheit, die nicht vergehen will" ("The Past That Will Not Pass") is the title of Ernst Nolte's notorious article in the *Frankfurter Allgemeine Zeitung* of June 6, 1986, in which the author attempts to minimize or displace Nazism's responsibility for the Holocaust. My use of this contextually appropriate phrase does not at all imply agreement with Nolte's views.

80. Matters are admittedly somewhat more complicated than this, as Delbo writes "Aucun de nous n'aurait dû revenir" (1:183), which could also be translated as "None of us should have returned," thus suggesting both a sense of survivor guilt and the despair of those whose return confronted them with the formidable difficulty of communicating traumatic experience to the world at large. "Aucun de nous ne devait revenir" corresponds more closely to "None of us was meant to return" but does not convey these additional meanings. I am grateful to Tim Clark, Tom Kavanagh, Susan Suleiman, and Monique Middleton for discussing this with me.

81. For essential reading on the question of community in *Auschwitz and After*, see David Caron, *My Father & I: The Marais & the Queerness of Community* (Ithaca: Cornell University Press, 2009), esp. 143–46, 158–59, 177–82, and 216–19.

82. Quoted by Langer, introduction to Auschwitz and After, x, and in the translator's preface to Charlotte Delbo, *Days and Memory*, trans. Rosette C. Lamont (Marlboro, Vt.: The Marlboro Press, 1990), vii / *La mémoire et les jours*, (Paris: Berg International, 1985). "Il faut donner à voir" conveys the imperative of *making seen* or *showing*. The expression *donner à voir* is particularly appropriate here in light of the author's involvement in the theater and the remarkably visual orientation of her testimony. Although Delbo is not frequently given to irony, one might also consider the nature of the "gift" (*don*) suggested by *donner*, that is, the nature of what is being shown.

83. Dominick LaCapra, *Writing History, Writing Trauma* (Baltimore: Johns Hopkins University Press, 2001), 41. See also Silverman's use of the term "heteropathic identification" (borrowed from Max Scheler) in *The Threshold of the Visible World*, 23.

84. Charlotte Delbo, *Days and Memory*, 4/14. In this passage, Delbo has just referred to the difficulty of verbally articulating traumatic experience and then says, as if to reprise the epigraph of *Auschwitz and After*: "This is why I say today that while knowing perfectly well that it corresponds to the facts, I no longer know if it is real [*C'est pourquoi je dis aujourd'hui que, tout en sachant très bien que c'est véridique, je ne sais plus si c'est vrai*]."

85. It may be asked how, in fact, Delbo could have witnessed the arrival of such a convoy, since she was transferred to Rajsko on August 3, 1943, well before the Nazis completed the spur leading underneath the guard tower at Birkenau and contiguous to Sector BI, the women's camp (the image of this spur and especially of the tower has become one of the most familiar of the Holocaust). However, it would not have been unusual for prisoners working in the fields outside the *kleine Kette* or internal perimeter of the camp to pass by the ramp in use throughout Delbo's imprisonment at Auschwitz-Birkenau, the so-called *Judenrampe* (see, e.g., *AA*, 166/2:87, where, in a short passage reminiscent of "Arrivals, Departures," she speaks of just such an occasion, although it is not immediately clear whether "the railway station" refers to this ramp or some more distant terminus). In any case, the *Judenrampe* stood only three hundred meters or so from Section BI, thus making it possible for inmates to observe activity there, even if not in a detailed manner. (And besides, it is not a question of determining whether what she describes corresponds in every respect to a particular, historically identifiable convoy, or of denying the possibility that her description may be based to some extent on information gathered over a period of time or from sources other than personal observation. The point is rather that nothing in this scene controverts the historical record.) See, e.g., Tadeusz Iwaszko, "Deportation to the Camp and Registration of Prisoners," in *Auschwitz: Nazi Death Camp*, 3rd ed., ed. Franciszek Piper and Teresa Świebocka, trans. Douglas Selvage (Oświęcim: Auschwitz-Birkenau State Museum, 2004), 58. For his indispensable assistance in this matter, I am very grateful to Tomasz Cebulski, a state-licensed guide currently researching the political history of Auschwitz-Birkenau, 1980–2005.

One may also wonder why, toward the very end of this passage, Delbo suddenly shifts to a gendered perspective ("with their children, *their wives*, their aged parents"). I know of no fully satisfactory answer to this question but would refer the reader to three sections, two in *None of Us Will Return* and one in *Useless Knowledge* and all entitled "The Men" (*AA*, 20–21/1:34–36; *AA*, 95–96/1:152–53; *AA*, 117–22/2:9–18). In these sections, Delbo suggests that in some respects, due to their culturally determined social role, the men suffered more than the women. Thus: "They experienced, more acutely than any other, the feeling of the decline in their strength and manly duty, since they could do nothing for the women. If we suffered from seeing them unhappy, hungry, deprived, they suffered even more from no longer being able to protect us, to defend us, to assume destiny on their own" (*AA*, 117/2:10). The claim need not be construed as invidious, however, since later in "Arrivals, Departures" and elsewhere as well Delbo alludes, for example, to the especially difficult plight of women with children. On the question of gender in *Auschwitz and After*, see David Caron's illuminating remarks in *My Father & I*, 167–74.

86. See Edmund Husserl, *Ideas Pertaining to a Pure Phenomenology and to a Phenomenological Philosophy*, in *Collected Works*, trans. F. Kersten (The Hague: Martinus Nijhoff, 1982), 1:51–62.

87. Viktor Shklovsky, "Art as Technique," in *Russian Formalist Criticism*, trans. Lee T. Lemon and Marion J. Reis (Lincoln: University of Nebraska Press, 1965), 5–24. A more recent translation, "Art as Device," can be found in Viktor Shklovsky, *Theory of Prose*, trans. Benjamin Sher (Elmwood Park, Ill.: Dalkey Archive Press, 1990), 1–14. In his translator's introduction, Sher takes issue with the translation of Shklovsky's term as "defamiliarization," preferring "enstrangement." However, I do not quite follow his argument, and it seems to me that Shklovksy's position justifies either term—as when, for example, he states that "the purpose of art . . . is to lead us to a knowledge of a thing through the organ of sight instead of recognition," so that we see that thing "as if it were perceived for the first time" (*Theory of Prose*, 6).

88. *AA*, 1:10, 12, 16. The translation reads "They do not know" (4), "They have no idea" (5), and "no one knows it" (7).

89. Let me recall that one of Lang's objections to the artistic representation of the Holocaust has precisely to do with such contingency. To quote him again: "The figurative assertion of alternative possibilities . . . suggests a denial of limitation: *no* possibilities are excluded. And although for some literary subjects openness of this sort may be warranted or even desirable, for others it represents a falsification, morally *and* conceptually" (*AI*, 145–46). A rebuttal no less forceful than Delbo's own is actually provided by Lang himself: "What is historically possible at any particular moment, even if partly indeterminate, is itself part of the historical record. And unless one seriously considers what might have been in place of what *is* now, an issue that requires more than only historical deliberation, the question of what was possible in the past becomes easily obscured" (*Holocaust Representation*, 135).

4. THEORY AND TESTIMONY

1. Adorno, *Negative Dialectics*, 366 / *Negative Dialektik*, GS, 6:359.
2. Ibid., 3 / 6:15.

3. My translation. See Karl Marx, "Thesen über Feuerbach," in *Marx-Engels Werke*, vol. 3 (Berlin: Dietz, 1969), 7.

4. *Negative Dialectics*, 3 / *GS*, 6:15.

5. Ibid., 362/6:355.

6. Ibid., 365/6:358.

7. I refer to the "protective shield" in Chapter 2 as a component of Freud's theory of trauma.

8. Saul Friedlander, "The 'Final Solution': On the Unease in Historical Interpretation," chap. 6 in *Memory, History, and the Extermination of the Jews of Europe* (Bloomington: Indiana University Press, 1993); originally published in *History & Memory* 1, no. 2 (Fall/Winter 1989): 61–76. Friedlander speaks of *"the noncongruence between intellectual probing and the blocking of intuitive comprehension"* (*Memory, History*, 111; author's italics).

9. The gloss "[*testimone*]" is mine, but "[*superstite*]" is in the published translation.

10. Moreover, as Levi points out, "the Lager, on a smaller scale but with amplified characteristics, reproduced the hierarchical structure of the totalitarian state" (*DS*, 47 / *O*, 2:1025).

11. The literature on this subject is immense. See, e.g., Hermann Langbein, *People in Auschwitz*, trans. Harry Zohn (Chapel Hill: University of North Carolina Press, 2004), 191–202; Franciszek Piper, "The Mass Extermination of Jews in the Gas Chambers," in *Auschwitz: Nazi Death Camp*, ed. Franciszek Piper and Teresa Świebocka, trans. Douglas Selvage (Oświęcim: Auschwitz-Birkenau State Museum, 1996), esp. 169–73; Wolfgang Sofsky, *The Order of Terror: The Concentration Camp*, trans. William Templer (Princeton: Princeton University Press, 1997), 267–72; and, for the account of a survivor, Filip Müller, *Eyewitness Auschwitz: Three Years in the Gas Chambers*, trans. Susanne Flatauer (Chicago: Ivan R. Dee, 1979), 57–71.

12. See Dr. Miklos Nyiszli, *Auschwitz: A Doctor's Eyewitness Account*, trans. Tibère Kremer and Richard Seaver (New York: Arcade Publishing, 1993), 68.

13. See esp. Sanyal, "A Soccer Match in Auschwitz," and Philippe Mesnard and Claudine Kahan, *Giorgio Agamben à l'épreuve d'Auschwitz* (Paris: Editions Kimé, 2001), 36–40. In more general terms, I am also indebted to Dominick LaCapra, "Approaching Limit Events: Siting Agamben," chap. 4 in *History in Transit: Experience, Identity, Critical Theory* (Ithaca: Cornell University Press, 2004), and Esther Marion, "The Nazi Genocide and the Writing of the Holocaust Aporia: Ethics and *Remnants of Auschwitz*," *Modern Language Notes* 121, no. 4 (2006): 1009–22.

14. Inga Clendinnen subscribes to the view that Agamben appears to repudiate. In contrast to Levi's characterization of the match, she states: "It is possible, however, to read the game differently—as men being allowed to recognize each other, however briefly, as fellow humans." This rather dubious reading

loses further credibility when she explains: "Both teams knew that at some unspecified time in the future one would eliminate the other, but in Auschwitz the future had little reality" ("Inside the Grey Zone: The Auschwitz *Sonderkommando*," chap. 5 in *Reading the Holocaust* [Cambridge: Cambridge University Press, 1999], 73). As in the case of Agamben's own syntax, the very phrasing of this sentence, especially the initial "Both teams knew . . . ," misleadingly places the SS and the SK on an equal footing, allowing for the vagueness of "one" (team) and "the other" (team) as well as the almost obscene ambiguity of the verb *eliminate* (from the playoffs?), and historically decontextualizing the claim that "in Auschwitz the future had little reality"—as though this were true for the SS, which it was not, rather than for the inmates alone, of whose future it must be specified that it had "little reality" precisely because they could be killed at any moment.

15. Mesnard and Kahan, *Giorgio Agamben à l'épreuve d'Auschwitz*, 39.

16. The quotation by Agamben is from Levi's "Shame," in *DS*, 85 / *O*, 2:1057.

17. The adjective "whatever" (*qualunque*) applies to substitutable singularities in Agamben's *The Coming Community*, trans. Michael Hardt (Minneapolis: University of Minnesota Press, 1993) / *La comunità che viene* (Turin: Einaudi, 1990).

18. This point is important enough to warrant further clarification. In a sense, one *could* say that judgment of the Special Squads is "impossible." However, this would reflect an understanding that they and the SS were *not* morally equivalent but rather that their agency was a product of the most extreme coercion.

19. Here, as with the Special Squads, there is a massive literature. To cite three important works (on which Agamben himself relies): Langbein, *People in Auschwitz*, 89–105; Zdisław Ryn and Stanisław Kłodziński, "An der Grenze zwischen Leben und Tod: Eine Studie über die Erscheinung des 'Muselmanns' im Konzentrationslager," in *Die Auschwitz-Hefte*, rev. ed. (Hamburg: Rogner & Bernhard, 1994), 1:89–154; Sofsky, *The Order of Terror*, 199–205.

20. See also Levi's broader but closely related reflections in the preface, *DS*, 16–21 / *O*, 2:1001–5.

21. This may be the most complete formulation. Earlier versions are to be found on *RA*, 34/31 and 82/76.

22. Agamben attempts to justify the use of this term in the reading of Levi as follows: "How can the non-human testify to the human, and how can the true witness be the one who by definition cannot bear witness? The Italian title of *Survival in Auschwitz*, 'If This Is a Man' [*Se questo è un uomo*], certainly has this meaning as well: the name 'man' applies first of all to a non-man, and the complete witness of man is he whose humanity has been wholly destroyed" (*RA*, 82/76). In his very question here Agamben already presupposes the "non-human,"

for which he then claims to find confirmation in a title whose meaning is not obviously or without qualification the one he asserts it to be. This is not to deny that a preoccupation with the nature of the "human" pervades Levi's testimony, often coupled with a concern for the possibility of testimony itself, as in the statement that "our language lacks words to express this offence, the demolition of a man" (Levi, *Survival in Auschwitz*, 26 / *O*, 1:20). The point here, however, is that in the context of the camp the word *non-human*, used in reference to the "Muslims," could never be purely descriptive, since it reflects the judgment of a perceiver who is anything but morally or affectively neutral.

23. Giorgio Agamben, *Homo Sacer: Sovereign Power and Bare Life*, trans. Daniel Heller-Roazen (Stanford: Stanford University Press, 1998) / *Homo Sacer: Il potere soverano et la vita nuda* (Turin: Einaudi, 1995).

24. LaCapra, *History in Transit*, 159. Of course, the subtext here is Kafka: just as the characterization of Levi as a "land-surveyor" alludes to K. in Kafka's *The Castle*, so the *Muselmann* as a "guard" recalls the doorkeeper in his parable "Before the Law." Agamben comments on this parable in *Homo Sacer*, 49–58/57–67. In the text quoted here and in two earlier essays ("What Is a Camp?" in *Means without End: Notes on Politics*, trans. Vincenzo Binetti and Cesare Casarino [Minneapolis: University of Minnesota Press, 2000], 37–45 / *Mezzi senza fine* [Turin: Bollati Boringhieri, 1996], 35–41, and "The Camp as the 'Nomos' of the Modern," in *Homo Sacer*, 166–80/185–201), it would appear that Agamben himself confuses law and ethics.

25. It may well be Agamben that Jorge Semprun has in mind when he remarks, in *Le mort qu'il faut* (Paris: Gallimard, 2001):

> Of course, the best witness, the only true witness, in fact, according to the specialists, is the one who did not survive, the one who went to the very end of the experience and who died from it. But neither historians nor sociologists have yet managed to resolve this contradiction: how to invite the true witnesses, that is, the dead, to their conferences? How to make them talk?
>
> This is a question, in any case, that the passage of time will settle by itself: soon there will no longer be any bothersome witnesses, with their cumbersome memory. (17, my translation)

This passage (with slight differences in translation) is also quoted by Susan Suleiman in her fine essay on Semprun, "Revision: Historical Trauma and Literary Testimony: The Buchenwald Memoirs of Jorge Semprun," chap. 6 in *Crises of Memory and the Second World War* (Cambridge: Harvard University Press, 2006), 156–57.

26. Sofsky, *The Order of Terror*, 199–200; quoted by Agamben, *RA*, 47–48/42.

27. Cited in Langbein, *People in Auschwitz*, 102.

28. The pronouns used to represent the *Muselmann* are masculine not so much because of the inflection of the German noun as because the camps were segregated and the witnesses cited on this subject are most often men. The fact remains, however, that the condition of the "Muslim" was just as common among female as among male inmates. In this connection, moreover, if on a somewhat different note, it is hardly insignificant that the figure chosen by Levi to convey the horror of the *Muselmann* condition is the Gorgon, a female. I regret very much not being able to explore here the wealth of social and psychological issues suggested by this figuration.

29. Emmanuel Levinas, *On Escape*, trans. Bettina Bergo (Stanford, Calif.: Stanford University Press, 2003)/"De l'évasion," *Recherches philosophiques* 5 (1935–36): 373–92; rpt. *De l'évasion* (Montpellier: Fata Morgana, 1982). See Samuel Moyn, *Origins of the Other: Emmanuel Levinas Between Revelation and Ethics* (Ithaca: Cornell University Press, 2005), 103–8, as well as James Creech, "La honte dans la théorie," *Le Coq-héron* 184 (2006), 100–8.

30. Emile Benveniste, "Subjectivity in Language," in *Problems in General Linguistics*, trans. Mary Elizabeth Meek (Coral Gables, Fla.: University of Miami Press, 1971), 223–30.

31. Benveniste, "The Nature of Pronouns," in *Problems in General Linguistics*, 218.

32. Ibid.

33. Ibid.

34. Ibid. Agamben quotes this in *RA*, 115–16/107–8.

35. Benveniste, "The Nature of Pronouns," 220.

36. Ibid., 219. I have modified the translation, especially its syntax. See Emile Benveniste, "La nature des pronoms," in *Problèmes de linguistique générale* (Paris: Gallimard, 1966), 1:254.

37. Roman Jakobson, "Shifters, Verbal Categories, and the Russian Verb," in *Selected Writings*, vol. 2, *Word and Language* (The Hague: Mouton, 1971), 132.

38. The English translation renders the first word, *L'istanza*, as "The event of language." This is certainly more elegant than my own rendition, but it is important here to reproduce the terminology that Agamben is borrowing from Benveniste.

39. Referring to "the constitutive desubjectification in every subjectification," Agamben notes: "(It is hardly astonishing that it was precisely from an analysis of the pronoun 'I' in Husserl that Derrida was able to draw his idea of an infinite deferral, an originary disjunction—writing—inscribed in the pure self-presence of consciousness)" (*RA*, 123/114). What Derrida demonstrates, however, is that, although an indicative sign such as the pronoun "I" remains

meaningful (*sinnvol*) in the absence of its referent, one cannot derive from this meaningfulness the claim that, in the instance of discourse, the "I" did not also refer to the subject of its enunciation. (Husserl's own reflections might have benefited from his observing the Fregean distinction, especially pertinent here, between *Sinn* [sense] and *Bedeutung* [initially translated as "meaning," now as "reference"].) See Jacques Derrida, *Speech and Phenomena*, in *Speech and Phenomena and Other Essays on Husserl's Theory of Signs*, trans. David B. Allison (Evanston, Ill.: Northwestern University Press, 1973), esp. 93–97, and also my discussion in *Into the Breach: Samuel Beckett and the Ends of Literature* (Princeton: Princeton University Press, 1990), 11–27.

40. Among the former Muselmänner quoted by Agamben, one, Edward Sokol, says: "I am a *Muselmann*" (instead of "I was a *Muselmann*"). In fact, in the German original, all of the verbs employed by Sokol to talk about his experience in Auschwitz are in the present tense (whereas in the Italian and English translations some are converted to the imperfect). The effect is uncanny—and worthy, no doubt, of further discussion. See *RA*, 166/155, and Ryn and Kłodziński, "An der Grenze zwischen Leben und Tod," 1:122.

41. A further complication arises if we consider that, in order to say "I was a *Muselmann*," the witness must remember a condition characterized by the loss of memory. The complication has to do not only with this difficulty, however, but also with the testimony of former Muselmänner at variance with the characterization itself, such as that of Lucjan Sobieraj, who opens by saying: "I can't forget the days when I was a *Muselmann*" (*RA*, 166/155; see also Ryn and Kłodziński, "An der Grenze zwischen Leben und Tod," 1:121).

42. See Levi, *Survival in Auschwitz*, 101–8 and 136–44/*Se questo é un uomo*, in *Opere*, 1:97–104 and 132–40.

43. This rootedness in particularity or singularity, in the historical experience of the individual survivor, can be ascertained as well if we consider that it is one thing for Levi to say that Holocaust survivors are not the true witnesses and quite another for a nonsurvivor to do so.

44. Levi, *Survival in Auschwitz*, 60/*Se questo è un uomo*, in *Opere*, 1:54.

45. Ibid.

46. Ibid., 29/1:23.

47. Ibid., 60/1:54.

5. THE SURVIVOR AS OTHER

1. *TI*, 215/190. This biblically inspired phrase or phrases like it recur throughout Levinas's work.

2. Emmanuel Levinas, "Signature," in *Difficult Freedom: Essays on Judaism*, trans. Seán Hand (Baltimore: Johns Hopkins University Press, 1990), 291 / *Difficile liberté: Essais sur le judaïsme* (Paris: Albin Michel, 1976), 406. Levinas was

mobilized by the French army in 1939, captured by the Germans in 1940, and eventually transported to a prisoner-of-war camp in Germany, where he remained until 1945 and where his military status protected him from the persecution to which, as a Jew, he would otherwise have been subjected. His wife and daughter survived the Occupation, but as he later and only gradually learned, his parents and siblings were shot by the Nazis in Lithuania in 1941.

3. Levinas, "Signature," 291/406.

4. However, in another text whose autobiographical thrust is unmistakable, entitled "Nameless" and first published in 1966 (under the title "Honneur sans drapeau," *Les Nouveaux Cahiers*, no. 6), Levinas discusses the Holocaust and its legacy at some length. "Nameless" is the last chapter in *Proper Names*, trans. Michael B. Smith (Stanford: Stanford University Press, 1996) / *Noms propres* (Montpellier: Fata Morgana, 1976). Levinas also tended to be more expansive about his life when interviewed. See *Ethics and Infinity: Conversations with Philippe Nemo*, trans. Richard A. Cohen (Pittsburgh: Duquesne University Press, 1985) / *Éthique et infini: Dialogues avec Philippe Nemo* (Paris: Fayard, 1982), and *Is It Righteous To Be?: Interviews with Emmanuel Levinas*, ed. Jill Robbins (Stanford: Stanford University Press, 2001). I would recommend as well Marie-Anne Lescourret's biography, *Emmanuel Levinas* (Paris: Flammarion, 1994), and Salomon Malka, *Emmanuel Levinas: His Life and Legacy*, trans. Michael Kigel and Sonja M. Embree (Pittsburgh: Duquesne University Press, 2006).

5. Levinas, "Signature," 289/403; trans. modified.

6. For editorial remarks, see Emmanuel Levinas, *Basic Philosophical Writings*, ed. Adriaan T. Peperzak, Simon Critchley, and Robert Bernasconi (Bloomington: Indiana University Press, 1996), 97.

7. Levinas underscores this mistake in his reflections on subjectivity as an *object* of disclosure:

> It is true that the role that is incumbent on the subject in the manifestation of being makes the subject part of the way being carries on. Then, as a participant in the event of being, the subject also manifests itself. The function of disclosing being is disclosed in its turn. That would be the self-consciousness of consciousness. As a moment of being, subjectivity shows itself to itself, and presents itself as an object to human sciences. As mortal, the ego is conceptualized. But as other than the true being, as different from the being that shows itself, subjectivity is nothing. Despite or because of its finiteness, being has an encompassing, absorbing, enclosing essence. The veracity of the subject would have no other signification than this effacing before presence, this representation. (*OB*, 134/171)

Strictly speaking, the function of disclosing being is not—or at least not fully—disclosed in self-consciousness, since this function can only be inferred from its effect, that is, from *what* it discloses. Thus, even where what it discloses is a self whose function is disclosive, the subject disclosing that self as such remains unseen. When Levinas observes that "the disclosure of truth is not a simple optical phenomenon" (*OB*, 132/168), he indicates, among other things, the inextricability of the optical from the temporal: if the subjectivity to which being owes its disclosure cannot, itself, be disclosed, this is because subjectivity can never temporally coincide with itself. As we shall see, this temporal nonidentity—what Levinas calls "diachrony"—pertains to the "other" subjectivity.

8. I have had to modify the translation of the second to last sentence here. The original reads "Le *concret du sujet* ou l'*être* est schématisé et que le critique ou l'historien ou le philosophe de l'art recherche—se place du côté de l'être" ("Vérité du dévoilement et vérité du témoignage," 103), and the published translation "The *concreteness of the subject or being*, investigated by the critic or the historian or the philosopher, is schematized and placed on the side of being." No doubt the translator was misled by *ou* ("or"), which should be *où* ("where, in which"), but both the sense and the grammar—*que* requiring an antecedent—make it clear that "le *concret du sujet*" is modified by "où l'*être* est schématisé."

9. Jill Robbins, *Altered Reading: Levinas and Literature* (Chicago: University of Chicago Press, 1999), 75.

10. See my review of *Proper Names* in *Comparative Literature Studies* 37, no. 3 (2000): 352–60.

11. Emmanuel Levinas, *Sur Maurice Blanchot* (Montpellier: Fata Morgana, 1975). This work brings together four texts published between 1956 and 1975. The English translation is included in *Proper Names*.

12. Robbins, *Altered Reading*, 75.

13. The tension alluded to here emerges from the ascription to aesthetic experience of "qualities" that also pertain, either at the same time or somewhat later in Levinas's thinking, to the ethical encounter of the other, most notably perhaps the passivity of the self. I will return to this point. See also Robbins, *Altered Reading*, 52.

14. RS 3/773. Although elsewhere Levinas sharply distinguishes revelation from disclosure (associating revelation with the nonphenomenal sphere of the ethical, as, e.g., in *TI*, 65–66/37), in this context he makes it clear, through the contrast of art with cognition (through disclosure), among other things, that revelation and disclosure are synonymous. Let me point out here as well that the studies of ethics and aesthetics in Levinas from which my own thinking has benefited include: Gerald L. Bruns, "The Concepts of Art and Poetry in Emmanuel Levinas's Writing," in *The Cambridge Companion to Levinas*, ed. Simon Critchley and Robert Bernasconi (Cambridge: Cambridge University Press, 2002), 206–33; Philippe Crignon, "Figuration: Emmanuel Levinas and

the Image," *Yale French Studies*, no. 104 (2004): 100–125; Robbins, *Altered Reading*; Alain P. Toumayan, *Encountering the Other: The Artwork and the Problem of Difference in Blanchot and Levinas* (Pittsburgh: Duquesne University Press, 2004); and Edith Wyschogrod, "The Art in Ethics: Aesthetics, Objectivity, and Alterity in the Philosophy of Emmanuel Levinas," in *Ethics as First Philosophy: The Significance of Emmanuel Levinas for Philosophy, Literature and Religion*, ed. Adriaan T. Peperzak (New York: Routledge, 1995), 137–48.

15. *EE*, 52/83. It is worth noting that Levinas's perspective on the practical world is indebted to Heidegger's, even where he takes a critical distance from it (see the analysis of *das Zuhandene*, or the "ready-to-hand," in Martin Heidegger, *Being and Time*, trans. John Macquarrie and Edward Robinson [New York: Harper & Row, 1962], 95–102, and, for Levinas, *EE*, 42–45/64–70, and *TI*, 130–34/103–8). The distance is less apparent, however, when it comes to the aesthetic as a disruption of this world.

16. On vision and touch as modes of cognition, see *TI*, 188–91/162–65. Although I cannot discuss the matter here, it strikes me that to deny any cognitive value to art, as Levinas does, rather begs the question. At the very least, it is not clear how one would recognize the unworlding or estrangement at issue here if its effect were not accessible to some form of cognition.

17. It is clear in this respect that Levinas's thinking of the aesthetic is related to a major tendency of the first half of the twentieth century represented, e.g., by Freud's reflections on the uncanny (*das Unheimliche*) and Shklovsky's notion of defamiliarization (*ostranenie*). See Sigmund Freud, "The 'Uncanny,'" in *SE*, 17:217–52, and Shklovsky, "Art as Technique," as well as this volume, Chapter 3, n. 87.

18. Heidegger, *Being and Time*, 149–68. For Levinas's critique of this notion, see esp. *EE*, 94–96/162–64.

19. Emmanuel Levinas, "The Trace of the Other," trans. Alphonso Lingis, in *Deconstruction in Context*, ed. Mark C. Taylor (Chicago: University of Chicago Press, 1986), 351–52. I have somewhat modified the translation; see Emmanuel Levinas, "La trace de l'autre," in *En découvrant l'existence avec Husserl et Heidegger*, 3rd ed. (Paris: Vrin, 1974), 194.

20. Maurice Blanchot, *Thomas the Obscure*, trans. Robert Lamberton (New York: David Lewis, 1973), esp. 7–9. A footnote in *Existence and Existents* (63/103) refers to the same work, albeit to the pages immediately following these (and presumably to the first rather than the second version). For a detailed analysis of the opening section, see Toumayan, *Encountering the Other*, 19–29.

21. The French reads: "Dans la jouissance, je suis absolument pour moi. Egoïste sans référence à autrui—je suis seul sans solitude, innocemment égoïste et seul. Pas contre les autres, pas 'quant à moi'—mais entièrement sourd à autrui, en dehors de toute communication et de tout refus de communiquer—sans

oreilles comme ventre affamé." I have modified the published translation, which uses "Other," "Others," and "Other" for *autrui*, *les autres*, and *autrui*, respectively, since in my view the framework of this description does not unambiguously confer on *autrui* or *les autres* the ethical sense conveyed by the capital *O* (as opposed, for example, to the sense of the "other" in *Mitsein*). Moreover, since Levinas's use of the capital *A* in *l'Autre* or *Autrui* is not entirely consistent and since I would like to avoid any unnecessary confusion in what follows, I will always use the lower case. It should be noted as well that although the proverb "ventre affamé n'a point d'oreilles" is normally translated as "it's no use reasoning with a hungry man," *affamé* is closer to "famished" than to "hungry."

22. We should keep in mind here that, like Adorno's condemnation of poetry after Auschwitz (see Chapter 3, above), Levinas's condemnation of art or its enjoyment may owe its severity to having been stated so soon after the Holocaust.

23. In Levinas's mature work, of course, there is no correlation between initiative and responsibility: not only do I not choose to be responsible, but my responsibility precedes and exceeds my power to assume it.

24. This may appear to contradict Levinas's claim that enjoyment "embraces all relations with things" or at least to imply that the claim is too sweeping. It is true that the term *enjoyment* admits of some fluctuation, since, in general, it designates "an ultimate relation with the substantial plenitude of being, with its materiality" (*TI*, 133/106), whereas that relation may in particular instances entail suffering—such as hunger—rather than enjoyment. But Levinas's overriding concern is to articulate a relation to materiality beyond the mere instrumental satisfaction of needs that he finds in Heidegger's analysis of *Zeughaftigkeit* ("equipmentality"), where, as he puts it, "*Dasein* . . . is never hungry" (*TI*, 134/108), that is, never seeks to *enjoy* the appeasement of hunger. Moreover, in the terms used below, that relation pertains essentially to the "day" (and its night), not to the "night" of the *there is*. Yet most remarkable in this respect is Levinas's unbridled affirmation of a material indulgence that— minus the plague, it is true—we have just seen him condemn in the severest manner. As though inspired by Georges Bataille, whom he so little resembles in other respects, he states: "To enjoy without utility, in pure loss, gratuitously, without referring to anything else, in pure expenditure—this is the human" (*TI*, 13/107).

25. Sigmund Freud, *Civilization and Its Discontents*, in *SE*, 21:64–65.

26. *Effrayant* (*Totalité et infini*, 165). The English translation has "terrifying" (*TI*, 190).

27. See *TI*, 142/116 and 190–93/164–67.

28. This "order," of crucial importance to Levinas's thought, is conveyed by the French title, *De l'existence à l'existant* (*From Existence to Existents*), but lost in the English *Existence and Existents*.

29. See Maurice Blanchot, *The Space of Literature*, trans. Ann Smock (Lincoln: University of Nebraska Press, 1982), esp. 32–33, and Joseph Libertson, *Proximity: Levinas, Blanchot, Bataille and Communication* (The Hague: Martinus Nijhoff, 1982), 242–53.

30. On the "other night" in Blanchot, see *The Space of Literature*, 163–70, Libertson, *Proximity*, 96–105, and Toumayan, *Encountering the Other*, 158–68. For Levinas's reading of Blanchot, see "Exercises on 'The Madness of the Day,'" in *Proper Names*, 156–70.

31. For a useful discussion of Levy-Bruhl's influence on Levinas, see Robbins, *Altered Reading*, 86–89.

32. *Time and the Other* was a series of lectures delivered in 1946–47 and first published as "Le temps et l'autre" in *Le Choix, le Monde, l'Existence*, ed. Jean Wahl (Grenoble-Paris: Arthaud, 1947), 125–96. It has since been republished as *Le temps et l'autre* (Montpellier: Fata Morgana, 1979; rpt. Paris: Presses Universitaires de France, 1983). For the English translation, see *Time and the Other*, trans. Richard A. Cohen (Pittsburgh: Duquesne University Press, 1987).

33. See, however, the last sentence of the essay (RS, 13/789) and my remarks below.

34. It is in this light that I would propose we read the following quite categorical statement:

> To poetic activity—where influences arise unbeknownst to us out of this nonetheless conscious activity, to envelop it and beguile it like a rhythm, and where action is borne along by the very work to which it has given rise, where in a dionysiac mode the artist, according to Nietzsche's expression, becomes a work of art—is opposed the language that at each instant dispels the charm of rhythm and prevents initiative from becoming a role. Discourse is rupture and commencement, a breaking of the rhythm that enraptures and transports interlocutors—prose. (*TI*, 203/177)

35. I reproduce verbatim Levinas's quotation of Hamlet, which is somewhat mangled in the published translation. Cf. *Hamlet*, act 3, scene 1.

36. Opinion varies on this. Seán Hand writes: "Great art, conceived unapologetically in European canonic terms, occupies a crucial place in Levinas's philosophy. We are as likely to encounter the texts of Dostoyevsky or Shakespeare, Agnon or Grossman, as those of Plato or Kant, in Levinas's philosophical examples and analogies. Nor are the artistic characters or dilemmas a mere *illustration* of philosophical concepts or principles; on the contrary, for Levinas they are the necessary dramatization of ethical being which has become elsewhere fatally compromised and reduced in the philosophical process of the comprehension of Being. They operate then as the ethical shadow within ontological language, as an aesthetic of the face-to-face relation otherwise threatened with suppression in the work of the metaphysician" ("Shadowing Ethics: Levinas's View of Art and Aesthetics," in *Facing the Other: The Ethics of*

Emmanuel Levinas, ed. Seán Hand [London : Routledge, 1996], 63). In theory, I find this quite plausible, but I am not at all convinced that Levinas's practice as a philosopher justifies such a claim.

37. I have modified the translation of Phaedra's lines as they appear in *Existence and Existents.* See Jean Racine, *Phèdre,* in *Oeuvres complètes,* vol. 1, ed. Raymond Picard (Paris: Gallimard, 1950), 808. The French reads: "Le ciel, tout l'univers est plein de mes aïeux./Où me cacher? Fuyons dans la nuit infernale./Mais que dis-je? Mon père y tient l'urne fatale" (act 4, scene 6).

38. The indissociability of ethics and sensation is stressed any number of times by Levinas, but perhaps nowhere more plainly than in "Language and Proximity" (originally published in 1974), where "the ethical relationship with the real" is equated with "the relationship of proximity which the sensible establishes." But here as well—that is, only a few lines further on—the indissociability of the ethical and the aesthetic is no less obvious, as Levinas states that "the proximity of things is poetry" (*Collected Philosophical Papers,* trans. Alphonso Lingis [Dordrecht: Martinus Nijhoff, 1987], 118/"Langage et proximité," in *En découvrant l'existence avec Husserl et Heidegger,* 228).

39. On the erotic, see in particular *Time and the Other,* 84–94/77–89, and *TI,* 254–77/232–54.

40. On exposure, see *EE,* 59/96, and *OB,* 49/63; on insomnia, *EE,* 65–67/109–13, and *OB,* 87/110; on invasion, *EE,* 58/95, and the hostage, *OB,* 112/142 and 114/145; on persecution, *OB,* 111–12/142–43. These are but a few from among a very large number of examples.

41. R. Clifton Spargo, *Vigilant Memory: Emmanuel Levinas, the Holocaust, and the Unjust Death* (Baltimore: Johns Hopkins University Press, 2006), 92.

42. Robbins, *Altered Reading,* 84.

43. "Language is already skepticism" (*OB,* 170/216).

44. This, however, does not entail privileging the verbal over the visual but attending to the signification that exceeds representation.

45. Of particular note in this respect are certain essays in *Proper Names,* such as "The Other in Proust" and especially "Paul Celan: From Being to the Other," in which Levinas—reading, it is true, the speech entitled "The Meridian" and not the poetry—sees in poetic language according to Celan "a saying without a said" and "an unheard-of modality of the *otherwise than being*" (40/59, 46/66).

46. The translation has been considerably modified. In particular, "Sight seeks to draw out of the light beings integrated into a whole" (*EE,* 56) misconstrues Levinas's sentence, "Elle cherche à arracher à la lumière les êtres intégrés dans un ensemble," where the antecedent of *Elle* is not *la vision* but *la peinture* (*De l'existence à l'existant,* 90). In the first paragraph, the phrase "D'où la guerre au sujet qui est la littérature de la peinture" (89) is admittedly somewhat enigmatic, but is probably best rendered by "Whence the hostility toward

the subject, which makes painting into literature" (essentially the same, in this case, as the published translation), since the literature in question appears to refer to the subordination of painting to expression evoked in the preceding sentence. See Adorno on fragmentation in *Aesthetic Theory*, 189–90.

47. See esp. chap. 4, "Substitution," of *Otherwise than Being*, originally published in 1968 in the *Revue Philosophique de Louvain* 66, no. 91: 487–508.

48. The English translation here renders *signification* as "meaning," which is not a problem provided that as a gerund "meaning" is understood at least as much in its verbal as in its nominal sense.

49. At the same time, Levinas repeatedly stresses the "logical" order of affairs, whereby the other comes from within, as when he refers to "this way for a command to sound in the mouth of the one who obeys" (*OB*, 147/187).

50. In *Totality and Infinity* (e.g. 74–75/46–47), Levinas's use of the expression *kath 'auto*, "according to itself," to define signification in the ethical encounter anticipates this "sign given of this giving of a sign," this Saying that refers to itself rather than identifying something *as* something in a Said. As I suggest immediately below, however, this begs a number of questions. See also Robbins, *Altered Reading*, 25–26.

51. On illeity, see Levinas, "The Trace of the Other," 358–59/201–2; "Phenomenon and Enigma," in *Collected Philosophical Papers*, 71 /"Énigme et phénomène," in *En découvrant l'existence avec Husserl et Heidegger*, 214; *OB*, 12–13/15–16. On the relation between the *il y a* and illeity, see Hent de Vries, "Adieu, à dieu, a-Dieu," in Peperzak, *Ethics as First Philosophy*, 218.

52. Benveniste, "The Nature of Pronouns," 218 (trans. modified; see "La nature des pronoms," 1:252); Husserl, *Logical Investigations*, 1:315.

53. Although, as I point out, Levinas sometimes uses the word *survivor* simply to designate one who continues to live after an event, we should not underestimate the dismissiveness of this usage in the post-Holocaust era, that is, its knowing disregard of the more common and weightier sense of *survivor* as one who has lived *through* the event. This, too, is the sense on which Semprun insists (see below).

54. "Language presupposes interlocutors" (*TI*, 73/45). In this connection, see Jacques Derrida, "At This Very Moment in This Work Here I Am," in *Re-Reading Levinas*, ed. Robert Bernasconi and Simon Critchley (Bloomington: Indiana University Press, 1991), 11–48.

55. Jakobson, "Linguistics and Poetics," 23.

56. Ibid., 24.

57. See, in this connection, Jean-François Lyotard, "Levinas' Logic," in *Face to Face with Levinas*, ed. Richard A. Cohen (Albany: State University of New York Press, 1986), 117–58.

58. Elie Wiesel, *Night*, trans. Stella Rodway, in *The Night Trilogy: Night, Dawn, The Accident* (New York: Hill and Wang, 1987), 17.

59. Ibid.

60. *Survival in Auschwitz*, 60.

61. Chambers, "Memory, Genre, Truth," 12.

62. Ibid.

63. Ibid., 15.

64. Ibid.

65. Ibid., 12.

66. What I wish to suggest is simply that this solidarity pertained most likely to a particular group of inmates, composed especially of former members of resistance groups, such as Halbwachs and Semprun, and of those who, also like Semprun, belonged to the political underground at Buchenwald—and for whom conditions in the camp were appreciably better than for other groups, especially the Jews. It is worth noting that before Semprun studied with Halbwachs at the Sorbonne Levinas had studied with him at the University of Strasbourg—and that Semprun was already reading Levinas during the Occupation (see *LL*, 89–93/122–25 and 168/221).

67. Chambers, "Memory, Genre, Truth," 14.

68. As Chambers points out, the *désordre concerté* that Semprun attributes to his writing is "reminiscent of the smoke that daily issued from the crematorium chimney at Buchenwald" (10) and, I would add, is not unrelated to the motif of ghostliness.

69. Levinas, *Proper Names*, 4/10.

70. Semprun strikes a more optimistic note regarding the receptivity of the public when he refers to the virtually simultaneous publication of his *Le grand voyage* and Primo Levi's *La tregua* in 1963 (*LL*, 250–51/322–23). It should also be noted that, although the translation of *L'écriture ou la vie* as *Literature or Life* is understandable both for its alliterative value and because Semprun's writing is so self-consciously literary, it does not do justice, as does the French— and the passage just quoted—to the author's focus on the relation between the act of writing and both life and death (the original title of the work having been *L'écriture ou la mort* [*LL*, 231/299]). On writing and life, see *LL*, 163/215 and 194/254, and for an illuminating account of the genesis of the memoir, esp. "The Gaze," see 227–31/295–99.

71. I refer to this relation as Levinas understands it in his critique of Martin Buber. See *TI*, 68–69/40–41, and my review of *Proper Names*, 356–57.

72. See, inter alia, Jacques Derrida, "Différance," in *Margins of Philosophy*, trans. Alan Bass (Chicago: University of Chicago Press, 1982), 1–28. Of course, when Levinas states here that "by virtue of time, indeed, being is not *yet*," that it is "at a distance from itself," one could say that the discourse of *Totality and Infinity* is being shadowed by the *entretemps* of "Reality and Its Shadow."

73. On Levinas and Christianity, esp. in connection with substitution, see Spargo's illuminating discussion in *Vigilant Memory*, 149–58.

74. See Lescourret, *Emmanuel Levinas*, 46–47, as well as 125 and 356, and also Alain Toumayan, "'I more than the others': Dostoevsky and Levinas," *Yale French Studies*, no. 104 (2004): 55–66.

75. Levinas, *Éthique et infini*, 19 (my translation; see *Ethics and Infinity*, 24). In the first chapter of *Otherwise than Being*, Levinas says of the book's itinerary that "it is doubtless not completely disengaged from prephilosophical experiences" (*OB*, 20/24).

76. Friedrich Nietzsche, *Beyond Good and Evil*, trans. Walter Kaufmann (New York: Vintage, 1966), 13.

77. Brison, *Aftermath*, 73–77.

78. *Proper Names*, 120/178.

79. Ibid., 119, 122 / 177, 181.

80. Ibid., 119/177–78.

81. Levinas speaks of "le gouffre béant," which could also be translated as, say, "the yawning abyss" and would in that case be less immediately evocative of killing operations although no less so of their effect on survivors.

82. I take it that Levinas is resorting to a not uncommon stylistic device expressive of modesty when he uses the first person plural *nous* instead of the singular *je*. Of course, this does not exclude the possibility that the *nous* might also represent other survivors.

83. "God writes straight with crooked lines" (*OB*, 147/187). Both the mention of God and the fact that Levinas is borrowing an epigraph from Paul Claudel, a conservative Catholic, could appear to render my paraphrase somewhat inappropriate. But these considerations aside, and given that the proverb is cited in the context of a discussion concerning testimony and language, its pertinence here strikes me as undeniable.

The following list includes all of the works cited in this book, as well as a selection of others that have proven important in the course of my research and writing. It is far from exhaustive but may at least indicate the substance and scope of the reading on which the book is based.

For the foreign authors who figure most prominently in the volume—namely, Adorno, Agamben, Delbo, Freud, Levi, Levinas, and Semprun—I first cite, whenever available (which is almost all of the time), the English translation of a work, followed by the foreign-language original. The same procedure is adopted for any additional work whose translation has been modified or given rise to questions of a substantive nature, or whose original date of publication is of note. In view of my readership, I have otherwise cited, whenever these, too, are available, the English translations of foreign works rather than the originals themselves.

Adorno, Theodor W. *Aesthetic Theory*. Translated by Robert Hullot-Kentor. Minneapolis: University of Minnesota Press, 1997. *Ästhetische Theorie*. Vol. 7 of *Gesammelte Schriften*, edited by Rolf Tiedemann. Frankfurt am Main: Suhrkamp, 1997.

———. "Commitment." In *Notes to Literature*, edited by Rolf Tiedemann, translated by Shierry Weber Nicholsen, 2:76–94. New York: Columbia University Press, 1992. "Engagement." In *Noten zur Literatur III, Gesammelte Schriften*, edited by Rolf Tiedemann, 11:409–30. Frankfurt am Main: Suhrkamp, 1997.

———. "Cultural Criticism and Society." In *Prisms*, translated by Samuel and Shierry Weber, 17–34. Cambridge: MIT Press, 1981. "Kulturkritik und Gesellschaft." In *Prismen, Gesammelte Schriften*, edited by Rolf Tiedemann, 10.1:11–30. Frankfurt am Main: Suhrkamp, 1997.

———. *Negative Dialectics*. Translated by E. B. Ashton. New York: Continuum, 1973. *Negative Dialektik*. Vol. 6 of *Gesammelte Schriften*, edited by Rolf Tiedemann. Frankfurt am Main: Suhrkamp, 1997.

————. "On Lyric Poetry and Society." In *Notes to Literature*, edited by Rolf Tiedemann, translated by Shierry Weber Nicholsen, 1:37–54. New York: Columbia University Press, 1991. "Rede über Lyrik und Gesellschaft." In *Noten zur Literatur I, Gesammelte Schriften*, edited by Rolf Tiedemann, 11:49–68. Frankfurt am Main: Suhrkamp, 1997.

————. "Trying to Understand *Endgame*." In *Notes to Literature*, edited by Rolf Tiedemann, translated by Shierry Weber Nicholsen, 1:241–75. New York: Columbia University Press, 1991. "Versuch, das Endspiel zu verstehen." In *Noten zur Literatur II, Gesammelte Schriften*, edited by Rolf Tiedemann, 11:281–321. Frankfurt am Main: Suhrkamp, 1997.

————. "What Does Coming to Terms with the Past Mean?" Translated by Timothy Bahti and Geoffrey Hartman. In *Bitburg in Moral and Political Perspective*, edited by Geoffrey Hartman, 115–29. Bloomington: Indiana University Press, 1986. "Was bedeutet: Aufarbeitung der Vergangenheit." In *Eingriffe: Neun kritische Modelle, Gesammelte Schriften*, edited by Rolf Tiedemann, 10.2:555–72. Frankfurt am Main: Suhrkamp, 1997.

Agamben, Giorgio. *The Coming Community*. Translated by Michael Hardt. Minneapolis: University of Minnesota Press, 1993. *La comunità che viene*. Turin: Einaudi, 1990.

————. *Homo Sacer: Sovereign Power and Bare Life*. Translated by Daniel Heller-Roazen. Stanford: Stanford University Press, 1998. *Homo sacer: Il potere sovrano e la nuda vita*. Turin: Einaudi, 1995.

————. *Means Without End: Notes on Politics*. Translated by Vincenzo Binetti and Cesare Casarino. Minneapolis: University of Minnesota Press, 2000. *Mezzi senza fine*. Turin: Bollati Boringhieri, 1996.

————. *Remnants of Auschwitz: The Witness and the Archive*. Translated by Daniel Heller-Roazen. New York: Zone Books, 1999. *Quel che resta di Auschwitz: L'archivio e il testimone*. Turin: Bollati Boringhieri, 1998.

Aichinger, Ilse. *Herod's Children*. Translated by Cornelia Schaeffer. New York: Atheneum, 1963.

Alexander, Edward. *The Resonance of Dust: Essays on Holocaust Literature and Jewish Fate*. Columbus: Ohio State University Press, 1979.

Alphen, Ernst van. *Caught by History: Holocaust Effects in Contemporary Art, Literature, and Theory*. Stanford, Calif.: Stanford University Press, 1997.

Alvarez, A. "The Literature of the Holocaust." *Commentary*, November 1964, 65–69.

Aly, Götz, and Susanne Heim. *Architects of Annihilation: Auschwitz and the Logic of Destruction*. Translated by A. G. Blunden. Princeton: Princeton University Press, 2002.

American Psychiatric Association. *Diagnostic and Statistical Manual of Mental Disorders*. 3rd ed. Washington, D.C.: American Psychiatric Association, 1980.

———. *Diagnostic and Statistical Manual of Mental Disorders.* 3rd rev. ed. Washington, D.C.: American Psychiatric Association, 1987.

———. *Diagnostic and Statistical Manual of Mental Disorders.* 4th ed. Washington, D.C.: American Psychiatric Association, 1994.

———. *Diagnostic and Statistical Manual of Mental Disorders.* 4th rev. edition. Washington, D.C.: American Psychiatric Association, 2000.

Améry, Jean. *At the Mind's Limits: Contemplations by a Survivor on Auschwitz and Its Realities.* Translated by Sidney Rosenfeld and Stella P. Rosenfeld. Bloomington: Indiana University Press, 1980.

———. *Radical Humanism: Selected Essays.* Translated and edited by Sidney Rosenfeld and Stella P. Rosenfeld. Bloomington: Indiana University Press, 1984.

Antelme, Robert. *The Human Race.* Translated by Jeffrey Haight and Annie Mahler. Marlboro, Vt.: The Marlboro Press, 1992.

Appelfeld, Aharon. *Badenheim 1939.* Translated by Dalya Bilu. Boston: David R. Godine, 1980.

———. *Beyond Despair.* Translated by Jeffrey M. Green. New York: Fromm International, 1994.

———. *The Immortal Bartfuss.* Translated by Jeffrey M. Green. New York: Grove Press, 1989.

———. *The Iron Tracks.* Translated by Jeffrey M. Green. New York: Schocken Books, 1998.

———. *The Retreat.* Translated by Dalya Bilu. New York: Schocken Books, 1984.

———. *Tzili.* Translated by Dalya Bilu. New York: Grove Press, 1983.

Appignanesi, Lisa. *Losing the Dead: A Family Memoir.* Toronto: McArthur & Company, 1999.

Arad, Yitzhak. *Belzec, Sobibor, Treblinka: The Operation Reinhard Death Camps.* Bloomington: Indiana University Press, 1987.

Arendt, Hannah. *Eichmann in Jerusalem: A Report on the Banality of Evil.* New York: Viking, 1963; rev. ed., New York: Penguin, 1994.

Aristotle. *The 'Poetics' of Aristotle.* Translated with commentary by Stephen Halliwell. Chapel Hill: University of North Carolina Press, 1987.

Auerhahn, Nanette, and Dori Laub. "Holocaust Testimony." *Holocaust and Genocide Studies* 5, no. 4 (1990): 447–62.

Auerhahn, Nanette, Dori Laub, and Harvey Peskin. "Psychotherapy with Holocaust Survivors." *Psychotherapy* 30, no. 3 (Fall 1993): 434–42.

Bal, Mieke. *Narratology: Introduction to the Theory of Narrative.* 3rd ed. Toronto: University of Toronto Press, 2009.

Ball, Karyn. "Ex/propriating Survivor Experience, or Auschwitz 'after' Lyotard." In *Witness and Memory: The Discourse of Trauma*, edited by Ana Douglass and Thomas A. Vogler, 249–73. New York: Routledge, 2003.

———. "Introduction: Trauma and Its Institutional Destinies." *Cultural Critique* 46 (Fall 2000): 1–44.

Barthes, Roland. "Historical Discourse." Translated by Peter Wexler. In *Introduction to Structuralism*, edited by Michael Lane, 145–55. New York: Basic Books, 1970.

Bartov, Omer, ed. *The Holocaust: Origins, Implementation, Aftermath*. London: Routledge, 2000.

———. *Mirrors of Destruction: War, Genocide, and Modern Identity*. Oxford: Oxford University Press, 2000.

Bauer, Yehuda. *A History of the Holocaust*. Danbury, Conn.: Franklin Watts, 1982.

———. *Rethinking the Holocaust*. New Haven, Conn.: Yale University Press, 2001.

Bauman, Zygmunt. *Modernity and the Holocaust*. Cambridge: Polity Press, 1989.

Becker, Jurek. *Jakob the Liar*. Translated by Leila Vennewitz. New York: Arcade Publishing, 1990.

Beckett, Samuel. *Endgame*. In *Samuel Beckett: The Grove Centenary Edition*, edited by Paul Auster, 3:89–154. New York: Grove Press, 2006.

———. *Malone Dies*. In *Samuel Beckett: The Grove Centenary Edition*, edited by Paul Auster, 2:171–281. New York: Grove Press, 2006.

———. *Molloy*. In *Samuel Beckett: The Grove Centenary Edition*, edited by Paul Auster, 2:1–170. New York: Grove Press, 2006.

———. *The Unnamable*. In *Samuel Beckett: The Grove Centenary Edition*, edited by Paul Auster, 2:283–407. New York: Grove Press, 2006.

Bellow, Saul. *Mr. Sammler's Planet*. New York: Viking, 1970.

Benjamin, Walter. "The Storyteller." In *Illuminations*, translated by Harry Zohn, edited by Hannah Arendt, 83–109. New York: Schocken Books, 1969.

———. "Theses on the Philosophy of History." In *Illuminations*, translated by Harry Zohn, edited by Hannah Arendt, 253–64. New York: Schocken Books, 1969.

Benveniste, Emile. "The Nature of Pronouns." In *Problems in General Linguistics*, translated by Mary Elizabeth Meek., 217–22. Coral Gables, Fla.: University of Miami Press, 1971. "La nature des pronoms." In *Problèmes de linguistique générale*, 1:251–57. Paris: Gallimard, 1966.

———. "Subjectivity in Language." In *Problems in General Linguistics*, translated by Mary Elizabeth Meek., 223–30. Coral Gables, Fla.: University of Miami Press, 1971. "De la subjectivité dans le langage." In *Problèmes de linguistique générale*, 1:258–66. Paris: Gallimard, 1966.

Berenbaum, Michael. *The World Must Know: The History of the Holocaust as Told in the United States Holocaust Memorial Museum*. Boston: Little, Brown and Company, 1993.

Bergmann, Martin S. "Reflections on the Psychological and Social Function of Remembering the Holocaust." In *Generations of the Holocaust*, edited by Martin S. Bergmann and Milton E. Jucovy, 317–32. New York: Columbia University Press, 1990.

Bernard-Donals, Michael, and Richard Glejzer. *Between Witness and Testimony: The Holocaust and the Limits of Representation.* Albany: State University of New York Press, 2001.

Bernasconi, Robert. "Deconstruction and the Possibility of Ethics." In *Deconstruction and Philosophy: The Texts of Jacques Derrida,* edited by John Sallis, 122–39. Chicago: University of Chicago Press, 1987.

———. "Levinas and Derrida: The Question of the Closure of Metaphysics." In *Face to Face with Levinas,* edited by Richard A. Cohen, 181–202. Albany: State University of New York Press, 1986.

Bernasconi, Robert, and David Wood, eds. *The Provocation of Levinas: Rethinking the Other.* London: Routledge, 1988.

Bettelheim, Bruno. *"Surviving" and Other Essays.* New York: Knopf, 1979.

Blanchot, Maurice. *The Space of Literature.* Translated by Ann Smock. Lincoln: University of Nebraska Press, 1982.

———. *Thomas the Obscure.* Translated by Robert Lamberton. New York: David Lewis, 1973.

———. *The Writing of the Disaster.* Translated by Ann Smock. Lincoln: University of Nebraska Press, 1995.

Borowski, Tadeusz. *This Way for the Gas, Ladies and Gentlemen.* Translated by Barbara Vedder. New York: Viking Penguin, 1967.

Bracher, Nathan. "Histoire, ironie et interprétation chez Charlotte Delbo: Une écriture d'Auschwitz." *French Forum* 19, no. 1 (January 1994): 81–93.

———. "Humanisme, violence et métaphysique: La thématique du visage chez Charlotte Delbo." *Symposium* 45 (Winter 1992): 255–72.

Breuer, Josef, and Sigmund Freud. *Studies on Hysteria.* Vol. 1 of *The Standard Edition of the Complete Psychological Works of Sigmund Freud,* edited and translated by James Strachey. London: Hogarth, 1955; London: rpt. Vintage, 2001. *Studien über Hysterie.* In Sigmund Freud, *Gesammelte Werke,* edited by Anna Freud et al, 1:77–312. London: Imago, 1952.

Brison, Susan J. *Aftermath: Violence and the Remaking of a Self.* Princeton, N.J.: Princeton University Press, 2002.

Broszat, Martin. "Hitler and the Genesis of the 'Final Solution.'" *Yad Vashem Studies* 13 (1979): 73–125.

Browning, Christopher R. *Collected Memories: Holocaust History and Postwar Testimony.* Madison: University of Wisconsin Press, 2003.

———. *Ordinary Men: Reserve Police Battalion 101 and the Final Solution in Poland.* New York: HarperCollins, 1992.

Bruns, Gerald L. "The Concepts of Art and Poetry in Emmanuel Levinas's Writing." In *The Cambridge Companion to Levinas,* edited by Simon Critchley and Robert Bernasconi, 206–33. Cambridge: Cambridge University Press, 2002.

Buber, Martin. *I and Thou.* Translated by Walter Kaufmann. New York: Scribner's, 1970.

Buck-Morss, Susan. *The Origin of Negative Dialectics: Theodor W. Adorno, Walter Benjamin and the Frankfurt Institute.* New York: Free Press, 1977.

Caron, David. *My Father and I: The Marais and the Queerness of Community.* Ithaca: Cornell University Press, 2009.

Caron, David, and Sharon Marquart, eds. *Les revenantes: Charlotte Delbo, la voix d'une communauté à jamais déportée.* Toulouse: Presses universitaires du Mirail, 2011.

Caruth, Cathy. *Unclaimed Experience: Trauma, Narrative, and History.* Baltimore: Johns Hopkins University Press, 1996.

Caruth, Cathy, ed. *Trauma: Explorations in Memory.* Baltimore: Johns Hopkins University Press, 1995.

Celan, Paul. *Selected Poems and Prose of Paul Celan.* Translated by John Felstiner. New York: W. W. Norton, 2001.

———. "Speech on the Occasion of Receiving the Literature Prize of the Free Hanseatic City of Bremen." In *Collected Prose,* translated by Rosmarie Waldrop, 33–36. Riverdale-on-Hudson, N.Y.: The Sheep Meadow Press, 1986. German original in Paul Celan, *Gesammelte Werke,* edited by Beda Allemann and Stefan Reichert, 3:185–86. Frankfurt am Main: Suhrkamp, 1983.

Chalier, Catherine, and Miguel Abensour, eds. *L'Herne: Emmanuel Levinas.* Paris: Editions de l'Herne, 1991.

Chambers, Ross. "Memory, Genre, Truth: Lucie Aubrac, Jorge Semprun, François Maspero and the *devoir de mémoire.*" *Contemporary French Civilization* 30, no. 1 (Winter/Spring 2006): 1–27.

———. *Untimely Interventions: AIDS Writing, Testimonial, and the Rhetoric of Haunting.* Ann Arbor: University of Michigan Press, 2004.

Chevrie, Marc, and Hervé Le Roux. "Site and Speech: An Interview with Claude Lanzmann about *Shoah.*" In *Claude Lanzmann's "Shoah": Key Essays,* edited by Stuart Liebman, 37–49. New York: Oxford University Press, 2007.

Clendinnen, Inga. *Reading the Holocaust.* Cambridge: Cambridge University Press, 1999.

Cohen, Richard A., ed. *Face to Face with Levinas.* Albany: State University of New York Press, 1986.

Creech, James. "La honte dans la théorie." *Le Coq-héron* 184 (2006): 100–108.

Crignon, Philippe. "Figuration: Emmanuel Levinas and the Image." *Yale French Studies,* no. 104 (2004): 100–125.

Critchley, Simon. *The Ethics of Deconstruction: Derrida and Levinas.* 2nd ed. Edinburgh: Edinburgh University Press, 1999.

Czech, Danuta. *Auschwitz Chronicle: 1939–1945.* Translated by Barbara Harshav, Martha Humphreys, and Stephen Shearier. New York: Henry Holt, 1990.

Czerniakow, Adam. *The Warsaw Diary of Adam Czerniakow.* Translated by Stanislaw Staron and the Staff of Vad Yashem. Edited by Raul Hilberg,

Stanislaw Staron, and Josef Kermisz. New York: Stein and Day, 1979; rpt. Chicago: Ivan R. Dee, in association with the United States Holocaust Memorial Museum, 1999.

Davis, Colin. *Levinas: An Introduction*. Notre Dame, Ind.: University of Notre Dame Press, 1996.

Dawidowicz, Lucy S. *From That Place and Time: A Memoir, 1938–1947*. New York: W. W. Norton, 1989.

———. *The Holocaust and the Historians*. Cambridge: Harvard University Press, 1981.

———. *The War Against the Jews, 1933–1945*. New York: Holt, Rinehart and Winston, 1975.

Dawidowicz, Lucy S. , ed. *A Holocaust Reader*. West Orange, N.J.: Behrman House, 1976.

Delbo, Charlotte. *Auschwitz and After*. Translated by Rosette C. Lamont. New Haven, Conn.: Yale University Press, 1995. *Auschwitz et après*. Vol. 1, *Aucun de nous reviendra*. Geneva: Gonthier, 1965; rpt. Paris: Minuit, 1970. Vol. 2, *Une connaissance inutile*. Paris: Minuit, 1970. Vol. 3, *Mesure de nos jours*. Paris: Minuit, 1971.

———. *Les Belles Lettres*. Paris: Minuit, 1961.

———. *Convoy to Auschwitz: Women of the French Resistance*. Translated by Carol Cosman. Boston: Northeastern University Press, 1997. *Le convoi du 24 janvier*. Paris: Minuit, 1965.

———. *Days and Memory*. Translated by Rosette C. Lamont. Marlboro, Vt.: The Marlboro Press, 1990. *La mémoire et les jours*. Paris: Berg International, 1985.

———. *Spectres, mes compagnons*. Lausanne: Maurice Bridel, 1977.

———. *La théorie et la pratique: Dialogue imaginaire mais non tout à fait apocryphe entre Herbert Marcuse et Henri Lefebvre*. Paris: editions anthropos paris, 1969.

———. *Who Will Carry the Word?* Translated by Cynthia Haft. In *The Theatre of the Holocaust: Four Plays*, edited by Robert Skloot, 267–325. Madison: University of Wisconsin Press, 1982. *Qui rapportera ces paroles?* Paris: Pierre Jean Oswald, 1974.

Derrida, Jacques. *Adieu to Emmanuel Levinas*. Translated by Pascale-Anne Brault and Michael Naas. Stanford, Calif.: Stanford University Press, 1999.

———. "At This Very Moment in This Work Here I Am." In *Re-Reading Levinas*, edited by Robert Bernasconi and Simon Critchley, 11–48. Bloomington: Indiana University Press, 1991.

———. "Différance." In *Margins of Philosophy*, translated by Alan Bass, 1–28. Chicago: University of Chicago Press, 1982.

———. *Speech and Phenomena*. In *"Speech and Phenomena" and Other Essays on Husserl's Theory of Signs*, translated by David B. Allison, 1–104. Evanston, Ill.: Northwestern University Press, 1973.

————. "Violence and Metaphysics: An Essay on the Thought of Emmanuel Levinas." In *Writing and Difference*, translated by Alan Bass, 79–153. Chicago: University of Chicago Press, 1978.

Des Pres, Terrence. *The Survivor*. Oxford: Oxford University Press, 1976.

Diner, Dan. "Historical Understanding and Counterrationality: The *Judenrat* as Epistemological Vantage." In *Probing the Limits of Representation: Nazism and the "Final Solution,"* edited by Saul Friedlander, 128–42. Cambridge: Harvard University Press, 1992.

Dobroszycki, Lucjan, ed. *The Chronicle of the Łódź Ghetto, 1941–1944*. Translated by Richard Lourie et al. New Haven, Conn.: Yale University Press, 1984.

Dwork, Debórah, and Robert Jan van Pelt. *Holocaust: A History*. New York: W. W. Norton, 2002.

Eaglestone, Robert. *Ethical Criticism: Reading after Levinas*. Edinburgh: Edinburgh University Press, 1997.

————. *The Holocaust and the Postmodern*. Oxford: Oxford University Press, 2004.

Epstein, Helen. *Children of the Holocaust: Conversations with Sons and Daughters of Survivors*. New York: Putnam, 1979.

Epstein, Leslie. *King of the Jews*. New York: W. W. Norton, 1979.

Ezrahi, Sidra. *By Words Alone: The Holocaust in Literature*. Chicago: University of Chicago Press, 1980.

————. "'The Grave in the Air': Unbound Metaphors in Post-Holocaust Poetry." In *Probing the Limits of Representation: Nazism and the "Final Solution,"* edited by Saul Friedlander, 259–76. Cambridge: Harvard University Press, 1992.

————. "Representing Auschwitz." *History & Memory* 7, no. 2 (Fall/Winter 1996): 121–54.

Felman, Shoshana, and Dori Laub. *Testimony: Crises of Witnessing in Literature, Psychoanalysis, and History*. New York: Routledge, 1992.

Felstiner, John. *Paul Celan: Poet, Survivor, Jew*. New Haven, Conn.: Yale University Press, 1995.

Fink, Ida. *"A Scrap of Time" and Other Stories*. Translated by Madeline Levine and Francine Prose. New York: Random House, 1987; rpt. Evanston, Ill.: Northwestern University Press, 1995.

Fortunoff Video Archive for Holocaust Testimonies. Yale University Library. T-179, Serena N.; T-183, Rose A.; T-65, Irene W. Website: http://www.library.yale.edu/testimonies.

Frank, Anne. *The Diary of a Young Girl*. Edited by Otto H. Frank and Mirjam Pressler. Translated by Susan Massotty. New York: Doubleday, 1995.

Frankl, Viktor E. *Man's Search for Meaning: An Introduction to Logotherapy*. Translated by Ilse Lasch. Boston: Beacon, 1962; rpt. New York: Simon & Schuster, 1984.

Fresco, Nadine. "Remembering the Unknown." *International Journal of Psychoanalysis* 65 (1984): 417–27. Originally published as "La diaspora des cendres." *La Nouvelle Revue de Psychanalyse*, no. 24 (1981): 205–20.

Freud, Sigmund. *Beyond the Pleasure Principle*. In *The Standard Edition of the Complete Psychological Works of Sigmund Freud*, edited and translated by James Strachey, 18:7–64. London: Hogarth, 1955; rpt. London: Vintage, 2001. *Jenseits des Lustprinzips*. In *Gesammelte Werke*, edited by Anna Freud et al., 13:3–69. London: Imago, 1940.

———. *Civilization and Its Discontents*. In *The Standard Edition of the Complete Psychological Works of Sigmund Freud*, edited and translated by James Strachey, 21:64–145. London: Hogarth, 1964; rpt. London: Vintage, 2001. *Das Unbehagen in der Kultur*. In *Gesammelte Werke*, edited by Anna Freud et al., 14:421–506. London: Imago, 1948.

———. *Group Psychology and the Analysis of the Ego*. In *The Standard Edition of the Complete Psychological Works of Sigmund Freud*, edited and translated by James Strachey,18:69–143. London: Hogarth, 1955; rpt. London: Vintage, 2001. *Massenpsychologie und Ich-Analyse*. In *Gesammelte Werke*, edited by Anna Freud et al., 13:71–161. London: Imago, 1940.

———. *Inhibitions, Symptoms and Anxiety*. In *The Standard Edition of the Complete Psychological Works of Sigmund Freud*, edited and translated by James Strachey, 20:87–172. London: Hogarth, 1959; rpt. London: Vintage, 2001. *Hemmung, Symptom und Angst*. In *Gesammelte Werke*, edited by Anna Freud et al.,14:113–205. London: Imago, 1948.

———. *The Interpretation of Dreams*. In *The Standard Edition of the Complete Psychological Works of Sigmund Freud*, edited and translated by James Strachey, vol. 4 and vol. 5, pp. 339–625. London: Hogarth, 1953; rpt. London: Vintage, 2001. *Die Traumdeutung*. Vols. 2 and 3 of *Gesammelte Werke*, edited by Anna Freud et al. London: Imago, 1942.

———. "Introduction to *Psychoanalysis and the War Neuroses*." In *The Standard Edition of the Complete Psychological Works of Sigmund Freud*, edited and translated by James Strachey, 17:207–10. London: Hogarth, 1955; rpt. London: Vintage, 2001. "Einleitung zu *Zur Psychoanalyse der Kriegsneurosen*." In *Gesammelte Werke*, edited by Anna Freud et al., 12:321–24. London: Imago, 1947.

———. *Introductory Lectures on Psycho-analysis*. Vols. 15 (Parts 1 and 2) and 16 (Part 3) of *The Standard Edition of the Complete Psychological Works of Sigmund Freud*, edited and translated by James Strachey. London: Hogarth, 1963; rpt. London: Vintage, 2001. *Vorlesungen zur Einführung in die Psychoanalyse*. Vol. 11 of *Gesammelte Werke*, edited by Anna Freud et al. London: Imago, 1940.

———. "A Metapsychological Supplement to the Theory of Dreams." In *The Standard Edition of the Complete Psychological Works of Sigmund Freud*, edited and translated by James Strachey, 14:221–35. London: Hogarth, 1957; rpt.

London: Vintage, 2001. "Metapsychologische Ergänzung zur Traumlehre." In *Gesammelte Werke*, edited by Anna Freud et al., 10:412–26. London: Imago, 1946.

———. *Moses and Monotheism*. In *The Standard Edition of the Complete Psychological Works of Sigmund Freud*, edited and translated by James Strachey, 23:7–137. London: Hogarth, 1964; rpt. London: Vintage, 2001. *Der Mann Moses und die monotheistische Religion*. In *Gesammelte Werke*, edited by Anna Freud et al., 16:101–246. London: Imago, 1950.

———. *An Outline of Psychoanalysis*. In *The Standard Edition of the Complete Psychological Works of Sigmund Freud*, edited and translated by James Strachey, 23:144–207. London: Hogarth, 1964; rpt. London: Vintage, 2001. *Abriss der Psychoanalyse*. In *Gesammelte Werke*, edited by Anna Freud et al., 17:63–138. London: Imago, 1941.

———. *Project for a Scientific Psychology*. In *The Standard Edition of the Complete Psychological Works of Sigmund Freud*, edited and translated by James Strachey, 1:295–387. London: Hogarth, 1966; rpt. London: Vintage, 2001. *Entwurf einer Psychologie*. In *Aus den Anfängen der Psychoanalyse*, edited by Marie Bonaparte, Anna Freud, and Ernst Kris. London: Imago, 1950.

———. *The Psychopathology of Everyday Life*. Vol. 6 of *The Standard Edition of the Complete Psychological Works of Sigmund Freud*, edited and translated by James Strachey. London: Hogarth, 1960; rpt. London: Vintage, 2001. *Zur Psychopathologie des Alltagslebens*. Vol. 4 of *Gesammelte Werke*, edited by Anna Freud et al. London: Imago, 1941.

———. "Remembering, Repeating and Working-Through." In *The Standard Edition of the Complete Psychological Works of Sigmund Freud*, edited and translated by James Strachey, 12:147–56. London: Hogarth, 1958; rpt. London: Vintage, 2001. "Erinnern, Wiederholen und Durcharbeiten." In *Gesammelte Werke*, edited by Anna Freud et al., 10:126–36. London: Imago, 1946.

———. "Splitting of the Ego in the Process of Defence." In *The Standard Edition of the Complete Psychological Works of Sigmund Freud*, edited and translated by James Strachey, 23:274–78. London: Hogarth, 1964; rpt. London: Vintage, 2001. "Die Ichspaltung im Abwehrvorgang." In *Gesammelte Werke*, edited by Anna Freud et al., 17:59–62. London: Imago, 1941.

———. *Totem and Taboo*. In *The Standard Edition of the Complete Psychological Works of Sigmund Freud*, edited and translated by James Strachey, 13:1–161. London: Hogarth, 1955; rpt. London: Vintage, 2001. *Totem und Tabu*. In *Gesammelte Werke*, edited by Anna Freud et al., 9:1–205. London: Imago, 1940.

———. "The Uncanny." In *The Standard Edition of the Complete Psychological Works of Sigmund Freud*, edited and translated by James Strachey, 17:219–56. London: Hogarth, 1955; rpt. London: Vintage, 2001. "Das Unheimliche." In *Gesammelte Werke*, edited by Anna Freud et al., 12:229–68. London: Imago, 1947.

Fridman, Lea Wernick. *Words and Witness: Narrative and Aesthetic Strategies in the Representation of the Holocaust*. Albany: State University of New York Press, 2000.

Friedlander, Saul. *Memory, History, and the Extermination of the Jews of Europe*. Bloomington: Indiana University Press, 1993.

———. *Nazi Germany and the Jews: The Years of Persecution, 1933–1939*. New York: HarperCollins, 1997.

———. *Reflections of Nazism: An Essay on Kitsch and Death*. Translated by Thomas Weyr. New York: Harper & Row, 1984; rpt. Bloomington: Indiana University Press, 1993.

———. *When Memory Comes*. Translated by Helen R. Lane. New York: Farrar, Straus, Giroux, 1979.

———. *The Years of Extermination: Nazi Germany and the Jews, 1939–1945*. New York: HarperCollins, 2007.

Funkenstein, Amos. "History, Counterhistory, and Narrative." In *Probing the Limits of Representation: Nazism and the "Final Solution,"* edited by Saul Friedlander, 66–81. Cambridge: Harvard University Press, 1992.

Gary, Romain. *The Dance of Genghis Cohn*. Translated by Romain Gary, with the assistance of Camilla Sykes. New York: World Publishing Company, 1968.

Genette, Gérard. *Narrative Discourse: An Essay in Method*. Translated by Jane E. Lewin. Ithaca: Cornell University Press, 1980.

Gilbert, Martin. *The Holocaust: A History of the Jews of Europe During the Second World War*. New York: Henry Holt, 1985.

Glazar, Richard. *Trap with a Green Fence*. Translated by Roslyn Theobald. Evanston, Ill.: Northwestern University Press, 1995.

Goldhagen, Daniel Jonah. *Hitler's Willing Executioners: Ordinary Germans and the Holocaust*. New York: Vintage, 1996.

Gossman, Eva. *Good Beyond Evil: Ordinary People in Extraordinary Times*. London: Valentine Mitchell, 2002.

Gossman, Lionel. "History and Literature." In *The Writing of History: Literary Form and Historical Understanding*, edited by Robert H. Canary and Henry Kozicki, 3–39. Madison: University of Wisconsin Press, 1978.

Gourevitch, Philip. "The Memory Thief." *New Yorker*, 14 June 1999: 48–68.

Haidu, Peter. "The Dialectics of Unspeakability: Language, Silence, and the Narratives of Desubjectification." In *Probing the Limits of Representation: Nazism and the "Final Solution,"* edited by Saul Friedlander, 277–99. Cambridge: Harvard University Press, 1992.

Hand, Seán. "Shadowing Ethics: Levinas's View of Art and Aesthetics." In *Facing the Other: The Ethics of Emmanuel Levinas*, edited by Seán Hand, 63–89. London: Routledge, 1996.

Hart, Kitty. *Return to Auschwitz: The Remarkable Life of a Girl Who Survived the Holocaust*. New York: Atheneum, 1983.

Hartman, Geoffrey. *Holocaust Remembrance: The Shapes of Memory*. Oxford: Blackwell, 1994.

———. *The Longest Shadow: In the Aftermath of the Holocaust*. Bloomington: Indiana University Press, 1996.

Hartman, Geoffrey, ed. *Bitburg in Moral and Political Perspective*. Bloomington: Indiana University Press, 1986.

Haskell, Thomas. "Objectivity Is Not Neutrality: Rhetoric Versus Practice in Peter Novick's *That Noble Dream*." In *History and Theory: Contemporary Readings*, edited by Brian Fay, Philip Pomper, and Richard T. Vann, 299–319. Oxford: Blackwell, 1998.

Hegel, G. W. F. *The Philosophy of History*. Translated by J. Sibree. New York: Dover, 1956; rpt. Mineola, N.Y.: Dover, 2004.

Heidegger, Martin. *Being and Time*. Translated by John Macquarrie and Edward Robinson. New York: Harper & Row, 1962.

Heinemann, Marlene E. *Gender and Destiny: Women Writers and the Holocaust*. Westport, Conn.: Greenwood Press, 1986.

Herman, Judith. *Trauma and Recovery*. New York: Basic Books, 1992.

Hersey, John. *The Wall*. New York: Knopf, 1950; rpt. New York: Vintage, 1988.

Heyen, William. *Erika: Poems of the Holocaust*. St. Louis: Time Being Books, 1991.

———. *Shoah Train: Poems*. Silver Spring, Md.: Etruscan Press, 2003.

———. *The Swastika Poems*. New York: Vanguard Press, 1977.

Hilberg, Raul. *The Destruction of the European Jews*. 3rd ed. 3 vols. New Haven, Conn.: Yale University Press, 2003.

———. "I Was Not There." In *Writing and the Holocaust*, edited by Berel Lang, 17–25. New York: Holmes & Meier, 1988.

———. *Perpetrators, Victims, Bystanders: The Jewish Catastrophe, 1933–1945*. New York: HarperCollins, 1992.

———. *The Politics of Memory: The Journey of a Holocaust Historian*. Chicago: Ivan R. Dee, 1996.

———. *Sources of Holocaust Research: An Analysis*. Chicago: Ivan R. Dee, 2001.

Hillesum, Etty. *"An Interrupted Life: The Diaries, 1941–1943" and "Letters from Westerbork."* Translated by Arnold J. Pomerans. New York: Henry Holt, 1996.

Hirsch, Marianne. *Family Frames: Photography, Narrative, and Postmemory*. Cambridge: Harvard University Press, 1997.

———. "Surviving Images: Holocaust Photographs and the Work of Postmemory." *The Yale Journal of Criticism* 14, no. 1 (2001): 5–38.

Hirsch, Marianne, and Leo Spitzer. *Ghosts of Home: The Afterlife of Czernowitz in Jewish Memory*. Berkeley: University of California Press, 2010.

Hoess, Rudolf. *Commandant of Auschwitz: The Autobiography of Rudolf Hoess*. Translated by Constantine FitzGibbon. London: Weidenfeld & Nicolson, 1959; rpt. London: Phoenix Press, 2000.

Hoffman, Eva. *After Such Knowledge: Memory, History, and the Legacy of the Holocaust*. New York: PublicAffairs, 2004.

Horkheimer, Max, and Theodor W. Adorno. *Dialectic of Enlightenment: Philosophical Fragments*. Translated by Edmond Jephcott. Edited by Gunzelin Schmid Noerr. Stanford, Calif.: Stanford University Press, 2002. *Dialektik der Aufklärung: Philosophische Fragmente*. In Theodor W. Adorno, *Gesammelte Schriften*, edited by Rolf Tiedemann, 3:19–234. Frankfurt am Main: Suhrkamp, 1997.

Howe, Irving. "Writing and the Holocaust." In *Writing and the Holocaust*, edited by Berel Lang, 175–99. New York: Holmes & Meier, 1988.

Husserl, Edmund. *Ideas Pertaining to a Pure Phenomenology and to a Phenomenological Philosophy*. Translated by F. Kersten. Vol. 1 of *Collected Works*. The Hague: Martinus Nijhoff, 1982.

———. *Logical Investigations*. Translated by J. N. Findlay. Vol. 1. New York: Humanities Press, 1970.

Iwaszko, Tadeusz. "Deportation to the Camp and Registration of Prisoners." In *Auschwitz: Nazi Death Camp*, 3rd ed., edited by Franciszek Piper and Teresa Świebocka, translated by Douglas Selvage, 54–69. Oświęcim: Auschwitz-Birkenau State Museum, 2004.

Jackson, Julian. *France: The Dark Years, 1940–1944*. Oxford: Oxford University Press, 2001.

Jakobson, Roman. "Linguistic and Poetics." In *Selected Writings*, Vol. 3, *Poetry of Grammar and Grammar of Poetry*, edited by Stephen Rudy, 18–51. The Hague: Mouton, 1981.

———. "Shifters, Verbal Categories, and the Russian Verb." In *Selected Writings*, Vol. 2, *Word and Language*, 130–47. The Hague: Mouton, 1971.

Jameson, Fredric. *Late Marxism: Adorno, or, the Persistence of the Dialectic*. London: Verso, 1990.

Janet, Pierre. *Psychological Healing: A Historical and Clinical Study*. Translated by Eden Paul and Cedar Paul. 2 vols. New York: Macmillan, 1925.

Jarosz, Barbara. "Organizations of the Camp Resistance Movement and Their Activities." In *Auschwitz: Nazi Death Camp*, ed. Franciszek Piper and Teresa Świebocka, translated by Douglas Selvage, 215–34. Oświęcim: The Auschwitz-Birkenau State Museum, 1996.

Jarvis, Simon. *Adorno: A Critical Introduction*. New York: Routledge, 1998.

Jaspers, Karl. *Philosophy*. Translated by E. B. Ashton. 2 vols. Chicago: University of Chicago Press, 1970.

Jay, Martin. *Adorno*. Cambridge: Harvard University Press, 1984.

Kaes, Anton. "Holocaust and the End of History: Postmodern Historiography in Cinema." In *Probing the Limits of Representation: Nazism and the "Final Solution*,*"* edited by Saul Friedlander, 206–22. Cambridge: Harvard University Press, 1992.

Kafka, Franz. "Before the Law." Translated by Willa and Edwin Muir. In *Franz Kafka: The Complete Stories*, edited by Nahum N. Glatzer, 3–4. New York: Schocken Books, 1946; rpt. 1983 .

————. *The Castle.* Translated by Mark Harman. New York: Schocken Books, 1998.

Kaplan, Chaim. *Scroll of Agony: The Warsaw Diary of Chaim A. Kaplan.* Translated and edited by Abraham I. Katsh. New York: Macmillan, 1965; rpt. Bloomington: Indiana University Press, in association with the United States Holocaust Memorial Museum, 1999.

Ka-tzetnik 135633. *Atrocity.* New York: Lyle Stuart, 1963.

————. *House of Dolls.* Translated by Moshe M. Kohn. New York: Simon & Schuster, 1955.

Keneally, Thomas. *Schindler's List: A Novel.* New York: Simon & Schuster, 1982.

Kertész, Imre. *Fatelessness.* Translated by Tim Wilkinson. New York: Vintage International, 2004.

Kielar, Wiesław. *Anus Mundi: 1,500 Days in Auschwitz/Birkenau.* Translated by Susanne Flatauer. New York: Times Books, 1980.

Klemperer, Victor. *I Will Bear Witness: A Diary of the Nazi Years, 1933–1941.* Translated by Martin Chalmers. New York: Random House, 1998.

————. *I Will Bear Witness: A Diary of the Nazi Years, 1942–1945.* Translated by Martin Chalmers. New York: Random House, 1999.

Kluger, Ruth. *Still Alive: A Holocaust Girlhood Remembered.* New York: The Feminist Press at the City University of New York, 2001.

Koestler, Arthur. *Scum of the Earth.* New York: Macmillan, 1941; rpt. London: Eland, 2006.

Kofman, Sarah. *Rue Ordener, Rue Labat.* Translated by Ann Smock. Lincoln: University of Nebraska Press, 1996.

————. *Smothered Words.* Translated by Madeleine Dobie. Evanston, Ill.: Northwestern University Press, 1999.

Kogon, Eugen. *The Theory and Practice of Hell: The German Concentration Camps and the System Behind Them.* Translated by Heinz Norden. New York: Farrar, Straus, 1950.

Kolk, Bessel A. van der. "The Body Keeps the Score: Approaches to the Psychobiology of Posttraumatic Stress Disorder." In *Traumatic Stress: The Effects of Overwhelming Experience on Mind, Body, and Society,* edited by Bessel A. van der Kolk, Alexander C. McFarlane, and Lars Weisaeth, 214–41. New York: The Guilford Press, 1996.

————. "Trauma and Memory." In *Traumatic Stress: The Effects of Overwhelming Experience on Mind, Body, and Society,* edited by Bessel A. van der Kolk, Alexander C. McFarlane, and Lars Weisaeth, 279–302. New York: The Guilford Press, 1996.

Kolk, Bessel A. van der, and Onno van der Hart. "The Intrusive Past: The Flexibility of Memory and the Engraving of Trauma." In *Trauma: Explorations in Memory,* edited by Cathy Caruth, 158–82. Baltimore: Johns Hopkins University Press, 1995.

Kolk, Bessel A. van der, Onno van der Hart, and Charles R. Marmar. "Dissociation and Information Processing in Posttraumatic Stress Disorder." In *Traumatic Stress: The Effects of Overwhelming Experience on Mind, Body, and Society*, edited by Bessel A. van der Kolk, Alexander C. McFarlane, and Lars Weisaeth, 303–27. New York: The Guilford Press, 1996.

Kolk, Bessel A. van der, and Alexander C. McFarlane. "The Black Hole of Trauma." In *Traumatic Stress: The Effects of Overwhelming Experience on Mind, Body, and Society*, edited by Bessel A. van der Kolk, Alexander C. McFarlane, and Lars Weisaeth, 3–23. New York: The Guilford Press, 1996.

Kolk, Bessel A. van der, Lars Weisaeth, and Onno van der Hart. "History of Trauma in Psychiatry." In *Traumatic Stress: The Effects of Overwhelming Experience on Mind, Body, and Society*, edited by Bessel A. van der Kolk, Alexander C. McFarlane, and Lars Weisaeth, 47–74. New York: The Guilford Press, 1996.

Kolk, Bessel A. van der, ed. *Post-Traumatic Stress Disorder: Psychological and Biological Sequelae*. Washington, D.C.: American Psychiatric Press, 1984.

Korczak, Janusz. *Ghetto Diary*. Translated by Jerzy Bachrach and Barbara Krzywicka. New Haven, Conn.: Yale University Press, 2003.

Kosinski, Jerzy. *The Painted Bird*. 2nd ed. New York: Grove Press, 1995.

Kovner, Abba. *A Canopy in the Desert*. Translated by Shirley Kaufman, with Ruth Adler and Nurit Orchan. Pittsburgh: University of Pittsburgh Press, 1973.

Krystal, Henry, ed. *Massive Psychic Trauma*. New York: International Universities Press, 1968.

Kuznetsov, A. Anatoli. *Babi Yar: A Document in the Form of a Novel*. Translated by David Floyd. New York: Farrar, Straus and Giroux, 1970.

LaCapra, Dominick. *History and Memory after Auschwitz*. Ithaca: Cornell University Press, 1998.

———. *History in Transit: Experience, Identity, Critical Theory*. Ithaca: Cornell University Press, 2004.

———. *Representing the Holocaust: History, Theory, Trauma*. Ithaca: Cornell University Press, 1994.

———. *Writing History, Writing Trauma*. Baltimore: Johns Hopkins University Press, 2001.

Lamont, Rosette C. Translator's preface to *Days and Memory*, by Charlotte Delbo. Marlboro, Vt.: The Marlboro Press, 1990.

Lang, Berel. *Act and Idea in the Nazi Genocide*. Chicago: University of Chicago Press, 1990; rpt. Syracuse: Syracuse University Press, 2003.

———. *The Future of the Holocaust: Between History and Memory*. Ithaca: Cornell University Press, 1999.

———. *Holocaust Representation: Art Within the Limits of History and Ethics*. Baltimore: Johns Hopkins University Press, 2000.

———. *Philosophical Witnessing: The Holocaust as Presence*. Waltham, Mass.: Brandeis University Press, 2009.

———. *Post-Holocaust: Interpretation, Misinterpretation, and the Claims of History*. Bloomington: Indiana University Press, 2005.

Langbein, Hermann. *Against All Hope: Resistance in the Nazi Concentration Camps, 1938–1945*. Translated by Harry Zohn. New York: Paragon House, 1994.

———. *People in Auschwitz*. Translated by Harry Zohn. Chapel Hill: University of North Carolina Press, 2004.

Langer, Lawrence L. *The Age of Atrocity: Death in Modern Literature*. Boston: Beacon Press, 1978.

———. *The Holocaust and the Literary Imagination*. New Haven, Conn.: Yale University Press, 1975.

———. *Holocaust Testimonies: The Ruins of Memory*. New Haven, Conn.: Yale University Press, 1991.

———. "Interpreting Survivor Testimony." In *Writing and the Holocaust*, edited by Berel Lang, 26–40. New York: Holmes & Meier, 1988.

———. Introduction to *Auschwitz and After*, by Charlotte Delbo, translated by Rosette C. Lamont. New Haven, Conn.: Yale University Press, 1995.

———. *Preempting the Holocaust*. New Haven, Conn.: Yale University Press, 1998.

Langfus, Anna. *The Lost Shore*. Translated by Peter Wiles. New York: Pantheon, 1964.

Lanzmann, Claude. "The Obscenity of Understanding: An Evening with Claude Lanzmann." In *Trauma: Explorations in Memory*, edited by Cathy Caruth, 200–220. Baltimore: Johns Hopkins University Press, 1995.

———. *Shoah: A Film by Claude Lanzmann*. New York: New Yorker Films Artwork, 1999. *Shoah*. Paris: Les Films Aleph, 1985.

———. *Shoah: The Complete Text of the Acclaimed Holocaust Film*. New York: Da Capo Press, 1995.

Laplanche, J., and J.-B. Pontalis. *The Language of Psychoanalysis*. Translated by Donald Nicholson-Smith. New York: W. W. Norton, 1973.

Laruelle, François, ed. *Textes pour Emmanuel Levinas*. Paris: Editions Jean-Michel Place, 1980.

Laub, Dori. "Bearing Witness, or the Vicissitudes of Listening." In Shoshana Felman and Dori Laub, *Testimony: Crises of Witnessing in Literature, Psychoanalysis, and History*, 57–74. New York: Routledge, 1992.

———. "The Empty Circle: Children of Survivors and the Limits of Reconstruction." *Journal of the American Psychoanalytic Association* 46, no. 2 (1998): 507–29.

———. "Erinnerungsprozesse beim Überlebenden und Tätern." In *Das Vermächtnis annehmen: Kulturelle und biographische Zugänge zum Holocaust—Beiträge aus den USA und Deutschland*, edited by Brigitta Huhnke and Björn Krondorfer, 251–73. Gießen: Psychosozial-Verlag, 2002.

————. "An Event Without a Witness: Truth, Testimony and Survival." In Shoshana Felman and Dori Laub, *Testimony: Crises of Witnessing in Literature, Psychoanalysis, and History*, 75–92. New York: Routledge, 1992.

————. "From Speechlessness to Narrative: The Cases of Holocaust Historians and of Psychiatrically Hospitalized Survivors." *Literature and Medicine* 24, no. 2 (Fall 2005): 253–65.

————. "Kann die Psychoanalyse dazu beitragen, den Völkermord historisch besser zu verstehen?" *Psyche: Zeitschrift für Psychoanalyse und ihre Anwendungen* 57, no. 9/10 (2003): 938–59.

————. "On Holocaust Testimony and Its 'Reception' Within Its Own Frame, as a Process in Its Own Right." *History & Memory* 21, no. 1 (Spring/Summer 2009): 127–50.

————. "Testimonies in the Treatment of Genocidal Trauma." *Journal of Applied Psychoanalytic Studies* 4, no. 1 (January 2002): 63–87.

Laub, Dori, with Marjorie Allard. "History, Memory, Truth." In *The Holocaust and History: The Known, the Unknown, the Disputed, and the Reexamined*, edited by Michael Berenbaum and Abraham J. Peck, 799–812. Bloomington: Indiana University Press, in association with the United States Holocaust Memorial Museum, 1998.

Laub, Dori, and Nanette Auerhahn. "Failed Empathy—A Theme in the Survivor's Holocaust Experience." *Psychoanalytic Psychology* 6, no. 4 (1989): 377–400.

Laub, Dori, and Susanna Lee. "Thanatos and Massive Psychic Trauma: The Impact of the Death Instinct on Knowing, Remembering and Forgetting." *Journal of the American Psychoanalytic Association* 51, no. 2 (2003): 433–64.

Laub, Dori, and Daniel Podell. "Art and Trauma." *International Journal of Psychoanalysis* 76, no. 5 (1995): 991–1005.

————. "Psychoanalytic Listening to Historical Trauma: The Conflict of Knowing and the Imperative to Act." *Mind and Human Interaction* 8, no. 4 (1997): 245–60.

Leak, Andrew, and George Paizis, eds. *The Holocaust and the Text: Speaking the Unspeakable*. New York: St. Martin's Press, 2000.

Lengyel, Olga. *Five Chimneys: A Woman Survivor's True Story of Auschwitz*. Chicago: Academy Chicago Publishers, 1995.

Lescourret, Marie-Anne. *Emmanuel Levinas*. Paris: Flammarion, 1994.

Levi, Primo. *The Drowned and the Saved*. Translated by Raymond Rosenthal. New York: Simon & Schuster, 1988; rpt. New York: Vintage International, 1989. *I sommersi e i salvati*. In *Opere*, edited by Marco Belpoliti, 2:995–1153. Turin: Einaudi, 1997.

————. *If Not Now, When?* Translated by William Weaver. New York: Summit Books, 1985. *Se non ora, quando?* In *Opere*, edited by Marco Belpoliti, 2:207–513. Turin: Einaudi, 1997.

————. *Other People's Trades.* Translated by Raymond Rosenthal. New York: Summit Books, 1989. *L'altrui mestiere.* In *Opere,* edited by Marco Belpoliti, 2:629–856. Turin: Einaudi, 1997.

————. *The Periodic Table.* Translated by Raymond Rosenthal. New York: Schocken Books, 1984. *Il sistema periodico.* In *Opere,* edited by Marco Belpoliti, 1:739–942. Turin: Einaudi, 1997.

————. *The Reawakening.* Translated by Stuart Woolf. London: The Bodley Head, 1965; rpt. New York: Macmillan, 1993. *La tregua.* In *Opere,* edited by Marco Belpoliti, 1:203–395. Turin: Einaudi, 1997.

————. *Survival in Auschwitz.* Translated by Stuart Woolf. New York: Macmillan, 1993; originally published under the title *If This Is a Man.* New York: Orion, 1959. *Se questo è un uomo.* In *Opere,* edited by Marco Belpoliti, 1:3–169. Turin: Einaudi, 1997.

Levin, Nora. "Some Reservations about Lanzmann's *Shoah.*" *Sh'ma: A Journal of Jewish Responsibility,* 18 April 1986: 91–93.

Levinas, Emmanuel. *Alterity and Transcendence.* Translated by Michael B. Smith. New York: Columbia University Press, 1999. *Altérité et transcendance.* Saint Clément: Fata Morgana, 1995.

————. *Basic Philosophical Writings.* Edited by Adriaan T. Peperzak, Simon Critchley, and Robert Bernasconi. Bloomington: Indiana University Press, 1996.

————. *Entre Nous: Thinking-of-the-Other.* Translated by Michael B. Smith and Barbara Harshav. New York: Columbia University Press, 1998. *Entre nous: Essais sur le penser-à-l'autre.* Paris: Grasset & Fasquelle, 1991.

————. *Ethics and Infinity: Conversations with Philippe Nemo.* Translated by Richard A. Cohen. Pittsburgh: Duquesne University Press, 1985. *Éthique et infini: Dialogues avec Philippe Nemo.* Paris: Fayard, 1982.

————. *Existence and Existents.* Translated by Alphonso Lingis. The Hague: Martinus Nijhoff, 1978. *De l'existence à l'existant.* 2nd ed. Paris: Vrin, 1963.

————. *God, Death, and Time.* Translated by Bettina Bergo. Stanford, Calif.: Stanford University Press, 2000. *Dieu, la mort et le temps.* Paris: Grasset & Fasquelle, 1993.

————. *Humanism of the Other.* Translated by Nidra Poller. Urbana: University of Illinois Press, 2003. *Humanisme de l'autre homme.* Montpellier: Fata Morgana, 1972.

————. *Is It Righteous To Be?: Interviews with Emmanuel Levinas.* Edited by Jill Robbins. Stanford, Calif.: Stanford University Press, 2001.

————. "Language and Proximity." In *Collected Philosophical Papers,* translated by Alphonso Lingis, 109–26. Dordrecht: Martinus Nijhoff, 1987. "Langage et proximité." In *En découvrant l'existence avec Husserl et Heidegger.* 3rd ed., 217–36. Paris: Vrin, 1974.

————. *The Levinas Reader.* Edited by Seán Hand. Oxford: Blackwell, 1989.

———. "Nameless." In *Proper Names*, translated by Michael B. Smith, 119–23. Stanford, Calif.: Stanford University Press, 1996. "San nom." In *Noms propres*, 177–82. Montpellier: Fata Morgana, 1976.

———. *On Escape / De l'évasion*. Translated by Bettina Bergo. Stanford, Calif.: Stanford University Press, 2003. *De l'évasion*. Montpellier: Fata Morgana, 1982.

———. *Otherwise than Being or Beyond Essence*. Translated by Alphonso Lingis. The Hague: Martinus Nijhoff, 1981; rpt. Pittsburgh: Duquesne University Press, 1998. *Autrement qu'être ou au-delà de l'essence*. The Hague: Martinus Nijhoff, 1974.

———. *Outside the Subject*. Translated by Michael B. Smith. Stanford, Calif.: Stanford University Press, 1994. *Hors sujet*. Saint Clément: Fata Morgana, 1987.

———. "Phenomenon and Enigma." In *Collected Philosophical Papers*, translated by Alphonso Lingis, 61–73. Dordrecht: Martinus Nijhoff, 1987. "Énigme et phénomène." In *En découvrant l'existence avec Husserl et Heidegger*. 3rd ed., 203–16. Paris: Vrin, 1974.

———. *Proper Names*. Translated by Michael B. Smith. Stanford, Calif.: Stanford University Press, 1996. *Noms propres*. Montpellier: Fata Morgana, 1976.

———. "Reality and Its Shadow." In *Collected Philosophical Papers*, translated by Alphonso Lingis, 1–13. Dordrecht: Martinus Nijhoff, 1987. "La réalité et son ombre." *Les Temps Modernes* 38 (1948): 771–89.

———. "Signature." In *Difficult Freedom: Essays on Judaism*. Translated by Seán Hand, 291–95. Baltimore: Johns Hopkins University Press, 1990. "Signature." In *Difficile liberté: Essais sur le judaïsme*, 371–79. Paris: Albin Michel, 1976.

———. "Substitution." Translated by Peter Atterton, Simon Critchley, and Graham Noctor. In *Basic Philosophical Writings*, edited by Adriaan T. Peperzak, Simon Critchley, and Robert Bernasconi, 80–95. Bloomington: Indiana University Press, 1996. "La substitution." *Revue Philosophique de Louvain* 66, no. 91 (1968): 487–508.

———. *Sur Maurice Blanchot*. Montpellier: Fata Morgana, 1975. English translation in *Proper Names*.

———. *Time and the Other*. Translated by Richard A. Cohen. Pittsburgh: Duquesne University Press, 1987. *Le temps et l'autre*. Montpellier: Fata Morgana, 1979; rpt. Paris: Presses Universitaires de France, 1983. Originally published as "Le temps et l'autre." In *Le Choix, le Monde, l'Existence*, edited by Jean Wahl, 125–96. Grenoble-Paris: Arthaud, 1947.

———. *Totality and Infinity: An Essay on Exteriority*. Translated by Alphonso Lingis. Pittsburgh: Duquesne University Press, 1969. *Totalité et infini: Essai sur l'extériorité*. The Hague: Martinus Nijhoff, 1961.

———. "The Trace of the Other." Translated by Alphonso Lingis. In *Deconstruction in Context: Literature and Philosophy*, edited by Mark C. Taylor, 345–59.

Chicago: University of Chicago Press, 1986. "La trace de l'autre." In *En dé-couvrant l'existence avec Husserl et Heidegger.* 3rd ed., 187–202. Paris: Vrin, 1974.

———. "Truth of Disclosure and Truth of Testimony." Translated by Iain MacDonald. In *Basic Philosophical Writings,* edited by Adriaan T. Peperzak, Simon Critchley, and Robert Bernasconi, 98–107. Bloomington: Indiana University Press, 1996. "Vérité du dévoilement et vérité du témoignage." In *Le témoignage,* edited by E. Castelli, 101–10. Paris: Aubier-Montaigne, 1972.

Levine, Michael G. *The Belated Witness: Literature, Testimony, and the Question of Holocaust Survival.* Stanford, Calif.: Stanford University Press, 2006.

Leys, Ruth. *Trauma: A Genealogy.* Chicago: University of Chicago Press, 2000.

Libertson, Joseph. *Proximity: Levinas, Blanchot, Bataille and Communication.* The Hague: Martinus Nijhoff, 1982.

Liebman, Stuart, ed. *Claude Lanzmann's "Shoah": Key Essays.* Oxford: Oxford University Press, 2007.

Lifton, Robert Jay. *The Broken Connection: On Death and the Continuity of Life.* New York: Basic Books, 1983.

Lind, Jakov. *Soul of Wood.* Translated by Ralph Manheim. New York: New York Review Books, 2010.

Lipstadt, Deborah. *Denying the Holocaust: The Growing Assault on Truth and Memory.* New York: Free Press, 1993.

Littell, Jonathan. *The Kindly Ones.* Translated by Charlotte Mandell. New York: HarperCollins, 2009. *Les bienveillantes.* Paris: Gallimard, 2006.

Llewelyn, John. *Emmanuel Levinas: The Genealogy of Ethics.* New York: Routledge, 1995.

Loftus, Elizabeth E. *Eyewitness Testimony.* Cambridge: Harvard University Press, 1979; rpt. 1996.

Lorenz, Chris. "Historical Knowledge and Historical Reality: A Plea for 'Internal Realism.'" In *History and Theory: Contemporary Readings,* edited by Brian Fay, Philip Pomper, and Richard T. Vann, 342–76. Oxford: Blackwell, 1998.

Luckhurst, Roger. *The Trauma Question.* London: Routledge, 2008.

Lyotard, Jean-François. *The Differend.* Translated by Georges Van Den Abbeele. Minneapolis: University of Minnesota Press, 1988.

———. *Heidegger and "the jews."* Translated by Andreas Michel and Mark Roberts. Minneapolis: University of Minnesota Press, 1990.

———. "Levinas' Logic." In *Face to Face with Levinas,* edited by Richard A. Cohen, 117–58. Albany: State University of New York Press, 1986.

Malka, Salomon. *Emmanuel Levinas: His Life and Legacy.* Translated by Michael Kigel and Sonja M. Embree. Pittsburgh: Duquesne University Press, 2006.

Marcuse, Herbert. "Existentialism: Remarks on Jean-Paul Sartre's *L'Être et le Néant.*" *Philosophy and Phenomenological Research* 8, no. 3 (March 1948): 309–

36; rpt. with revisions as "Sartre's Existentialism." In *Studies in Critical Philosophy*, 157–90. Boston: Beacon, 1973.

Marion, Esther. "The Nazi Genocide and the Writing of the Holocaust Aporia: Ethics and *Remnants of Auschwitz*." *Modern Language Notes* 121, no. 4 (2006): 1009–22.

Mark, Ber. *The Scrolls of Auschwitz*. Translated by Sharon Neemani. Tel Aviv: Am Oved, 1985.

Marrus, Michael R., and Robert O. Paxton. *Vichy France and the Jews*. New York: Basic Books, 1981; rpt. Stanford, Calif.: Stanford University Press, 1995.

Marx, Karl. "Thesen über Feuerbach." In *Marx-Engels Werke*, 3:5–7. Berlin: Dietz, 1969.

Mayer, Arno J. *Why Did the Heavens Not Darken?: The "Final Solution" in History*. New York: Pantheon, 1988.

McFarlane, Alexander C., and Giovanni de Girolamo. "The Nature of Traumatic Stressors and the Epidemiology of Posttraumatic Reactions." In *Traumatic Stress: The Effects of Overwhelming Experience on Mind, Body, and Society*, edited by Bessel A. van der Kolk, Alexander C. McFarlane, and Lars Weisaeth, 129–54. New York: The Guilford Press, 1996.

Mendelsohn, Daniel. *The Lost: A Search for Six of Six Million*. New York: HarperCollins, 2006.

Mermelstein, Mel. *By Bread Alone: The Story of a Survivor of the Nazi Holocaust*. Huntington Beach, Calif.: Auschwitz Study Foundation, 1979.

Mesnard, Philippe, and Claudine Kahan. *Giorgio Agamben à l'épreuve d'Auschwitz*. Paris: Editions Kimé, 2001.

Michaels, Anne. *Fugitive Pieces*. New York: Knopf, 1997.

Mink, Louis O. "Narrative Form as a Cognitive Instrument." In *The Writing of History: Literary Form and Historical Understanding*, edited by Robert H. Canary and Henry Kozicki, 129–49. Madison: University of Wisconsin Press, 1978.

Mitscherlich, Alexander, and Margarete Mitscherlich. *The Inability to Mourn: Principles of Collective Behavior*. Translated by Beverley R. Placzek. New York: Grove Press, 1975.

Modiano, Patrick. *Dora Bruder*. Translated by Joanna Kilmartin. Berkeley: University of California Press, 1999.

———. *La place de l'étoile*. Paris: Gallimard, 1968.

Moyn, Samuel. *Origins of the Other: Emmanuel Levinas Between Revelation and Ethics*. Ithaca: Cornell University Press, 2005.

Müller, Filip. *Eyewitness Auschwitz: Three Years in the Gas Chambers*. Translated by Susanne Flatauer. Chicago: Ivan R. Dee, 1999.

Nancy, Jean-Luc. *The Inoperative Community*. Edited by Peter Connor. Translated by Peter Connor et al. Minneapolis: University of Minnesota Press, 1991.

Némirovsky, Irène. *Suite Française: A Novel.* Translated by Sandra Smith. New York: Vintage International, 2006.

Nietzsche, Friedrich. *Beyond Good and Evil.* Translated by Walter Kaufmann. New York: Vintage, 1966.

Nolte, Ernst. "Die Vergangenheit, die nicht vergehen will." *Frankfurter Allgemeine Zeitung,* 6 June 1986.

Nomberg-Przytyk, Sara. *Auschwitz: True Tales from a Grotesque Land.* Translated by Roslyn Hirsch. Edited by Eli Pfefferkorn and David H. Hirsch. Chapel Hill: University of North Carolina Press, 1985.

Novick, Peter. *That Noble Dream: The "Objectivity Question" and the American Historical Profession.* Cambridge: Cambridge University Press, 1988.

Nyiszli, Miklos. *Auschwitz: A Doctor's Eyewitness Account.* Translated by Tibère Kremer and Richard Seaver. New York: Arcade Publishing, 1993.

Ofer, Dalia, and Lenore J. Weitzman, eds. *Women in the Holocaust.* New Haven, Conn.: Yale University Press, 1998.

Ophuls, Marcel. *Hotel Terminus: The Life and Times of Klaus Barbie.* The Memory Pictures Company, 1988; Santa Monica, Calif.: MGM Home Entertainment, 2000.

———. *The Sorrow and the Pity: Chronicle of a French City under the Occupation.* Harrington Park, N.J.: Milestone Film & Video, 2000. *Le chagrin et la pitié: Chronique d'une ville française sous l'Occupation.* France/Germany/Switzerland: Productions Télévision Rencontre S.A., 1969.

Ozick, Cynthia. *The Shawl.* New York: Knopf, 1989.

Pagis, Dan. *Points of Departure.* Translated by Stephen Mitchell. Philadelphia: The Jewish Publication Society of America, 1981.

Paxton, Robert O. *Vichy France: Old Guard and New Order, 1940–1944.* New York: Knopf, 1972; rpt. New York: Columbia University Press, 2001.

Peperzak, Adriaan T. *Beyond: The Philosophy of Emmanuel Levinas.* Evanston, Ill.: Northwestern University Press, 1997.

———. *To the Other: An Introduction to the Philosophy of Emmanuel Levinas.* West Lafayette, Ind.: Purdue University Press, 1993.

Perec, Georges. *W, or, The Memory of Childhood.* Translated by David Bellos. London: Collins Harvill, 1988.

Piper, Franciszek. "The Mass Extermination of Jews in the Gas Chambers." In *Auschwitz: Nazi Death Camp,* edited by Franciszek Piper and Teresa Świebocka, translated by Douglas Selvage, 165–73. Oświęcim: Auschwitz-Birkenau State Museum, 1996.

Piper, Franciszek, and Teresa Świebocka, eds. *Auschwitz: Nazi Death Camp.* Translated by Douglas Selvage. Oświęcim: The Auschwitz-Birkenau State Museum, 1996.

Pollack, Michael. *L'expérience concentrationnaire: Essai sur le maintien de l'identité sociale.* Paris: Métailié, 1990.

Popper, Karl. *The Logic of Scientific Discovery.* Translated by the author with the assistance of Julius Freed and Ian Freed. New York: Basic Books, 1959; rpt. London: Routledge, 2002.

Prince, Gerald. *A Dictionary of Narratology.* Rev. ed. Lincoln: University of Nebraska Press, 2003.

Racine, Jean. *Phèdre.* In *Oeuvres complètes,* edited by Raymond Picard, 1:763–821. Paris: Gallimard, Bibliothèque de la Pléiade, 1950.

Raczymow, Henri. *Contes d'exil et d'oubli.* Paris: Gallimard, 1979.

———. *Writing the Book of Esther.* Translated by Dori Katz. New York: Holmes & Meier, 1995.

Rashke, Richard. *Escape from Sobibor.* Boston: Houghton Mifflin, 1982.

Rawicz, Piotr. *Blood from the Sky.* Translated by Peter Wiles. New York: Harcourt, Brace & World, 1964.

Reitlinger, Gerald. *The Final Solution: The Attempt to Exterminate the Jews of Europe.* 2nd ed. South Brunswick, N.J.: T. Yoseloff, 1968.

Reznikoff, Charles. *Holocaust.* Los Angeles: Black Sparrow Press, 1975; rpt. Boston: David R. Godine, 2007.

Ricoeur, Paul. "Otherwise: A Reading of Emmanuel Levinas's *Otherwise than Being or Beyond Essence.*" Translated by Matthew Escobar. *Yale French Studies,* no. 104 (2004): 82–99.

Ringelblum, Emmanuel. *Notes from the Warsaw Ghetto.* Translated and edited by Jacob Sloan. New York: McGraw-Hill, 1958; rpt. New York: ibooks, 2006.

Rittner, Carol, and John K. Roth, eds. *Different Voices: Women and the Holocaust.* St. Paul, Minn.: Paragon House, 1993.

Robbins, Jill. *Altered Reading: Levinas and Literature.* Chicago: University of Chicago Press, 1999.

Rose, Sven-Erik. "Auschwitz as Hermeneutic Rupture, Differend, and Image *malgré tout*: Jameson, Lyotard, Didi-Huberman." In *Visualizing the Holocaust: Documents, Aesthetics, Memory,* edited by David Bathrick, Brad Prager, and Michael D. Richardson, 114–137. Rochester, N.Y.: Camden House, 2008.

Rosenbaum, Alan S., ed. *Is the Holocaust Unique?: Perspectives on Comparative Genocide.* Boulder, Colo.: Westview Press, 1996.

Rosenfeld, Alvin H. *A Double Dying: Reflections on Holocaust Literature.* Bloomington: Indiana University Press, 1980.

Rosenman, Anny Dayan. *Les alphabets de la Shoah: Survivre. Témoigner. Écrire.* Paris: CNRS Editions, 2007.

Roskies, David. *Against the Apocalypse: Responses to Catastrophe in Modern Jewish Culture.* Cambridge: Harvard University Press, 1984.

Roskies, David, ed. *The Literature of Destruction: Jewish Responses to Catastrophe.* Philadelphia: Jewish Publication Society of America, 1989.

Rotem, Simha (Kazik). *Memoirs of a Warsaw Ghetto Fighter.* Translated and edited by Barbara Harshav. New Haven, Conn.: Yale University Press, 1994.

Roth, John K., and Michael Berenbaum, eds. *Holocaust: Religious & Philosophical Implications*. New York: Paragon House, 1989.

Rothberg, Michael. *Traumatic Realism: The Demands of Holocaust Representation*. Minneapolis: University of Minnesota Press, 2000.

Rousset, David. *The Other Kingdom*. Translated by Ramon Guthrie. New York: Reynal and Hitchcock, 1947. *L'univers concentrationnaire*. Paris: Editions du Pavois, 1946.

Rousso, Henry. *The Vichy Syndrome: History and Memory in France since 1944*. Translated by Arthur Goldhammer. Cambridge: Harvard University Press, 1991. Originally published as *Le syndrome de Vichy: De 1944 à nos jours*. Paris: Editions du Seuil, 1987.

Rubenstein, Richard L., and John K. Roth. *Approaches to Auschwitz: The Holocaust and Its Legacy*. Rev. ed. Louisville, Ky.: Westminster John Knox Press, 2003.

Ryn, Zdzisław, and Stanisław Kłodziński. "An der Grenze zwischen Leben und Tod: Eine Studie über die Erscheinung des 'Muselmanns' im Konzentrationslager." In *Die Auschwitz-Hefte*, rev. ed., 1:89–154. Hamburg: Rogner & Bernhard, 1994.

Sachs, Nelly. *O The Chimneys: Selected Poems*. Translated by Michael Hamburger, Christopher Holme, Ruth Mead and Matthew Mead, and Michael Roloff. New York: Farrar, Straus and Giroux, 1967.

Santner, Eric. *Stranded Objects: Mourning, Memory, and Film in Postwar Germany*. Ithaca: Cornell University Press, 1990.

Sanyal, Debarati. "A Soccer Match in Auschwitz: Passing Culpability in Holocaust Criticism." *Representations* 79 (Summer 2002): 1–27.

Sartre, Jean-Paul. *Anti-Semite and Jew*. Translated by George. J. Becker. New York: Schocken Books, 1948.

———. *Being and Nothingness: An Essay on Phenomenological Ontology*. Translated by Hazel E. Barnes. New York: Philosophical Library, 1956; rpt. London: Routledge, 2003.

———. *Dirty Hands*. Translated by Lionel Abel. In *"No Exit" and Three Other Plays*, 125–242. New York: Vintage International, 1989.

———. *No Exit*. Translated by Stuart Gilbert. In *"No Exit" and Three Other Plays*, 1–46. New York: Vintage International, 1989.

———. *What Is Literature?* Translated by Bernard Frechtman. In *"What Is Literature?" and Other Essays*, 21–245. Cambridge: Harvard University Press, 1988.

Schlink, Bernhard. *The Reader: A Novel*. Translated by Carol Brown Janeway. New York: Vintage International, 1997.

Schwarz, Daniel R. *Imagining the Holocaust*. New York: St. Martin's Press, 1999.

Schwarz-Bart, André. *The Last of the Just*. Translated by Stephen Becker. New York: Atheneum, 1960; rpt. Woodstock and New York: The Overlook Press, 2000.

Segal, Lore. *Other People's Houses: A Novel.* New York: Harcourt Brace Jovanovich, 1963; rpt. New York: The New Press, 2004.

Semprun, Jorge. *Literature or Life.* Translated by Linda Coverdale. New York: Viking 1997. *L'écriture ou la vie.* Paris: Gallimard, 1994; rpt. Collection Folio, 1996.

———. *The Long Voyage.* Translated by Richard Seaver. New York: Grove Press, 1964. *Le grand voyage.* Paris: Gallimard, 1963.

———. *Le mort qu'il faut.* Paris: Gallimard, 2001.

———. *What a Beautiful Sunday!* Translated by Alan Sheridan. New York: Harcourt Brace Jovanovich, 1982. *Quel beau dimanche!* Paris: Grasset, 1980.

Semprun, Jorge, and Elie Wiesel. *Se taire est impossible.* Paris: Editions Mille et une nuits, 1997.

Sereny, Gitta. *Into that Darkness: An Examination of Conscience.* London: Deutsch, 1974; rpt. New York, Vintage, 1983.

Shakespeare, William. *Hamlet.* In *The Riverside Shakespeare,* edited by G. Blakemore Evans, 1135–97. Boston: Houghton Mifflin, 1974.

Shermer, Michael, and Alex Grobman. *Denying History: Who Says the Holocaust Never Happened and Why Do They Say It?* Berkeley: University of California Press, 2000.

Shklovsky, Viktor. "Art as Technique." In *Russian Formalist Criticism,* translated by Lee T. Lemon and Marion J. Reis, 5–24. Lincoln: University of Nebraska Press, 1965. Also: "Art as Device." In *Theory of Prose,* by Viktor Shklovskii, translated by Benjamin Sher, 1–14. Elmwood Park, Ill.: Dalkey Archive Press, 1990.

Silverman, Kaja. *The Threshold of the Visible World.* New York: Routledge, 1996.

Singer, Isaac Bashevis. *Enemies, A Love Story.* New York: Farrar, Straus and Giroux, 1972.

Sobolewicz, Tadeusz. *But I Survived.* Translated by Witold Zbirohowski-Kościa. Oświęcim: Auschwitz-Birkenau State Museum, 1998.

Sofsky, Wolfgang. *The Order of Terror: The Concentration Camp.* Translated by William Templer. Princeton: Princeton University Press, 1997.

Spargo, R. Clifton. *Vigilant Memory: Emmanuel Levinas, the Holocaust, and the Unjust Death.* Baltimore: Johns Hopkins University Press, 2006.

Spiegelman, Art. *Maus: A Survivor's Tale.* Vol. 1. *My Father Bleeds History.* New York: Pantheon, 1973.

———. *Maus: A Survivor's Tale.* Vol. 2. *And Here My Troubles Began.* New York: Pantheon, 1986.

Spitzer, Leo. *Hotel Bolivia: The Culture of Memory in a Refuge from Nazism.* New York: Hill and Wang, 1998.

Steinberg, Paul. *Speak You Also: A Survivor's Reckoning.* Translated by Linda Coverdale, with Bill Ford. New York: Henry Holt, Metropolitan Books, 2000.

Steiner, George. *Language and Silence: Essays on Language, Literature, and the Inhuman.* New York: Atheneum, 1967.

———. "The Long Life of Metaphor: An Approach to the 'Shoah.'" In *Writing and the Holocaust,* edited by Berel Lang, 154–71. New York: Holmes & Meier, 1988.

———. *The Portage to San Cristobal of A.H.: A Novel.* New York: Simon & Schuster, 1982; rpt. Chicago: University of Chicago Press, 1999.

Steiner, Jean-François. *Treblinka.* Translated by Helen Weaver. New York: Simon & Schuster, 1967.

Stern, Kenneth S. *Holocaust Denial.* New York: American Jewish Committee, 1993.

Styron, William. *Sophie's Choice.* New York: Random House, 1979; rpt. New York: Vintage International, 1992.

Suleiman, Susan Rubin. *Crises of Memory and the Second World War.* Cambridge: Harvard University Press, 2006.

———. "When the Perpetrator Becomes a Reliable Witness of the Holocaust: On Jonathan Littell's *Les bienveillantes.*" *New German Critique* no. 106 (Winter 2009): 1–19.

Sutzkever, Abraham. *A. Sutzkever: Selected Poetry and Prose.* Translated by Barbara and Benjamin Harshav. Berkeley: University of California Press, 1991.

Świebocki, Henryk, ed. *London Has Been Informed . . . : Reports by Auschwitz Escapees.* Translated by Michael Jacobs and Laurence Weinbaum. Oświęcim: Auschwitz-Birkenau State Museum, 2002.

Szmaglewska, Seweryna. *Smoke over Birkenau.* Translated by Jadwiga Rynas. New York: Henry Holt, 1947; rpt. Warsaw: Książka i Wiedza, 2001.

Szpilman, Wladyslaw. *The Pianist: The Extraordinary True Story of One Man's Survival in Warsaw, 1939–1945.* Translated by Anthea Bell. London: Victor Gollanz, 1999; New York: Picador, 2000.

Tal, Uriel. "On the Study of the Holocaust and Genocide." *Yad Vashem Studies* 13 (1979): 7–52.

Tec, Nechama. *Resilience and Courage: Women, Men, and the Holocaust.* New Haven, Conn.: Yale University Press, 2003.

Thatcher, Nicole. *Charlotte Delbo: Une voix singulière.* Paris: L'Harmattan, 2003.

Thomas, D. M. *The White Hotel.* New York: Viking, 1981; rpt. New York: Penguin, 1993.

Thomson, Ian. *Primo Levi.* London: Vintage, 2003.

Todorov, Tzvetan. *Facing the Extreme: Moral Life in the Concentration Camps.* Translated by Arthur Denner and Abigail Pollak. New York: Henry Holt, 1996.

Toumayan, Alain P. *Encountering the Other: The Artwork and the Problem of Difference in Blanchot and Levinas.* Pittsburgh: Duquesne University Press, 2004.

————. "'I more than the others': Dostoevsky and Levinas." *Yale French Studies*, no. 104 (2004): 55–66.

Trezise, Thomas. "Between History and Psychoanalysis: A Case Study in the Reception of Holocaust Survivor Testimony." *History & Memory* 20, no. 1 (Spring/Summer 2008): 7–47.

————. *Into the Breach: Samuel Beckett and the Ends of Literature.* Princeton, N.J.: Princeton University Press, 1990.

————. "The Question of Community in Charlotte Delbo's *Auschwitz and After.*" *Modern Language Notes* 117, no. 4 (September 2002): 858–86.

————. Review of *Proper Names,* by Emmanuel Levinas. *Comparative Literature Studies* 37, no. 3 (2000): 352–60.

————. "Unspeakable." *The Yale Journal of Criticism* 14, no. 1 (2001): 39–66.

Vidal-Naquet, Pierre. *Assassins of Memory: Essays on the Denial of the Holocaust.* Translated by Jeffrey Mehlman. New York: Columbia University Press, 1992.

Vrba, Rudolf. *I Escaped from Auschwitz.* Fort Lee, N.J.: Barricade Books, 2002.

Vries, Hent de. "Adieu, à dieu, a-Dieu." In *Ethics as First Philosophy: The Significance of Emmanuel Levinas for Philosophy, Literature and Religion,* edited by Adriaan T. Peperzak, 211–20. New York: Routledge, 1995.

————. *Minimal Theologies: Critiques of Secular Reason in Adorno and Levinas.* Translated by Geoffrey Hale. Baltimore: Johns Hopkins University Press, 2005.

Waintrater, Régine. *Sortir du génocide: Témoigner pour réapprendre à vivre.* Paris: Payot, 2003.

Wallant, Edward Lewis. *The Pawnbroker.* San Diego: Harcourt Brace & Company, 1989.

White, Hayden. *The Content of the Form.* Baltimore: Johns Hopkins University Press, 1987.

————. "Historical Emplotment and the Problem of Truth." In *Probing the Limits of Representation: Nazism and the "Final Solution,"* edited by Saul Friedlander, 37–53. Cambridge: Harvard University Press, 1992.

————. *Metahistory: The Historical Imagination in Nineteenth-Century Europe.* Baltimore: Johns Hopkins University Press, 1973.

————. *Tropics of Discourse: Essays in Cultural Criticism.* Baltimore: Johns Hopkins University Press, 1978.

Wiesel, Elie. *The Accident.* Translated by Anne Borchardt. In *The Night Trilogy: Night, Dawn, The Accident,* 205–318. New York: Hill and Wang, 1987.

————. *Dawn.* Translated by Frances Frenaye. In *The Night Trilogy: Night, Dawn, The Accident,* 121–204. New York: Hill and Wang, 1987.

————. *Night.* Translated by Stella Rodway. In *The Night Trilogy: Night, Dawn, The Accident,* 5–119. New York: Hill and Wang, 1987.

Wieviorka, Annette. *The Era of the Witness.* Translated by Jared Stark. Ithaca: Cornell University Press, 2006.

Wilkomirski, Binjamin. *Fragments: Memories of a Wartime Childhood*. Translated by Carol Brown Janeway. New York: Schocken Books, 1996.

Wyschogrod, Edith. "The Art in Ethics: Aesthetics, Objectivity, and Alterity in the Philosophy of Emmanuel Levinas." In *Ethics as First Philosophy: The Significance of Emmanuel Levinas for Philosophy, Literature and Religion*, edited by Adriaan T. Peperzak, 137–48. New York: Routledge, 1995.

———. *Emmanuel Levinas: The Problem of Ethical Metaphysics*. 2nd ed. New York: Fordham University Press, 2000.

Young, James E. *Writing and Rewriting the Holocaust: Narrative and the Consequences of Interpretation*. Bloomington: Indiana University Press, 1988.

Zeitlin, Froma. "The Vicarious Witness." *History & Memory* 10, no. 2 (Fall 1998): 5–42.

Zuccotti, Susan. *The Holocaust, the French, and the Jews*. New York: Basic Books, 1993; rpt. Lincoln: University of Nebraska Press, 1999.

Żywulska, Krystyna. *I Survived Auschwitz*. Translated by Krystyna Cenkalska. Warsaw: tCHu Publishing House, 2004.

other, 21, 27, 29, 78, 160, 169, 170, 171,
182, 215, 267n.21; absolute, 194;
confusion of same and, 194; embodied, 215; ethical relation to, 6, 153, 92,
159, 191, 192, 194–95, 199, 206, 208–9,
217; for-the-other, 191–92; identity of,
194–95; mortality of, 182–83, 184,
216–17; other-in-the-same, 191, 215;
survivor as, 195, 208, 224; and time,
183, 191
Ozick, Cynthia, 96

particularity, 73, 77–78, 100, 110, 116,
118, 123, 127–28, 188–89, 200, 221;
contrasted with generality or
universality, 15, 100, 144, 146, 147–48,
160, 173, 193, 196, 198, 212. *See also*
singularity
performative, 4, 15–17, 22–24, 28, 90,
107, 117, 231n.15, 235n.25
perpetrators, 6, 82, 83–85, 107, 137–38,
139, 148, 194; testimony of, 33, 34. *See
also* executioner; victims: and
perpetrators
personal pronouns, 29, 77–78, 81, 104–8,
110, 116–21, 144–46, 193, 196–97, 209.
See also voice
phenomenality, 168–69, 173–74, 176–77,
208. *See also* Levinas, Emmanuel:
disclosure
phenomenology, 70, 112, 162, 168,
173–74, 183, 211
philosophy, 7, 29, 72–74, 122–23,
160–62; language of, 7, 160, 184,
192–96, 215, 221; and literature, 72–74,
160, 199–200, 221; philosophical
critique of art, 183–84; as testimony,
160, 217–22
poetry, 36, 63–68, 76, 90, 95, 96, 101–3,
109, 119–20
poiēsis, 90
post-traumatic stress disorder (PTSD),
43, 49, 50, 53, 56
power: political, 139, 151; of the subject,
178, 182, 191, 215

psychiatry, 46–48
psychoanalysis, 4, 9, 22–24, 27, 29, 43,
53; and the body, 54–56
psychotherapy, 23–24, 33, 57–59

Racine, Jean, 179; *Phaedra*, 179
Ravensbrück concentration camp, 104
reception, 1–4, 7, 8–9, 19–20, 24, 28–39,
41, 59–60, 64, 95, 101, 104, 121, 159,
160, 166, 168, 184, 200–206, 210,
223–24, 226
reenactment, 3, 35, 46–48, 60, 62, 98,
99–101, 108, 116–17, 218
reification. *See* individual.
relationality, 29–30, 92, 117, 118, 136,
153, 191, 197, 208, 216, 225
religion, 125–26, 153–54, 192;
Christianity, 215; Judaism, 211
repetition, 182, 215; and difference,
53–55, 177, 191, 213–14; traumatic, 4,
43–48, 51–56
representation: artistic, 2, 5, 6, 70, 91,
98–100, 188, 199, 259n.89; figurative,
43–45, 48, 55, 59, 61, 97–100, 203;
historical, 17, 79–80, 98–101; literal,
44–46, 48, 53, 56, 61, 97–100; as
mediation, 45–46, 60, 68, 98, 141;
contrasted with signification, 89, 186,
192, 196, 206; of trauma, 2, 4, 40, 43,
46–48, 58–60, 89, 117–18, 209–10; and
traumatic dreams, 43–45. *See also* art;
figuration; historiography
responsibility, 6, 7, 19, 21, 25, 82, 92, 95,
112, 120, 125–29, 131–32, 134, 142,
152–53, 156, 206, 226. *See also under*
Levinas, Emmanuel
return. *See* haunting
Robbins, Jill, 164, 165, 181
Rothberg, Michael, 63, 66; *Traumatic
Realism*, 63
Rousso, Henry, 33; *The Vichy Syndrome*, 33
Rumkowski, Chaim, 142

sacralization. *See under* Holocaust
Santner, Eric, 65